# PMQ
## EXAM PREP
# ESSAYS

Your Study Guide to Passing the APM
Project Management Qualification

GEORGE GLOVER

British Library cataloguing in the publication data is available.

ISBN: 978-1-7393629-0-4

"The best way to predict the future is to create it."

Peter Drucker

# TABLE OF CONTENTS

# INTRODUCTION

The APM PMQ exam is a challenging exam that requires a thorough understanding of project management principles and practices. It covers a range of topics that are essential for project managers to know, including project planning, risk management, procurement, and quality management, among others. Passing the exam requires a significant amount of time and effort, and many candidates struggle to find the right resources to help them prepare.

That's where the PMQ Exam Prep Essays come in. This comprehensive study guide has been designed to help you prepare for the PMQ exam by providing you with all the information you need to pass the exam with flying colours. The guide covers all 11 learning outcomes and 67 assessment criteria that align with the APM Body of Knowledge 7th edition. Each chapter corresponds to one of the learning outcomes, and each essay addresses a specific assessment criterion.

The guide is organized in a way that is easy to follow and understand. Each essay is written in clear, concise language and provides a comprehensive overview of the topic it covers. By studying each essay thoroughly, you will gain an in-depth understanding of the knowledge required to excel on the exam. You can also create customized essays based on the content of the guide's essays as revision material, which can help reinforce your understanding of the exam's content.

One of the key benefits of the PMQ Exam Prep Essays is that it prepares you for the essay questions that are part of the PMQ exam. Writing 10 essays during the exam can be challenging, but with the material provided in this study guide, you'll be well-prepared to tackle these questions with confidence. By reading and compiling your own essays from the guide, you can gain a deeper understanding of the exam's content and increase your chances of passing.

In conclusion, if you are looking for a comprehensive study guide that covers all the necessary information you need to pass the APM PMQ exam on your first attempt, the PMQ Exam Prep Essays are the ideal resource.

# CHAPTER ONE

## *UNDERSTANDING THE STRUCTURE OF ORGANIZATIONS AND PROJECTS*

# 1.1 UNDERSTANDING THE DIFFERENT TYPES OF PERMANENT AND TEMPORARY ORGANIZATIONAL STRUCTURES

Organizational structure refers to the way a company is organized to achieve its objectives. It defines the roles, responsibilities, and relationships between individuals and departments within the organization. Having a well-defined organizational structure is crucial for efficient and effective decision-making, communication, and coordination of activities. It also helps to clarify the hierarchy of authority and the reporting lines for different positions within the organization.

There are two main types of organizational structures: permanent and temporary. Permanent structures are designed to be stable and enduring, while temporary structures are formed to achieve specific goals and then disbanded. In this section, we will discuss the different types of permanent and temporary organizational structures, including functional, matrix, and project structures. We will also explore the advantages and disadvantages of each structure, and how to choose the right structure for your business.

## PERMANENT ORGANIZATIONAL STRUCTURES

Permanent organizational structures are designed to be long-lasting and stable, with clearly defined roles, responsibilities, and reporting lines. These structures are typically used by large organizations that require a hierarchical structure to manage their operations effectively. There are several types of permanent organizational structures, including:

a. Functional Organizational Structure: In a functional organizational structure, employees are grouped based on their area of expertise or function, such as marketing, finance, operations, or human resources. This structure is best suited for organizations with a single product or service line and a limited geographical scope. The advantage of this structure is that it allows for specialization and expertise in different functional areas, but it can lead to silos and communication barriers between departments.

b. Divisional Organizational Structure: In a divisional organizational structure, employees are grouped based on the products or services they provide, with each division operating as a separate entity. This structure is best suited for organizations with multiple product lines or services and a larger geographical scope. The advantage of this structure is that it allows for greater autonomy and flexibility for each division, but it can lead to duplication of resources and lack of coordination between divisions.

c. Geographic Organizational Structure: In a geographic organizational structure, employees are grouped based on their location or region, with each geographic region operating as a separate entity. This structure is best suited for organizations with a diverse customer base and a wide geographical spread. The advantage of this structure is that it allows for greater responsiveness to local market conditions and customer needs, but it can lead to duplication of resources and lack of coordination between regions.

Overall, permanent organizational structures are designed to provide stability, clarity, and consistency in the management of organizational functions. However, they can also become rigid and inflexible, limiting the ability of the organization to adapt to changing market conditions or pursue new opportunities. It is important for organizations to regularly review and revise their organizational structure to ensure that it aligns with their strategic goals and objectives.

## TEMPORARY ORGANIZATIONAL STRUCTURES

Temporary organizational structures are designed to achieve a specific goal or objective and then disbanded once the goal is accomplished. These structures are typically used for projects, events, or other temporary initiatives that require a different structure than the permanent organization. There are several types of temporary organizational structures, including:

a. Matrix Organizational Structure: In a matrix organizational structure, employees are assigned to both a functional manager and a project manager. This structure is best suited for organizations that have complex projects or initiatives that require collaboration across functional areas. The advantage of this structure is that it allows for flexibility and adaptability to changing project needs, but it can lead to confusion and conflict over roles and responsibilities.

b. Project Organizational Structure: In a project organizational structure, employees are organized around a specific project or initiative, with a project manager overseeing the team. This structure is best suited for organizations that have a large, complex project that requires a dedicated team to complete. The advantage of this structure is that it allows for clear accountability and a focus on achieving project goals, but it can lead to duplication of resources and lack of integration with the permanent organization.

c. Network Organizational Structure: In a network organizational structure, the organization works with external partners, contractors, or other organizations to achieve a specific goal or objective. This structure is best suited for organizations that have limited resources or expertise in a particular area. The advantage of this structure is that it allows for flexibility and access to specialized resources, but it can lead to challenges in coordination and control.

Temporary organizational structures are designed to be agile and adaptable to changing circumstances. They allow organizations to pursue new opportunities or respond to unexpected challenges without disrupting the permanent organizational structure. However, they can also lead to confusion and a lack of clarity over roles and responsibilities. It is important for organizations to establish clear objectives, roles, and reporting lines for temporary structures to ensure their success.

## FUNCTIONAL ORGANIZATIONAL STRUCTURE

A functional organizational structure groups employees based on their expertise or function, such as marketing, finance, operations, or human resources. Each department is headed by a functional manager who is responsible for overseeing the activities of their department and ensuring that they align with the organization's strategic objectives.

The advantages of a functional organizational structure include:

a. Specialization: Employees can focus on their area of expertise and develop specialized skills and knowledge.

b. Efficiency: Functional departments can develop efficient processes and procedures to streamline operations and reduce costs.

c. Clear Career Path: Employees can clearly see their career path and opportunities for advancement within their functional area.

However, there are also disadvantages to a functional organizational structure:

a. Silos: Departments may become isolated and develop their own goals and priorities, leading to a lack of collaboration and communication between departments.

b. Lack of Flexibility: Functional departments may become resistant to change or new ideas that do not align with their area of expertise.

c. Slow Decision-Making: Decisions may take longer to make as they need to be approved by multiple functional departments.

To overcome the disadvantages of a functional organizational structure, organizations can implement cross-functional teams or committees to facilitate communication and collaboration between departments. This can help to break down silos and encourage a more holistic approach to decision-making.

Overall, a functional organizational structure is best suited for organizations with a single product or service line and a limited geographical scope. It allows for specialization and expertise in different functional areas, but it can lead to silos and communication barriers between departments.

## Matrix Organizational Structure

In a matrix organizational structure, employees are assigned to both a functional manager and a project manager. This structure is designed to facilitate collaboration and communication across functional departments to achieve a specific project or goal.

The advantages of a matrix organizational structure include:

a. Flexibility: The structure allows for flexibility and adaptability to changing project needs.

b. Improved Communication: The structure promotes communication and collaboration across functional departments, leading to better decision-making.

c. Efficient Use of Resources: Resources can be shared across projects, leading to a more efficient use of resources.

However, there are also disadvantages to a matrix organizational structure:

a. Role Confusion: Employees may become confused over their roles and responsibilities, leading to conflicts and reduced productivity.

b. Dual Reporting: Employees may have conflicting priorities as they report to both a functional manager and a project manager.

c. Complex Decision-Making: Decisions may take longer to make as multiple stakeholders need to be consulted.

To overcome the disadvantages of a matrix organizational structure, organizations can establish clear reporting lines, roles, and responsibilities for each employee. They can also provide training to employees on how to work in a matrix structure and how to manage conflicts effectively.

Overall, a matrix organizational structure is best suited for organizations that have complex projects or initiatives that require collaboration across functional areas. It allows for flexibility and adaptability to changing project needs, but it can lead to confusion and conflict over roles and responsibilities.

## PROJECT ORGANIZATIONAL STRUCTURE

In a project organizational structure, employees are organized around a specific project or initiative, with a project manager overseeing the team. This structure is designed to facilitate a clear focus on achieving project goals and objectives.

The advantages of a project organizational structure include:

a. Clear Accountability: Each project has a dedicated team with clear roles and responsibilities, leading to clear accountability for project outcomes.

b. Efficient Resource Allocation: Resources are allocated specifically to the project, leading to more efficient use of resources.

c. Flexibility: The structure allows for flexibility in responding to changing project needs and priorities.

However, there are also disadvantages to a project organizational structure:

a. Duplication of Resources: There may be duplication of resources across multiple projects, leading to inefficient use of resources.

b. Limited Integration: The project team may become isolated from the permanent organization, leading to a lack of integration and coordination.

c. Limited Career Path: Employees may have limited opportunities for career advancement within a project team.

To overcome the disadvantages of a project organizational structure, organizations can establish clear communication and reporting lines between the project team and the permanent organization. They can also implement knowledge management systems to ensure that knowledge and expertise are shared between projects and the permanent organization.

Overall, a project organizational structure is best suited for organizations that have a large, complex project that requires a dedicated team to complete. It allows for clear accountability and a focus on achieving project goals, but it can lead to duplication of resources and lack of integration with the permanent organization.

## COMPARING AND CONTRASTING PERMANENT AND TEMPORARY ORGANIZATIONAL STRUCTURES

Permanent and temporary organizational structures have their own advantages and disadvantages, and choosing the right structure for your business depends on several factors, such as the size of the organization, the complexity of the projects, and the strategic objectives of the organization.

Permanent organizational structures provide stability, clarity, and consistency in the management of organizational functions. They are best suited for organizations with a single product or service line and a limited geographical scope. The functional, divisional, and geographic structures are examples of permanent organizational structures.

On the other hand, temporary organizational structures provide agility and adaptability to changing circumstances. They are best suited for projects, events, or other temporary initiatives that require a different structure than the permanent organization. The matrix, project, and network structures are examples of temporary organizational structures.

When comparing and contrasting permanent and temporary organizational structures, the following factors should be considered:

a. Flexibility: Temporary organizational structures are more flexible and adaptable to changing circumstances than permanent organizational structures.

b. Accountability: Permanent organizational structures provide clear accountability and a defined hierarchy of authority, while temporary organizational structures may have less clear accountability and reporting lines.

c. Resource Allocation: Permanent organizational structures allocate resources based on functional areas, while temporary organizational structures allocate resources based on projects or initiatives.

d. Integration: Permanent organizational structures are more integrated with the organization's culture and values, while temporary organizational structures may be less integrated and have their own culture and values.

In conclusion, both permanent and temporary organizational structures have their own advantages and disadvantages. Choosing the right structure for your business depends on several factors, such as the size of the organization, the complexity of the projects, and the strategic objectives of the organization. It is important to regularly review and revise the organizational structure to ensure that it aligns with the organization's strategic goals and objectives.

## SELECTING THE RIGHT ORGANIZATIONAL STRUCTURE FOR YOUR BUSINESS

Choosing the right organizational structure is crucial for the success of your business. The organizational structure you choose will impact your communication, decision-making processes, resource allocation, and overall performance. Here are some factors to consider when selecting the right organizational structure for your business:

a. Size of the Organization: The size of your organization will determine the level of complexity and the number of functional areas or projects you have. A functional structure is best suited for smaller organizations with a limited number of functional areas, while a matrix or project structure is better suited for larger organizations with more complex projects.

b. Nature of the Business: The nature of your business will also determine the organizational structure that is most appropriate. For example, a manufacturing business may benefit from a functional structure, while a consulting firm may benefit from a matrix structure.

c. Geographical Scope: The geographical scope of your business will also impact the organizational structure you choose. A geographic structure is best suited for organizations with a wide geographical spread, while a functional or divisional structure may be more appropriate for organizations with a limited geographical scope.

d. Strategic Objectives: Your organization's strategic objectives should guide the selection of the organizational structure. For example, if your strategic objective is to increase innovation, a matrix or project structure may be more appropriate.

e. Culture and Values: Your organizational structure should align with your organization's culture and values. For example, if your organization values collaboration and teamwork, a matrix structure may be more appropriate.

It is important to note that there is no one-size-fits-all organizational structure, and it may be necessary to make changes to the structure as the business evolves. Regularly reviewing and revising the organizational structure is important to ensure that it continues to align with the organization's strategic goals and objectives.

In conclusion, selecting the right organizational structure for your business requires careful consideration of several factors. It is important to choose a structure that aligns with your organization's size, nature of the business, geographical scope, strategic objectives, and culture and values. Regularly reviewing and revising the organizational structure is important to ensure that it continues to support the organization's growth and success.

## CHALLENGES ASSOCIATED WITH DIFFERENT TYPES OF ORGANIZATIONAL STRUCTURES

While different types of organizational structures have their own advantages, they also come with unique challenges that organizations need to address. Here are some challenges associated with different types of organizational structures:

Functional Organizational Structure:

a. Silos: Departments may become isolated and develop their own goals and priorities, leading to a lack of collaboration and communication between departments.

b. Lack of Flexibility: Functional departments may become resistant to change or new ideas that do not align with their area of expertise.

c. Slow Decision-Making: Decisions may take longer to make as they need to be approved by multiple functional departments.

Matrix Organizational Structure:

a. Role Confusion: Employees may become confused over their roles and responsibilities, leading to conflicts and reduced productivity.

b. Dual Reporting: Employees may have conflicting priorities as they report to both a functional manager and a project manager.

c. Complex Decision-Making: Decisions may take longer to make as multiple stakeholders need to be consulted.

Project Organizational Structure:

a. Duplication of Resources: There may be duplication of resources across multiple projects, leading to inefficient use of resources.

b. Limited Integration: The project team may become isolated from the permanent organization, leading to a lack of integration and coordination.

c. Limited Career Path: Employees may have limited opportunities for career advancement within a project team.

Geographic Organizational Structure:

a. Duplication of Efforts: Departments in different regions may work on similar projects, leading to duplication of efforts and resources.

b. Communication Barriers: There may be language and cultural barriers that hinder effective communication and collaboration between regions.

c. Limited Autonomy: Regions may have limited autonomy and decision-making power, leading to a lack of responsiveness to local market conditions.

Divisional Organizational Structure:

a. Duplication of Resources: Divisions may have their own resources and systems, leading to duplication of resources and inefficiencies.

b. Lack of Collaboration: Divisions may become focused on their own goals and objectives, leading to a lack of collaboration and coordination between divisions.

c. Limited Sharing of Best Practices: Divisions may not share best practices and knowledge, leading to missed opportunities for improvement and growth.

In conclusion, different types of organizational structures come with their own set of challenges that organizations need to address to ensure success. Organizations should identify and address these challenges to create an effective and efficient organizational structure.

## IMPORTANCE OF REGULARLY REVIEWING AND REVISING ORGANIZATIONAL STRUCTURE

Regularly reviewing and revising organizational structure is critical for ensuring the success of the organization. Organizational structure should be evaluated against the organization's strategic goals and objectives to ensure that it is aligned and effective. Here are some reasons why regularly reviewing and revising organizational structure is important:

a. Ensures Alignment with Strategic Goals: As the organization's strategic goals and objectives change, the organizational structure must also change to ensure alignment. Regularly reviewing and revising the organizational structure helps to ensure that the structure is aligned with the organization's strategic goals and objectives.

b. Improves Efficiency and Effectiveness: Regularly reviewing and revising the organizational structure can help to identify inefficiencies and areas for improvement. This can lead to a more efficient and effective organization.

c. Increases Collaboration and Communication: Organizational structure can impact collaboration and communication between departments and teams. Regularly reviewing and revising the structure can help to identify barriers to collaboration and communication and implement solutions to improve them.

d. Enhances Agility and Adaptability: Organizational structure should be able to adapt to changes in the business environment. Regularly reviewing and revising the structure can help to ensure that the organization is agile and adaptable to changes.

e. Supports Growth and Development: As the organization grows and develops, the organizational structure must also evolve to support the growth and development. Regularly reviewing and revising the structure can help to identify areas for growth and development and implement changes to support them.

In conclusion, regularly reviewing and revising organizational structure is important for ensuring alignment with strategic goals, improving efficiency and effectiveness, increasing collaboration and communication, enhancing agility and adaptability, and supporting growth and development. Organizations should establish a process for regularly reviewing and revising the organizational structure to ensure that it continues to support the organization's growth and success.

# 1.2 Understanding the Role of Organizational Breakdown Structure in Responsibility Assignment Matrix Creation

An Organizational Breakdown Structure (OBS) is a hierarchical representation of an organization's structure, including departments, teams, and individuals. It is typically used in project management to help define and communicate the roles and responsibilities of each team member involved in a project. An OBS provides a visual representation of the organizational structure, outlining who reports to whom, who is responsible for what tasks, and who has decision-making authority.

In an OBS, the organization is divided into various levels, with each level representing a different aspect of the organization's structure. At the top level, the organization is typically divided into major departments or divisions, such as finance, marketing, or operations. The next level may represent teams within each department, and the subsequent levels may represent individual employees within each team.

An OBS can be used to facilitate communication and collaboration within the organization. By clearly defining the organizational structure and the roles and responsibilities of each team member, team members can better understand their place within the organization and work together more effectively towards achieving the project goals. An OBS can also be used to facilitate decision-making by identifying the appropriate stakeholders and decision-makers for each aspect of the project.

## How Does OBS Help in Project Management?

In project management, an Organizational Breakdown Structure (OBS) plays a crucial role in defining the organizational structure and project roles. It helps project managers to identify the key stakeholders and team members involved in a project, and to define the roles and responsibilities of each team member. OBS is often used in conjunction with a Work Breakdown Structure (WBS), which breaks down the project into smaller, more manageable tasks.

An OBS is helpful in project management because it provides a clear understanding of the organizational structure of the project team. It helps project managers to identify the appropriate team members for each task, and to assign specific roles and responsibilities to each team member. This ensures that each team member understands their role in the project and is held accountable for their assigned tasks.

Moreover, an OBS helps to identify potential communication channels and decision-making pathways. By outlining the reporting and decision-making structure of the project team, an OBS helps to ensure that team members communicate effectively and that the project progresses smoothly.

An OBS can also be used to identify any potential conflicts or bottlenecks in the project team structure. For example, if two team members are assigned conflicting roles or responsibilities, this can be identified and resolved through the OBS. By clearly defining the project team structure and roles, an OBS helps to prevent such conflicts from arising and ensures that the project progresses smoothly. Overall, OBS is an essential tool for project managers to effectively manage the project team and ensure the success of the project.

## What is a Responsibility Assignment Matrix (RAM)?

A Responsibility Assignment Matrix (RAM), also known as a RACI matrix, is a project management tool used to clarify and communicate the roles and responsibilities of each team member involved in a project. It defines who is responsible, accountable, consulted, and informed (RACI) for each task or activity in the project. The RAM is often created in conjunction with the Work Breakdown Structure (WBS) and the Organizational Breakdown Structure (OBS).

The RAM assigns roles and responsibilities to each team member based on their expertise, authority, and level of involvement in the project. The RACI matrix is organized into rows and columns, with each row representing a specific task or activity, and each column representing a specific team member or group.

The four roles defined in a RAM are:

- Responsible (R): The team member who is responsible for completing the task or activity.

- Accountable (A): The team member who has overall responsibility for the task or activity and is accountable for its completion.

- Consulted (C): The team member who provides input or advice on the task or activity.

- Informed (I): The team member who is kept informed about the progress of the task or activity.

By using a RAM, project managers can ensure that each team member understands their role in the project and is held accountable for their assigned tasks. The RAM also helps to prevent confusion and misunderstandings about who is responsible for each task or activity. Additionally, the RAM can be used to identify any gaps or overlaps in the project team's responsibilities and ensure that all tasks are covered. Overall, the RAM is a valuable tool for effective project management and communication.

## How is RAM Created Using OBS?

A Responsibility Assignment Matrix (RAM) is often created using an Organizational Breakdown Structure (OBS) in project management. The OBS helps to identify the roles and responsibilities of each team member involved in the project, and the RAM helps to clarify and communicate these roles and responsibilities to the team.

To create a RAM using an OBS, follow these steps:

1. Identify the project tasks: The first step in creating a RAM is to identify the tasks and activities involved in the project. This can be done using a Work Breakdown Structure (WBS).

2. Assign each task to a team member: Using the OBS, identify the team member or group responsible for each task or activity. This helps to ensure that each task is assigned to the appropriate team member based on their expertise and level of involvement in the project.

3. Define the roles and responsibilities: Once each task is assigned to a team member or group, the RAM can be created. Define the roles and responsibilities of each team member using the RACI framework: Responsible, Accountable, Consulted, and Informed. Be sure to clearly define the level of authority and decision-making power for each role.

4. Review and refine: Once the RAM is created, review it to ensure that all tasks are covered and that there are no gaps or overlaps in the team's responsibilities. Refine the RAM as needed to ensure that it accurately reflects the project team's roles and responsibilities.

Creating a RAM using an OBS helps to ensure that each team member understands their role in the project and is held accountable for their assigned tasks. It also helps to prevent confusion and misunderstandings about who is responsible for each task or activity. By creating a clear and effective RAM, the project team can work together more efficiently and effectively towards achieving the project goals. Overall, using an OBS to create a RAM is an important step in effective project management.

## BENEFITS OF USING OBS IN RAM CREATION

Using an Organizational Breakdown Structure (OBS) in creating a Responsibility Assignment Matrix (RAM) offers several benefits in project management. Some of these benefits include:

a. Clear communication: An OBS provides a clear and visual representation of the project team's structure and roles. Using the OBS in creating the RAM ensures that each team member understands their role in the project and is held accountable for their assigned tasks. This helps to prevent confusion and misunderstandings about who is responsible for each task or activity.

b. Improved efficiency: By using an OBS in creating the RAM, project managers can ensure that each task is assigned to the appropriate team member based on their expertise and level of involvement in the project. This helps to ensure that the team works more efficiently towards achieving the project goals.

c. Identifying potential issues: Using the OBS in creating the RAM helps to identify potential conflicts or bottlenecks in the project team's structure. For example, if two team members are assigned conflicting roles or responsibilities, this can be identified and resolved through the OBS. By clearly defining the project team structure and roles, an OBS helps to prevent such conflicts from arising and ensures that the project progresses smoothly.

d. Effective decision-making: By outlining the reporting and decision-making structure of the project team, the OBS helps to ensure that team members communicate effectively and that the project progresses smoothly. Using the OBS in creating the RAM helps to identify the appropriate stakeholders and decision-makers for each aspect of the project.

e. Flexibility: The OBS can be easily modified as the project progresses. This allows project managers to adjust the project team structure and roles as needed to ensure that the project progresses smoothly.

Overall, using an OBS in creating a RAM offers several benefits in project management, including clear communication, improved efficiency, identifying potential issues, effective decision-making, and flexibility.

## EXAMPLES OF RAM CREATED USING OBS

Here are a few examples of how a Responsibility Assignment Matrix (RAM) can be created using an Organizational Breakdown Structure (OBS):

Example 1: A software development project

Task: Develop a new software application

Roles and Responsibilities:

- Project Manager (Accountable): Overall responsibility for the project, including budget, schedule, and quality.

- Development Team (Responsible): Develops the software application according to the project requirements.

- Quality Assurance Team (Consulted): Provides input and advice on the software development process and ensures that the software meets quality standards.

- Marketing Team (Informed): Receives updates on the progress of the project and provides input on marketing strategies for the software application.

Example 2: A construction project

Task: Build a new office building

Roles and Responsibilities:

- Project Manager (Accountable): Overall responsibility for the project, including budget, schedule, and quality.

- Architectural Team (Responsible): Designs the building according to the project requirements.

- Construction Team (Responsible): Builds the office building according to the architectural design.

- Safety Team (Consulted): Provides input and advice on safety requirements for the construction site and ensures that the construction process meets safety standards.

- Building Owner (Informed): Receives updates on the progress of the project and provides input on any changes to the building design.

Example 3: A marketing campaign project

Task: Launch a new product

Roles and Responsibilities:

- Project Manager (Accountable): Overall responsibility for the project, including budget, schedule, and quality.

- Marketing Team (Responsible): Develops and executes the marketing campaign for the new product.

- Sales Team (Consulted): Provides input and advice on sales strategies for the new product and ensures that the marketing campaign meets sales targets.

- Product Development Team (Consulted): Provides input and advice on the product development process and ensures that the marketing campaign aligns with the product's features and benefits.

- Customer Service Team (Informed): Receives updates on the progress of the project and provides input on customer service strategies for the new product.

These examples demonstrate how an OBS can be used to create a RAM that clearly defines the roles and responsibilities of each team member involved in a project. The RAM ensures that each team member understands their role in the project and is held accountable for their assigned tasks. Overall, using an OBS to create a RAM is an effective way to manage projects and ensure project success.

## CONCLUSION: IMPORTANCE OF OBS IN PROJECT MANAGEMENT

In project management, an Organizational Breakdown Structure (OBS) plays a crucial role in defining the organizational structure and project roles. It helps project managers to identify the key stakeholders and team members involved in a project, and to define the roles and responsibilities of each team member. An OBS provides a visual representation of the organizational structure, outlining who reports to whom, who is responsible for what tasks, and who has decision-making authority.

Using an OBS in creating a Responsibility Assignment Matrix (RAM) offers several benefits in project management, including clear communication, improved efficiency, identifying potential issues, effective decision-making, and flexibility. The RAM ensures that each team member understands their role in the project and is held accountable for their assigned tasks. It also helps to prevent confusion and misunderstandings about who is responsible for each task or activity. By creating a clear and effective RAM, the project team can work together more efficiently and effectively towards achieving the project goals.

Overall, an OBS is an essential tool for project managers to effectively manage the project team and ensure the success of the project. By clearly defining the organizational structure and the roles and responsibilities of each team member, team members can better understand their place within the organization and work together more effectively towards achieving the project goals. Using an OBS in project management helps to ensure that the project progresses smoothly and that the project team is able to deliver a successful project outcome.

# 1.3 THE ROLE OF A PROJECT MANAGER: RESPONSIBILITIES AND KEY TASKS

The success of any project depends largely on the effective management of resources, time, and people. The project manager plays a critical role in achieving project goals and objectives. The project manager is responsible for planning, organizing, leading, and controlling the project from start to finish. The project manager is the person who is accountable for delivering the project within the agreed time, budget, and quality parameters.

In this section, we will delve deeper into the key responsibilities of a project manager. We will explore the skills, competencies, and attributes that are essential for a successful project manager. We will also examine the different types of project managers, their roles and responsibilities, and the key challenges they face. By the end of this section, you should have a clear understanding of the project manager's role in delivering successful projects.

## PLANNING AND ORGANIZING

One of the most critical responsibilities of a project manager is planning and organizing the project. This involves defining the project's scope, goals, objectives, and deliverables, and creating a comprehensive project plan. The project plan should include a detailed timeline, milestones, tasks, and resources required to complete the project.

To plan effectively, the project manager needs to have a thorough understanding of the project's requirements, constraints, and risks. They must also identify the project's stakeholders and their expectations, as well as the project's dependencies and interdependencies. The project manager should use a range of tools and techniques to plan and organize the project, such as Gantt charts, work breakdown structures, risk matrices, and project management software.

Effective planning and organizing also involve managing the project's budget and resources. The project manager should ensure that the project is financially feasible and that adequate resources are available to complete the project on time and within budget. They should also allocate resources effectively and efficiently, taking into account the project's priorities and critical path.

Overall, planning and organizing are critical to the success of a project. A well-planned project provides a clear roadmap for the team, minimizes risks, and ensures that the project stays on track. The project manager's ability to plan and organize effectively can make the difference between a successful project and a failed one.

## TEAM MANAGEMENT AND LEADERSHIP

Another critical responsibility of a project manager is team management and leadership. The project manager is responsible for assembling the project team, assigning roles and responsibilities, and ensuring that the team is motivated, productive, and engaged.

Effective team management requires strong leadership skills, including the ability to inspire and motivate the team, provide clear direction and guidance, and foster a positive team culture. The project manager should also encourage open communication, collaboration, and knowledge sharing within the team. They should be able to manage conflicts and ensure that the team is working towards the project's goals and objectives.

In addition to managing the team, the project manager should also identify and address any skills gaps or training needs within the team. They should provide opportunities for professional development and ensure that the team has the necessary resources and tools to carry out their tasks effectively.

Overall, team management and leadership are essential to the success of a project. A well-managed team is more likely to be productive, engaged, and committed to the project's goals. The project manager's ability to lead and motivate the team can make the difference between a successful project and a failed one.

## COMMUNICATION AND STAKEHOLDER MANAGEMENT

Effective communication and stakeholder management are critical responsibilities of a project manager. The project manager must be able to communicate effectively with the project team, stakeholders, and other key players involved in the project. They should ensure that everyone is aware of the project's objectives, scope, timelines, risks, and issues.

Stakeholder management involves identifying and engaging with all stakeholders who have an interest in or impact on the project. This includes the project sponsor, customers, end-users, suppliers, regulators, and other relevant parties. The project manager should understand the stakeholders' expectations, concerns, and needs and communicate with them regularly throughout the project lifecycle.

Effective communication and stakeholder management require excellent interpersonal and negotiation skills. The project manager should be able to listen actively, manage conflicts, and build relationships with stakeholders. They should also be able to manage expectations and adapt their communication style to suit different stakeholders' needs.

Overall, effective communication and stakeholder management are critical to the success of a project. Good communication helps ensure that the project stays on track, stakeholders are engaged and satisfied, and issues are resolved promptly. The project manager's ability to communicate effectively and manage stakeholders can make the difference between a successful project and a failed one.

## RISK MANAGEMENT AND PROBLEM-SOLVING

Risk management and problem-solving are critical responsibilities of a project manager. Every project faces risks, such as budget overruns, schedule delays, scope changes, technical issues, and external factors. The project manager should identify, assess, and manage these risks throughout the project lifecycle.

Risk management involves identifying potential risks, assessing their likelihood and impact, and developing strategies to mitigate or avoid them. The project manager should work with the project team and other stakeholders to identify risks and develop risk management plans. They should also monitor and review the risk management plans regularly to ensure they remain effective.

In addition to risk management, the project manager should also be skilled in problem-solving. When issues arise, the project manager should be able to analyse the situation, identify the root cause of the problem, and develop and implement effective solutions. They should work collaboratively with the project team and other stakeholders to address problems promptly and minimize their impact on the project.

Overall, effective risk management and problem-solving are critical to the success of a project. A well-managed project can anticipate and mitigate risks and handle problems promptly, ensuring that the project stays on track. The project manager's ability to manage risks and solve problems can make the difference between a successful project and a failed one.

## BUDGETING AND RESOURCE ALLOCATION

Budgeting and resource allocation are critical responsibilities of a project manager. The project manager should be able to manage the project's financial resources effectively and allocate them efficiently to achieve the project's objectives.

Budgeting involves estimating the costs associated with completing the project, including labour, materials, equipment, and overhead. The project manager should develop a comprehensive budget that takes into account all project costs, including contingencies and unforeseen expenses. They should also track actual project costs and compare them to the budget regularly to ensure the project remains financially viable.

Resource allocation involves identifying the project's resource requirements, such as personnel, equipment, and materials, and allocating them effectively. The project manager should ensure that the project has adequate resources to complete the project on time and within budget. They should also manage the project's resources efficiently, taking into account the project's priorities and critical path.

Effective budgeting and resource allocation require strong analytical and financial management skills. The project manager should be able to develop and manage budgets, track expenses, and forecast costs accurately. They should also be able to negotiate effectively with suppliers and vendors to obtain the best value for money.

Overall, effective budgeting and resource allocation are critical to the success of a project. Adequate financial resources and efficient allocation of resources can help ensure that the project is completed on time and within budget. The project manager's ability to manage budgets and allocate resources effectively can make the difference between a successful project and a failed one.

## MONITORING AND EVALUATION

Monitoring and evaluation are critical responsibilities of a project manager. The project manager should track the project's progress regularly and evaluate its performance against the project plan. This involves monitoring project activities, tracking milestones, and assessing progress against the project timeline.

The project manager should also evaluate the project's performance against its goals and objectives. This involves assessing the project's outcomes and impacts, identifying any gaps or deficiencies, and developing strategies to address them. The project manager should also evaluate the project's strengths and successes and identify opportunities for improvement.

Effective monitoring and evaluation require strong analytical and project management skills. The project manager should be able to use a range of monitoring and evaluation techniques, such as performance metrics, progress reports, and quality reviews. They should also be able to use this information to make informed decisions and adjustments to the project plan.

Overall, monitoring and evaluation are critical to the success of a project. Regular monitoring and evaluation can help ensure that the project stays on track and achieves its objectives. The project manager's ability to monitor and evaluate effectively can make the difference between a successful project and a failed one.

## ADAPTABILITY AND FLEXIBILITY

Adaptability and flexibility are critical skills for a project manager. Projects are often complex and unpredictable, and the project manager must be able to adapt to changing circumstances and adjust the project plan as needed. This involves being flexible and open-minded, able to pivot when necessary, and to be agile in their approach to project management.

The project manager should be able to identify and respond to changes in the project's environment, such as changes in stakeholder requirements or unexpected events. They should also be able to adjust the project plan to accommodate changes and ensure that the project remains on track.

Effective adaptability and flexibility require a strong understanding of the project's objectives and scope, as well as the ability to anticipate potential risks and challenges. The project manager should be able to work collaboratively with the project team and stakeholders to identify and address issues promptly.

Overall, adaptability and flexibility are critical to the success of a project. The ability to adapt to changing circumstances and adjust the project plan as needed can help ensure that the project stays on track and achieves its objectives. The project manager's ability to be adaptable and flexible can make the difference between a successful project and a failed one.

## The Importance of Effective Project Management

In conclusion, effective project management is essential to the success of any project. A project manager's role is to plan, organize, lead, and control the project from start to finish. This involves managing resources, time, and people, communicating effectively with stakeholders, and adapting to changing circumstances.

The key responsibilities of a project manager include planning and organizing the project, managing the project team, communicating with stakeholders, managing risks and problem-solving, budgeting and resource allocation, monitoring and evaluation, and being adaptable and flexible.

Effective project management requires a range of skills and competencies, including leadership, communication, problem-solving, analytical, and financial management skills. The project manager must be able to manage the project's resources effectively and allocate them efficiently to achieve the project's objectives.

Overall, effective project management is critical to delivering successful projects. The project manager's ability to plan, organize, lead, and control the project can make the difference between a successful project and a failed one. By mastering the key responsibilities of a project manager, the project manager can help ensure that the project is completed on time, within budget, and to the required quality standards.

# 1.4 THE PROJECT SPONSOR: KEY ROLES AND RESPONSIBILITIES

The project sponsor is a critical role in project management, and is typically a senior executive or leader within the organization that is funding the project. They are responsible for initiating, guiding, and providing oversight for the project, with the goal of achieving successful outcomes. The sponsor plays a critical role in ensuring that the project aligns with the organization's strategic goals and objectives, and has the necessary resources and support to be successful.

The project sponsor is responsible for providing the project team with the necessary resources, authority, and support to carry out the project successfully. They are also responsible for providing guidance and direction to the project team, and ensuring that the project remains aligned with the organization's strategic objectives. The project sponsor is typically not involved in the day-to-day management of the project, but rather provides high-level oversight and guidance.

In many cases, the project sponsor is responsible for securing funding for the project, and may need to justify the costs and benefits of the project to the organization's leadership. They also play a key role in communicating the project's progress and outcomes to the organization's stakeholders, including executives, customers, and employees. Overall, the project sponsor is critical to the success of the project, and their support and guidance can make a significant difference in the project's outcomes.

## KEY RESPONSIBILITIES OF THE PROJECT SPONSOR

The project sponsor has several key responsibilities that are critical to the success of the project. These responsibilities include:

a. Initiating the Project: The project sponsor is responsible for identifying the need for the project and initiating it. They must ensure that the project aligns with the organization's strategic goals and objectives and has the necessary resources and support to be successful.

b. Providing Resources and Support: The project sponsor is responsible for providing the project team with the necessary resources, support, and authority to carry out the project. This includes funding, personnel, equipment, and any other resources needed to complete the project.

c. Defining the Project Scope: The project sponsor is responsible for defining the scope of the project, including its goals, objectives, and deliverables. They must ensure that the project remains focused on its goals and does not deviate from its intended purpose.

d. Setting the Project Budget: The project sponsor is responsible for setting the budget for the project and ensuring that it remains within budget throughout the project lifecycle. They must also ensure that the project delivers value for the money spent.

e. Managing Stakeholder Expectations: The project sponsor is responsible for managing the expectations of stakeholders, including executives, customers, and employees. They must communicate the project's progress and outcomes to stakeholders and ensure that their needs and expectations are met.

f. Removing Obstacles: The project sponsor is responsible for removing any obstacles that may impede the project's progress. This includes addressing any issues that arise during the project lifecycle and ensuring that the project team has the necessary support to overcome them.

g. Approving Project Deliverables: The project sponsor is responsible for approving the project deliverables, including the final product or service. They must ensure that the deliverables meet the project's goals and objectives and are of high quality.

h. Ensuring Project Success: The project sponsor is ultimately responsible for ensuring the success of the project. They must monitor the project's progress, identify any risks or issues, and take action to mitigate them. They must also ensure that the project is delivered on time, within budget, and to the satisfaction of stakeholders.

## PROJECT SPONSOR VS. PROJECT MANAGER: UNDERSTANDING THE DIFFERENCES

While the project sponsor and project manager are both critical roles in project management, there are significant differences between the two. Understanding these differences is essential to effective project management.

a. Responsibilities: The project sponsor is responsible for the overall success of the project, while the project manager is responsible for managing the day-to-day activities of the project. The sponsor provides high-level guidance and oversight, while the project manager focuses on the details of the project.

b. Authority: The project sponsor has the authority to approve major decisions and changes to the project, while the project manager is responsible for implementing those decisions and changes.

c. Focus: The project sponsor focuses on the business objectives of the project, while the project manager focuses on the technical aspects of the project.

d. Stakeholder Management: The project sponsor manages the expectations of stakeholders, while the project manager manages the relationships with stakeholders.

e. Accountability: The project sponsor is ultimately accountable for the success of the project, while the project manager is accountable for the delivery of the project within the established constraints of time, cost, and quality.

f. Role in the Project Team: The project sponsor is typically not a member of the project team, while the project manager is a member of the project team and is responsible for leading and managing the team.

Understanding the differences between the project sponsor and project manager is critical to effective project management. Both roles are essential to project success and must work together closely to ensure that the project is delivered on time, within budget, and to the satisfaction of stakeholders.

## IMPORTANCE OF THE PROJECT SPONSOR FOR SUCCESSFUL PROJECT DELIVERY

The project sponsor is critical to the success of the project, and their role cannot be overstated. The following are some of the reasons why the project sponsor is important for successful project delivery:

a. Strategic Alignment: The project sponsor ensures that the project is aligned with the organization's strategic goals and objectives. This ensures that the project is focused on achieving outcomes that are important to the organization, and that the project delivers value to the organization.

b. Resource Management: The project sponsor is responsible for providing the project team with the necessary resources, support, and authority to carry out the project. This includes funding, personnel, equipment, and any other resources needed to complete the project. Without adequate resources, the project is likely to fail.

c. Stakeholder Management: The project sponsor manages the expectations of stakeholders, including executives, customers, and employees. This ensures that the project team has the necessary support to carry out the project successfully.

d. Risk Management: The project sponsor is responsible for identifying and managing risks associated with the project. This includes addressing any issues that arise during the project lifecycle and ensuring that the project team has the necessary support to overcome them.

e. Communication: The project sponsor communicates the project's progress and outcomes to stakeholders and ensures that their needs and expectations are met. This ensures that stakeholders remain engaged and supportive of the project.

f. Decision Making: The project sponsor has the authority to approve major decisions and changes to the project. This ensures that the project remains focused on its goals and objectives and that any changes are aligned with the organization's strategic goals.

In summary, the project sponsor plays a critical role in ensuring the success of the project. They provide guidance and oversight, ensure that the project is aligned with the organization's strategic goals and objectives, and provide the project team with the necessary resources and support to carry out the project successfully. Without the project sponsor, the project is unlikely to be successful.

## BEST PRACTICES FOR EFFECTIVE PROJECT SPONSORSHIP

Effective project sponsorship is critical to the success of the project. The following are some best practices for effective project sponsorship:

a. Clearly Define Roles and Responsibilities: It is important to clearly define the roles and responsibilities of the project sponsor and project manager to avoid confusion and ensure that everyone understands their role in the project.

b. Establish a Governance Structure: Establish a governance structure that provides the necessary oversight and guidance for the project. This includes setting up a steering committee, project board, or other governance body to provide oversight and ensure that the project remains aligned with the organization's strategic goals.

c. Ensure Adequate Resources: The project sponsor must ensure that the project team has the necessary resources, support, and authority to carry out the project successfully. This includes funding, personnel, equipment, and any other resources needed to complete the project.

d. Communicate Effectively: The project sponsor must communicate effectively with stakeholders, including executives, customers, and employees. This includes providing regular updates on the project's progress, outcomes, and any issues that arise during the project lifecycle.

e. Manage Stakeholder Expectations: The project sponsor must manage the expectations of stakeholders and ensure that their needs and expectations are met. This includes addressing any concerns or issues that stakeholders may have and keeping them engaged and supportive of the project.

f. Foster Collaboration: The project sponsor must foster collaboration and teamwork among the project team and stakeholders. This includes promoting open communication, resolving conflicts, and encouraging collaboration and cooperation.

g. Take a Long-term View: The project sponsor must take a long-term view of the project and its outcomes. This includes considering the project's impact on the organization and ensuring that it delivers long-term value.

h. Review and Evaluate: The project sponsor must review and evaluate the project's progress and outcomes regularly. This includes identifying any issues or risks and taking action to mitigate them.

In summary, effective project sponsorship requires clear roles and responsibilities, adequate resources, effective communication, stakeholder management, collaboration, a long-term view, and regular review and evaluation. Following these best practices can help ensure the success of the project and maximize its value to the organization.

# 1.5 OTHER KEY ROLES IN PROJECT MANAGEMENT

## USERS AND STAKEHOLDERS:

Users and stakeholders are crucial to the success of a project. They are the individuals or groups who will ultimately benefit from the project's outcome or be impacted by it. Understanding their needs, expectations, and requirements is essential to ensure that the project delivers its intended value.

Some of the key roles within users and stakeholders include:

a. Customers: They are the individuals who will use or purchase the product or service resulting from the project. Their feedback and satisfaction are critical to the success of the project.

b. End-users: They are the individuals who will directly use the product or service. Their feedback on usability, functionality, and design is essential to ensure that the product meets their needs.

c. Business sponsors: They are the individuals who provide the funding for the project and have a vested interest in its success. They often play a critical role in defining the project's scope and approving its deliverables.

d. Regulators: They are the individuals or organizations who oversee the project's compliance with relevant laws, regulations, and policies. Their input and approval are often necessary for the project to move forward.

It is important to engage users and stakeholders throughout the project lifecycle to ensure that their needs are met, and the project delivers its intended value. This may involve conducting user research, gathering feedback through surveys or focus groups, or involving stakeholders in project governance and decision-making processes.

## PROJECT TEAM MEMBERS:

Project team members are the individuals who work together to plan, execute, and deliver the project's objectives. They are responsible for completing specific tasks and delivering the project within the agreed-upon timeframe, budget, and quality standards.

Some of the key roles within project team members include:

a. Project manager: They are responsible for the overall success of the project, including planning, execution, monitoring, and control. They manage the project team and communicate with stakeholders to ensure that the project's objectives are met.

b. Project coordinator: They support the project manager by coordinating project activities and ensuring that the project team is on track to meet its deliverables.

c. Business analyst: They gather and analyze requirements, identify gaps and risks, and provide recommendations to improve the project's outcomes.

d. Technical lead: They are responsible for the technical aspects of the project, including architecture, design, and implementation. They provide guidance to the development team and ensure that the project's technical requirements are met.

e. Quality assurance (QA) lead: They ensure that the project meets the specified quality standards by reviewing deliverables, identifying defects, and providing feedback to the development team.

It is important to have a diverse and skilled project team that can collaborate effectively to achieve the project's objectives. The project manager should ensure that team members have clearly defined roles and responsibilities and that they have the necessary resources and support to deliver their tasks on time and within budget. Effective communication and collaboration among team members are critical to ensuring project success.

## PROJECT STEERING GROUP/BOARD:

The project steering group/board is a group of senior-level stakeholders who provide oversight, guidance, and decision-making support for the project. They are responsible for ensuring that the project aligns with the organization's goals, priorities, and strategic vision.

Some of the key roles within the project steering group/board include:

a. Sponsor: They provide the highest level of support for the project, including funding, resources, and strategic guidance. They have the ultimate responsibility for the project's success and are accountable to the organization's executive leadership.

b. Chair: They lead the project steering group/board, ensuring that meetings are conducted efficiently, decisions are made, and actions are taken to support the project's success.

c. Members: They are typically senior-level executives from various departments and functions within the organization who have a vested interest in the project's outcomes. They provide guidance, expertise, and oversight to ensure that the project aligns with the organization's goals and priorities.

The project steering group/board is responsible for setting the project's strategic direction, providing oversight, and making critical decisions that affect the project's success. They also serve as a link between the project team and the organization's executive leadership, ensuring that the project aligns with the organization's overall strategic vision. Effective communication, collaboration, and decision-making within the project steering group/board are critical to ensuring project success.

## PRODUCT OWNER:

The product owner is a key role within Agile project management methodology, and they are responsible for defining and prioritizing the product backlog. The product backlog is a list of features, enhancements, and bug fixes that the project team will deliver during the project.

Some of the key roles within the product owner include:

a. Defining requirements: The product owner is responsible for defining the product vision and requirements, based on market research, user feedback, and stakeholder needs. They work closely with the project team to ensure that the requirements are understood, and the project is aligned with the product vision.

b. Prioritizing the product backlog: The product owner is responsible for prioritizing the items on the product backlog based on the business value they provide, stakeholder needs, and project constraints.

c. Reviewing and accepting deliverables: The product owner is responsible for reviewing and accepting the project deliverables to ensure that they meet the product requirements and are aligned with the product vision.

The product owner works closely with the project team, stakeholders, and other key roles, such as the Scrum master, to ensure that the project delivers a high-quality product that meets customer needs and provides business value. Effective communication, collaboration, and decision-making among the product owner, project team, and stakeholders are critical to ensuring project success.

# 1.6 Understanding Different Types of Project Offices: Functions and Benefits

In today's fast-paced business world, organizations often face significant challenges in managing multiple projects, programs, and portfolios concurrently. To address this challenge, many companies have established Project Offices (POs) to manage projects efficiently, reduce risk, and ensure the timely delivery of project outcomes.

A Project Office can be defined as a centralized unit responsible for coordinating, standardizing, and controlling project-related activities across an organization. This unit provides the necessary support and guidance to project teams to ensure the successful completion of projects while meeting the organization's strategic goals.

The importance of a Project Office in project management cannot be overstated. Project Offices provide a structured approach to project management, which leads to consistency in project delivery, a reduction in risks and costs, improved communication, and collaboration between teams. The use of Project Offices is becoming increasingly popular, and different types of Project Offices have emerged over the years to meet specific organizational needs. This paper seeks to describe the functions and benefits of different types of Project Offices, including Project/Programme/Portfolio Management Office (PMO), Embedded PMO, Central PMO, and Hub-and-Spoke PMO.

## Project/Programme/Portfolio Management Office (PMO)

A Project/Programme/Portfolio Management Office, commonly known as PMO, is a centralized unit responsible for managing project portfolios, programs, and individual projects. The PMO provides governance and oversight for project-related activities to ensure that the organization's strategic objectives are met. The PMO is typically responsible for establishing and maintaining project management standards, processes, and methodologies across the organization.

Functions and Benefits:

The primary functions of a PMO include:

a. Project Portfolio Management: PMOs help organizations manage their project portfolios by identifying, prioritizing, and selecting projects aligned with the organization's strategic goals.

b. Standardization of Processes and Procedures: PMOs establish and maintain project management standards, processes, and methodologies across the organization to ensure consistency in project delivery and reduce risks and costs.

c. Resource Allocation and Management: PMOs manage project resources by identifying the required resources, assigning them to projects, and ensuring they are utilized efficiently.

d. Risk Management: PMOs identify and manage project risks by developing risk management plans, monitoring and controlling risks, and mitigating them when necessary.

The benefits of having a PMO in an organization include:

a. Improved Project Performance: PMOs help ensure that projects are delivered on time, within budget, and meet the required quality standards.

b. Consistency in Project Delivery: PMOs establish and maintain project management standards, processes, and methodologies across the organization to ensure consistency in project delivery.

c. Increased Visibility and Control: PMOs provide greater visibility into project-related activities, enabling better decision-making, and control over project outcomes.

d. Enhanced Collaboration and Communication: PMOs facilitate collaboration and communication between project teams, stakeholders, and senior management, ensuring everyone is on the same page and working towards the same goals.

Key Characteristics:

The key characteristics of a PMO include:

a. Centralized: The PMO is a centralized unit responsible for managing project portfolios, programs, and individual projects.

b. Strategic: The PMO is aligned with the organization's strategic goals and objectives.

c. Governance and Oversight: The PMO provides governance and oversight for project-related activities.

d. Standardization: The PMO establishes and maintains project management standards, processes, and methodologies across the organization.

e. Resource Management: The PMO manages project resources, including human, financial, and material resources.

In summary, a PMO is a centralized unit responsible for managing project portfolios, programs, and individual projects. The PMO provides governance and oversight for project-related activities, establishes and maintains project management standards, processes, and methodologies across the organization, and manages project resources. The benefits of having a PMO in an organization include improved project performance, consistency in project delivery, increased visibility and control, and enhanced collaboration and communication.

## EMBEDDED PMO

An Embedded PMO is a project management office that is integrated into an existing business unit or department within an organization. The Embedded PMO is responsible for managing the projects within that specific business unit or department, and its activities are closely aligned with the unit's objectives and goals. The Embedded PMO has a strong understanding of the business unit's operations, processes, and culture, which enables it to provide targeted support to the unit's project teams.

Functions and Benefits:

The primary functions of an Embedded PMO include:

a. Project Management Support: The Embedded PMO provides project management support to the business unit's project teams, including planning, execution, monitoring, and controlling of projects.

b. Process Improvement: The Embedded PMO works with the business unit to identify process improvement opportunities and implement changes to improve project delivery.

c. Resource Management: The Embedded PMO manages project resources, including human, financial, and material resources, to ensure they are utilized efficiently.

d. Risk Management: The Embedded PMO identifies and manages project risks by developing risk management plans, monitoring and controlling risks, and mitigating them when necessary.

The benefits of having an Embedded PMO in an organization include:

a. Improved Project Delivery: The Embedded PMO provides project management support to the business unit's project teams, resulting in improved project delivery.

b. Increased Efficiency: The Embedded PMO works with the business unit to identify process improvement opportunities, resulting in increased efficiency in project delivery.

c. Better Resource Management: The Embedded PMO manages project resources, including human, financial, and material resources, resulting in better utilization of resources and cost savings.

d. Improved Risk Management: The Embedded PMO identifies and manages project risks, resulting in better risk management and mitigation.

Key Characteristics:

The key characteristics of an Embedded PMO include:

a. Integration: The Embedded PMO is integrated into an existing business unit or department within an organization.

b. Business Unit Focus: The Embedded PMO's activities are closely aligned with the business unit's objectives and goals.

c. Supportive: The Embedded PMO provides project management support to the business unit's project teams.

d. Process Improvement: The Embedded PMO works with the business unit to identify process improvement opportunities and implement changes to improve project delivery.

e. Resource Management: The Embedded PMO manages project resources, including human, financial, and material resources.

In summary, an Embedded PMO is a project management office that is integrated into an existing business unit or department within an organization. The Embedded PMO provides project management support to the business unit's project teams, works with the unit to identify process improvement opportunities, manages project resources, and identifies and manages project risks. The benefits of having an Embedded PMO in an organization include improved project delivery, increased efficiency, better resource management, and improved risk management.

## CENTRAL PMO

A Central PMO is a project management office that operates independently of any specific business unit or department within an organization. The Central PMO is responsible for managing the organization's project portfolios, programs, and individual projects, and its activities are aligned with the organization's strategic goals and objectives. The Central PMO has a comprehensive understanding of the organization's operations, processes, and culture, which enables it to provide broad-based support to all project teams within the organization.

Functions and Benefits:

The primary functions of a Central PMO include:

a. Project Portfolio Management: The Central PMO is responsible for managing the organization's project portfolios, including identifying, prioritizing, and selecting projects aligned with the organization's strategic goals.

b. Standardization of Processes and Procedures: The Central PMO establishes and maintains project management standards, processes, and methodologies across the organization to ensure consistency in project delivery and reduce risks and costs.

c. Resource Allocation and Management: The Central PMO manages project resources, including human, financial, and material resources, to ensure they are utilized efficiently.

d. Risk Management: The Central PMO identifies and manages project risks by developing risk management plans, monitoring and controlling risks, and mitigating them when necessary.

The benefits of having a Central PMO in an organization include:

a. Improved Project Performance: The Central PMO helps ensure that projects are delivered on time, within budget, and meet the required quality standards.

b. Consistency in Project Delivery: The Central PMO establishes and maintains project management standards, processes, and methodologies across the organization to ensure consistency in project delivery.

c. Increased Visibility and Control: The Central PMO provides greater visibility into project-related activities, enabling better decision-making and control over project outcomes.

d. Enhanced Collaboration and Communication: The Central PMO facilitates collaboration and communication between project teams, stakeholders, and senior management, ensuring everyone is on the same page and working towards the same goals.

Key Characteristics:

The key characteristics of a Central PMO include:

a. Independence: The Central PMO operates independently of any specific business unit or department within an organization.

b. Strategic: The Central PMO's activities are aligned with the organization's strategic goals and objectives.

c. Governance and Oversight: The Central PMO provides governance and oversight for project-related activities.

d. Standardization: The Central PMO establishes and maintains project management standards, processes, and methodologies across the organization.

e. Resource Management: The Central PMO manages project resources, including human, financial, and material resources.

In summary, a Central PMO is a project management office that operates independently of any specific business unit or department within an organization. The Central PMO is responsible for managing the organization's project portfolios, programs, and individual projects, establishes and maintains project management standards, processes, and methodologies across the organization, manages project resources, and identifies and manages project risks. The benefits of having a Central PMO in an organization include improved project performance, consistency in project delivery, increased visibility and control, and enhanced collaboration and communication.

# HUB-AND-SPOKE PMO

A Hub-and-Spoke PMO is a project management office that comprises both a central hub and multiple satellite offices or spokes. The central hub is responsible for overall project portfolio management, while the satellite offices are responsible for managing individual projects within their respective business units or departments. The Hub-and-Spoke PMO is designed to provide flexibility and tailored support to the business units or departments, while maintaining overall governance and control over the organization's project portfolio.

Functions and Benefits:

The primary functions of a Hub-and-Spoke PMO include:

a. Project Portfolio Management: The central hub is responsible for managing the organization's project portfolios, including identifying, prioritizing, and selecting projects aligned with the organization's strategic goals. The satellite offices manage individual projects within their respective business units or departments.

b. Standardization of Processes and Procedures: The central hub establishes and maintains project management standards, processes, and methodologies across the organization to ensure consistency in project delivery and reduce risks and costs. The satellite offices can customize these processes and methodologies to suit their specific business unit or department's needs.

c. Resource Allocation and Management: The central hub manages project resources, including human, financial, and material resources, to ensure they are utilized efficiently. The satellite offices can request additional resources as needed to support their individual projects.

d. Risk Management: The central hub identifies and manages project risks by developing risk management plans, monitoring and controlling risks, and mitigating them when necessary. The satellite offices can also identify and manage project risks specific to their business unit or department.

The benefits of having a Hub-and-Spoke PMO in an organization include:

a. Tailored Support: The Hub-and-Spoke PMO provides tailored support to individual business units or departments while maintaining overall governance and control over the organization's project portfolio.

b. Increased Flexibility: The Hub-and-Spoke PMO provides flexibility in project delivery by allowing the satellite offices to customize project management processes and methodologies to suit their specific needs.

c. Consistency in Project Delivery: The central hub establishes and maintains project management standards, processes, and methodologies across the organization to ensure consistency in project delivery.

d. Enhanced Collaboration and Communication: The Hub-and-Spoke PMO facilitates collaboration and communication between the central hub, satellite offices, stakeholders, and senior management, ensuring everyone is on the same page and working towards the same goals.

Key Characteristics:

The key characteristics of a Hub-and-Spoke PMO include:

a. Centralized and Decentralized: The Hub-and-Spoke PMO comprises both a central hub and multiple satellite offices or spokes.

b. Strategic: The Hub-and-Spoke PMO's activities are aligned with the organization's strategic goals and objectives.

c. Governance and Oversight: The central hub provides governance and oversight for project-related activities.

d. Standardization and Customization: The central hub establishes and maintains project management standards, processes, and methodologies across the organization, while the satellite offices can customize these processes and methodologies to suit their specific needs.

e. Resource Management: The central hub manages project resources, including human, financial, and material resources, while the satellite offices can request additional resources as needed to support their individual projects.

In summary, a Hub-and-Spoke PMO is a project management office that comprises both a central hub and multiple satellite offices or spokes. The central hub is responsible for overall project portfolio management, while the satellite offices are responsible for managing individual projects within their respective business units or departments. The Hub-and-Spoke PMO provides tailored support to individual business units or departments while maintaining overall governance and control over the organization's project portfolio. The benefits of having a Hub-and-Spoke PMO in an organization include increased flexibility, consistency in project delivery, enhanced collaboration and communication, and tailored support.

## CONCLUSION

In conclusion, project offices play a crucial role in ensuring the successful delivery of projects, programs, and portfolios in organizations. Different types of project offices have emerged over the years to meet specific organizational needs, including Project/Programme/Portfolio Management Office (PMO), Embedded PMO, Central PMO, and Hub-and-Spoke PMO. Each type of project office has its own functions, benefits, and key characteristics.

A PMO is a centralized unit responsible for managing project portfolios, programs, and individual projects. It provides governance and oversight for project-related activities, establishes and maintains project management standards, processes, and methodologies, and manages project resources. An Embedded PMO is integrated into an existing business unit or department within an organization and provides project management support, process improvement, resource management, and risk management. A Central PMO operates independently of any specific business unit or department within an organization and is responsible for managing the organization's project portfolios, establishing and maintaining project management standards, processes, and methodologies, managing project resources, and identifying and managing project risks. A Hub-and-Spoke PMO comprises both a central hub and multiple satellite offices or spokes, providing tailored support to individual business units or departments while maintaining overall governance and control over the organization's project portfolio.

Choosing the right project office model for an organization requires careful consideration of the organization's needs, culture, and strategic goals. Organizations should evaluate each type of project office against their specific requirements and select the one that best meets their needs.

In summary, the establishment of a project office can provide numerous benefits to an organization, including improved project performance, consistency in project delivery, increased visibility and control, and enhanced collaboration and communication. By understanding the functions and benefits of different types of project offices, organizations can select the right project office model to meet their specific needs and improve their project management practices.

# 1.7 UNDERSTANDING THE IMPORTANCE OF PROJECT MANAGEMENT GOVERNANCE

Project management governance refers to the system of policies, regulations, functions, processes, procedures, and delegated responsibilities that an organization uses to manage its projects. It is a framework that defines the rules, procedures, and decision-making processes for project management.

The purpose of project management governance is to ensure that projects are completed on time, within budget, and to the desired quality standards. It helps organizations to manage risks, avoid conflicts, and ensure compliance with laws and regulations.

Project management governance is important for organizations of all sizes and types, whether they are in the private or public sector. It provides a structured approach to project management, which helps to minimize risks and maximize the chances of success.

Effective project management governance requires the involvement of all stakeholders, including project managers, sponsors, team members, and external partners. It is a collaborative process that requires communication, coordination, and cooperation among all parties involved in the project.

## THE NEED FOR POLICIES AND REGULATIONS IN PROJECT MANAGEMENT GOVERNANCE

Policies and regulations are essential components of project management governance. They provide guidelines and standards that help organizations to ensure that their projects are aligned with their strategic objectives, comply with laws and regulations, and meet stakeholder expectations.

Policies are high-level statements that define the principles, values, and objectives of the organization. They provide guidance on how projects should be managed, what resources should be used, and how risks should be managed.

Regulations, on the other hand, are specific rules that must be followed to comply with legal, ethical, or other requirements. They can include industry standards, safety guidelines, environmental regulations, or contractual obligations.

By implementing policies and regulations in project management governance, organizations can ensure that their projects are aligned with their overall strategy, vision, and mission. They can also ensure that their projects are managed consistently, transparently, and ethically.

Policies and regulations can help organizations to avoid project failures, minimize risks, and enhance stakeholder trust and confidence. They provide a framework for decision-making, resource allocation, and performance measurement, which helps to ensure that projects are completed successfully and deliver value to the organization.

## KEY FUNCTIONS IN PROJECT MANAGEMENT GOVERNANCE

Project management governance involves several key functions that are essential for effective project management. These functions include:

a.  Project Portfolio Management (PPM): PPM is the process of selecting, prioritizing, and managing a portfolio of projects to achieve organizational objectives. It involves evaluating projects based on their strategic fit, resource requirements, risk profiles, and expected returns. PPM helps organizations to allocate resources effectively, balance risks and rewards, and optimize their project portfolio.

b.  Project Governance: Project governance is the process of setting up a governance framework for a specific project. It involves defining the roles and responsibilities of project stakeholders, establishing decision-making processes, and ensuring compliance with policies and regulations. Project governance helps to ensure that projects are managed effectively, risks are managed appropriately, and stakeholders are engaged throughout the project lifecycle.

c. Project Management Office (PMO): A PMO is a centralized unit that provides project management support, guidance, and governance to project teams. It helps to standardize project management processes, methodologies, and tools across the organization. PMOs can improve project outcomes by providing project teams with the necessary resources, skills, and expertise.

d. Risk Management: Risk management is the process of identifying, assessing, and mitigating risks that could impact project objectives. It involves analyzing potential risks, developing risk mitigation strategies, and monitoring risk exposure throughout the project lifecycle. Effective risk management helps organizations to minimize the likelihood of project failures, reduce project costs, and improve project outcomes.

e. Quality Management: Quality management is the process of ensuring that project deliverables meet the required quality standards. It involves defining quality requirements, developing quality assurance processes, and conducting quality control activities. Quality management helps organizations to deliver projects that meet or exceed stakeholder expectations, enhance customer satisfaction, and improve organizational performance.

These key functions are essential components of project management governance. By implementing these functions effectively, organizations can ensure that their projects are aligned with their strategic objectives, managed consistently, and deliver value to the organization.

## PROCESSES AND PROCEDURES IN PROJECT MANAGEMENT GOVERNANCE

Processes and procedures are critical components of project management governance. They provide a standardized approach to project management, which helps to ensure that projects are managed consistently, effectively, and efficiently. Processes and procedures in project management governance include:

1. Project Concept: This process involves identifying project objectives, defining scope, developing a project charter, and identifying stakeholders. It sets the foundation for the project and provides a clear direction for the project team.

2. Project Definition: This process involves developing a detailed project plan, which includes defining project scope, developing a work breakdown structure (WBS), identifying project tasks and activities, and developing a project schedule. Project planning helps to ensure that the project is completed on time, within budget, and to the desired quality standards.

3. Project Deployment: This process involves implementing the project plan, monitoring project progress, and managing project risks. It includes managing project scope, managing project resources, managing project communications, and managing project stakeholders. Project deployment helps to ensure that the project is completed according to the project plan.

4. Project Monitoring and Control: This process involves monitoring project progress, identifying variances, and implementing corrective actions. It includes monitoring project schedule, monitoring project budget, monitoring project quality, and monitoring project risks. Project monitoring and control helps to ensure that the project is on track and within the desired scope, budget, and quality.

5. Project Transition: This process involves finalizing project deliverables, obtaining acceptance from stakeholders, and closing out the project. It includes conducting a post-project review, documenting lessons learned, and archiving project

documents. Project transition helps to ensure that the project is completed successfully and that the organization benefits from the project outcomes.

By implementing processes and procedures in project management governance, organizations can ensure that their projects are managed consistently, effectively, and efficiently. It helps to minimize risks, avoid conflicts, and ensure compliance with laws and regulations.

## DELEGATED RESPONSIBILITIES IN PROJECT MANAGEMENT GOVERNANCE

Delegated responsibilities are an essential component of project management governance. They involve assigning responsibilities and authority to individuals or groups who are responsible for managing various aspects of the project. Delegated responsibilities in project management governance include:

a. Project Sponsor: The project sponsor is the individual who provides funding and support for the project. The project sponsor is responsible for defining project objectives, setting project priorities, and ensuring that the project aligns with the organization's strategic objectives.

b. Project Manager: The project manager is the individual responsible for managing the project. The project manager is responsible for developing the project plan, coordinating project activities, managing project risks, and ensuring that the project is completed on time, within budget, and to the desired quality standards.

c. Project Team: The project team is a group of individuals who work together to complete the project. The project team is responsible for carrying out project activities, communicating with stakeholders, and ensuring that project deliverables meet the required quality standards.

d. Steering Committee: The steering committee is a group of individuals who provide guidance and oversight for the project.

The steering committee is responsible for reviewing project progress, making decisions on key project issues, and ensuring that the project aligns with the organization's strategic objectives.

e. Project Review Board: The project review board is a group of individuals who review the project's progress and provide recommendations for improvement. The project review board is responsible for identifying project risks, evaluating project outcomes, and providing feedback to the project team.

By delegating responsibilities in project management governance, organizations can ensure that the right people are assigned the right roles and responsibilities. It helps to ensure that project activities are managed effectively and that project risks are managed appropriately. It also helps to ensure that stakeholders are engaged throughout the project lifecycle and that project outcomes meet stakeholder expectations.

## BENEFITS OF EFFECTIVE PROJECT MANAGEMENT GOVERNANCE

Effective project management governance provides several benefits to organizations. Some of these benefits include:

a. Improved Project Outcomes: Effective project management governance helps organizations to deliver projects that meet or exceed stakeholder expectations. It helps to ensure that projects are completed on time, within budget, and to the desired quality standards.

b. Increased Transparency: Project management governance provides a structured approach to project management, which helps to increase transparency and accountability. It helps to ensure that project activities are documented and communicated effectively to stakeholders.

c. Minimized Risks: Project management governance helps to minimize project risks by identifying and assessing potential risks, developing risk mitigation strategies, and monitoring risk exposure throughout the project lifecycle.

d. Increased Efficiency: Project management governance provides a standardized approach to project management, which helps to increase efficiency and productivity. It helps to ensure that project activities are carried out consistently and that resources are allocated effectively.

e. Enhanced Stakeholder Engagement: Project management governance ensures that stakeholders are engaged throughout the project lifecycle. It helps to ensure that stakeholders are involved in decision-making processes, are kept informed of project progress, and have opportunities to provide feedback.

f. Improved Resource Management: Project management governance helps organizations to allocate resources effectively. It ensures that resources are used efficiently, and that project activities are aligned with organizational goals and objectives.

Overall, effective project management governance helps organizations to deliver projects that meet stakeholder expectations, minimize risks, and maximize value to the organization. It provides a structured approach to project management, which helps to increase efficiency, productivity, and transparency.

## CHALLENGES IN IMPLEMENTING PROJECT MANAGEMENT GOVERNANCE

Implementing project management governance can be challenging for organizations, particularly for those that are new to project management or have limited resources. Some of the challenges that organizations may face when implementing project management governance include:

a. Resistance to Change: Implementing project management governance can involve significant changes to an organization's culture, processes, and procedures. This can be met with resistance from stakeholders who are accustomed to the status quo.

b. Lack of Resources: Effective project management governance requires dedicated resources, including skilled project managers, project management tools, and project management processes. Organizations may struggle to allocate the necessary resources to implement project management governance.

c. Lack of Senior Management Support: Senior management support is critical to the success of project management governance. Without the support of senior management, it can be difficult to obtain the necessary resources and to implement the necessary changes to organizational culture and processes.

d. Lack of Project Management Expertise: Effective project management governance requires individuals with project management expertise to manage projects effectively. Organizations may struggle to find individuals with the necessary skills and experience to manage projects.

e. Inadequate Training: Project management governance requires individuals to have the necessary training and skills to manage projects effectively. Organizations may struggle to provide the necessary training and support to individuals involved in project management.

f. Insufficient Stakeholder Engagement: Effective project management governance requires stakeholder engagement throughout the project lifecycle. Organizations may struggle to engage stakeholders effectively, leading to conflicts, delays, and suboptimal project outcomes.

To overcome these challenges, organizations must be committed to implementing project management governance and willing to invest the necessary resources to ensure its success. This includes providing training and support to individuals involved in project management, engaging stakeholders effectively, and ensuring senior management support for the project management governance framework.

# BEST PRACTICES FOR PROJECT MANAGEMENT GOVERNANCE

Implementing project management governance requires organizations to adopt best practices to ensure its success. Some best practices for project management governance include:

a. Aligning Project Management with Organizational Strategy: Project management governance should be aligned with the organization's strategic objectives to ensure that projects are in line with the organization's overall goals.

b. Establishing Clear Roles and Responsibilities: Clear roles and responsibilities should be defined for all stakeholders involved in the project to ensure accountability and ownership.

c. Developing Standardized Processes and Procedures: Standardized processes and procedures should be developed to ensure consistency and efficiency in project management.

d. Providing Adequate Resources: Adequate resources should be allocated to support project management governance, including skilled project managers, project management tools, and project management processes.

e. Engaging Stakeholders: Stakeholders should be engaged throughout the project lifecycle to ensure that their needs and expectations are met.

f. Implementing Risk Management Strategies: Risk management strategies should be implemented to identify, assess, and mitigate risks that could impact project outcomes.

g. Providing Training and Support: Training and support should be provided to individuals involved in project management to ensure that they have the necessary skills and knowledge to manage projects effectively.

h. Conducting Post-Project Reviews: Post-project reviews should be conducted to evaluate project outcomes, identify lessons learned, and implement improvements for future projects.

By adopting these best practices, organizations can ensure the success of project management governance. It helps to ensure that projects are completed on time, within budget, and to the desired quality standards. It also helps to ensure that project outcomes meet stakeholder expectations, minimize risks, and maximize value to the organization.

# CHAPTER TWO

## *NAVIGATING THE PHASES OF PROJECT LIFE CYCLES*

# 2.1 UNDERSTANDING THE DIFFERENCES BETWEEN LINEAR, ITERATIVE, AND HYBRID LIFE CYCLES IN PROJECT MANAGEMENT

Project management is the practice of planning, executing, controlling, and closing projects efficiently and effectively. One of the critical aspects of project management is choosing the right life cycle for your project. A life cycle is a series of phases or stages that a project goes through from start to finish.

There are different types of life cycles, including linear, iterative, and hybrid life cycles. Each life cycle has its unique characteristics, advantages, and disadvantages.

Understanding the differences between these life cycles is crucial to selecting the most appropriate life cycle for your project. It helps project managers to optimize their resources, reduce risks, and improve project outcomes.

In the following sections, we will explore each of these life cycles and how they differ from one another. We will also examine the benefits and drawbacks of each life cycle and how to choose the right life cycle for your project.

## THE LINEAR LIFE CYCLE:

The linear life cycle, also known as the waterfall model, is a traditional approach to project management. This life cycle consists of a sequential and linear flow of phases. Each phase is completed before moving on to the next phase. The linear life cycle typically includes the following phases:

76

1. Requirements Gathering: In this phase, the project team identifies the project's objectives, deliverables, and stakeholders' requirements.

2. Design: In this phase, the project team designs a plan for the project, including its scope, schedule, budget, and resources.

3. Implementation: In this phase, the project team executes the plan according to the design specifications.

4. Testing: In this phase, the project team tests the project to ensure that it meets the stakeholders' requirements and specifications.

5. Deployment: In this phase, the project team delivers the final product or service to the stakeholders.

The linear life cycle is suitable for projects with well-defined requirements and stable environments. It is often used in manufacturing, construction, and software development projects. The advantages of this life cycle include clear and straightforward planning, easy monitoring, and control of project progress.

However, the linear life cycle has some drawbacks. Its sequential nature makes it challenging to accommodate changes in requirements during the implementation phase. It is also inflexible and does not allow for feedback from stakeholders until the testing phase. As a result, the linear life cycle may result in delayed delivery, increased costs, and dissatisfied stakeholders.

## THE ITERATIVE LIFE CYCLE:

The iterative life cycle, also known as the Agile model, is an adaptive approach to project management. This life cycle consists of a series of iterations, each of which is a mini project in itself. Each iteration includes the following phases:

1. Planning: In this phase, the project team plans the iteration's objectives, scope, and deliverables.

2. Execution: In this phase, the project team executes the iteration, including design, implementation, testing, and deployment.

3. Review: In this phase, the project team reviews the iteration's results and identifies areas for improvement.

4. Refinement: In this phase, the project team refines the plan for the next iteration based on the results and feedback from the previous iteration.

The iterative life cycle is suitable for projects with changing requirements, high uncertainty, and complex environments. It is often used in software development, product development, and research projects. The advantages of this life cycle include flexibility, adaptability, and continuous improvement.

However, the iterative life cycle also has some drawbacks. It can be challenging to manage, and the constant changes and feedback may lead to scope creep and budget overruns. It also requires a high level of collaboration and communication among team members and stakeholders.

## THE HYBRID LIFE CYCLE:

The hybrid life cycle is a combination of the linear and iterative life cycles. It involves using both sequential and adaptive approaches in a project. The hybrid life cycle is tailored to fit the specific requirements and constraints of a project. The project team determines the appropriate mix of linear and iterative phases based on the project's needs.

For example, a project may start with a linear phase for requirements gathering, followed by an iterative phase for design and implementation, and then end with a linear phase for testing and deployment. Alternatively, a project may use a linear phase for project planning and an iterative phase for execution.

The hybrid life cycle is suitable for projects that have both well-defined requirements and changing requirements. It allows for flexibility and adaptability while maintaining control and structure. It is often used in software development, product development, and construction projects.

The advantages of the hybrid life cycle include flexibility, control, and the ability to manage changing requirements. It allows the project team to tailor the life cycle to fit the project's unique needs.

However, the hybrid life cycle also has some drawbacks. It requires a high level of project management expertise to determine the appropriate mix of linear and iterative phases. It can also be challenging to manage and may result in increased project complexity and cost.

## COMPARISON OF LINEAR, ITERATIVE, AND HYBRID LIFE CYCLES:

Linear, iterative, and hybrid life cycles differ in several aspects, including their approach to planning, execution, control, and adaptation. The following are some of the key differences between these life cycles:

a. Planning: The linear life cycle involves detailed planning before the deployment phase, while the iterative life cycle involves planning each iteration before execution. The hybrid life cycle involves a combination of both detailed planning and planning for each iteration.

b. Execution: The linear life cycle involves executing each phase sequentially without feedback until the testing phase. The iterative life cycle involves executing each iteration with continuous feedback and improvement. The hybrid life cycle involves a combination of sequential execution and iterative execution.

c. Control: The linear life cycle is easier to control and monitor since each phase has well-defined outputs and inputs. The iterative life cycle is more challenging to control since each iteration may have different objectives and deliverables. The hybrid life cycle requires a flexible and adaptive approach to control and monitoring.

d. Adaptation: The linear life cycle is inflexible and does not allow for significant changes in requirements during the deployment phase. The iterative life cycle allows for changes and feedback during each iteration. The hybrid life cycle allows for some changes during iterative phases but has more rigid requirements during linear phases.

e. Risks: The linear life cycle is more susceptible to risks due to its inflexible nature, while the iterative life cycle is more adaptable and can reduce risks through continuous feedback and improvement. The hybrid life cycle can reduce risks through a combination of both inflexible and adaptive approaches.

f. Stakeholder involvement: The linear life cycle involves minimal stakeholder involvement until the testing phase, while the iterative life cycle involves continuous stakeholder involvement and feedback. The hybrid life cycle involves a mix of stakeholder involvement during sequential and iterative phases.

Each life cycle has its advantages and disadvantages, and the appropriate life cycle depends on the project's specific requirements and constraints. Understanding the differences between these life cycles can help project managers select the most appropriate life cycle for their projects.

## Choosing the Right Life Cycle for Your Project:

Selecting the appropriate life cycle for your project is crucial for its success. The following are some factors to consider when choosing a life cycle for your project:

a. Project Requirements: The project's requirements and objectives should guide the selection of the life cycle. Projects with well-defined requirements may benefit from the linear life cycle, while projects with changing requirements may benefit from the iterative life cycle. Projects with a mix of requirements may benefit from the hybrid life cycle.

b. Project Complexity: The project's complexity should also guide the selection of the life cycle. Projects with high complexity may benefit from the iterative or hybrid life cycle, while less complex projects may benefit from the linear life cycle.

c. Project Environment: The project's environment, including the stakeholders and resources, should also guide the selection of the life cycle. The linear life cycle may be suitable for projects with a stable environment, while the iterative or hybrid life cycle may be suitable for projects with a dynamic environment.

d. Project Team Expertise: The project team's expertise and experience should also guide the selection of the life cycle. The iterative or hybrid life cycle may require a higher level of project management expertise and experience than the linear life cycle.

e. Project Timeline: The project's timeline should also guide the selection of the life cycle. The linear life cycle may be suitable for projects with tight deadlines, while the iterative or hybrid life cycle may require more time due to the continuous feedback and improvement.

By considering these factors, project managers can select the most appropriate life cycle for their projects. It is important to note that selecting the life cycle is not a one-time decision and may require adjustments as the project progresses.

## CONCLUSION: BENEFITS AND DRAWBACKS OF EACH LIFE CYCLE APPROACH:

Each life cycle approach - linear, iterative, and hybrid - has its advantages and disadvantages. Understanding these benefits and drawbacks can help project managers select the appropriate approach for their projects.

The linear life cycle provides a structured approach to project management, making it easy to control and monitor. However, it can be inflexible, making it challenging to accommodate changes in requirements during the deployment phase.

The iterative life cycle provides a flexible approach to project management, allowing for continuous feedback and improvement. However, it can be challenging to control and monitor, and it may result in scope creep and budget overruns.

The hybrid life cycle combines the advantages of both the linear and iterative life cycles, providing a tailored approach to project management. However, it can be challenging to manage and may result in increased project complexity and cost.

In conclusion, selecting the appropriate life cycle approach for your project depends on several factors, including the project's requirements, complexity, environment, team expertise, and timeline. Project managers should carefully evaluate these factors and select the life cycle approach that best fits their project's unique needs. By doing so, project managers can optimize their resources, reduce risks, and improve project outcomes.

## 2.2 THE IMPORTANCE OF PHASED PROJECT MANAGEMENT IN A LINEAR LIFE CYCLE

Linear life cycle is a traditional approach to project management, where projects are structured into a sequence of phases that follow a linear progression from start to finish. Each phase is usually marked by a deliverable, such as a document or a prototype, which is reviewed and approved before proceeding to the next phase. This approach is often used in industries such as construction, engineering, and manufacturing, where projects tend to be more predictable and have a clear start and end date.

The linear life cycle typically consists of four main phases: concept, definition, deployment, and transition. During the concept phase, the project is defined, and its feasibility is assessed. In the definition phase, the project scope is defined, and a detailed plan is created, including timelines, resources, and budget. The deployment phase is where the project work is completed, and the deliverables are produced. Finally, in the transition phase, the project is formally closed, and the final deliverables are handed over to the customer.

Although the linear life cycle approach has been criticized for being inflexible and not suitable for complex projects, it still remains a popular choice for many organizations. This is because it provides a clear structure and helps project teams to manage resources, time, and budgets effectively. By breaking down the project into manageable phases, it also allows for better control and monitoring of progress and helps to identify potential issues early on.

## PHASED PROJECT MANAGEMENT DEFINED

Phased project management is an approach to project management that breaks down a project into distinct phases or stages, each with its own set of activities, deliverables, and milestones. The phases are usually organized in a linear sequence, where each phase builds on the previous one and leads to the next one. This approach is used to manage projects that have a clear start and end date, and where the deliverables are well defined.

Phased project management typically involves the following phases:

1. Concept: This phase involves defining the project scope, objectives, and stakeholders. It also includes the identification of project risks, assumptions, and constraints.

2. Definition: In this phase, the project plan is developed, including the detailed scope, schedule, budget, and resource requirements. A risk management plan is also created, and the project team is assembled.

3. Deployment: This is the phase where the actual project work is performed. The project team works on the tasks identified in the project plan, and the deliverables are produced.

4. Transition: This is the final phase, where the project is formally closed, and the final deliverables are handed over to the customer. This phase also involves conducting a post-project review to identify lessons learned and best practices for future projects.

Phased project management is a popular approach to project management because it provides a clear structure and helps to manage resources, time, and budgets effectively. By breaking down the project into manageable phases, it allows for better control and monitoring of progress, and helps to identify potential issues early on. It also enables project teams to focus on specific deliverables and milestones, which can help to improve the quality of the final product or service.

# Benefits of Phased Project Management

Phased project management offers several benefits to organizations, including:

a. Improved project planning: By breaking down a project into distinct phases, project teams can create a detailed plan for each phase, including timelines, resources, and budget. This enables better management of resources and helps to identify potential issues early on.

b. Better control and monitoring: Phased project management allows project teams to monitor progress against the project plan, identify variances, and take corrective action. This helps to ensure that the project stays on track and that issues are addressed before they become major problems.

c. Reduced risk: By conducting a risk assessment at the beginning of the project and creating a risk management plan, project teams can identify and mitigate potential risks. This can help to reduce the likelihood of project delays or failure.

d. Improved quality: By focusing on specific deliverables and milestones, project teams can ensure that each deliverable meets the required quality standards. This can help to improve the overall quality of the final product or service.

e. Clear communication: Phased project management provides a clear structure for communication between the project team, stakeholders, and customers. This helps to ensure that everyone is aware of the project status, and that any issues or concerns are addressed in a timely manner.

f. Better alignment with business goals: Phased project management helps to ensure that the project is aligned with the organization's business goals and objectives. By defining the project scope and objectives at the beginning of the project, project teams can ensure that the project delivers the desired outcomes.

Overall, phased project management offers a structured approach to project management that helps organizations to manage projects more effectively and efficiently. It provides a framework for planning, executing, monitoring, and controlling projects, and enables project teams to deliver projects that meet the required quality standards, within budget and on time.

## LIMITATIONS OF PHASED PROJECT MANAGEMENT

Although phased project management offers several benefits, there are also some limitations to this approach, including:

a. Inflexibility: The linear nature of phased project management can make it difficult to adapt to changes in the project scope or requirements. Once a phase is completed, it can be challenging to make changes without impacting the rest of the project.

b. Limited collaboration: Phased project management can sometimes lead to silos of work, where each phase is completed by a different team or group of people. This can limit collaboration and communication between team members, and can lead to delays or misunderstandings.

c. Overemphasis on planning: Phased project management places a lot of emphasis on planning, which can sometimes result in too much time spent on planning and not enough time spent on executing the project work.

d. Unforeseen issues: Despite careful planning, unforeseen issues can arise during the project, which can lead to delays or require changes to the project plan. Phased project management can sometimes make it difficult to adapt to these issues quickly.

e. Limited creativity: Phased project management can sometimes stifle creativity, as each phase is focused on specific deliverables and milestones. This can make it difficult to explore new ideas or approaches that may emerge during the project.

f. Costly: Phased project management can be costly, as each phase requires a separate set of resources and deliverables. This can sometimes result in duplication of effort and can lead to higher project costs.

Overall, while phased project management is a popular approach to project management, it is not suitable for every project. Organizations should carefully consider the project scope, complexity, and requirements before deciding to use this approach. They should also be aware of the limitations and potential challenges associated with this approach and should take steps to address these issues to ensure project success.

## EXAMPLES OF PHASED PROJECT MANAGEMENT IN ACTION

Phased project management is used in many industries, including construction, engineering, and manufacturing, where projects tend to be more predictable and have a clear start and end date. Here are some examples of how phased project management is used in different industries:

a. Construction: In the construction industry, phased project management is used to manage large-scale construction projects. The project is broken down into distinct phases, such as site preparation, foundation, framing, electrical and plumbing, and finishing. Each phase has its own set of activities, deliverables, and milestones, and must be completed before the next phase can begin.

b. Software development: In software development, phased project management is used to manage the development of software applications. The project is typically broken down into distinct phases, such as requirements gathering, design, development, testing, and deployment. Each phase has its own set of activities, deliverables, and milestones, and must be completed before the next phase can begin.

c. Product development: In product development, phased project management is used to manage the development of new products. The project is typically broken down into distinct phases, such as ideation, research, design, prototyping, testing, and production. Each phase has its own set of activities, deliverables, and milestones, and must be completed before the next phase can begin.

d. Manufacturing: In manufacturing, phased project management is used to manage the production of goods. The project is typically broken down into distinct phases, such as planning, sourcing, production, and delivery. Each phase has its own set of activities, deliverables, and milestones, and must be completed before the next phase can begin.

Overall, phased project management is a versatile approach to project management that can be used in many different industries and contexts. It provides a clear structure and helps project teams to manage resources, time, and budgets effectively. By breaking down the project into manageable phases, it also allows for better control and monitoring of progress and helps to identify potential issues early on.

## Choosing the Right Project Management Approach for Your Organization

While phased project management can be an effective approach to project management, it is not suitable for every project. Organizations must carefully consider the project scope, complexity, and requirements before deciding to use this approach. Here are some factors to consider when choosing the right project management approach for your organization:

a. Project scope: The project scope will determine the level of detail required for project planning and management. Projects with a well-defined scope and clear deliverables are typically better suited for phased project management.

b. Project complexity: Projects that are more complex and involve multiple stakeholders or require a high degree of collaboration may require a more flexible project management approach, such as agile or hybrid project management.

c. Project timeline: Projects with a short timeline and a fixed deadline may require a more structured approach to project management, such as phased project management.

d. Resource availability: The availability of resources, including personnel, time, and budget, can also impact the choice of project management approach. Projects with limited resources may require a more structured approach to project management to ensure that resources are used effectively.

e. Organizational culture: The organizational culture can also impact the choice of project management approach. Organizations that value stability and predictability may prefer a more structured approach to project management, such as phased project management. Organizations that value flexibility and innovation may prefer a more flexible approach, such as agile project management.

Overall, the choice of project management approach will depend on a variety of factors, including project scope, complexity, timeline, resource availability, and organizational culture. It is important to carefully evaluate these factors and choose the approach that is best suited for your organization and the specific project at hand. By choosing the right project management approach, organizations can ensure that projects are completed on time, within budget, and to the required quality standards.

# 2.3 UNDERSTANDING THE DIFFERENCES BETWEEN PROJECT LIFE CYCLE AND EXTENDED LIFE CYCLE

In project management, a life cycle refers to a series of phases or stages that a project goes through from concept to transition. A project life cycle provides a framework for managing and controlling the project from start to finish. It is a roadmap that guides the project team through the various stages of defining, deploying, monitoring, and controlling, and ultimately, transitioning the project.

The choice of a project life cycle is based on several factors such as project scope, complexity, and the level of risk involved. Project managers need to select a life cycle that aligns with the project's objectives and goals to ensure that it is completed successfully.

In addition to the traditional project life cycle, there is also an extended life cycle approach that can be used in certain situations. In this approach, the project life cycle is extended beyond the typical concept, definition, deployment, and transition phases. Instead, it may include additional phases, such as benefits realization, operations, and maintenance.

This section aims to differentiate between project life cycle and extended life cycle, their definitions, characteristics, and key differences, and when to use each approach in project management.

## PROJECT LIFE CYCLE: DEFINITION AND CHARACTERISTICS

A project life cycle is a series of sequential phases that a project goes through from concept to transition. It defines the project's framework, including the tasks, deliverables, milestones, and resources required to complete the project successfully. The project life cycle approach provides a structured and organized way of managing projects and helps to ensure that all project stakeholders are aligned with the project goals and objectives.

The typical project life cycle consists of four phases:

1. Concept: This phase involves the identification and definition of the project's objectives, stakeholders, and deliverables. It also involves conducting a feasibility study to determine if the project is viable and aligns with the organization's goals and objectives.

2. Definition: In this phase, the project manager develops a detailed project plan, including the scope, schedule, budget, and resources required to complete the project successfully.

3. Deployment: This phase involves the actual implementation of the project plan. The project team performs the tasks outlined in the project plan, and the project manager monitors progress against the plan.

4. Transition: In this final phase, the project is completed, and the project team conducts a post-project review to assess the project's success and identify areas for improvement.

The project life cycle approach is suitable for projects that have a well-defined scope, clear objectives, and a finite timeline. This approach is commonly used for construction projects, software development projects, and other types of projects that have a defined beginning and end.

## PHASES OF PROJECT LIFE CYCLE

The project life cycle approach consists of several sequential phases that a project must go through to achieve its objectives. These phases are as follows:

1. Concept Phase: This phase marks the beginning of the project and involves identifying the project's objectives, goals, and stakeholders. The project team also conducts a feasibility study to determine whether the project is viable, and if it aligns with the organization's goals and objectives.

2. Definition Phase: In this phase, the project manager develops a detailed project plan that outlines the project's scope, objectives, timeline, budget, and resources required to complete the project successfully. This phase also involves creating a project team structure, defining the roles and responsibilities of team members, and identifying potential risks and constraints that may impact the project's success.

3. Deployment Phase: This phase involves the actual implementation of the project plan. The project team performs the tasks outlined in the project plan, and the project manager monitors progress against the plan. The deployment phase involves executing the tasks, making sure they are performed efficiently and effectively, and using the right resources to ensure the project's objectives are achieved.

4. Transition Phase: In this final phase, the project is completed, and the project team conducts a post-project review to assess the project's success and identify areas for improvement. This phase also involves closing out the project, including finalizing all project deliverables and archiving project documentation.

These phases form a cycle that repeats for each project that is undertaken, with each cycle resulting in a completed project. The project life cycle approach provides a structured and organized way of managing projects and helps to ensure that all project stakeholders are aligned with the project goals and objectives.

# EXTENDED LIFE CYCLE: DEFINITION AND CHARACTERISTICS

An extended life cycle is an approach to project management that extends beyond the typical concept, definition, deployment, monitoring and control, and transition phases of the project life cycle. Instead, it may include additional phases, such as benefits realization, operations, and maintenance.

The extended life cycle approach is often used for projects that have a long-term impact on an organization or require ongoing support after the project is completed. This approach considers the entire life cycle of the project, including the post-project phase, which involves ensuring that the project's benefits are realized and that the project continues to meet its objectives in the long term.

The extended life cycle approach is suitable for projects that involve implementing new systems, processes, or technology that require ongoing support, maintenance, and improvement. For example, a project to implement a new customer relationship management (CRM) system would require ongoing maintenance and support to ensure that it continues to meet the organization's needs and provides the expected benefits.

The extended life cycle approach involves several additional phases, including:

a. Benefits Realization: This phase involves identifying and quantifying the benefits that the project will deliver and developing a plan to realize those benefits. The project team works with stakeholders to ensure that the benefits are achievable and align with the organization's goals and objectives.

b. Operations: This phase involves implementing the project's deliverables and ensuring that they are integrated into the organization's operations. This includes training employees, creating standard operating procedures, and developing a plan to support the ongoing use of the project deliverables.

c. Maintenance: This phase involves ensuring that the project deliverables continue to meet the organization's needs and operate efficiently. This includes monitoring system performance, identifying and addressing issues, and making necessary upgrades or modifications.

The extended life cycle approach provides a more holistic view of the project and considers its long-term impact on the organization. It ensures that the project's benefits are realized and that the project continues to meet the organization's needs in the long term.

## KEY DIFFERENCES BETWEEN PROJECT LIFE CYCLE AND EXTENDED LIFE CYCLE

The main difference between the project life cycle and extended life cycle is the length of time that each approach considers. The project life cycle is a traditional approach that focuses on the phases required to complete a project from concept to transition, while the extended life cycle approach considers the entire life cycle of the project, including the post-project phase.

Other key differences between the project life cycle and extended life cycle include:

a. Emphasis on benefits realization: The extended life cycle approach places more emphasis on benefits realization, which involves identifying and quantifying the benefits that the project will deliver and developing a plan to realize those benefits.

b. Focus on operations and maintenance: The extended life cycle approach considers the ongoing operational and maintenance requirements of the project deliverables, while the project life cycle approach focuses on completing the project on time and within budget.

c. Timeframe: The project life cycle approach has a defined timeframe, while the extended life cycle approach can continue for an extended period, depending on the project's needs and objectives.

d. Complexity: The extended life cycle approach is typically more complex than the project life cycle approach, as it involves more phases and considers a longer period.

e. Scope: The project life cycle approach is suitable for projects with a well-defined scope, while the extended life cycle approach is more suitable for projects with a broader scope or those that require ongoing support and maintenance.

Choosing between the project life cycle and extended life cycle approaches depends on the project's objectives, complexity, and scope. Project managers need to assess the project's requirements and select the approach that best aligns with the project's goals and objectives.

## WHEN TO USE PROJECT LIFE CYCLE VERSUS EXTENDED LIFE CYCLE

The choice between the project life cycle and extended life cycle approaches depends on the project's objectives, complexity, and scope. Here are some factors to consider when deciding which approach to use:

a. Project Scope: The project life cycle approach is suitable for projects with a well-defined scope, while the extended life cycle approach is more suitable for projects with a broader scope or those that require ongoing support and maintenance.

b. Complexity: The extended life cycle approach is typically more complex than the project life cycle approach, as it involves more phases and considers a longer period. If a project is straightforward and requires little maintenance, the project life cycle approach may be more appropriate.

c. Timeline: The project life cycle approach has a defined timeframe, while the extended life cycle approach can continue for an extended period, depending on the project's needs and objectives. If the project has a defined timeline, the project life cycle approach may be more appropriate.

d. Organizational Culture: The organizational culture can also influence the choice of life cycle approach. If an organization values long-term planning and continuous improvement, the extended life cycle approach may be more suitable.

e. Stakeholder Needs: The stakeholders' needs and requirements can also influence the choice of life cycle approach. For example, if the project's stakeholders require ongoing support and maintenance, the extended life cycle approach may be more appropriate.

In general, the project life cycle approach is suitable for projects that have a well-defined scope, clear objectives, and a finite timeline. This approach is commonly used for construction projects, software development projects, and other types of projects that have a defined beginning and end.

The extended life cycle approach is more suitable for projects that involve implementing new systems, processes, or technology that require ongoing support, maintenance, and improvement. This approach considers the entire life cycle of the project, including the post-project phase, and ensures that the project's benefits are realized and that the project continues to meet the organization's needs in the long term.

Ultimately, the choice of life cycle approach should align with the project's objectives and the organization's goals and objectives.

## CONCLUSION: WHICH APPROACH TO CHOOSE FOR YOUR PROJECT?

Choosing between the project life cycle and extended life cycle approaches can be challenging, as each approach has its advantages and disadvantages. The choice depends on the project's requirements, objectives, and scope, as well as the organizational culture and stakeholders' needs.

The project life cycle approach is suitable for projects with a well-defined scope, clear objectives, and a finite timeline. This approach is commonly used for construction projects, software development projects, and other types of projects that have a defined beginning and end. The project life cycle approach is more straightforward and easier to manage, and it provides a clear roadmap for completing the project on time and within budget.

On the other hand, the extended life cycle approach is more suitable for projects that involve implementing new systems, processes, or technology that require ongoing support, maintenance, and improvement. This approach considers the entire life cycle of the project, including the post-project phase, and ensures that the project's benefits are realized and that the project continues to meet the organization's needs in the long term. The extended life cycle approach provides a more holistic view of the project and allows for continuous improvement over time.

In conclusion, project managers should carefully assess the project's requirements and objectives to determine which life cycle approach is best suited for their project. While the project life cycle approach is more straightforward and easier to manage, the extended life cycle approach provides a more comprehensive approach that considers the long-term impact of the project on the organization.

# 2.4 THE CRUCIAL ROLE OF KNOWLEDGE AND INFORMATION MANAGEMENT IN DECISION MAKING

Making informed decisions is a critical aspect of any organization, and knowledge and information management play a crucial role in informing decision-making processes. Knowledge management involves creating, sharing, and utilizing knowledge within an organization to support decision making, while information management involves collecting, organizing, and analysing data to provide insights that inform decision making.

Organizations that effectively manage their knowledge and information resources have a significant advantage in making informed decisions, as they can draw on a wealth of internal and external knowledge and information to support their decision-making processes. Effective knowledge and information management help organizations to identify trends, anticipate changes, and make decisions that align with their strategic goals and objectives.

Moreover, knowledge and information management can enhance an organization's ability to learn from past experiences and mistakes, and incorporate that learning into future decision-making processes. By managing knowledge and information, organizations can build a knowledge base that enables them to make better decisions, increase efficiency, and remain competitive in their respective markets.

Overall, the effective management of knowledge and information is essential to support informed decision making, and organizations that prioritize these activities are better positioned to succeed in today's fast-paced and dynamic business environment.

## KNOWLEDGE MANAGEMENT: CREATING, SHARING, AND UTILIZING KNOWLEDGE FOR INFORMED DECISION MAKING

Knowledge management is the process of creating, sharing, and utilizing knowledge within an organization. Effective knowledge management helps organizations to capture knowledge from various sources, including employees, customers, partners, and competitors. This knowledge is then stored in a variety of formats, such as documents, databases, and knowledge repositories.

One key aspect of knowledge management is the creation of a knowledge-sharing culture within an organization. This involves encouraging employees to share their knowledge and experiences with others, providing training and resources to support knowledge sharing, and fostering a collaborative environment that encourages learning and innovation.

Another critical component of knowledge management is knowledge utilization. This involves using the knowledge that has been captured and stored to inform decision-making processes. By drawing on their internal knowledge resources, organizations can make better-informed decisions, identify new opportunities, and improve their overall performance.

Effective knowledge management can also help organizations to manage risks more effectively. By capturing and sharing knowledge about potential risks and their potential impact, organizations can develop risk mitigation strategies that enable them to proactively address potential issues before they become problems.

Overall, knowledge management plays a crucial role in informed decision making by enabling organizations to leverage their knowledge resources to make better decisions, manage risks more effectively, and remain competitive in their respective markets.

## INFORMATION MANAGEMENT: COLLECTING, ORGANIZING, AND ANALYSING INFORMATION TO SUPPORT DECISION MAKING

Information management involves collecting, organizing, and analysing data to provide insights that inform decision making. The process of information management begins with identifying the data sources that are relevant to an organization's decision-making processes. This may include data from internal sources, such as customer databases, financial records, and operational data, as well as external sources, such as market research and competitive intelligence.

Once data sources have been identified, the next step is to collect and store the data in a structured manner. This may involve using databases or other information management systems to store and organize data in a way that facilitates analysis and decision making.

The next step in the information management process is data analysis. This involves using tools and techniques such as data mining, predictive analytics, and machine learning to extract insights from the data. By analysing data, organizations can identify patterns, trends, and correlations that provide valuable insights into their operations, customers, and markets.

Finally, the insights generated through data analysis are used to inform decision making. By drawing on these insights, organizations can make better-informed decisions, develop more effective strategies, and improve their overall performance.

Effective information management requires a range of skills, including data collection, data analysis, and data visualization. It also requires organizations to invest in technology and tools that enable them to collect, store, and analyse data effectively.

Overall, information management plays a crucial role in informed decision making by enabling organizations to collect, organize, and analyse data to provide insights that inform decision making. By leveraging their information resources, organizations can make better-informed decisions, improve their performance, and remain competitive in their respective markets.

## DECISION MAKING PROCESSES: HOW KNOWLEDGE AND INFORMATION MANAGEMENT CAN IMPACT DECISION MAKING

Effective decision making is critical to the success of any organization. The decision-making process involves identifying problems or opportunities, gathering information and knowledge, analysing the options, and selecting the best course of action. Knowledge and information management can impact decision making in several ways.

Firstly, knowledge and information management can provide decision makers with a comprehensive understanding of the problem or opportunity. By collecting and analysing relevant data, decision makers can gain valuable insights into the nature of the problem or opportunity, the potential risks and benefits, and the possible courses of action.

Secondly, knowledge and information management can enable decision makers to identify and evaluate a range of options. By drawing on internal and external knowledge resources, decision makers can identify a range of potential solutions to the problem or opportunity, evaluate the pros and cons of each option, and select the best course of action.

Thirdly, knowledge and information management can help decision makers to monitor and evaluate the outcomes of their decisions. By tracking key performance indicators and other metrics, decision makers can evaluate the effectiveness of their decisions, identify areas for improvement, and adjust their strategies accordingly.

Overall, effective knowledge and information management can have a significant impact on decision making by providing decision makers with a comprehensive understanding of the problem or opportunity, enabling them to evaluate a range of options, and helping them to monitor and evaluate the outcomes of their decisions. By leveraging their knowledge and information resources, organizations can make better-informed decisions, improve their performance, and remain competitive in their respective markets.

## CHALLENGES OF KNOWLEDGE AND INFORMATION MANAGEMENT IN DECISION MAKING: OVERCOMING BARRIERS TO EFFECTIVE DECISION MAKING

While knowledge and information management are essential to informed decision making, several challenges can hinder organizations' ability to manage their knowledge and information effectively. These challenges include the following:

a. Data quality and availability: Poor data quality and limited data availability can limit the effectiveness of knowledge and information management. Data must be accurate, relevant, and up to date to support effective decision making.

b. Siloed information: Information silos can develop within organizations, where information is not shared between departments or teams. This can limit the effectiveness of knowledge and information management, as decision makers may not have access to all the information they need to make informed decisions.

c. Limited technology resources: Effective knowledge and information management often require organizations to invest in technology resources, such as information management systems, data analytics tools, and knowledge management platforms. Limited technology resources can limit an organization's ability to manage their knowledge and information effectively.

d. Lack of skills and expertise: Effective knowledge and information management requires a range of skills and expertise, including data analysis, data management, and knowledge management. A lack of skills and expertise can limit an organization's ability to manage their knowledge and information effectively.

e. Resistance to change: Resistance to change can hinder organizations' ability to adopt new knowledge and information management practices, such as knowledge sharing and collaboration. Resistance to change can limit an organization's ability to manage their knowledge and information effectively.

To overcome these challenges, organizations must adopt a range of strategies, including investing in technology resources, providing training and support for employees, and fostering a culture of knowledge sharing and collaboration. By addressing these challenges, organizations can effectively manage their knowledge and information resources and make better-informed decisions.

## THE FUTURE OF KNOWLEDGE AND INFORMATION MANAGEMENT IN DECISION MAKING: ADVANCEMENTS IN TECHNOLOGY AND PRACTICES

Advancements in technology and practices are transforming the way organizations manage their knowledge and information resources, and these changes will continue to shape the future of knowledge and information management in decision making. Here are some of the key trends that are likely to shape the future of knowledge and information management:

a. Artificial intelligence and machine learning: Advances in artificial intelligence and machine learning are transforming the way organizations analyze and make decisions based on large amounts of data. These technologies enable organizations to automate many aspects of the decision-making process, identify patterns and insights in data that might be missed by human analysts, and generate more accurate and reliable predictions.

b. Cloud-based solutions: Cloud-based solutions are becoming increasingly popular for managing knowledge and information resources, as they offer scalability, flexibility, and cost-effectiveness. Cloud-based solutions enable organizations to store, share, and analyze data from anywhere, on any device, and can be easily integrated with other software and applications.

c. Collaborative tools: Collaborative tools, such as social media platforms, wikis, and instant messaging apps, are increasingly being used for knowledge sharing and collaboration within organizations. These tools enable employees to share knowledge, exchange ideas, and collaborate on projects in real-time, regardless of their location.

d. Agile methodologies: Agile methodologies, such as Agile project management, are becoming increasingly popular for managing knowledge and information resources. Agile methodologies emphasize flexibility, collaboration, and continuous improvement, enabling organizations to respond quickly to changing conditions and optimize their decision-making processes.

e. Data privacy and security: Data privacy and security are becoming increasingly important considerations for knowledge and information management. Organizations must ensure that their data management practices comply with relevant laws and regulations and take steps to protect their data from cyber threats and other risks.

Overall, the future of knowledge and information management in decision making is likely to be shaped by advances in technology and practices that enable organizations to manage their data more effectively, collaborate more easily, and make more informed decisions. By adopting these new approaches, organizations can stay ahead of the curve and remain competitive in their respective markets.

# 2.5 THE IMPORTANCE OF CONDUCTING REVIEWS THROUGHOUT THE PROJECT LIFE CYCLE

Project management involves the application of knowledge, skills, tools, and techniques to meet project requirements within a defined timeline, budget, and scope. To ensure project success, project managers must monitor and control the project progress to identify issues and implement corrective actions. One way to achieve this is by conducting reviews throughout the project life cycle. Reviews refer to systematic assessments of project documents, processes, and results. These assessments are designed to provide stakeholders with insights into project performance, identify areas of improvement, and make informed decisions.

In this section, we will discuss the benefits of conducting reviews throughout the project life cycle, including at decision gates, during benefits reviews, and audits. We will also explore the benefits of reviews and why they are important. Finally, we will conclude with an overview of the benefits of conducting reviews throughout the project life cycle.

## WHAT ARE REVIEWS AND WHY ARE THEY IMPORTANT?

Reviews refer to a process of examining project documentation, processes, and results to determine whether they meet specific criteria or standards. Reviews can take different forms, including peer reviews, technical reviews, quality reviews, and management reviews. The purpose of reviews is to identify issues and risks early in the project life cycle, assess progress, and make informed decisions.

Reviews are important because they help project managers and stakeholders to monitor and control project performance. Reviews enable project managers to identify issues and risks early, before they become major problems. By conducting reviews, project managers can ensure that the project remains on track and that project requirements are met within the specified budget, timeline, and scope. Reviews also provide stakeholders with insights into project performance, enabling them to make informed decisions about project status, risks, and opportunities.

Reviews are also important because they promote transparency, accountability, and continuous improvement. By conducting reviews, project managers can ensure that project processes and practices are effective and efficient. Reviews can help identify best practices, areas of improvement, and lessons learned, which can be applied to future projects. Finally, reviews promote collaboration and communication among project team members, enabling them to work together effectively to achieve project goals.

## REVIEWS AT DECISION GATES

Reviews at decision gates refer to assessments that are conducted at specific points in the project life cycle, typically at the end of project phases. Decision gates are important because they enable project managers and stakeholders to assess project progress, determine whether the project is on track, and make informed decisions about project continuation. Decision gates are also known as stage gates or phase gates.

Reviews at decision gates involve a comprehensive assessment of project documentation, processes, and results. The purpose of these reviews is to ensure that project requirements have been met, assess project risks and issues, and make decisions about project continuation. Reviews at decision gates typically involve project sponsors, stakeholders, and subject matter experts. The review team assesses project documentation, such as the project charter, project plan, and status reports, to determine whether the project has met specific criteria for success. The review team may also conduct interviews with project team members to obtain additional insights into project performance.

Reviews at decision gates are important because they enable project managers and stakeholders to make informed decisions about project continuation. If the project has not met specific criteria, the review team may recommend that the project be re-planned or terminated. If the project has met specific criteria, the review team may recommend that the project move to the next phase. Reviews at decision gates also promote transparency and accountability, enabling project managers and stakeholders to understand project status, risks, and opportunities. Finally, reviews at decision gates promote continuous improvement, enabling project managers to identify best practices, areas of improvement, and lessons learned that can be applied to future projects.

## BENEFITS REVIEWS

Benefits reviews refer to assessments that are conducted to determine whether the benefits of a project have been realized. Benefits reviews are typically conducted after project completion, during the project transition phase. The purpose of benefits reviews is to assess whether the project has delivered the expected benefits, whether those benefits have been sustained, and whether the benefits have been realized in a cost-effective manner.

Benefits reviews involve a comprehensive assessment of project documentation, processes, and results. The review team assesses whether the project has achieved its intended benefits, such as increased revenue, improved customer satisfaction, or reduced costs. The review team also assesses whether the benefits have been sustained over time and whether the project has delivered the benefits in a cost-effective manner. Benefits reviews typically involve project sponsors, stakeholders, and subject matter experts. The review team may also conduct interviews with project team members and stakeholders to obtain additional insights into project performance.

Benefits reviews are important because they enable project managers and stakeholders to determine whether the project has delivered the expected benefits. Benefits reviews provide insights into the effectiveness of project processes and practices and enable project managers to identify areas for improvement. Benefits reviews also promote transparency and accountability, enabling project managers and stakeholders to understand the impact of the project on the organization. Finally, benefits reviews promote continuous improvement, enabling project managers to identify best practices, areas of improvement, and lessons learned that can be applied to future projects.

## AUDITS

Audits refer to independent assessments of project documentation, processes, and results. Audits are typically conducted by internal or external auditors and are designed to provide objective assessments of project performance. The purpose of audits is to identify issues, risks, and opportunities that may not have been identified through other review processes.

Audits involve a comprehensive assessment of project documentation, processes, and results. The audit team assesses whether project processes and practices are effective, efficient, and comply with relevant standards and regulations. The audit team also assesses whether project documentation is complete, accurate, and reflects project performance. Audits typically involve project sponsors, stakeholders, and subject matter experts. The audit team may also conduct interviews with project team members and stakeholders to obtain additional insights into project performance.

Audits are important because they provide objective assessments of project performance. Audits promote transparency and accountability, enabling project managers and stakeholders to understand project status, risks, and opportunities. Audits also promote compliance with relevant standards and regulations, enabling project managers to mitigate risks associated with non-compliance. Finally, audits promote continuous improvement, enabling project managers to identify best practices, areas of improvement, and lessons learned that can be applied to future projects.

## BENEFITS OF CONDUCTING REVIEWS THROUGHOUT THE PROJECT LIFE CYCLE

Conducting reviews throughout the project life cycle offers several benefits to project managers and stakeholders. These benefits include:

a. Early Identification of Issues and Risks: By conducting reviews throughout the project life cycle, project managers can identify issues and risks early, before they become major problems. Early identification of issues and risks enables project managers to implement corrective actions and keep the project on track.

b. Improved Project Performance: Reviews throughout the project life cycle promote continuous improvement, enabling project managers to identify best practices, areas of improvement, and lessons learned that can be applied to future projects. This can lead to improved project performance and increased efficiency.

c. Informed Decision-Making: Reviews throughout the project life cycle provide stakeholders with insights into project performance, enabling them to make informed decisions about project status, risks, and opportunities. This promotes transparency and accountability, and ensures that project decisions are based on objective data.

d. Compliance with Standards and Regulations: Reviews throughout the project life cycle promote compliance with relevant standards and regulations, enabling project managers to mitigate risks associated with non-compliance.

e. Reduced Costs: Reviews throughout the project life cycle can help identify areas where costs can be reduced, such as inefficient processes or unnecessary activities. This can lead to cost savings and increased profitability.

f. Improved Communication and Collaboration: Reviews throughout the project life cycle promote collaboration and communication among project team members, enabling them to work together effectively to achieve project goals.

In summary, conducting reviews throughout the project life cycle can help project managers and stakeholders to monitor and control project performance, improve project outcomes, and make informed decisions. It promotes transparency, accountability, and continuous improvement, and helps ensure project success.

## CONCLUSION

Conducting reviews throughout the project life cycle is an essential component of project management. Reviews provide project managers and stakeholders with insights into project performance, identify issues and risks early, and enable informed decision-making. Reviews can take different forms, including at decision gates, benefits reviews, and audits. Each of these review types offers unique benefits and insights into project performance.

Reviews throughout the project life cycle promote transparency, accountability, and continuous improvement, and help ensure project success. They enable project managers to identify best practices, areas of improvement, and lessons learned that can be applied to future projects. They also promote compliance with relevant standards and regulations, enabling project managers to mitigate risks associated with non-compliance.

In conclusion, conducting reviews throughout the project life cycle is essential for project success. Project managers and stakeholders should ensure that reviews are conducted regularly and that review findings are used to improve project outcomes. By leveraging the benefits of reviews, project managers can ensure that their projects are delivered on time, within budget, and to the satisfaction of stakeholders.

## 2.6 Understanding Why Projects May Close Early: Exploring Common Causes and Solutions

When we talk about a project "closing early," we mean that it ended before it was supposed to or before achieving its intended goals. In other words, the project was terminated prematurely, and its intended outcomes were not fully achieved.

Early project closure can be a frustrating experience for everyone involved, from the project team to stakeholders and sponsors. It can be a significant waste of resources, time, and money, and may also damage the reputation of the organization. Therefore, it is essential to understand the reasons why projects may close early and learn how to prevent them from happening in the future.

In this section, we will explore some common causes of early project closure and provide some solutions to help you keep your projects on track and ensure their success. We will discuss the importance of proper planning and execution, sufficient budget and resources, managing unforeseen circumstances, and changes in priorities, aligning project goals with business objectives, promoting communication and collaboration, and engaging stakeholders and sponsors. Finally, we will conclude with some final thoughts and recommendations for preventing projects from closing early.

### Lack of Proper Planning and Execution

One of the most common reasons why projects close early is the lack of proper planning and execution. The failure to plan the project adequately or to execute the plan effectively can lead to delays, cost overruns, and a failure to achieve the desired outcomes. Poor planning and execution can also lead to miscommunication, confusion, and conflicts among team members.

Effective planning is crucial to the success of any project. It involves defining the project objectives, setting realistic timelines, identifying the required resources, and creating a detailed plan for each project phase. When planning a project, it is also essential to consider potential risks and develop strategies to mitigate them.

Execution is the process of implementing the plan and delivering the project outcomes. Effective execution involves assigning roles and responsibilities, monitoring progress, and ensuring that the project is on track. It also involves effective communication and collaboration among team members to ensure that everyone is working towards the same goals.

To prevent early project closure due to poor planning and execution, it is essential to invest time and resources in the definition phase. The project team should work together to create a detailed plan that outlines the project's scope, timeline, resources, and risks. They should also establish clear communication channels and ensure that everyone understands their roles and responsibilities. Effective monitoring and reporting can help to identify potential issues and address them before they become critical. Finally, it is essential to regularly evaluate progress against the plan and make adjustments as necessary.

## INSUFFICIENT BUDGET OR RESOURCES

Another common reason why projects may close early is the lack of sufficient budget or resources. Without adequate funding or resources, the project team may struggle to complete the project on time or to the desired standard. This can lead to scope creep, where additional work is added to the project without additional resources, further stretching the team's capacity and resources.

To prevent early project closure due to insufficient budget or resources, it is essential to develop a realistic budget and resource plan during the definition phase. The project team should work with stakeholders and sponsors to ensure that the budget is sufficient to cover all necessary expenses, including personnel, materials, and equipment. They should also consider any potential risks that could impact the project's cost and develop contingency plans to address them.

During the project's execution, the project team should closely monitor the budget and resources, keeping track of expenses and progress against the plan. If additional resources are needed, they should work with sponsors and stakeholders to secure the necessary funding or resources.

Effective communication is essential in this process to ensure that everyone involved in the project understands the budget and resource constraints and the consequences of exceeding them. Clear communication will also help to manage stakeholder expectations and reduce the risk of misunderstandings or conflicts. Finally, the project team should regularly evaluate the project's progress against the budget and resource plan and adjust as necessary.

## Unforeseen Circumstances and Changes in Priorities

Sometimes, external factors can cause projects to close early, such as unforeseen circumstances or changes in priorities. These factors may be beyond the project team's control, such as changes in market conditions, government regulations, or natural disasters. They may also be internal factors, such as changes in business strategy or shifts in stakeholder priorities.

To prevent early project closure due to unforeseen circumstances or changes in priorities, it is essential to develop contingency plans during the definition phase. The project team should identify potential risks and develop strategies to mitigate them. They should also consider the impact of external factors and have plans in place to address them if they occur.

During the project's execution, the project team should regularly monitor external factors and changes in stakeholder priorities that could impact the project's progress. They should also be prepared to adjust the project plan as necessary to adapt to changing circumstances.

Effective communication is critical in this process to ensure that stakeholders and sponsors are aware of any changes and their impact on the project. Clear communication will help to manage expectations and reduce the risk of misunderstandings or conflicts. Finally, the project team should regularly evaluate the project's progress against the plan and adjust as necessary. By being prepared for unforeseen circumstances and changes in priorities, the project team can reduce the risk of early project closure.

## MISALIGNMENT OF PROJECT GOALS AND BUSINESS OBJECTIVES

Another reason why projects may close early is the misalignment of project goals and business objectives. This can occur when the project's objectives are not closely tied to the organization's overall strategy or when there is a lack of clarity regarding the project's intended outcomes. In these cases, the project team may struggle to secure the necessary resources or support, or the project may fail to deliver the expected benefits.

To prevent early project closure due to misalignment of project goals and business objectives, it is essential to ensure that the project's objectives are closely aligned with the organization's overall strategy. The project team should work closely with stakeholders and sponsors to ensure that the project's intended outcomes are clearly defined and aligned with the organization's goals.

Effective communication and collaboration are crucial in this process. The project team should engage stakeholders and sponsors early in the planning process and regularly communicate with them throughout the project's execution. They should also work closely with other departments and teams within the organization to ensure that the project's outcomes are consistent with the overall business objectives.

During the project's execution, the project team should regularly evaluate the project's progress against the intended outcomes and adjust as necessary. They should also work closely with stakeholders and sponsors to ensure that the project's benefits are clearly communicated and understood. By ensuring that the project's objectives are closely aligned with the organization's overall strategy, the project team can reduce the risk of early project closure and increase the project's overall success.

## POOR COMMUNICATION AND COLLABORATION

Poor communication and collaboration can also lead to early project closure. When team members fail to communicate effectively, misunderstandings and conflicts can arise, leading to delays and decreased productivity. Similarly, when team members fail to collaborate effectively, they may duplicate efforts, overlook critical details, or miss important deadlines, further exacerbating delays and leading to early project closure.

To prevent early project closure due to poor communication and collaboration, it is essential to establish clear communication channels and promote effective collaboration from the outset. The project team should establish regular communication protocols and ensure that everyone understands their roles and responsibilities. They should also establish clear lines of authority and decision-making to reduce the risk of misunderstandings or conflicts.

Effective collaboration is essential in this process. The project team should work closely together, leveraging each other's strengths and expertise to achieve the project's objectives. They should also be open to feedback and willing to adjust their approach based on input from other team members.

During the project's execution, the project team should regularly evaluate the effectiveness of their communication and collaboration strategies and adjust as necessary. They should also be willing to address conflicts and misunderstandings as soon as they arise, to prevent them from escalating and impacting the project's progress. By promoting effective communication and collaboration, the project team can reduce the risk of early project closure and increase the project's overall success.

## LACK OF STAKEHOLDER ENGAGEMENT AND SUPPORT

Another reason why projects may close early is the lack of stakeholder engagement and support. Stakeholders, including sponsors, customers, and users, play a critical role in the success of a project. When stakeholders are not engaged or do not support the project, the project team may struggle to secure the necessary resources or achieve the desired outcomes.

To prevent early project closure due to a lack of stakeholder engagement and support, it is essential to engage stakeholders early in the project's definition phase. The project team should work closely with stakeholders to understand their needs and expectations and to ensure that the project's objectives align with their goals.

Effective communication is crucial in this process. The project team should regularly communicate with stakeholders, providing updates on the project's progress and seeking feedback on the project's outcomes. They should also be willing to adjust the project plan based on stakeholder feedback to ensure that the project's outcomes align with stakeholder needs and expectations.

During the project's execution, the project team should continue to engage stakeholders regularly. They should work closely with sponsors to secure the necessary resources and support and ensure that stakeholders understand the project's progress and expected outcomes. By engaging stakeholders early and often and ensuring their support throughout the project's execution, the project team can reduce the risk of early project closure and increase the project's overall success.

## How to Prevent Projects from Closing Early

To prevent projects from closing early, it is essential to address the common causes of early project closure. Here are some steps you can take to prevent early project closure:

a. Invest time and resources in the definition phase to ensure that the project's objectives, scope, timeline, budget, and resources are well-defined and aligned with the organization's overall strategy.

b. Establish clear communication channels and promote effective collaboration among team members to prevent misunderstandings and conflicts that could lead to delays and decreased productivity.

c. Regularly monitor the project's progress against the plan and adjust as necessary to ensure that the project stays on track.

d. Develop contingency plans to address potential risks and unforeseen circumstances that could impact the project's progress.

e. Engage stakeholders early and often, seeking their input and feedback and ensuring that they understand the project's objectives and expected outcomes.

f.  Secure the necessary resources and support from sponsors and stakeholders to ensure that the project has the necessary funding and resources to succeed.

g.  Evaluate the project's progress regularly against the intended outcomes and adjust as necessary to ensure that the project's benefits are realized.

By following these steps and addressing the common causes of early project closure, you can increase the likelihood of project success and reduce the risk of early project closure.

## CONCLUSION: FINAL THOUGHTS AND RECOMMENDATIONS

In conclusion, early project closure can be a frustrating and costly experience for everyone involved. However, by understanding the common causes of early project closure and taking steps to prevent them, you can increase the likelihood of project success and reduce the risk of early project closure.

Proper planning and execution, sufficient budget and resources, managing unforeseen circumstances, aligning project goals with business objectives, promoting communication and collaboration, and engaging stakeholders and sponsors are all essential to preventing early project closure.

To ensure project success, it is important to invest time and resources in the definition phase, establish clear communication channels, monitor progress regularly, develop contingency plans, engage stakeholders early and often, secure necessary resources and support, and evaluate progress against the intended outcomes.

By taking these steps and working closely with your project team, sponsors, and stakeholders, you can increase the chances of project success and reduce the risk of early project closure. Remember that effective communication and collaboration are critical to project success, so be sure to maintain open lines of communication and encourage collaboration throughout the project's execution.

# CHAPTER THREE

## *ASSESSING THE SITUATIONAL CONTEXT OF PROJECTS*

# 3.1 UNDERSTANDING THE DIFFERENCE BETWEEN PROJECTS AND BUSINESS AS USUAL (BAU)

Projects are temporary endeavours that are designed to achieve specific objectives within a defined period, budget, and scope. They are unique in nature and require a distinct set of skills, resources, and management techniques to ensure their successful completion.

Projects usually involve a series of activities that are planned, executed, and monitored to achieve a specific outcome. They can be complex or simple, depending on the scope of work, the size of the team, and the available resources. Projects can range from building a new product, launching a marketing campaign, developing a new software application, constructing a building, and many other endeavours that require a significant investment of time, money, and effort.

Characteristics of Projects:

a. Temporary: Projects have a specific start and end date and are not ongoing.

b. Unique: Projects are distinct and require a specific set of resources and management techniques.

c. Specific Goals and Objectives: Projects have clear and defined outcomes that they are designed to achieve.

d. Cross-Functional Teams: Projects usually require the involvement of multiple teams with different skill sets.

e. Risk Management: Projects often require a risk management plan to ensure that potential issues are identified and addressed.

f. Change Management: Projects may require a change management plan to ensure that stakeholders are informed and involved in the project's progress.

Understanding the definition and characteristics of projects is critical for differentiating them from business as usual (BAU) activities. While both projects and BAU are essential for organizational success, they require different management approaches and resources.

## DEFINITION AND CHARACTERISTICS OF BUSINESS AS USUAL (BAU)

Business as usual (BAU) refers to the routine and ongoing operations of an organization. BAU activities are the day-to-day tasks that a company performs to maintain its current level of service or production. BAU activities include tasks such as managing customer relationships, processing orders, paying bills, managing inventory, and maintaining facilities. These activities are essential for the organization to continue functioning but do not involve the creation of new products or services.

BAU activities are usually performed by the same team or department on a continuous basis, and they do not have a specific end date. Unlike projects, BAU activities do not have a clear set of deliverables, and they do not involve a significant investment of resources or time.

Characteristics of Business as Usual (BAU):

a. Ongoing: BAU activities are part of the regular, daily operations of an organization and are continuous.

b. Repetitive: BAU activities involve the same set of tasks or processes that are repeated on a regular basis.

c. Maintain Existing Processes: BAU activities are focused on maintaining the current level of service or production of an organization.

d. Team Responsibility: BAU activities are usually performed by the same team or department responsible for their management.

e. Limited Risk Management: BAU activities may involve some risk management, but the risk is typically lower than that of a project.

Understanding the definition and characteristics of BAU is essential for differentiating it from projects. While BAU activities are essential for maintaining the day-to-day operations of an organization, they do not involve the creation of new products or services. Thus, they require different management approaches and resources than projects.

## KEY DIFFERENCES BETWEEN PROJECTS AND BUSINESS AS USUAL (BAU)

Projects and business as usual (BAU) are two distinct types of work that require different management approaches and resources. Understanding the differences between them is crucial for organizations to manage their resources effectively and achieve their strategic goals.

Here are the key differences between projects and business as usual (BAU):

a. Objectives: Projects have specific objectives and outcomes to achieve, while BAU activities aim to maintain the status quo.

b. Duration: Projects have a specific start and end date, while BAU activities are ongoing and do not have a specific end date.

c. Resources: Projects require a significant investment of resources, including time, money, and human resources, while BAU activities require minimal investment in resources.

d. Teams: Projects require cross-functional teams with specialized skills to achieve specific objectives, while BAU activities are usually performed by a specific team or department.

e. Risk: Projects involve higher levels of risk due to their unique nature and the need to achieve specific objectives within a defined period. In contrast, BAU activities are generally less risky as they involve the maintenance of existing processes.

f. Management: Projects require a distinct management approach, including project planning, risk management, and change management, while BAU activities require a different management approach, including process improvement and continuous improvement.

g. Budget: Projects have a specific budget allocated to them, while BAU activities are funded from the organization's ongoing operational budget.

Understanding these differences is essential for organizations to manage their resources effectively, allocate budgets appropriately, and achieve their strategic goals. Successful organizations strike a balance between projects and BAU activities, ensuring that both are appropriately managed and aligned with the organization's overall strategy.

## EXAMPLES OF PROJECTS VS. BUSINESS AS USUAL (BAU)

Examples of projects include:

a. Developing a new product: This involves designing, prototyping, and testing a new product before it can be launched into the market. It requires a dedicated team, a specific budget, and a defined timeline to achieve the desired outcome.

b. Launching a new marketing campaign: This involves developing a comprehensive plan for promoting a product or service to the target audience. It requires a specialized team of marketers, creative designers, and content writers to achieve the desired outcome.

c. Building a new office: This involves designing, constructing, and equipping a new office space to accommodate the organization's growing workforce. It requires a specialized team of architects, engineers, contractors, and project managers to achieve the desired outcome.

Examples of business as usual (BAU) activities include:

a. Responding to customer inquiries: This involves answering phone calls, responding to emails, and addressing customer concerns or complaints. It is a routine activity that is performed by the customer service team on a daily basis.

b. Paying bills: This involves processing invoices, issuing payments, and reconciling accounts. It is a routine activity that is performed by the accounting team on a regular basis.

c. Managing inventory: This involves tracking inventory levels, placing orders, and restocking products. It is a routine activity that is performed by the operations team on a regular basis.

Understanding the difference between projects and BAU activities is crucial for organizations to allocate resources effectively and prioritize their initiatives. Projects require a significant investment of time, money, and human resources, while BAU activities are essential for maintaining the daily operations of the organization. By understanding the differences between the two, organizations can strike a balance between their ongoing operational needs and their strategic objectives.

## IMPORTANCE OF DISTINGUISHING BETWEEN PROJECTS AND BUSINESS AS USUAL (BAU)

Distinguishing between projects and business as usual (BAU) activities is crucial for organizations for the following reasons:

a. Resource Allocation: Projects require a significant investment of time, money, and human resources. Distinguishing them from BAU activities ensures that resources are allocated effectively, and project goals are met without impacting the ongoing operational needs of the organization.

b. Budgeting: Projects have specific budgets allocated to them, while BAU activities are funded from the organization's ongoing operational budget. Distinguishing between the two ensures that budgets are allocated appropriately, and the organization's financial resources are utilized effectively.

c. Risk Management: Projects involve higher levels of risk due to their unique nature and the need to achieve specific objectives within a defined period. Distinguishing them from BAU activities ensures that risk management strategies are put in place to identify and mitigate potential issues.

d. Change Management: Projects involve significant changes to an organization's existing processes, while BAU activities are focused on maintaining the status quo. Distinguishing between the two ensures that change management strategies are put in place to ensure that stakeholders are informed and involved in the project's progress.

e. Prioritization: Projects and BAU activities are essential for organizational success, but they require different management approaches and resources. Distinguishing between the two ensures that initiatives are prioritized appropriately, and resources are allocated to the initiatives that align with the organization's overall strategy.

By distinguishing between projects and BAU activities, organizations can effectively manage their resources, allocate budgets appropriately, identify potential risks, and prioritize initiatives that align with their overall strategy. A clear understanding of the difference between the two ensures that organizations can achieve their strategic goals while maintaining their ongoing operational needs.

## CONCLUSION: BALANCING PROJECTS AND BUSINESS AS USUAL (BAU) FOR ORGANIZATIONAL SUCCESS

Projects and business as usual (BAU) activities are essential for organizational success. Projects enable organizations to innovate, develop new products and services, and pursue strategic objectives, while BAU activities enable organizations to maintain their existing operations and provide consistent service to their customers.

To achieve success, organizations must strike a balance between projects and BAU activities. This requires effective management, allocation of resources, and prioritization of initiatives. Organizations must allocate resources effectively to ensure that projects are completed on time, within budget, and with the desired outcome. Similarly, they must also allocate resources to BAU activities to ensure that the day-to-day operations of the organization are running smoothly.

Effective management of projects and BAU activities requires different management approaches. Project management requires specific tools, techniques, and strategies to plan, execute, and monitor the project's progress. In contrast, BAU management requires continuous improvement and process improvement strategies to ensure that the organization's ongoing operational needs are met.

Organizations must also prioritize their initiatives to ensure that resources are allocated to those initiatives that align with their overall strategy. Prioritizing projects and BAU activities requires a clear understanding of the difference between the two, and the strategic goals that the initiatives are designed to achieve.

In conclusion, balancing projects and business as usual (BAU) activities is essential for organizational success. Effective management of resources, prioritization of initiatives, and different management approaches are necessary for achieving this balance. By striking a balance between projects and BAU activities, organizations can innovate, develop new products and services, and maintain their ongoing operational needs, leading to sustained success over the long term.

# 3.2 Understanding the Differences Between Project Management, Program Management, and Portfolio Management

Effective management is essential to achieving organizational objectives, particularly in complex and dynamic environments. Three management approaches commonly used in organizations are project management, program management, and portfolio management. While they share some similarities, each approach has distinct goals, scope, and requirements. Understanding the differences between project management, program management, and portfolio management can help organizations choose the right approach for their needs and maximize their resources and investments.

Project management focuses on the management of specific projects. A project is a temporary endeavour undertaken to create a unique product, service, or result. Project management involves defining project objectives, developing project plans, coordinating project activities, monitoring project progress, and delivering project outcomes. Project managers are responsible for ensuring that projects are completed on time, within budget, and to the desired quality standards.

Program management involves the management of a group of related projects. A program is a group of projects that are managed together to achieve strategic objectives. Program management involves defining program objectives, developing program plans, coordinating project activities, monitoring program progress, and delivering program outcomes. Program managers are responsible for ensuring that the program's projects are aligned with the organization's strategic objectives and that the program delivers the intended benefits.

Portfolio management involves the management of a group of programs and projects. A portfolio is a collection of programs, projects, and other activities that are managed together to achieve strategic objectives. Portfolio management involves defining portfolio objectives, developing portfolio plans, monitoring portfolio performance, and making decisions about portfolio investments. Portfolio managers are responsible for ensuring that the organization's resources are allocated to the most strategically important programs and projects and that the portfolio delivers the intended benefits.

## DEFINING PROJECT MANAGEMENT: GOALS AND SCOPE

Project management is a management approach that focuses on achieving specific objectives within a defined timeframe and budget. A project is a temporary endeavour undertaken to create a unique product, service, or result. Project management involves defining project objectives, developing project plans, coordinating project activities, monitoring project progress, and delivering project outcomes.

The goals of project management are to deliver a project that meets the specified objectives, within the defined timeframe and budget, and to the desired quality standards. The scope of project management includes all activities required to plan, execute, monitor, and control a project. This includes defining project requirements, developing project plans, managing project resources, monitoring project progress, and delivering project outcomes.

Project managers play a critical role in project management. They are responsible for leading project teams, managing project resources, monitoring project progress, and communicating project status to stakeholders. Project managers must be skilled in project planning, risk management, communication, stakeholder management, and team leadership.

Examples of projects that might be managed using project management include developing a new product, implementing a new system or process, constructing a building or infrastructure, or organizing an event. Successful project management requires a combination of technical skills, management skills, and interpersonal skills.

## DEFINING PROGRAM MANAGEMENT: GOALS AND SCOPE

Program management is a management approach that involves managing a group of related projects that are managed together to achieve strategic objectives. A program is a group of projects that are coordinated and managed together to achieve benefits that cannot be obtained by managing the projects individually.

The goals of program management are to ensure that the program delivers the intended benefits, that the program's projects are aligned with the organization's strategic objectives, and that the program is managed efficiently and effectively. The scope of program management includes all activities required to plan, execute, monitor, and control a group of related projects. This includes defining program objectives, developing program plans, coordinating project activities, monitoring program progress, and delivering program outcomes.

Program managers play a critical role in program management. They are responsible for leading program teams, managing program resources, monitoring program progress, and communicating program status to stakeholders. Program managers must be skilled in program planning, risk management, communication, stakeholder management, and team leadership.

Examples of programs that might be managed using program management include product development programs, technology implementation programs, construction programs, or business transformation programs. Successful program management requires a combination of technical skills, management skills, and interpersonal skills. It also requires a deep understanding of the organization's strategic objectives and how the program contributes to those objectives.

Program management is often used when an organization has several related projects that need to be managed together to achieve a common goal. By coordinating and managing the projects together as a program, the organization can achieve benefits that could not be obtained by managing the projects individually.

## DEFINING PORTFOLIO MANAGEMENT: GOALS AND SCOPE

Portfolio management is a management approach that involves managing a group of programs, projects, and other activities that are managed together to achieve strategic objectives. A portfolio is a collection of programs, projects, and other activities that are managed together to achieve benefits that cannot be obtained by managing them individually.

The goals of portfolio management are to ensure that the organization's resources are allocated to the most strategically important programs and projects, that the portfolio delivers the intended benefits, and that the portfolio is managed efficiently and effectively. The scope of portfolio management includes all activities required to plan, execute, monitor, and control a group of programs, projects, and other activities. This includes defining portfolio objectives, developing portfolio plans, monitoring portfolio performance, and making decisions about portfolio investments.

Portfolio managers play a critical role in portfolio management. They are responsible for leading portfolio teams, managing portfolio resources, monitoring portfolio progress, and communicating portfolio status to stakeholders. Portfolio managers must be skilled in portfolio planning, risk management, communication, stakeholder management, and team leadership.

Examples of activities that might be managed using portfolio management include programs, projects, ongoing operations, and other strategic initiatives. Successful portfolio management requires a deep understanding of the organization's strategic objectives, its resources, and its capabilities. It also requires the ability to make strategic decisions about which programs and projects to invest in and which to deprioritize or terminate.

Portfolio management is often used when an organization has several programs and projects that need to be managed together to achieve a common goal, but also need to be aligned with the organization's overall strategic objectives. By managing them together as a portfolio, the organization can ensure that its resources are allocated to the most strategically important activities and that the portfolio delivers the intended benefits.

## KEY DIFFERENCES BETWEEN PROJECT, PROGRAM, AND PORTFOLIO MANAGEMENT

While project management, program management, and portfolio management share some similarities, each approach has distinct goals, scope, and requirements. Understanding the differences between these approaches is essential to choosing the right management approach for an organization's needs. Some of the key differences between project management, program management, and portfolio management include:

  a. Scope: Project management focuses on the management of specific projects, program management focuses on a group of related projects, and portfolio management focuses on a collection of programs, projects, and other activities that are managed together to achieve strategic objectives.

b. Goals: Project management aims to deliver a project that meets the specified objectives, within the defined timeframe and budget, and to the desired quality standards. Program management aims to ensure that the program delivers the intended benefits, that the program's projects are aligned with the organization's strategic objectives, and that the program is managed efficiently and effectively. Portfolio management aims to ensure that the organization's resources are allocated to the most strategically important programs and projects, that the portfolio delivers the intended benefits, and that the portfolio is managed efficiently and effectively.

c. Timeframe: Project management has a relatively short timeframe, typically ranging from a few months to a few years. Program management has a longer timeframe, typically ranging from several years to a decade or more. Portfolio management has the longest timeframe, typically ranging from several years to decades.

d. Management Approach: Project management typically follows a structured approach, with a focus on delivering specific outputs within a defined timeframe and budget. Program management follows a more flexible approach, with a focus on delivering benefits that cannot be achieved by managing the projects individually. Portfolio management follows a strategic approach, with a focus on aligning the organization's resources with its strategic objectives.

e. Management Roles: Project management typically involves a project manager who is responsible for managing the project team and delivering the project outcomes. Program management typically involves a program manager who is responsible for managing a group of related projects and ensuring that the program delivers the intended benefits. Portfolio management typically involves a portfolio manager who is responsible for managing a collection of programs, projects, and other activities and ensuring that the portfolio delivers the intended benefits.

Understanding these differences is critical to choosing the right management approach for an organization's needs. Depending on the organization's goals, resources, and capabilities, it may choose to use one or more of these management approaches.

## THE ROLE OF PROJECT, PROGRAM, AND PORTFOLIO MANAGERS

Project, program, and portfolio managers play critical roles in their respective management approaches. Each manager has a unique set of responsibilities that are essential to the success of the management approach.

Project managers are responsible for managing a specific project from start to finish. They work closely with the project team to develop project plans, allocate resources, monitor progress, and deliver project outcomes. Project managers are also responsible for managing project risks, communicating with stakeholders, and ensuring that the project is completed on time, within budget, and to the desired quality standards.

Program managers are responsible for managing a group of related projects that are managed together to achieve strategic objectives. They work closely with project managers to ensure that the program's projects are aligned with the organization's strategic objectives and that the program delivers the intended benefits. Program managers are also responsible for managing program risks, communicating with stakeholders, and ensuring that the program is managed efficiently and effectively.

Portfolio managers are responsible for managing a collection of programs, projects, and other activities that are managed together to achieve strategic objectives. They work closely with program managers to ensure that the organization's resources are allocated to the most strategically important programs and projects and that the portfolio delivers the intended benefits. Portfolio managers are also responsible for managing portfolio risks, communicating with stakeholders, and ensuring that the portfolio is managed efficiently and effectively.

In addition to their specific responsibilities, project, program, and portfolio managers also play important leadership roles. They are responsible for motivating and guiding their teams, managing conflicts, and making difficult decisions. They must also be skilled communicators, able to effectively communicate with stakeholders, team members, and senior leaders.

Effective project, program, and portfolio management requires skilled and experienced managers who can navigate complex environments, manage risks, and deliver outcomes that meet or exceed expectations. Organizations that invest in their project, program, and portfolio management capabilities are more likely to achieve their strategic objectives and maximize their resources and investments.

## CHOOSING THE RIGHT MANAGEMENT APPROACH FOR YOUR ORGANIZATION

Choosing the right management approach for an organization depends on a variety of factors, including the organization's goals, resources, capabilities, and environment. Each management approach has its own strengths and weaknesses, and organizations must carefully consider their options before choosing a particular approach.

When choosing a management approach, organizations should consider the following factors:

a. Goals: The first step in choosing a management approach is to identify the organization's goals. Are the goals short-term or long-term? Are they specific or general? Depending on the goals, one management approach may be more appropriate than another.

b. Resources: The second factor to consider is the organization's resources. How much time, money, and personnel can the organization dedicate to the management approach? Some management approaches require more resources than others, and organizations must ensure that they have the necessary resources to implement the approach effectively.

c. Capabilities: The third factor to consider is the organization's capabilities. Does the organization have the skills and experience necessary to implement the management approach? If not, the organization may need to invest in training or hire outside expertise.

d. Environment: The fourth factor to consider is the organization's environment. Is the environment stable or dynamic? Are there external factors that could impact the management approach? Depending on the environment, one management approach may be more suitable than another.

Once organizations have considered these factors, they can choose the management approach that best aligns with their goals, resources, capabilities, and environment. In some cases, organizations may choose to use multiple management approaches, depending on the nature of their projects and programs.

Effective management is essential to achieving organizational objectives, particularly in complex and dynamic environments. By choosing the right management approach and investing in their management capabilities, organizations can maximize their resources and investments and achieve their strategic objectives.

## CONCLUSION: THE IMPORTANCE OF EFFECTIVE MANAGEMENT IN ACHIEVING ORGANIZATIONAL OBJECTIVES

Effective management is critical to achieving organizational objectives, particularly in complex and dynamic environments. Project management, program management, and portfolio management are three management approaches that organizations can use to manage their projects, programs, and other activities.

While project management, program management, and portfolio management share some similarities, each approach has distinct goals, scope, and requirements. Understanding the differences between these approaches is essential to choosing the right management approach for an organization's needs.

Project management is focused on delivering a specific project within a defined timeframe and budget. Program management is focused on managing a group of related projects to achieve strategic objectives. Portfolio management is focused on managing a collection of programs, projects, and other activities to achieve strategic objectives.

Choosing the right management approach depends on a variety of factors, including the organization's goals, resources, capabilities, and environment. Organizations must carefully consider their options and choose the management approach that best aligns with their goals and resources.

Effective project, program, and portfolio management requires skilled and experienced managers who can navigate complex environments, manage risks, and deliver outcomes that meet or exceed expectations. Organizations that invest in their project, program, and portfolio management capabilities are more likely to achieve their strategic objectives and maximize their resources and investments.

In conclusion, effective management is critical to achieving organizational objectives, and project management, program management, and portfolio management are three management approaches that organizations can use to manage their projects, programs, and other activities. By choosing the right management approach and investing in their management capabilities, organizations can achieve their strategic objectives and maximize their resources and investments.

# 3.3 THE INTERPLAY BETWEEN PROGRAMMES, PROJECTS, AND STRATEGIC CHANGE

Programmes, projects, and strategic change are three concepts that are closely related and interconnected. Understanding the relationship between these concepts is essential for any organization that wants to achieve its strategic objectives effectively.

Programmes refer to a group of related projects that are managed together in a coordinated way to achieve a common goal. In other words, programmes are a collection of projects that are organized in a way that enables the organization to achieve a strategic objective. Programmes are often used in complex projects, where there are many interrelated tasks that need to be carried out in a coordinated way to achieve the desired outcome.

Projects, on the other hand, are specific, time-limited initiatives that are undertaken to achieve a specific goal or objective. Projects are usually smaller in scale than programmes and are often used to achieve specific objectives that are part of a larger programme. Projects are typically managed by a project manager who is responsible for delivering the project on time, within budget, and to the required quality standards.

Strategic change refers to the process of making significant changes to an organization's direction, structure, culture, or operations. Strategic change is usually driven by external factors such as changes in the competitive environment, changes in customer preferences, or changes in government regulations. Strategic change is often necessary for organizations to remain competitive and achieve their long-term objectives.

The relationship between programmes, projects, and strategic change is that programmes and projects are the vehicles that organizations use to implement strategic change. Programmes and projects are used to deliver the changes that are necessary for the organization to achieve its strategic objectives. The success of a strategic change initiative often depends on the effective implementation of programmes and projects. Therefore, it is essential to have a clear understanding of the relationship between these concepts to ensure that strategic change is implemented successfully.

## PROGRAMMES AND PROJECTS: TWO KEY CONCEPTS

Programmes and projects are two key concepts that are often used interchangeably but have distinct differences. Understanding these differences is essential for effective project management and strategic change implementation.

A project is a temporary endeavour that is designed to achieve a specific goal or objective. Projects are usually time-bound, have defined objectives and deliverables, and require specific resources to achieve their objectives. Projects can be of different sizes, from small-scale initiatives to complex, multi-year projects that involve many stakeholders.

Programmes, on the other hand, are a collection of related projects that are managed together to achieve a common goal. Programmes are designed to achieve strategic objectives and are made up of multiple projects that are interdependent and coordinated. Programmes are usually longer-term than projects, and they require a higher level of strategic planning and coordination.

One of the key differences between programmes and projects is that programmes33 have a broader scope than projects. Projects are usually designed to achieve specific, narrow objectives, while programmes are designed to achieve broader strategic goals that require a more comprehensive and integrated approach.

Another difference is that programmes are designed to manage the interdependencies between projects. Projects that are part of a programme are often interrelated, and changes in one project can impact other projects in the programme. Programmes provide a framework for managing these interdependencies and ensuring that all projects are aligned with the overall strategic objectives.

Programme management is, therefore, more complex than project management. It requires a higher level of coordination, communication, and stakeholder engagement to ensure that all projects within the programme are aligned with the overall strategic objectives. Effective programme management also requires a strong focus on benefits realization, ensuring that the intended benefits of the programme are achieved.

In summary, programmes and projects are two distinct concepts that are used to achieve different objectives. While projects are designed to achieve specific goals and objectives, programmes are designed to achieve broader strategic objectives that require a coordinated and integrated approach. Understanding the differences between these concepts is essential for effective project management and strategic change implementation.

## THE ROLE OF PROGRAMMES AND PROJECTS IN ACHIEVING STRATEGIC CHANGE

Strategic change is a critical process for organizations looking to remain competitive and achieve long-term success. However, implementing strategic change can be complex and challenging, requiring a coordinated and integrated approach. Programmes and projects play a crucial role in implementing strategic change, ensuring that organizations can achieve their objectives effectively.

One of the key roles of programmes and projects in implementing strategic change is to provide a structured framework for managing change. Programmes and projects enable organizations to break down complex strategic change initiatives into smaller, more manageable projects that can be executed in a coordinated and integrated way. This helps to ensure that change is implemented in a structured and controlled manner, reducing the risk of failure.

Programmes and projects also help to ensure that strategic change is aligned with the organization's overall strategic objectives. By breaking down strategic change initiatives into smaller projects, it becomes easier to ensure that each project is aligned with the overall strategic direction of the organization. This helps to ensure that strategic change is not only implemented effectively but is also focused on achieving the organization's long-term objectives.

Another important role of programmes and projects in implementing strategic change is to manage risks effectively. Strategic change initiatives are often complex and involve a high degree of uncertainty. By breaking down strategic change initiatives into smaller projects, it becomes easier to identify and manage risks effectively. Programme and project managers can use project management tools and techniques to identify, analyse, and manage risks, reducing the likelihood of failure.

Programmes and projects also help to ensure that the benefits of strategic change are realized effectively. By breaking down strategic change initiatives into smaller projects, it becomes easier to identify and track the benefits of each project. Programme and project managers can use benefits management techniques to ensure that the intended benefits of each project are realized, helping to ensure that the overall strategic change initiative delivers the expected benefits.

In summary, programmes and projects play a crucial role in implementing strategic change. They provide a structured framework for managing change, ensure that strategic change is aligned with the organization's overall strategic objectives, manage risks effectively, and ensure that the benefits of strategic change are realized. By using programmes and projects to implement strategic change, organizations can achieve their long-term objectives effectively and efficiently.

## KEY RELATIONSHIPS BETWEEN PROGRAMMES, PROJECTS, AND STRATEGIC CHANGE

Programmes, projects, and strategic change are interrelated concepts that are critical for the success of any organization. Understanding the key relationships between these concepts is essential for effective project management and strategic change implementation.

One of the key relationships between programmes, projects, and strategic change is that programmes are used to implement strategic change initiatives. Strategic change initiatives often involve multiple interrelated projects that are managed together as a programme. The programme provides a structured framework for managing change and ensures that each project is aligned with the overall strategic objectives of the organization.

Another key relationship is that projects are used to deliver specific objectives that are part of a larger programme. Projects are designed to achieve specific goals or objectives that contribute to the overall strategic objectives of the programme. By breaking down the larger programme into smaller projects, it becomes easier to manage the interdependencies between projects and ensure that each project is aligned with the overall strategic direction of the organization.

Programmes and projects also play a crucial role in managing risks associated with strategic change initiatives. Programme and project managers use project management tools and techniques to identify, analyse, and manage risks, reducing the likelihood of failure. Effective risk management is critical for the success of strategic change initiatives, as they often involve a high degree of uncertainty and complexity.

Programmes and projects also help to ensure that the benefits of strategic change are realized effectively. By breaking down strategic change initiatives into smaller projects, it becomes easier to identify and track the benefits of each project. Programme and project managers can use benefits management techniques to ensure that the intended benefits of each project are realized, helping to ensure that the overall strategic change initiative delivers the expected benefits.

Finally, effective communication and stakeholder engagement are essential for the success of programmes, projects, and strategic change initiatives. Programme and project managers must communicate effectively with stakeholders, ensuring that they understand the objectives of the programme or project and the role they play in achieving those objectives. Effective communication and stakeholder engagement help to ensure that stakeholders are supportive of the programme or project and are willing to contribute to its success.

In summary, understanding the key relationships between programmes, projects, and strategic change is critical for effective project management and strategic change implementation. Programmes are used to implement strategic change initiatives, while projects are used to deliver specific objectives that contribute to the overall strategic objectives of the programme. Effective risk management, benefits management, and communication and stakeholder engagement are essential for the success of programmes, projects, and strategic change initiatives.

## CHALLENGES IN IMPLEMENTING PROGRAMMES AND PROJECTS TO DRIVE STRATEGIC CHANGE

While programmes and projects are essential for implementing strategic change, there are several challenges that organizations may face when implementing them. Understanding these challenges is critical for effective project management and strategic change implementation.

One of the key challenges in implementing programmes and projects to drive strategic change is the complexity of managing multiple interrelated projects. Programmes involve multiple projects that are interdependent and coordinated. Managing these projects requires a high degree of coordination and communication, which can be challenging, particularly in large organizations.

Another challenge is managing the risks associated with strategic change initiatives. Strategic change initiatives often involve a high degree of uncertainty and complexity, which can make risk management challenging. Programme and project managers must identify, analyse, and manage risks effectively to reduce the likelihood of failure.

Another challenge is managing stakeholder expectations and engagement. Effective communication and stakeholder engagement are essential for the success of programmes and projects. Programme and project managers must ensure that stakeholders are engaged and supportive of the programme or project, which can be challenging, particularly in organizations with many stakeholders.

Resource management is another challenge in implementing programmes and projects to drive strategic change. Projects and programmes require specific resources, including human resources, financial resources, and technological resources. Managing these resources effectively is critical for the success of the programme or project, and inadequate resource management can lead to delays, cost overruns, and project failure.

Finally, a lack of alignment between the programme or project and the overall strategic objectives of the organization can be a significant challenge. Programmes and projects must be aligned with the overall strategic direction of the organization to ensure that they contribute to the achievement of the organization's long-term objectives.

In summary, implementing programmes and projects to drive strategic change can be challenging, particularly in large organizations. Challenges include managing multiple interrelated projects, managing risks, managing stakeholder expectations and engagement, resource management, and ensuring alignment with the overall strategic objectives of the organization. Understanding these challenges is critical for effective project management and strategic change implementation.

## BEST PRACTICES FOR EFFECTIVE IMPLEMENTATION OF PROGRAMMES AND PROJECTS

While implementing programmes and projects to drive strategic change can be challenging, there are several best practices that organizations can follow to ensure their success. These best practices can help organizations overcome common challenges and ensure that their programmes and projects are implemented effectively.

One best practice is to establish a clear and compelling business case for the programme or project. The business case should clearly outline the objectives of the programme or project, the benefits it will deliver, and the resources required to implement it. A compelling business case can help to secure the necessary support and funding for the programme or project.

Another best practice is to establish a governance structure for the programme or project. The governance structure should include clear roles and responsibilities for all stakeholders involved in the programme or project, as well as clear decision-making processes. This helps to ensure that the programme or project is managed effectively and that stakeholders are engaged and supportive of the initiative.

Effective communication and stakeholder engagement are also essential best practices for implementing programmes and projects. Programme and project managers should communicate regularly with stakeholders, providing updates on progress and seeking input and feedback. Effective communication and stakeholder engagement can help to ensure that stakeholders are supportive of the programme or project and are willing to contribute to its success.

Managing risks effectively is another best practice for implementing programmes and projects. Programme and project managers should identify, analyse, and manage risks throughout the programme or project lifecycle, using project management tools and techniques. This helps to ensure that risks are identified early and managed effectively, reducing the likelihood of failure.

Finally, measuring and tracking benefits is an essential best practice for implementing programmes and projects. Programme and project managers should establish clear benefits management processes, identifying the intended benefits of the programme or project and tracking their realization. This helps to ensure that the programme or project delivers the expected benefits and that the overall strategic objectives of the organization are achieved.

In summary, following best practices is essential for effective implementation of programmes and projects. Best practices include establishing a clear business case, establishing a governance structure, effective communication and stakeholder engagement, managing risks effectively, and measuring and tracking benefits. By following these best practices, organizations can ensure the successful implementation of programmes and projects and achieve their strategic objectives effectively.

## CONCLUSION: THE IMPORTANCE OF A COHESIVE APPROACH TO PROGRAMMES, PROJECTS, AND STRATEGIC CHANGE

In conclusion, programmes, projects, and strategic change are closely interrelated concepts that are critical for the success of any organization. Programmes and projects are used to implement strategic change initiatives, and understanding the key relationships between these concepts is essential for effective project management and strategic change implementation.

Implementing programmes and projects to drive strategic change can be challenging, but there are several best practices that organizations can follow to ensure their success. These best practices include establishing a clear business case, establishing a governance structure, effective communication and stakeholder engagement, managing risks effectively, and measuring and tracking benefits.

Adopting a cohesive approach to programmes, projects, and strategic change is essential for organizations looking to achieve their long-term objectives. A cohesive approach involves aligning programmes and projects with the overall strategic direction of the organization, managing risks effectively, engaging stakeholders, and measuring and tracking benefits.

Effective programme and project management is critical for implementing strategic change initiatives successfully. By adopting a structured and coordinated approach to programme and project management, organizations can ensure that they achieve their strategic objectives effectively and efficiently.

In summary, implementing programmes and projects to drive strategic change is a complex and challenging process, but it is critical for the success of any organization. By adopting best practices and a cohesive approach to programme and project management, organizations can overcome common challenges and achieve their long-term objectives effectively.

# 3.4 Situations Where Program Management is Appropriate

## Large-Scale Projects with Multiple Components:

Program management is especially effective when dealing with large-scale projects that have multiple components. These types of projects are often complex and require coordination across various departments and stakeholders. In such situations, program management provides a framework for managing the various components of the project in an integrated manner.

By using program management, the different components of a project can be aligned with the overall project goals, which helps ensure that everyone is working towards a common objective. Additionally, program management provides a mechanism for tracking progress across the different components of the project and identifying any issues or roadblocks that may arise.

For example, if a company is developing a new product, program management can help coordinate the development of the product, the marketing strategy, and the supply chain management. This allows the project to be managed as a cohesive program, rather than individual projects that may not be aligned with each other.

In summary, program management is appropriate in situations where there are multiple components to a large-scale project that require coordination and alignment towards a common goal.

## CROSS-FUNCTIONAL TEAMS AND COLLABORATION:

Program management is particularly useful in situations where cross-functional teams need to collaborate on a project. When a project requires input and expertise from multiple departments or teams, program management provides a structured framework for effective collaboration and communication.

By using program management, all stakeholders can be involved in the planning, execution, and monitoring of the project, ensuring that everyone is on the same page and working towards the same objectives. This helps to reduce silos between different departments or teams, enabling a more seamless flow of information and resources.

For example, in the development of a new software application, cross-functional teams such as developers, quality assurance, user experience, and marketing teams all need to work together. Program management helps ensure that everyone is working towards the same objectives, and that everyone is aware of the progress and issues across the different components of the project.

In summary, program management is appropriate when projects require input and expertise from multiple departments or teams and effective collaboration is required for successful project outcomes.

## LONG-TERM AND COMPLEX INITIATIVES:

Program management is particularly useful in situations where the project is complex and involves multiple interdependent initiatives that may span over a longer period of time. These types of initiatives often require a comprehensive approach to project management to ensure that all aspects of the project are integrated, and that the project is being delivered effectively.

Program management provides a structured approach to managing complex and long-term initiatives by breaking them down into smaller, more manageable components. This helps to identify and manage risks, mitigate issues, and track progress across the various components of the initiative.

For example, a company that is looking to expand into a new market may require a long-term initiative that involves multiple components such as market research, product development, marketing, and distribution. Program management can help ensure that all of these components are integrated and aligned with the overall objective of entering the new market.

In summary, program management is appropriate in situations where initiatives are long-term and complex, and require a comprehensive approach to project management to ensure successful project outcomes.

## RESOURCE ALLOCATION AND BUDGETING:

Program management is useful in situations where resource allocation and budgeting are critical to project success. Program management provides a structured approach to managing resources and budgets across multiple projects and components of a program.

By using program management, resource allocation and budgeting can be done in a more systematic and efficient manner. The program manager can ensure that resources are allocated appropriately across the different components of the program, and that the budget is being managed effectively.

For example, a company that is developing a new product line may have multiple projects that need to be completed as part of the program. By using program management, the program manager can ensure that resources such as staff, equipment, and materials are allocated appropriately across the different projects to ensure the successful delivery of the overall program.

In summary, program management is appropriate in situations where resource allocation and budgeting are critical to project success, and a structured approach is needed to manage resources and budgets effectively.

## MANAGING RISKS AND MITIGATING ISSUES:

Program management is useful in situations where risks need to be managed and issues need to be mitigated across multiple projects or components of a program. By using program management, risks can be identified and managed more effectively, and issues can be addressed in a timely manner before they become bigger problems.

The program manager can develop a risk management plan that outlines the potential risks associated with the program, and strategies for mitigating those risks. Additionally, program management provides a mechanism for identifying and addressing issues that arise during the course of the program.

For example, in the development of a new product, there may be risks associated with manufacturing, distribution, and marketing. Program management can help identify these risks and develop strategies for mitigating them. Additionally, if issues arise during the course of the program, program management provides a framework for addressing these issues in a timely manner.

In summary, program management is appropriate in situations where risks need to be managed and issues need to be addressed across multiple projects or components of a program to ensure the successful delivery of the program.

## MEASURING SUCCESS AND DELIVERING BENEFITS:

Program management is useful in situations where it is critical to measure the success of a program and deliver benefits to stakeholders. By using program management, a program manager can define clear objectives and success criteria for the program, and ensure that these objectives are being met.

Program management provides a framework for measuring progress towards the objectives of the program, and for delivering benefits to stakeholders. This can include monitoring the return on investment, tracking customer satisfaction, and measuring the impact of the program on the business.

For example, if a company is implementing a new customer relationship management system, program management can help ensure that the system is meeting the objectives of the program, such as improving customer satisfaction and increasing sales. Program management can also help track the return on investment of the program to ensure that it is delivering value to the company.

In summary, program management is appropriate in situations where it is critical to measure the success of a program and deliver benefits to stakeholders. Program management provides a framework for defining clear objectives, measuring progress, and delivering benefits to ensure the successful delivery of the program.

# 3.5 SITUATIONS WHERE PORTFOLIO MANAGEMENT CAN BENEFIT PROJECTS

Portfolio Management is a strategic approach to managing a collection of projects or programs in a coordinated way that achieves specific business objectives. In project management, portfolio management focuses on identifying, prioritizing, selecting, and managing a group of projects or programs that align with an organization's goals and objectives.

Portfolio Management helps organizations to manage multiple projects, prioritize resources, and align project portfolios with organizational strategies and goals. This approach provides a holistic view of projects and programs, which enables better decision-making and improves the success rate of projects.

In today's fast-paced business environment, organizations face numerous challenges in managing multiple projects and programs effectively. These challenges include limited resources, competing priorities, changing market conditions, and evolving customer needs. As a result, there is a growing need for portfolio management in project management to help organizations manage these challenges efficiently.

Portfolio management provides a framework for selecting, prioritizing, and managing a group of projects or programs that align with an organization's goals and objectives. It helps organizations to focus on projects that have the highest potential to deliver the greatest value and align with the organization's strategic objectives.

In summary, portfolio management is an essential approach to managing projects in today's business environment. It provides a structured framework for managing a group of projects and programs that align with an organization's goals and objectives, enabling better decision-making, and improving the success rate of projects.

## MANAGING MULTIPLE PROJECTS WITH PORTFOLIO MANAGEMENT:

In today's complex business environment, organizations often have to manage multiple projects simultaneously. Managing multiple projects can be challenging, especially when resources are limited and competing priorities exist. Portfolio management can help organizations manage multiple projects effectively by providing a framework for selecting, prioritizing, and managing a group of projects or programs that align with an organization's goals and objectives.

Portfolio management enables organizations to group similar projects together into portfolios based on their strategic importance, resource requirements, risk, and other criteria. This approach helps organizations to prioritize projects, allocate resources effectively, and ensure that project portfolios align with organizational strategies and goals.

Effective portfolio management also involves establishing governance processes and controls to ensure that projects are managed consistently and according to established standards. This includes defining project management methodologies, governance structures, reporting requirements, and project management tools and templates.

Portfolio management also helps organizations to identify and manage risks associated with multiple projects. It enables organizations to monitor and manage risks across the project portfolio, identify potential conflicts and dependencies, and take corrective action where necessary.

By managing multiple projects through portfolio management, organizations can improve their ability to deliver projects on time, within budget, and to the expected quality. They can also improve their ability to manage resources effectively and prioritize projects that provide the greatest value to the organization.

In summary, managing multiple projects with portfolio management is essential for organizations operating in today's complex business environment. It provides a structured framework for prioritizing and managing projects that align with organizational strategies and goals, improves resource allocation, and reduces risks associated with managing multiple projects.

## PRIORITIZING PROJECTS WITH PORTFOLIO MANAGEMENT:

Prioritizing projects is an essential part of project management, and it becomes even more critical when organizations have to manage multiple projects simultaneously. Prioritization helps organizations to allocate resources effectively, ensure that projects align with organizational strategies and goals, and maximize the value of project investments. Portfolio management provides a framework for prioritizing projects based on their strategic importance, resource requirements, and other criteria.

The first step in prioritizing projects with portfolio management is to define the organization's strategic objectives and goals. This enables the organization to identify projects that align with its strategies and goals and eliminate projects that do not. Projects that do not align with the organization's goals and objectives can consume valuable resources without providing significant benefits to the organization.

Next, the organization should define criteria for prioritizing projects, such as the potential return on investment (ROI), the impact on the organization's mission, the level of risk associated with the project, and the resource requirements. By defining these criteria, organizations can evaluate projects based on their strategic importance and allocate resources accordingly.

Portfolio management also involves developing a project portfolio that balances risk, return, and resources. This means selecting a mix of projects that have different levels of risk and return, as well as different resource requirements. By selecting a mix of projects, organizations can spread their risk and maximize their return on investment.

Effective portfolio management also involves monitoring and reviewing the project portfolio regularly to ensure that it remains aligned with organizational strategies and goals. This enables organizations to adjust their project portfolio if necessary and ensure that they are investing in the projects that provide the greatest value.

In summary, prioritizing projects with portfolio management is essential for organizations to ensure that they are investing in the projects that align with their strategies and goals and provide the greatest value. Portfolio management provides a framework for selecting a mix of projects that balance risk, return, and resources and enables organizations to adjust their project portfolio regularly to remain aligned with organizational strategies and goals.

## RESOURCE ALLOCATION WITH PORTFOLIO MANAGEMENT:

Effective resource allocation is essential for project success. In project management, resource allocation refers to the process of assigning and managing resources such as people, time, and money to specific tasks or activities within a project. Portfolio management provides a framework for allocating resources effectively across a group of projects or programs.

Portfolio management helps organizations to prioritize projects based on their strategic importance, resource requirements, and other criteria. This enables organizations to allocate resources effectively to the projects that provide the greatest value to the organization. By allocating resources to high-priority projects first, organizations can ensure that they are investing their resources in projects that align with their strategies and goals.

Portfolio management also helps organizations to identify and manage resource constraints across the project portfolio. This includes identifying resource gaps, conflicts, and dependencies and taking corrective action where necessary. By identifying and managing resource constraints, organizations can ensure that they have the resources necessary to complete projects on time, within budget, and to the expected quality.

Effective resource allocation with portfolio management also involves developing and maintaining a resource management plan. The resource management plan outlines how resources will be allocated and managed across the project portfolio, including the roles and responsibilities of project managers, resource managers, and stakeholders. The resource management plan also includes contingency plans for managing resource constraints and unforeseen events.

Finally, portfolio management helps organizations to optimize their resource utilization by identifying and eliminating redundant or unnecessary projects. By eliminating redundant or unnecessary projects, organizations can free up resources and allocate them to high-priority projects.

In summary, resource allocation with portfolio management is essential for project success. It provides a framework for allocating resources effectively across a group of projects or programs, identifying and managing resource constraints, developing a resource management plan, and optimizing resource utilization by eliminating redundant or unnecessary projects.

## RISK MANAGEMENT WITH PORTFOLIO MANAGEMENT:

Risk management is an essential part of project management. In project management, risk refers to the potential for loss, damage, or failure of a project or program. Portfolio management provides a framework for managing risks across a group of projects or programs.

Effective risk management with portfolio management involves identifying and assessing risks across the project portfolio, prioritizing risks based on their likelihood and impact, and developing risk mitigation strategies. Portfolio management also involves monitoring and controlling risks throughout the project lifecycle to ensure that they are managed effectively.

Portfolio management enables organizations to manage risks at the portfolio level, rather than at the individual project level. This approach provides a holistic view of risks across the project portfolio, enabling organizations to identify potential conflicts and dependencies and take corrective action where necessary.

Portfolio management also involves developing a risk management plan that outlines how risks will be managed across the project portfolio. The risk management plan includes processes for identifying, assessing, prioritizing, and mitigating risks, as well as roles and responsibilities for managing risks.

Effective risk management with portfolio management also involves developing contingency plans for managing unforeseen events and risks. Contingency plans help organizations to manage risks that were not identified or anticipated during the project definition phase.

Finally, portfolio management involves monitoring and controlling risks throughout the project lifecycle to ensure that they are managed effectively. This includes regular risk assessments, risk mitigation strategies, and contingency planning.

In summary, risk management with portfolio management is essential for managing risks across a group of projects or programs. It involves identifying and assessing risks, prioritizing risks based on their likelihood and impact, developing risk mitigation strategies, developing a risk management plan, developing contingency plans, and monitoring and controlling risks throughout the project lifecycle. By managing risks effectively with portfolio management, organizations can improve project success rates and achieve their strategic objectives.

## MANAGING CHANGE WITH PORTFOLIO MANAGEMENT:

Change is an inevitable part of project management. In project management, change refers to any modification or deviation from the original project plan. Portfolio management provides a framework for managing change across a group of projects or programs.

Effective change management with portfolio management involves identifying potential changes to the project portfolio, assessing the impact of these changes, and developing a change management plan to manage the changes effectively. This includes identifying stakeholders and communicating the changes to them, assessing the risks associated with the changes, and developing contingency plans to manage the changes if necessary.

Portfolio management enables organizations to manage changes at the portfolio level, rather than at the individual project level. This approach provides a holistic view of changes across the project portfolio, enabling organizations to identify potential conflicts and dependencies and take corrective action where necessary.

Effective change management with portfolio management also involves developing a change control process to manage changes throughout the project lifecycle. The change control process includes defining the scope of the change, assessing the impact of the change, and obtaining approval from relevant stakeholders before implementing the change.

Finally, portfolio management involves monitoring and controlling changes throughout the project lifecycle to ensure that they are managed effectively. This includes regular change assessments, change management strategies, and contingency planning.

In summary, managing change with portfolio management is essential for managing changes across a group of projects or programs. It involves identifying potential changes, assessing the impact of these changes, developing a change management plan, developing a change control process, and monitoring and controlling changes throughout the project lifecycle. By managing changes effectively with portfolio management, organizations can achieve their strategic objectives and improve project success rates.

## ALIGNING PROJECTS WITH ORGANIZATIONAL GOALS USING PORTFOLIO MANAGEMENT:

One of the key benefits of portfolio management is its ability to align projects with organizational strategies and goals. This alignment is essential for organizations to achieve their strategic objectives and maximize the value of project investments.

Effective alignment of projects with organizational goals with portfolio management involves defining the organization's strategic objectives and goals, identifying projects that align with these goals, and prioritizing these projects based on their strategic importance.

Portfolio management also involves developing a project portfolio that balances risk, return, and resources. This means selecting a mix of projects that have different levels of risk and return, as well as different resource requirements. By selecting a mix of projects, organizations can spread their risk and maximize their return on investment.

Effective alignment of projects with organizational goals also involves establishing governance processes and controls to ensure that projects are managed consistently and according to established standards. This includes defining project management methodologies, governance structures, reporting requirements, and project management tools and templates.

Portfolio management also involves developing a performance management system that measures and monitors project performance against established objectives and goals. This enables organizations to identify and address performance gaps and take corrective action where necessary.

Finally, portfolio management involves regular review and evaluation of the project portfolio to ensure that it remains aligned with organizational strategies and goals. This enables organizations to adjust their project portfolio if necessary and ensure that they are investing in the projects that provide the greatest value.

In summary, aligning projects with organizational goals using portfolio management is essential for organizations to achieve their strategic objectives and maximize the value of project investments. It involves defining strategic objectives and goals, identifying projects that align with these goals, developing a project portfolio that balances risk, return, and resources, establishing governance processes and controls, developing a performance management system, and regular review and evaluation of the project portfolio.

## CONCLUSION AND RECOMMENDATIONS FOR IMPLEMENTING PORTFOLIO MANAGEMENT IN PROJECTS:

Portfolio management provides a structured approach to managing a group of projects or programs that align with an organization's goals and objectives. It helps organizations to manage multiple projects, prioritize resources, align project portfolios with organizational strategies and goals, manage risks, and manage changes effectively.

To implement portfolio management in projects effectively, organizations should start by defining their strategic objectives and goals. They should then identify projects that align with these goals and prioritize these projects based on their strategic importance. This involves developing a project portfolio that balances risk, return, and resources and establishing governance processes and controls to ensure that projects are managed consistently and according to established standards.

Organizations should also develop a resource management plan that outlines how resources will be allocated and managed across the project portfolio and a risk management plan that outlines how risks will be managed across the project portfolio. Effective change management is also essential for managing changes across a group of projects or programs.

Finally, organizations should regularly review and evaluate the project portfolio to ensure that it remains aligned with organizational strategies and goals. This involves developing a performance management system that measures and monitors project performance against established objectives and goals.

In conclusion, implementing portfolio management in projects is essential for organizations operating in today's complex business environment. It provides a structured framework for managing a group of projects and programs that align with an organization's goals and objectives, enabling better decision-making and improving the success rate of projects. By following the recommendations outlined above, organizations can implement portfolio management effectively and achieve their strategic objectives.

# 3.6 TOOLS AND TECHNIQUES FOR IDENTIFYING FACTORS AFFECTING PROJECTS

In today's complex and dynamic business environment, projects are influenced by a variety of factors that can impact their success. From technological advancements and changing customer preferences to regulatory compliance and economic factors, it's essential for project managers to identify and analyse the different factors that can affect their projects.

To achieve this, project managers often use different tools and techniques to gather data and insights about the internal and external factors that can impact their projects. These tools and techniques provide a structured and systematic approach to project analysis, helping project managers make informed decisions and mitigate potential risks.

In this section, we will explore some of the popular tools and techniques used by project managers to identify and analyse the different factors that can affect their projects. We will discuss the PESTLE, SWOT, and VUCA frameworks in detail, along with other additional tools and techniques that can help project managers ensure project success.

## UNDERSTANDING THE IMPORTANCE OF IDENTIFYING FACTORS AFFECTING PROJECTS:

Project managers need to understand the importance of identifying the different factors that can impact their projects. By identifying these factors, project managers can assess the risks and opportunities associated with their projects and develop appropriate strategies to mitigate the risks and leverage the opportunities.

Identifying factors affecting projects can also help project managers develop a comprehensive project plan. The insights gained from the analysis can be used to define the project's objectives, scope, timeline, and budget, ensuring that the project is aligned with the organization's goals.

Furthermore, identifying the different factors that can impact projects can help project managers manage stakeholder expectations effectively. Project stakeholders, including clients, sponsors, and team members, have different expectations, goals, and requirements. By understanding the factors that can impact their projects, project managers can manage stakeholder expectations and develop effective communication strategies.

In summary, identifying factors affecting projects is essential for project success. It helps project managers assess risks, develop comprehensive project plans, and manage stakeholder expectations. The tools and techniques discussed in this section provide a structured and systematic approach to identifying and analysing factors that can impact projects.

## PESTLE ANALYSIS: A COMPREHENSIVE FRAMEWORK FOR PROJECT ANALYSIS:

PESTLE analysis is a popular framework used by project managers to identify and analyse external factors that can impact their projects. The framework considers six external factors that can influence projects, including political, economic, social, technological, legal, and environmental factors.

Political factors: These factors refer to the political environment in which the project operates. It includes government policies, regulations, and political stability. Political factors can impact projects by affecting funding, approvals, and licenses.

Economic factors: Economic factors refer to the economic environment in which the project operates. It includes inflation, interest rates, exchange rates, and economic growth. Economic factors can impact projects by affecting the availability of funding and resources.

Social factors: Social factors refer to the social environment in which the project operates. It includes cultural norms, demographics, and consumer behaviour. Social factors can impact projects by affecting customer preferences and market demand.

Technological factors: Technological factors refer to the technological environment in which the project operates. It includes technological advancements, innovation, and infrastructure. Technological factors can impact projects by affecting the availability of resources and the project's competitiveness.

Legal factors: Legal factors refer to the legal environment in which the project operates. It includes laws, regulations, and compliance requirements. Legal factors can impact projects by affecting the project's feasibility, funding, and timeline.

Environmental factors: Environmental factors refer to the natural environment in which the project operates. It includes weather patterns, natural disasters, and climate change. Environmental factors can impact projects by affecting the availability of resources and the project's sustainability.

By analysing these six external factors, project managers can gain insights into the opportunities and risks associated with their projects. The insights gained from the analysis can be used to develop appropriate strategies to mitigate risks and leverage opportunities, ensuring project success.

# SWOT ANALYSIS: ASSESSING STRENGTHS, WEAKNESSES, OPPORTUNITIES, AND THREATS:

SWOT analysis is another popular framework used by project managers to identify and analyse internal and external factors that can impact their projects. The framework considers four factors, including strengths, weaknesses, opportunities, and threats.

Strengths: These factors refer to the project's internal strengths, including resources, capabilities, and expertise. Identifying strengths can help project managers leverage them to achieve project success.

Weaknesses: These factors refer to the project's internal weaknesses, including lack of resources, expertise, or capabilities. Identifying weaknesses can help project managers develop strategies to mitigate them and prevent them from negatively impacting the project.

Opportunities: These factors refer to the external opportunities that can positively impact the project, including market trends, emerging technologies, and changes in customer preferences. Identifying opportunities can help project managers develop strategies to capitalize on them and achieve project success.

Threats: These factors refer to the external threats that can negatively impact the project, including competition, changing regulations, and economic downturns. Identifying threats can help project managers develop strategies to mitigate them and minimize their impact on the project.

By analysing these four factors, project managers can gain insights into the internal and external factors that can impact their projects. The insights gained from the analysis can be used to develop appropriate strategies to leverage strengths, mitigate weaknesses, capitalize on opportunities, and minimize threats, ensuring project success. SWOT analysis can also help project managers make informed decisions about resource allocation, stakeholder management, and project prioritization.

## VUCA ANALYSIS: EXAMINING VOLATILITY, UNCERTAINTY, COMPLEXITY, AND AMBIGUITY:

VUCA analysis is a framework used by project managers to analyse the external environment in which the project operates. The framework considers four factors, including volatility, uncertainty, complexity, and ambiguity.

Volatility: This factor refers to the level of instability and unpredictability in the external environment. Volatility can impact projects by affecting resource availability, project scope, and timeline.

Uncertainty: This factor refers to the lack of information and the level of unpredictability in the external environment. Uncertainty can impact projects by affecting decision-making, risk management, and stakeholder management.

Complexity: This factor refers to the level of complexity in the external environment, including interdependent variables and systems. Complexity can impact projects by affecting project planning, resource allocation, and stakeholder management.

Ambiguity: This factor refers to the lack of clarity and the level of ambiguity in the external environment. Ambiguity can impact projects by affecting decision-making, stakeholder management, and project planning.

By analysing these four factors, project managers can gain insights into the external environment in which the project operates. The insights gained from the analysis can be used to develop appropriate strategies to mitigate the impact of external factors and ensure project success. VUCA analysis can also help project managers develop contingency plans and adapt to changes in the external environment, ensuring project resilience.

Overall, VUCA analysis provides project managers with a framework for understanding the external environment's complexity and unpredictability and developing strategies to mitigate the impact of external factors on the project.

## COMBINING PESTLE, SWOT, AND VUCA FOR A HOLISTIC APPROACH:

While PESTLE, SWOT, and VUCA are standalone frameworks that provide unique insights into the external and internal factors that can impact projects, project managers can combine them to gain a holistic understanding of the project environment. By combining these frameworks, project managers can gain a comprehensive view of the external and internal factors that can impact their projects and develop appropriate strategies to mitigate risks and leverage opportunities.

For example, project managers can use PESTLE analysis to gain insights into the external factors that can impact their projects, including political, economic, social, technological, legal, and environmental factors. They can then use SWOT analysis to identify the project's internal strengths, weaknesses, opportunities, and threats. By combining PESTLE and SWOT analysis, project managers can develop appropriate strategies to leverage strengths, mitigate weaknesses, capitalize on opportunities, and minimize threats.

Furthermore, project managers can use VUCA analysis to gain insights into the external environment's complexity and unpredictability. By combining VUCA analysis with PESTLE and SWOT analysis, project managers can develop contingency plans, adapt to changes in the external environment, and ensure project resilience.

In summary, project managers can combine PESTLE, SWOT, and VUCA analysis to gain a holistic understanding of the external and internal factors that can impact their projects. By developing appropriate strategies to leverage strengths, mitigate weaknesses, capitalize on opportunities, and minimize threats, project managers can ensure project success and adapt to changes in the external environment.

## ADDITIONAL TOOLS AND TECHNIQUES FOR IDENTIFYING FACTORS AFFECTING PROJECTS:

Apart from PESTLE, SWOT, and VUCA analysis, project managers can use additional tools and techniques to identify and analyse the factors that can impact their projects. These tools and techniques provide project managers with a structured and systematic approach to project analysis, helping them make informed decisions and mitigate potential risks.

Some of the additional tools and techniques include:

a. Stakeholder Analysis: This tool helps project managers identify and analyze the stakeholders who are affected by the project. Stakeholder analysis helps project managers understand stakeholder expectations, interests, and requirements, enabling them to manage stakeholder relationships effectively.

b. Cost-Benefit Analysis: This tool helps project managers identify and analyze the costs and benefits associated with the project. Cost-benefit analysis helps project managers understand the financial implications of the project, enabling them to make informed decisions about resource allocation and project prioritization.

c. Risk Analysis: This tool helps project managers identify and analyze the risks associated with the project. Risk analysis helps project managers understand the potential risks and their likelihood, enabling them to develop appropriate risk management strategies.

d. Force Field Analysis: This tool helps project managers identify and analyze the forces that drive and restrain the project. Force field analysis helps project managers understand the factors that can impact the project's success and develop appropriate strategies to mitigate the restraining forces and leverage the driving forces.

e. Root Cause Analysis: This tool helps project managers identify the underlying causes of a problem. Root cause analysis helps project managers understand the reasons behind the problem and develop appropriate strategies to prevent similar problems in the future.

By using these additional tools and techniques, project managers can gain a comprehensive understanding of the factors that can impact their projects and develop appropriate strategies to ensure project success.

## CONCLUSION: LEVERAGING TOOLS AND TECHNIQUES TO ENSURE PROJECT SUCCESS:

In today's complex and dynamic business environment, project managers need to identify and analyse the different factors that can impact their projects. By using tools and techniques such as PESTLE, SWOT, VUCA, stakeholder analysis, cost-benefit analysis, risk analysis, force field analysis, and root cause analysis, project managers can gain insights into the external and internal factors that can impact their projects and develop appropriate strategies to mitigate risks and leverage opportunities.

Moreover, leveraging these tools and techniques can help project managers ensure project success by developing comprehensive project plans, managing stakeholder expectations effectively, making informed decisions about resource allocation and project prioritization, and adapting to changes in the external environment.

In summary, project managers must leverage different tools and techniques to identify and analyse the factors that can impact their projects. By doing so, they can develop appropriate strategies to mitigate risks and leverage opportunities, ensuring project success and delivering value to their organizations.

# 3.7 UNDERSTANDING THE INFLUENCE OF LEGAL AND REGULATORY ENVIRONMENT ON PROJECTS

In today's business world, legal and regulatory requirements play a crucial role in shaping the overall environment in which projects operate. Legal and regulatory compliance has become a critical aspect of project management. It ensures that projects are carried out within a framework of laws, regulations, and standards. Non-compliance with these regulations can result in penalties, legal issues, and reputational damage.

The legal and regulatory environment affects different aspects of project management, including working conditions, risk management, governance, and sustainability. As a project manager, it is important to understand the legal and regulatory environment and its impact on the project to ensure successful project delivery.

Legal requirements refer to laws, rules, and regulations that have been set by the government or regulatory bodies. Compliance with these laws and regulations is mandatory for businesses and organizations. Regulatory requirements, on the other hand, are specific requirements that organizations must meet to operate in a particular industry or sector.

The legal and regulatory environment is constantly changing, which makes it essential for project managers to keep themselves updated with the latest regulations and laws. Failure to comply with legal and regulatory requirements can result in fines, legal issues, and reputational damage, all of which can impact the success of a project.

Therefore, understanding the legal and regulatory environment is critical for project managers to ensure successful project delivery.

## IMPACT ON WORKING CONDITIONS OF PROJECTS

The legal and regulatory environment has a significant impact on the working conditions of projects. The working conditions of a project include factors such as health and safety, employment law, and labour regulations. These factors can impact the project's success, team morale, and overall productivity.

One of the most significant impacts of the legal and regulatory environment on working conditions is the health and safety regulations. Occupational health and safety (OHS) regulations aim to protect the health and safety of workers by identifying potential hazards and implementing measures to prevent accidents and injuries. Failure to comply with OHS regulations can lead to severe consequences such as lawsuits, fines, and damage to the organization's reputation.

Another area of concern is employment law. Employment laws regulate the relationship between employers and employees. They cover various aspects such as minimum wages, working hours, leave entitlements, discrimination, and harassment. Project managers must ensure that the project team's employment conditions comply with the relevant employment laws to avoid legal issues and maintain a healthy work environment.

Labour regulations are also an important aspect of the legal and regulatory environment that can impact working conditions. These regulations govern the relationship between employers and employees and cover issues such as collective bargaining, labour disputes, and union representation. Compliance with labour regulations is essential to prevent labour unrest and maintain a positive working environment.

In conclusion, the legal and regulatory environment has a significant impact on the working conditions of projects. Project managers must be aware of the relevant regulations and laws and ensure that the project team complies with them. Compliance with these regulations and laws can help maintain a positive working environment, prevent legal issues, and ensure successful project delivery.

## RISK MANAGEMENT AND COMPLIANCE IN PROJECT ENVIRONMENT

Risk management is an essential aspect of project management that involves identifying, assessing, and mitigating risks that could impact the project's success. The legal and regulatory environment has a significant impact on risk management in project environments. Compliance with legal and regulatory requirements is critical to managing risks and avoiding legal issues that could delay or derail the project.

One of the most significant risks that legal and regulatory compliance can help manage is the risk of non-compliance. Non-compliance with legal and regulatory requirements can lead to lawsuits, fines, legal issues, and reputational damage. By complying with the relevant regulations, project managers can mitigate these risks and ensure the project's success.

Another area of concern is data protection and privacy regulations. Projects often involve collecting and processing personal data, which makes compliance with data protection and privacy regulations essential. Failure to comply with these regulations can result in significant legal issues and reputational damage. Project managers must ensure that the project team complies with relevant data protection and privacy regulations to avoid such risks.

Intellectual property (IP) regulations are another critical aspect of the legal and regulatory environment that impacts risk management in project environments. Projects often involve developing new products, processes, or services, which can result in the creation of intellectual property. Compliance with IP regulations is essential to protect the organization's intellectual property rights and prevent legal issues.

In conclusion, legal and regulatory compliance plays a significant role in risk management in project environments. Project managers must be aware of the relevant regulations and laws and ensure that the project team complies with them. Compliance with these regulations and laws can help manage risks, avoid legal issues, and ensure the project's success.

## GOVERNANCE AND REGULATORY COMPLIANCE IN PROJECT MANAGEMENT

Governance and regulatory compliance are essential aspects of project management that ensure projects are carried out within a framework of laws, regulations, and standards. The legal and regulatory environment has a significant impact on governance and regulatory compliance in project management. Failure to comply with governance and regulatory requirements can result in severe consequences such as lawsuits, fines, and damage to the organization's reputation.

One of the critical aspects of governance and regulatory compliance in project management is financial regulations. Projects involve significant financial investments, and compliance with financial regulations is essential to prevent financial fraud and ensure the project's financial viability. Financial regulations include accounting standards, tax regulations, and investment regulations.

Another area of concern is environmental regulations. Projects often have environmental impacts, and compliance with environmental regulations is essential to prevent environmental damage and protect the environment. Environmental regulations include regulations related to pollution, waste management, and conservation.

Project managers must also ensure compliance with corporate governance regulations. Corporate governance regulations aim to ensure that the organization is managed in a responsible and ethical manner. Compliance with these regulations is essential to prevent unethical practices, maintain the organization's reputation, and promote social responsibility.

In conclusion, governance and regulatory compliance play a crucial role in project management. Project managers must be aware of the relevant regulations and laws and ensure that the project team complies with them. Compliance with these regulations and laws can help prevent legal issues, maintain the organization's reputation, and ensure the project's success.

## ENSURING SUSTAINABILITY IN PROJECT MANAGEMENT AMIDST LEGAL AND REGULATORY ENVIRONMENT

Sustainability is an essential aspect of project management that focuses on meeting the needs of the present without compromising the ability of future generations to meet their needs. The legal and regulatory environment has a significant impact on sustainability in project management. Compliance with environmental regulations is essential to ensure sustainable project outcomes.

One of the critical aspects of sustainability in project management is the use of sustainable materials and resources. Projects involve significant resource consumption, and the use of sustainable materials and resources can reduce the environmental impact of the project. Compliance with environmental regulations related to resource consumption, such as waste management, is essential to ensure sustainable project outcomes.

Another area of concern is the impact of the project on the environment. Projects often have significant environmental impacts, and compliance with environmental regulations is essential to prevent environmental damage and ensure sustainable project outcomes. Compliance with environmental regulations related to pollution, water use, and land use is essential to ensure sustainable project outcomes.

Project managers must also ensure that the project is socially responsible. Social responsibility involves considering the impact of the project on society and ensuring that the project benefits the community. Compliance with social responsibility regulations is essential to ensure that the project benefits the community and contributes to sustainable development.

In conclusion, sustainability is an essential aspect of project management, and compliance with environmental and social responsibility regulations is essential to ensure sustainable project outcomes. Project managers must be aware of the relevant regulations and laws and ensure that the project team complies with them. Compliance with these regulations and laws can help prevent legal issues, ensure sustainable project outcomes, and contribute to the development of a sustainable society.

## CONCLUSION: NAVIGATING THE LEGAL AND REGULATORY LANDSCAPE IN PROJECT MANAGEMENT

The legal and regulatory environment has a significant impact on project management. It affects different aspects of project management, including working conditions, risk management, governance, and sustainability. As a project manager, it is important to navigate the legal and regulatory landscape to ensure successful project delivery.

To navigate the legal and regulatory landscape, project managers must be aware of the relevant regulations and laws and ensure that the project team complies with them. Compliance with these regulations and laws can help manage risks, prevent legal issues, and ensure the project's success.

Project managers must also keep themselves updated with the latest legal and regulatory changes. The legal and regulatory environment is constantly changing, and project managers must keep themselves informed of the latest developments to ensure compliance and avoid legal issues.

In addition, project managers must collaborate with legal and regulatory experts to navigate the legal and regulatory landscape successfully. Legal and regulatory experts can provide valuable insights and guidance on compliance issues and help project managers navigate legal and regulatory challenges.

In conclusion, navigating the legal and regulatory landscape is critical for project managers to ensure successful project delivery. By understanding the impact of legal and regulatory requirements on different aspects of project management and collaborating with legal and regulatory experts, project managers can ensure compliance, manage risks, and achieve sustainable project outcomes.

# CHAPTER FOUR

## *Effective Communication in Project Management*

# 4.1 THE IMPORTANCE OF A COMMUNICATION PLAN FOR PROJECT SUCCESS

A communication plan is a document that outlines the communication goals, objectives, strategies, and tactics for a project. It is a crucial tool for ensuring that everyone involved in the project has a shared understanding of the project goals, timelines, deliverables, and expectations. The communication plan also establishes the channels, frequency, and tone of communication among the project team, stakeholders, and other relevant parties.

A well-designed communication plan provides clarity, consistency, and transparency throughout the project lifecycle, enabling the team to manage risks, resolve issues, and achieve project success. Without a communication plan, project stakeholders may be misinformed, misaligned, or disconnected, leading to confusion, delays, and failures.

In the following sections, we will explore the benefits of a communication plan in detail and how it can help a project succeed.

## CLEAR COMMUNICATION REDUCES RISKS

One of the most significant benefits of having a communication plan is that it reduces project risks. Effective communication ensures that everyone on the project team understands the project's objectives, timelines, milestones, and deliverables. It also enables team members to identify potential issues or risks early on, before they escalate into more significant problems.

A communication plan helps to establish a framework for how information is shared, who is responsible for sharing it, and when it should be shared. This ensures that critical information is communicated to the right people at the right time, reducing the likelihood of miscommunication, misunderstandings, or delays.

Clear communication also helps to establish a culture of transparency and accountability. When team members know what is expected of them and have a clear understanding of their roles and responsibilities, they are more likely to take ownership of their tasks and work collaboratively to achieve project goals. This reduces the likelihood of errors, rework, or delays, ultimately reducing project risks.

In summary, a communication plan helps to reduce project risks by establishing clear communication channels and expectations, promoting transparency and accountability, and enabling team members to identify and address potential issues early on.

## EFFICIENT USE OF RESOURCES

Another significant benefit of a communication plan is that it helps to ensure efficient use of resources. A well-designed communication plan outlines the communication goals, objectives, and strategies for the project, enabling team members to prioritize and allocate resources accordingly.

A communication plan also helps to establish clear communication channels and protocols, which can save time and resources by avoiding unnecessary or redundant communication. For example, if project stakeholders are informed of the project's status through regular status reports or meetings, they may not need to receive additional updates or communications unless there are significant changes or issues to address.

Additionally, a communication plan can help to prevent unnecessary meetings or discussions by establishing clear guidelines for when and how communication should occur. This helps to reduce interruptions and distractions, allowing team members to focus on their tasks and responsibilities and ultimately increasing productivity.

In summary, a communication plan helps to ensure efficient use of resources by establishing clear communication goals, channels, and protocols, which can save time and reduce interruptions and distractions, allowing team members to focus on their tasks and responsibilities.

## IMPROVED COLLABORATION AND COORDINATION

A communication plan can also improve collaboration and coordination among project team members. Clear and consistent communication helps to establish a shared understanding of the project's goals, objectives, and priorities, which promotes teamwork and collaboration.

A communication plan can help to establish regular communication channels and protocols, enabling team members to stay informed and up to date on project progress, issues, and risks. This helps to ensure that everyone is on the same page and working towards the same goals.

Effective communication can also help to identify and address conflicts or disagreements among team members. By encouraging open and honest communication, team members can share their perspectives and work together to find solutions that best meet the project's objectives and priorities.

In summary, a communication plan promotes collaboration and coordination by establishing regular communication channels and protocols, ensuring everyone is on the same page and working towards the same goals, and facilitating open and honest communication to address conflicts or disagreements.

## ENHANCED STAKEHOLDER ENGAGEMENT

A communication plan can also help to enhance stakeholder engagement in a project. Stakeholders are individuals or groups who have an interest or stake in the project, such as clients, customers, vendors, or regulators.

A communication plan helps to identify and engage stakeholders early on in the project, enabling project teams to understand their needs, expectations, and priorities. By involving stakeholders in the project planning and decision-making processes, project teams can ensure that the project aligns with stakeholders' needs and objectives, ultimately increasing stakeholder satisfaction.

Effective communication also helps to keep stakeholders informed and engaged throughout the project lifecycle. A communication plan can establish regular communication channels, such as progress reports, meetings, or updates, enabling stakeholders to track project progress and provide feedback or input when necessary.

Finally, a communication plan can help to manage stakeholder expectations and prevent misunderstandings or conflicts. By establishing clear communication channels and protocols, stakeholders can understand what to expect and when to expect it, reducing the likelihood of miscommunication or delays.

In summary, a communication plan can enhance stakeholder engagement by involving stakeholders early on in the project, keeping them informed and engaged throughout the project lifecycle, and managing their expectations and needs effectively.

## EFFECTIVE CHANGE MANAGEMENT

Change is inevitable in any project, and a communication plan can help to manage change effectively. A communication plan outlines the project's goals, objectives, and strategies, and establishes communication channels and protocols, which are critical components of effective change management.

When changes occur, a communication plan can help project teams communicate these changes to all stakeholders effectively. This includes providing clear and concise information about the changes, their impact on the project, and any necessary adjustments to project timelines, resources, or budgets.

Effective communication also helps to manage stakeholder expectations during periods of change. By keeping stakeholders informed and engaged, project teams can minimize resistance to change and ensure that stakeholders understand the reasons for the changes and their potential benefits.

Finally, a communication plan can help project teams to track and manage the impact of changes on the project's objectives and priorities. By establishing regular communication channels and protocols, project teams can monitor the effects of changes on project timelines, budgets, and resources, and make any necessary adjustments to keep the project on track.

In summary, a communication plan is an essential component of effective change management, enabling project teams to communicate changes effectively, manage stakeholder expectations, and track the impact of changes on project objectives and priorities.

## CONCLUSION: KEY TAKEAWAYS ON COMMUNICATION PLAN BENEFITS

In summary, a communication plan is a critical tool for project success, providing the following benefits:

    a. Clear communication reduces risks by establishing clear communication channels and expectations, promoting transparency and accountability, and enabling team members to identify and address potential issues early on.

b. Efficient use of resources is achieved by establishing clear communication goals, channels, and protocols, which can save time and reduce interruptions and distractions, allowing team members to focus on their tasks and responsibilities.

c. Improved collaboration and coordination are promoted by establishing regular communication channels and protocols, ensuring everyone is on the same page and working towards the same goals, and facilitating open and honest communication to address conflicts or disagreements.

d. Enhanced stakeholder engagement is achieved by involving stakeholders early on in the project, keeping them informed and engaged throughout the project lifecycle, and managing their expectations and needs effectively.

e. Effective change management is facilitated by establishing clear communication channels and protocols, enabling project teams to communicate changes effectively, manage stakeholder expectations, and track the impact of changes on project objectives and priorities.

In conclusion, a communication plan is a critical component of project success, enabling project teams to communicate effectively, manage risks and change, and engage stakeholders to achieve project goals and objectives. By establishing clear communication goals, channels, and protocols, project teams can ensure that everyone involved in the project has a shared understanding of the project's objectives, timelines, deliverables, and expectations, ultimately leading to successful project outcomes.

# 4.2 THE INTERCONNECTEDNESS OF STAKEHOLDER ANALYSIS AND EFFECTIVE COMMUNICATION MANAGEMENT PLAN

Stakeholder analysis is a process of identifying individuals, groups, or organizations that may affect, be affected by, or perceive themselves to be affected by a particular project, program, or decision. It is an essential step in any project or program management process, as it helps in identifying stakeholders' interests, expectations, and potential impact on the project's success.

The stakeholder analysis process involves identifying and categorizing stakeholders based on their level of interest, power, and influence on the project. Stakeholders are often classified into categories such as primary, secondary, and tertiary, depending on their level of importance to the project's success.

In addition to identifying stakeholders, stakeholder analysis also involves understanding their needs, expectations, and potential concerns related to the project. This information is crucial for developing effective communication strategies that ensure stakeholders are engaged, informed, and supportive of the project.

Stakeholder analysis is an ongoing process that should be revisited periodically throughout the project lifecycle to ensure that stakeholders' needs and expectations are continually met.

## IMPORTANCE OF IDENTIFYING STAKEHOLDERS

Identifying stakeholders is crucial for effective project management, as it allows project managers to understand who will be impacted by the project and who can influence its success. Stakeholders can include individuals, groups, or organizations that have a vested interest in the project, including project sponsors, team members, customers, vendors, regulators, and the community.

Effective stakeholder analysis helps project managers to prioritize stakeholders and identify their needs and expectations. By doing so, project managers can develop communication strategies that engage stakeholders in the project, ensuring that they remain supportive and informed throughout the project lifecycle.

Failure to identify stakeholders and understand their needs can result in miscommunication, delays, and even project failure. For example, if a project team fails to engage stakeholders who have the power to derail the project, it may face opposition or resistance that can halt progress or cause significant delays.

By identifying stakeholders and understanding their needs and expectations, project managers can tailor their communication strategies to ensure that stakeholders are engaged, informed, and supportive of the project. This can help to build trust and goodwill, which are essential for project success.

## COMPONENTS OF AN EFFECTIVE COMMUNICATION MANAGEMENT PLAN

An effective communication management plan is essential for ensuring that stakeholders are engaged, informed, and supportive of the project. A communication management plan outlines how communication will be managed throughout the project lifecycle and identifies the key stakeholders, communication channels, and messaging strategies.

The following are the components of an effective communication management plan:

   a. Stakeholder identification: The first step in developing a communication management plan is to identify the stakeholders who will be impacted by the project. This includes identifying primary, secondary, and tertiary stakeholders and understanding their needs and expectations.

b. Communication goals and objectives: The communication plan should include clear goals and objectives that define what the project team hopes to achieve through communication. This may include increasing stakeholder engagement, reducing misunderstandings, or building trust.

c. Communication channels: The communication plan should identify the communication channels that will be used to reach stakeholders. This may include email, social media, newsletters, project status reports, or face-to-face meetings.

d. Messaging strategies: The messaging strategy outlines how the project team will communicate with stakeholders. This includes defining the tone and style of communication, the frequency of updates, and the key messages that need to be communicated.

e. Communication schedule: The communication schedule outlines when communication will take place and who will be responsible for delivering it. It may also include deadlines for delivering updates or responding to stakeholder feedback.

f. Feedback mechanisms: The communication plan should include feedback mechanisms that allow stakeholders to provide input, ask questions, or provide feedback on the project. This may include surveys, focus groups, or regular stakeholder meetings.

An effective communication management plan ensures that stakeholders are engaged, informed, and supportive of the project. It helps to reduce misunderstandings, build trust, and ensure that the project is completed successfully.

## COMMUNICATION STRATEGIES FOR STAKEHOLDERS

Developing effective communication strategies is crucial for engaging stakeholders and ensuring their support throughout the project. The communication strategy should be tailored to the specific needs and expectations of each stakeholder group and should use appropriate channels and messaging to achieve the desired outcomes.

Here are some communication strategies that can be used to engage stakeholders:

a. Tailored messaging: Messages should be tailored to the needs and expectations of each stakeholder group. This may include using different language, tone, and style of communication for different groups.

b. Clear and concise messaging: Messages should be clear, concise, and easy to understand. This ensures that stakeholders can quickly grasp the key information and are not confused or overwhelmed by complex information.

c. Use of visuals: Visuals such as charts, graphs, and infographics can be used to convey complex information in a simple and easy-to-understand format.

d. Two-way communication: Two-way communication is crucial for engaging stakeholders and ensuring that their feedback is heard and acted upon. This can include regular stakeholder meetings, surveys, or feedback mechanisms.

e. Regular updates: Regular updates keep stakeholders informed about the progress of the project and help to build trust and goodwill. This may include weekly or monthly status reports, newsletters, or social media updates.

f. Engage with influential stakeholders: Engaging with influential stakeholders can help to build support for the project and reduce the risk of opposition or resistance. This may include meeting with community leaders, industry associations, or regulatory bodies.

Effective communication strategies help to ensure that stakeholders are engaged, informed, and supportive of the project. By tailoring communication to the needs and expectations of stakeholders and using appropriate channels and messaging, project managers can build trust and goodwill and ensure project success.

## FEEDBACK MECHANISMS AND CONTINUOUS IMPROVEMENT

Feedback mechanisms are essential components of a communication management plan as they provide an opportunity for stakeholders to provide input, ask questions, and provide feedback on the project. Feedback mechanisms help to ensure that stakeholders are engaged in the project, their concerns are addressed, and their expectations are met.

Here are some ways to incorporate feedback mechanisms into a communication management plan:

a. Surveys: Surveys can be used to gather feedback from stakeholders about their level of satisfaction with the project, their concerns, and their expectations. Surveys can be conducted online or in person.

b. Focus groups: Focus groups are a form of qualitative research that allows project managers to gather feedback from stakeholders in a group setting. This can help to identify common concerns and expectations and inform communication strategies.

c. Regular stakeholder meetings: Regular stakeholder meetings provide an opportunity for stakeholders to ask questions, provide feedback, and discuss concerns with the project team.

d. Continuous improvement: Feedback mechanisms can be used to identify areas where the project team can improve communication and engagement with stakeholders. This can help to ensure that the project is responsive to stakeholder needs and expectations.

By incorporating feedback mechanisms into a communication management plan, project managers can ensure that stakeholders remain engaged, informed, and supportive of the project. Feedback mechanisms can also help to identify areas where the project team can improve communication and engagement, leading to continuous improvement and increased stakeholder satisfaction.

# 4.3 THE INFLUENCE OF FACTORS ON COMMUNICATION: POSITIVE AND NEGATIVE EFFECTS

## PHYSICAL FACTORS AND COMMUNICATION

Physical factors refer to the physical attributes of the communicators and the environment in which the communication takes place. Physical factors can either positively or negatively affect communication.

a. Health conditions and communication: A person's physical health condition can impact their ability to communicate effectively. For instance, hearing impairment, speech impediments, or visual impairments can make it difficult for people to understand or express themselves.

b. Environment and communication: The physical environment can have a significant impact on communication. Loud noise, poor lighting, or uncomfortable seating can distract or impede communication. On the other hand, a quiet and comfortable environment can promote effective communication.

c. Body language and communication: Body language can also impact communication, as it conveys nonverbal cues that can either enhance or detract from the verbal message. Positive body language, such as eye contact, nodding, and smiling, can enhance the message being conveyed, while negative body language, such as crossed arms or slouching, can indicate disinterest or hostility.

d. Physical proximity and communication: Physical proximity, or the distance between communicators, can also impact communication. Close physical proximity can promote intimacy and trust, while too much distance can create a sense of detachment or discomfort.

In conclusion, physical factors are important to consider in communication as they can impact both the message being conveyed and the receiver's understanding of the message. Understanding how physical factors can positively or negatively affect communication can help individuals improve their communication skills and create more effective communication strategies.

## PSYCHOLOGICAL FACTORS AND COMMUNICATION

Psychological factors refer to the mental and emotional states of the communicators that can either positively or negatively affect communication.

a.  Attitude and communication: One's attitude towards the topic or the person they are communicating with can have a significant impact on communication. A positive attitude can promote open and effective communication, while a negative attitude can create tension and mistrust.

b.  Emotions and communication: Emotions can also affect communication. Strong emotions, such as anger, sadness, or fear, can lead to misinterpretation or miscommunication. Therefore, it is important to manage one's emotions effectively when communicating.

c.  Perception and communication: Perception refers to how an individual interprets and understands the message being conveyed. Perception is subjective and can be influenced by an individual's biases, experiences, and beliefs. Therefore, it is essential to be aware of one's perception and to consider the other person's perspective to avoid misunderstandings.

d.  Self-esteem and communication: One's self-esteem can also affect communication. Individuals with low self-esteem may struggle to express themselves or assert their needs, while individuals with high self-esteem may dominate the conversation or come across as arrogant.

e. Anxiety and communication: Anxiety can also negatively impact communication. Individuals with anxiety may struggle to express themselves, experience difficulty in maintaining eye contact, or have trouble following the conversation. Therefore, it is important to manage anxiety effectively to prevent it from hindering communication.

In conclusion, psychological factors can significantly impact communication. Understanding how these factors can positively or negatively affect communication can help individuals improve their communication skills and create more effective communication strategies. By being aware of one's own psychological state and considering the psychological state of the other person, individuals can create an environment that promotes open and effective communication.

## SOCIAL FACTORS AND COMMUNICATION

Social factors refer to the societal and cultural context in which communication takes place. Social factors can either positively or negatively affect communication.

a. Social norms and communication: Social norms are the unwritten rules of behavior that govern social interactions. Social norms can influence the way individuals communicate, and deviation from social norms can lead to misunderstandings or conflict. Therefore, it is essential to be aware of the social norms in a particular context and adjust communication accordingly.

b. Power dynamics and communication: Power dynamics refer to the unequal distribution of power between individuals or groups. Power dynamics can affect communication, as the person with more power may dominate the conversation, while the person with less power may struggle to assert their needs. Therefore, it is important to be aware of power dynamics and create an environment that promotes equal participation.

c. Cultural differences and communication: Cultural differences can significantly impact communication, as individuals from different cultures may have different communication styles, values, and expectations. Therefore, it is essential to be aware of cultural differences and adjust communication accordingly to prevent misunderstandings or offense.

d. Gender and communication: Gender can also affect communication, as individuals of different genders may have different communication styles or expectations. For instance, women may be socialized to use more indirect communication, while men may be socialized to use more direct communication. Therefore, it is important to be aware of gender differences and adjust communication accordingly.

e. Social media and communication: Social media has become an essential communication tool in modern society. Social media can positively impact communication by providing a platform for individuals to connect and share information. However, it can also negatively impact communication by promoting online harassment, cyberbullying, and misinformation.

In conclusion, social factors can significantly impact communication. Understanding how these factors can positively or negatively affect communication can help individuals improve their communication skills and create more effective communication strategies. By being aware of the social context of communication and adjusting communication accordingly, individuals can create an environment that promotes open and effective communication.

## CULTURAL FACTORS AND COMMUNICATION

Cultural factors refer to the values, beliefs, and practices of a particular culture. Cultural factors can significantly impact communication, as individuals from different cultures may have different communication styles, values, and expectations.

a. Language and communication: Language is an essential part of culture and can significantly impact communication. Individuals who speak different languages may struggle to communicate effectively, leading to misunderstandings or misinterpretations. Therefore, it is important to be aware of language barriers and use appropriate strategies to overcome them, such as using interpreters or translation tools.

b. Nonverbal communication and culture: Nonverbal communication, such as facial expressions, gestures, and tone of voice, can also be influenced by culture. Different cultures may interpret nonverbal cues differently, leading to misunderstandings or offense. Therefore, it is essential to be aware of cultural differences in nonverbal communication and adjust communication accordingly.

c. Cultural values and communication: Cultural values, such as individualism or collectivism, can significantly impact communication. For instance, individuals from individualistic cultures may value independence and direct communication, while individuals from collectivistic cultures may value group harmony and indirect communication. Therefore, it is essential to be aware of cultural values and adjust communication accordingly.

d. Cultural norms and communication: Cultural norms, such as the appropriate level of formality or the use of humor, can also affect communication. Individuals who are not aware of cultural norms may unintentionally offend or misunderstand others. Therefore, it is important to be aware of cultural norms and adjust communication accordingly.

e. Cultural stereotypes and communication: Cultural stereotypes can also negatively impact communication. Stereotypes can lead to assumptions about individuals based on their cultural background, leading to misunderstandings or discrimination. Therefore, it is essential to be aware of cultural stereotypes and avoid making assumptions about individuals based on their cultural background.

In conclusion, cultural factors can significantly impact communication. Understanding how cultural factors can positively or negatively affect communication can help individuals improve their communication skills and create more effective communication strategies. By being aware of cultural differences and adjusting communication accordingly, individuals can create an environment that promotes open and effective communication across cultures.

## TECHNOLOGICAL FACTORS AND COMMUNICATION

Technological factors refer to the tools and technologies used to facilitate communication. Technological factors can either positively or negatively impact communication.

a. Digital communication tools and communication: Digital communication tools, such as email, instant messaging, and video conferencing, have become essential communication tools in modern society. These tools can positively impact communication by enabling individuals to communicate across distances and time zones. However, they can also negatively impact communication by promoting a lack of face-to-face interaction and misunderstandings due to the lack of nonverbal cues.

b. Social media and communication: Social media platforms, such as Facebook, Twitter, and Instagram, have become popular communication tools in recent years. These platforms can positively impact communication by enabling individuals to connect and share information. However, they can also negatively impact communication by promoting online harassment, cyberbullying, and the spread of misinformation.

c. Mobile devices and communication: Mobile devices, such as smartphones and tablets, have become essential communication tools in modern society. These devices can positively impact communication by enabling individuals to communicate on-the-go. However, they can also negatively impact communication by promoting a lack of face-to-face interaction and creating a sense of constant connectivity that can be distracting and overwhelming.

d. Artificial intelligence and communication: Artificial intelligence (AI) has the potential to significantly impact communication. AI-powered tools, such as chatbots and voice assistants, can provide automated communication solutions that can enhance communication efficiency. However, they can also negatively impact communication by promoting a lack of human interaction and potentially replacing human jobs.

e. Accessibility tools and communication: Accessibility tools, such as closed captioning and text-to-speech software, can positively impact communication by making communication more accessible to individuals with disabilities. However, these tools can also negatively impact communication if they are not implemented effectively, leading to inaccurate or incomplete communication.

In conclusion, technological factors can significantly impact communication. Understanding how these factors can positively or negatively affect communication can help individuals improve their communication skills and create more effective communication strategies. By using technological tools effectively and being aware of their limitations, individuals can create an environment that promotes open and effective communication.

## ENVIRONMENTAL FACTORS AND COMMUNICATION

Environmental factors refer to the physical and social context in which communication takes place. Environmental factors can either positively or negatively impact communication.

a. Noise and communication: Noise can significantly impact communication. Excessive noise can make it difficult for individuals to hear or understand each other, leading to miscommunication. Therefore, it is important to select a quiet location for communication whenever possible or to use noise-cancelling devices when necessary.

b. Lighting and communication: Lighting can also impact communication. Poor lighting can make it difficult for individuals to see each other's facial expressions or body language, leading to misunderstandings. Therefore, it is important to select a well-lit location for communication whenever possible.

c. Temperature and communication: Temperature can also impact communication. Extreme temperatures, such as extreme heat or cold, can make individuals uncomfortable and distract from the communication. Therefore, it is important to select a location with a comfortable temperature for communication whenever possible.

d. Time and communication: Time can also affect communication. Different times of day can impact communication effectiveness, as individuals may be more or less alert or receptive depending on the time of day. Therefore, it is important to select a time that is appropriate for the communication, taking into account the schedules and availability of all parties.

e. Distance and communication: Distance can also impact communication. Physical distance can create a sense of detachment or discomfort, while too much closeness can create a sense of invasion or discomfort. Therefore, it is important to consider the appropriate distance for communication based on the relationship between individuals and the purpose of the communication.

In conclusion, environmental factors can significantly impact communication. Understanding how these factors can positively or negatively affect communication can help individuals improve their communication skills and create more effective communication strategies. By selecting appropriate locations, times, and distances for communication, individuals can create an environment that promotes open and effective communication.

## EMOTIONAL FACTORS AND COMMUNICATION

Emotional factors refer to the feelings and emotions of the communicators. Emotional factors can either positively or negatively impact communication.

a. Empathy and communication: Empathy is the ability to understand and share the feelings of others. Empathy can positively impact communication by promoting understanding and creating a sense of connection. Therefore, it is important to cultivate empathy when communicating with others.

b. Trust and communication: Trust is the belief that the other person is reliable and honest. Trust can positively impact communication by creating a sense of safety and openness. Therefore, it is important to establish trust when communicating with others.

c. Respect and communication: Respect is the recognition of the other person's worth and dignity. Respect can positively impact communication by promoting a sense of equality and creating a positive communication climate. Therefore, it is important to demonstrate respect when communicating with others.

d. Self-disclosure and communication: Self-disclosure is the act of revealing personal information to others. Self-disclosure can positively impact communication by promoting trust and creating a sense of connection. However, it is important to be mindful of the appropriateness of self-disclosure and to respect the boundaries of the other person.

e. Active listening and communication: Active listening is the act of listening attentively and responding appropriately to the other person's message. Active listening can positively impact communication by promoting understanding and creating a sense of connection. Therefore, it is important to practice active listening when communicating with others.

In conclusion, emotional factors can significantly impact communication. Understanding how these factors can positively or negatively affect communication can help individuals improve their communication skills and create more effective communication strategies. By cultivating empathy, trust, respect, and active listening, individuals can create an environment that promotes open and effective communication.

## COGNITIVE FACTORS AND COMMUNICATION

Cognitive factors refer to the mental processes involved in communication. Cognitive factors can either positively or negatively impact communication.

a. Clarity and communication: Clarity refers to the ability to express oneself clearly and effectively. Clarity can positively impact communication by promoting understanding and reducing misunderstandings. Therefore, it is important to use clear language and organize one's thoughts when communicating.

b. Memory and communication: Memory refers to the ability to retain and recall information. Memory can positively impact communication by enabling individuals to remember important details and follow-up actions. Therefore, it is important to use memory aids, such as notes or reminders, when necessary.

c. Attention and communication: Attention refers to the ability to focus on the task at hand. Attention can positively impact communication by enabling individuals to listen attentively and respond appropriately. Therefore, it is important to eliminate distractions and maintain focus when communicating.

d. Reasoning and communication: Reasoning refers to the ability to think logically and make connections between ideas. Reasoning can positively impact communication by promoting problem-solving and creative thinking. Therefore, it is important to use reasoning skills when communicating to find solutions to problems or to generate new ideas.

e. Perception and communication: Perception refers to how an individual interprets and understands the message being conveyed. Perception can positively or negatively impact communication depending on whether it is accurate or inaccurate. Therefore, it is important to be aware of one's own perception and to consider the other person's perspective to avoid misunderstandings.

In conclusion, cognitive factors can significantly impact communication. Understanding how these factors can positively or negatively affect communication can help individuals improve their communication skills and create more effective communication strategies. By using clear language, memory aids, and reasoning skills and by being aware of perception and maintaining focus, individuals can create an environment that promotes open and effective communication.

## PHYSIOLOGICAL FACTORS AND COMMUNICATION

Physiological factors refer to the physical state of the communicators that can either positively or negatively affect communication.

a. Health and communication: Health can significantly impact communication. Individuals who are in poor health may struggle to communicate effectively, leading to misunderstandings or misinterpretations. Therefore, it is important to maintain good physical health to facilitate effective communication.

b. Fatigue and communication: Fatigue can also negatively impact communication. Individuals who are tired may struggle to concentrate or express themselves effectively, leading to miscommunication. Therefore, it is important to get adequate rest to prevent fatigue from hindering communication.

c. Hunger and communication: Hunger can also negatively impact communication. Individuals who are hungry may be distracted or irritable, leading to miscommunication or conflict. Therefore, it is important to eat regularly and maintain adequate nutrition to prevent hunger from hindering communication.

d. Substance use and communication: Substance use, such as alcohol or drugs, can significantly impact communication. Substance use can impair cognitive and physical functioning, leading to misunderstandings or misinterpretations. Therefore, it is important to avoid substance use or to use substances responsibly to prevent them from hindering communication.

e. Physical disabilities and communication: Physical disabilities can also significantly impact communication. Individuals with physical disabilities may require accommodations, such as assistive technology or interpretation services, to communicate effectively. Therefore, it is important to be aware of the needs of individuals with physical disabilities and to provide appropriate accommodations when necessary.

In conclusion, physiological factors can significantly impact communication. Understanding how these factors can positively or negatively affect communication can help individuals improve their communication skills and create more effective communication strategies. By maintaining good physical health, getting adequate rest, and avoiding substance use, individuals can create an environment that promotes open and effective communication. Additionally, by providing appropriate accommodations for individuals with physical disabilities, individuals can ensure that everyone has an equal opportunity to communicate effectively.

## PERSONAL FACTORS AND COMMUNICATION

Personal factors refer to the individual characteristics of the communicators that can either positively or negatively impact communication.

a. Personality and communication: Personality refers to an individual's characteristic patterns of behavior, thoughts, and emotions. Personality can significantly impact communication, as individuals with different personalities may have different communication styles, values, and expectations. Therefore, it is important to be aware of one's own personality and adjust communication accordingly to prevent misunderstandings or conflict.

b. Attitudes and communication: Attitudes refer to an individual's beliefs, feelings, and values toward a particular topic or situation. Attitudes can impact communication, as individuals with different attitudes may have different perspectives and expectations. Therefore, it is important to be aware of one's own attitudes and be open to understanding the attitudes of others to prevent misunderstandings or conflict.

c. Self-esteem and communication: Self-esteem refers to an individual's sense of self-worth and confidence. Self-esteem can impact communication, as individuals with low self-esteem may struggle to express themselves effectively or may avoid communication altogether. Therefore, it is important to work on improving one's own self-esteem to facilitate effective communication.

d. Communication skills and communication: Communication skills refer to the ability to communicate effectively in a particular context or situation. Communication skills can significantly impact communication, as individuals with strong communication skills may be more effective at expressing themselves and understanding others. Therefore, it is important to work on improving communication skills to facilitate effective communication.

e. Personal goals and communication: Personal goals refer to the individual's aspirations and objectives. Personal goals can impact communication, as individuals with different goals may have different communication needs and expectations. Therefore, it is important to be aware of one's own personal goals and to adjust communication accordingly to prevent misunderstandings or conflict.

In conclusion, personal factors can significantly impact communication. Understanding how these factors can positively or negatively affect communication can help individuals improve their communication skills and create more effective communication strategies. By being aware of one's own personality, attitudes, self-esteem, communication skills, and personal goals, individuals can create an environment that promotes open and effective communication. Additionally, by being open to understanding the personal factors of others, individuals can facilitate effective communication and prevent misunderstandings or conflict.

# 4.4 EXPLORING SOURCES OF CONFLICT WITHIN A PROJECT: UNDERSTANDING THE CAUSES AND RESOLUTIONS

Conflict is an inevitable part of project management, as it arises from differences in perspectives, opinions, goals, and expectations of team members. Project teams are comprised of individuals with different personalities, experiences, and backgrounds, and it is natural for these differences to lead to conflicts. However, if these conflicts are not addressed in a timely and constructive manner, they can negatively impact project outcomes and team morale.

In this section, we will explore the nature of conflicts in project management and their impact on project success. We will also discuss why it is important for project managers to proactively identify and address potential sources of conflict to minimize their impact on the project. By gaining a better understanding of the nature of conflicts in project management, project managers can develop effective strategies to prevent, manage, and resolve conflicts in their projects.

## PERSONALITY CLASHES: DEALING WITH DIFFERENCES IN COMMUNICATION STYLES, WORK ETHICS AND VALUES

Personality clashes are one of the most common sources of conflict in project management. They occur when team members have different communication styles, work ethics, and values that are not aligned with the project goals. For example, a team member who is highly assertive and confrontational may clash with a team member who is more reserved and prefers to avoid conflict.

To address personality clashes, project managers should encourage open communication among team members and foster a culture of respect and empathy. They can also implement conflict management strategies, such as active listening, mediation, and negotiation, to help team members find common ground and resolve conflicts constructively.

Another effective approach is to create a team charter that outlines the team's shared goals, values, and expectations. This can help to establish a common understanding of how team members should interact with each other and what behaviour is acceptable. By addressing personality clashes proactively, project managers can promote a positive team dynamic and improve project outcomes.

## ROLE AMBIGUITY: ADDRESSING CONFLICTS ARISING FROM UNCLEAR ROLES AND RESPONSIBILITIES

Role ambiguity is another source of conflict that can arise in project management. This occurs when team members are uncertain about their roles and responsibilities, or when there is overlap or conflict between roles. For example, if two team members are responsible for different aspects of a project deliverable, but there is no clear definition of who is responsible for what, it can lead to conflict and confusion.

To address role ambiguity, project managers should ensure that all team members have a clear understanding of their roles and responsibilities. This can be achieved by defining each team member's role and responsibilities in the project charter, and by ensuring that each team member has a clear understanding of the project's objectives and expectations.

Project managers should also encourage regular communication among team members to ensure that everyone is aware of each other's roles and responsibilities. If conflicts do arise due to role ambiguity, project managers should take a proactive approach to resolve them, such as by clarifying roles and responsibilities, revising the project plan, or reallocating tasks among team members.

By addressing role ambiguity proactively, project managers can minimize the risk of conflict and ensure that team members are working together effectively towards a common goal.

## SCOPE CREEP: MANAGING CHANGES IN PROJECT SCOPE TO AVOID CONFLICT

Scope creep refers to the gradual expansion of project scope beyond its original boundaries. It occurs when additional requirements or changes are introduced during the project that were not originally planned for, which can cause conflict and delays in project delivery. For example, if a stakeholder requests additional features or functionality to be added to a project that is already in progress, it can lead to scope creep.

To address scope creep, project managers should establish clear project scope boundaries at the outset of the project, and communicate them effectively to all stakeholders. This can be achieved by creating a detailed project plan that outlines the project's scope, objectives, and deliverables.

Project managers should also establish a formal process for managing changes to project scope, such as a change management plan. This plan should outline how changes will be identified, evaluated, and approved, and should involve all stakeholders in the decision-making process.

Finally, project managers should track project progress regularly and adjust the project plan as needed to ensure that the project remains on track and within scope. If scope creep does occur, project managers should address it proactively by communicating with stakeholders, revaluating the project plan, and managing stakeholder expectations.

By managing scope creep proactively, project managers can minimize the risk of conflict and ensure that project outcomes are achieved on time and within budget.

## RESOURCE ALLOCATION: BALANCING DEMANDS AND CONSTRAINTS TO AVOID CONFLICT

Resource allocation is another source of conflict that can arise in project management. This occurs when team members have competing demands for resources, such as time, budget, and personnel, which can lead to conflict and delays in project delivery. For example, if two team members require the same resource, such as a piece of equipment or a software license, it can cause conflict and impact project progress.

To address resource allocation conflicts, project managers should establish clear priorities and allocate resources based on project needs and constraints. This can be achieved by creating a detailed resource plan that outlines the availability of resources, their intended use, and any constraints that may impact their allocation.

Project managers should also encourage regular communication among team members to ensure that everyone is aware of resource availability and any potential conflicts. If conflicts do arise, project managers should take a proactive approach to resolve them, such as by prioritizing tasks or reallocating resources.

Finally, project managers should monitor resource usage regularly and adjust resource allocation as needed to ensure that the project remains on track and within budget. If additional resources are needed, project managers should communicate this to stakeholders and explore alternative solutions, such as outsourcing or automation.

By managing resource allocation proactively, project managers can minimize the risk of conflict and ensure that team members have the resources they need to complete their tasks effectively. This can lead to improved project outcomes and a more positive team dynamic.

## TIMELINE AND DEADLINE PRESSURES: ADDRESSING ISSUES OF TIME MANAGEMENT AND PROJECT SCHEDULE

Timeline and deadline pressures are common sources of conflict in project management. These conflicts arise when team members have different priorities or approaches to time management, or when there are unexpected delays that impact project timelines. For example, if a team member is consistently late with deliverables, it can impact the overall project schedule and lead to conflict with other team members who are dependent on those deliverables.

To address timeline and deadline pressures, project managers should establish clear project timelines and deadlines that are communicated effectively to all stakeholders. This can be achieved by creating a detailed project schedule that outlines the tasks, milestones, and deadlines for each phase of the project.

Project managers should also encourage regular communication among team members to ensure that everyone is aware of project timelines and any potential delays. If delays do occur, project managers should take a proactive approach to resolve them, such as by reassigning tasks, adjusting the project schedule, or providing additional resources.

Finally, project managers should monitor project progress regularly and adjust the project schedule as needed to ensure that the project remains on track and within deadlines. If additional time is needed, project managers should communicate this to stakeholders and explore alternative solutions, such as reducing project scope or extending project timelines.

By managing timeline and deadline pressures proactively, project managers can minimize the risk of conflict and ensure that project outcomes are achieved on time and within budget. This can lead to improved project outcomes and a more positive team dynamic.

## BUDGET AND FINANCIAL ISSUES: MANAGING CONFLICTS RELATED TO PROJECT BUDGET AND RESOURCES

Budget and financial issues are another source of conflict that can arise in project management. These conflicts occur when team members have competing demands for project resources, such as funding, materials, and equipment. For example, if one team member requires additional funding to complete a task, it can cause conflict with another team member who requires the same funding for a different task.

To address budget and financial conflicts, project managers should establish a clear project budget that is communicated effectively to all stakeholders. This can be achieved by creating a detailed project plan that outlines the project's financial needs and constraints.

Project managers should also encourage regular communication among team members to ensure that everyone is aware of project financials and any potential conflicts. If conflicts do arise, project managers should take a proactive approach to resolve them, such as by prioritizing tasks or reallocating resources.

Finally, project managers should monitor project financials regularly and adjust the project budget as needed to ensure that the project remains on track and within budget. If additional funding is needed, project managers should communicate this to stakeholders and explore alternative solutions, such as seeking additional funding sources or reducing project scope.

By managing budget and financial issues proactively, project managers can minimize the risk of conflict and ensure that project outcomes are achieved within the available resources. This can lead to improved project outcomes and a more positive team dynamic.

## CONFLICT RESOLUTION: STRATEGIES FOR RESOLVING CONFLICTS WITHIN A PROJECT TEAM

Conflict resolution is an important skill for project managers to possess. Even with proactive measures in place to prevent and manage conflicts, conflicts can still arise within a project team. Conflict resolution involves identifying the source of the conflict, evaluating potential solutions, and implementing a resolution that is acceptable to all parties involved.

To effectively resolve conflicts within a project team, project managers should encourage open communication and active listening among team members. This can help to ensure that all parties are aware of the issues at hand and that each team member has an opportunity to express their concerns and perspectives.

Project managers should also use conflict management techniques, such as negotiation, mediation, and compromise, to identify potential solutions and reach an agreement that is acceptable to all parties. It may also be helpful to involve a neutral third party, such as a mediator, to facilitate the resolution process.

Finally, project managers should implement the agreed-upon solution and monitor the situation to ensure that the conflict does not resurface. This may involve adjusting project plans, revising team roles and responsibilities, or reallocating resources as needed.

By effectively resolving conflicts within a project team, project managers can promote a positive team dynamic and improve project outcomes. It is important to remember that conflict resolution is an ongoing process, and that conflicts may arise throughout the life of a project. Project managers should be prepared to address conflicts as they arise and adapt their conflict resolution strategies as needed.

## CONCLUSION: MITIGATING CONFLICT TO ACHIEVE PROJECT SUCCESS

In conclusion, conflicts are an inevitable part of project management, but by proactively identifying potential sources of conflict and implementing effective conflict management strategies, project managers can minimize the impact of conflicts on project outcomes and team morale.

To mitigate conflicts within a project team, project managers should:

a. Understand the nature of conflicts in project management and their impact on project success

b. Address personality clashes by fostering a culture of respect and empathy, and implementing conflict management strategies

c. Address role ambiguity by defining roles and responsibilities clearly, and establishing a formal process for managing changes to project scope

d. Manage scope creep by establishing clear project boundaries and a formal process for managing changes to project scope

e. Manage resource allocation by establishing clear priorities and allocating resources based on project needs and constraints

f. Address timeline and deadline pressures by establishing clear project timelines and deadlines, and monitoring project progress regularly

g. Address budget and financial issues by establishing a clear project budget and communicating effectively with stakeholders

h. Resolve conflicts within a project team by encouraging open communication and active listening, using conflict management techniques, and implementing agreed-upon solutions

By implementing these strategies, project managers can promote a positive team dynamic, improve project outcomes, and ultimately achieve project success.

# 4.5 EFFECTIVE APPROACHES FOR RESOLVING CONFLICT

Conflict is an inevitable part of human interaction, and it can arise in various settings, including workplaces, families, and social circles. Conflict can stem from various sources, including differences in opinions, values, interests, and goals. If not resolved effectively, conflict can lead to stress, reduced productivity, and negative relationships.

Conflict resolution involves the management and resolution of disagreements, disputes, and conflicts between individuals, groups, or organizations. It aims to find a mutually acceptable solution to a conflict that satisfies the needs and interests of all parties involved. The process involves identifying the root causes of the conflict, exploring possible solutions, and selecting the best approach for resolving the conflict.

Effective conflict resolution involves active listening, empathy, and the ability to communicate clearly and assertively. It also involves the use of conflict resolution tools and techniques that can help individuals and groups address their differences constructively. The Thomas-Kilmann Conflict Mode Instrument (TKI) is one such tool that can help individuals understand their conflict resolution styles and choose the most appropriate approach for a given conflict.

## THE THOMAS-KILMANN CONFLICT MODE INSTRUMENT (TKI)

The Thomas-Kilmann Conflict Mode Instrument (TKI) is a widely used tool for assessing individual conflict resolution styles. It was developed by Kenneth Thomas and Ralph Kilmann in the 1970s and is based on a model that identifies five distinct conflict resolution styles:

1. Collaborating: This style involves working together to find a solution that meets the needs and interests of all parties involved. This approach requires active listening, empathy, and open communication.

2. Compromising: This style involves finding a middle ground where each party gives up something to reach a mutually acceptable solution. This approach is useful when time is limited, and the parties involved are equal in power.

3. Competing: This style involves asserting one's own needs and interests at the expense of others. This approach is useful when quick and decisive action is needed, or when the parties involved have incompatible goals.

4. Avoiding: This style involves avoiding or postponing the conflict, hoping that it will go away on its own. This approach is useful when the issue at hand is minor, or when the parties involved need time to cool off and reflect.

5. Accommodating: This style involves meeting the needs and interests of the other party at the expense of one's own. This approach is useful when maintaining relationships is more important than achieving a specific goal.

The TKI is a self-assessment tool that helps individuals identify their preferred conflict resolution style and understand how it may impact their interactions with others. It can also be used in group settings to identify the dominant conflict resolution style within a team and facilitate discussions about how to address conflicts effectively. By understanding their own and others' conflict resolution styles, individuals can choose the most appropriate approach for a given conflict and work towards finding a mutually acceptable solution.

## COLLABORATIVE APPROACH

The collaborative approach is a conflict resolution style that involves working together to find a solution that meets the needs and interests of all parties involved. It is an effective approach when the parties involved have a long-term relationship and a mutual interest in finding a solution that benefits everyone.

The collaborative approach requires active listening, empathy, and open communication. It involves exploring the root causes of the conflict and brainstorming possible solutions. The parties involved need to be willing to share their needs, interests, and concerns openly and honestly. They must also be willing to consider and incorporate the needs and interests of the other party into the solution.

The collaborative approach can be time-consuming, as it requires the parties involved to work together to find a mutually acceptable solution. However, it can lead to better relationships, increased trust, and improved decision-making. It can also lead to creative solutions that may not have been apparent with other conflict resolution styles.

When using the collaborative approach, it is essential to establish ground rules for the discussion, such as no interrupting, no personal attacks, and respect for different viewpoints. It is also essential to keep the discussion focused on the issues at hand and not let it devolve into personal attacks or irrelevant topics.

Overall, the collaborative approach is an effective conflict resolution style when the parties involved have a mutual interest in finding a solution that benefits everyone. It requires active listening, empathy, and open communication and can lead to better relationships, increased trust, and improved decision-making.

## COMPROMISING APPROACH

The compromising approach is a conflict resolution style that involves finding a middle ground where each party gives up something to reach a mutually acceptable solution. It is an effective approach when time is limited, and the parties involved are equal in power.

The compromising approach requires active listening, empathy, and open communication. It involves identifying the needs and interests of each party and finding a solution that meets some of those needs and interests. The parties involved need to be willing to compromise and give up something to reach a solution.

The compromising approach can be useful when a quick resolution is needed, or when the parties involved are equal in power and unable to achieve their goals through competing. However, it can also lead to a suboptimal solution where neither party gets everything they want.

When using the compromising approach, it is important to establish clear guidelines for what can and cannot be compromised. It is also important to ensure that both parties feel that their needs and interests have been taken into account and that the solution is fair.

Overall, the compromising approach is an effective conflict resolution style when time is limited and the parties involved are equal in power. It requires active listening, empathy, and open communication and can lead to a quick resolution. However, it can also lead to a suboptimal solution where neither party gets everything they want.

## COMPETING APPROACH

The competing approach is a conflict resolution style that involves asserting one's own needs and interests at the expense of others. It is an effective approach when quick and decisive action is needed or when the parties involved have incompatible goals.

The competing approach requires assertiveness, confidence, and a willingness to stand up for one's own needs and interests. It involves identifying and advocating for one's own position and not compromising unless it is absolutely necessary. The parties involved need to be willing to assert their power and influence to achieve their goals.

The competing approach can be useful when a quick decision is needed or when there is a clear winner and loser. However, it can also lead to a win-lose situation where one party gets everything they want, and the other party gets nothing.

When using the competing approach, it is important to ensure that the other party feels heard and respected. It is also important to be aware of power imbalances and to avoid using power to intimidate or coerce the other party.

Overall, the competing approach is an effective conflict resolution style when quick and decisive action is needed, or when the parties involved have incompatible goals. It requires assertiveness, confidence, and a willingness to stand up for one's own needs and interests. However, it can also lead to a win-lose situation where one party gets everything they want, and the other party gets nothing.

## AVOIDING APPROACH

The avoiding approach is a conflict resolution style that involves avoiding or postponing the conflict, hoping that it will go away on its own. It is an effective approach when the issue at hand is minor or when the parties involved need time to cool off and reflect.

The avoiding approach requires patience, restraint, and the ability to recognize when a conflict is not worth pursuing. It involves putting the issue aside for the time being and focusing on other things. The parties involved need to be willing to let go of the issue and move on to other things.

The avoiding approach can be useful when the issue is not important, when there are more important issues to deal with, or when the parties involved need time to reflect and cool off. However, it can also lead to unresolved conflicts that may resurface later.

When using the avoiding approach, it is important to communicate clearly and respectfully with the other party. It is important to explain why the issue is not worth pursuing and to ensure that the other party feels heard and understood.

Overall, the avoiding approach is an effective conflict resolution style when the issue at hand is minor, when there are more important issues to deal with, or when the parties involved need time to reflect and cool off. It requires patience, restraint, and the ability to recognize when a conflict is not worth pursuing. However, it can also lead to unresolved conflicts that may resurface later.

## ACCOMMODATING APPROACH

The accommodating approach is a conflict resolution style that involves meeting the needs and interests of the other party at the expense of one's own. It is an effective approach when maintaining relationships is more important than achieving a specific goal.

The accommodating approach requires empathy, selflessness, and the ability to put oneself in the other party's shoes. It involves understanding the other party's needs and interests and finding a solution that meets those needs, even if it means giving up something in return. The parties involved need to be willing to prioritize the relationship over their own needs and interests.

The accommodating approach can be useful when maintaining relationships is more important than achieving a specific goal or when the other party has significantly more power. However, it can also lead to a situation where one party consistently gives up their needs and interests and becomes resentful.

When using the accommodating approach, it is important to ensure that the other party understands and appreciates the sacrifice being made. It is also important to communicate one's own needs and interests and to find a balance between meeting the needs of the other party and ensuring that one's own needs and interests are met.

Overall, the accommodating approach is an effective conflict resolution style when maintaining relationships is more important than achieving a specific goal. It requires empathy, selflessness, and the ability to prioritize the relationship over one's own needs and interests. However, it can also lead to a situation where one party consistently gives up their needs and interests and becomes resentful.

## CHOOSING THE RIGHT APPROACH

Choosing the right conflict resolution approach is crucial for resolving conflicts effectively. Each approach has its own advantages and disadvantages, and the choice of approach depends on several factors, including the nature of the conflict, the parties involved, and the desired outcome.

When choosing the right approach, it is essential to understand the root causes of the conflict, the needs and interests of all parties involved, and the potential consequences of each approach. It is also important to consider the power dynamics between the parties involved and to ensure that the approach chosen is appropriate for the situation.

For example, the collaborative approach is an effective conflict resolution style when the parties involved have a long-term relationship and a mutual interest in finding a solution that benefits everyone. On the other hand, the competing approach is effective when quick and decisive action is needed or when the parties involved have incompatible goals.

The compromising approach is useful when time is limited, and the parties involved are equal in power, while the avoiding approach is effective when the issue at hand is minor, or when the parties involved need time to cool off and reflect. The accommodating approach is effective when maintaining relationships is more important than achieving a specific goal.

Choosing the right approach also involves considering the potential consequences of each approach. For example, the competing approach may lead to a win-lose situation where one party gets everything they want, and the other party gets nothing. On the other hand, the accommodating approach may lead to a situation where one party consistently gives up their needs and interests and becomes resentful.

Overall, choosing the right approach is crucial for resolving conflicts effectively. It requires understanding the root causes of the conflict, the needs and interests of all parties involved, and the potential consequences of each approach. By choosing the right approach, individuals and groups can work towards finding a mutually acceptable solution that satisfies the needs and interests of all parties involved.

## IMPLEMENTING CONFLICT RESOLUTION STRATEGIES

Implementing conflict resolution strategies involves putting the chosen approach into action and working towards resolving the conflict effectively. The following are some key steps involved in implementing conflict resolution strategies:

1. Establish a clear goal: The first step in implementing conflict resolution strategies is to establish a clear goal. This involves identifying what the parties involved hope to achieve and what a successful outcome would look like.

2. Communicate effectively: Effective communication is essential for implementing conflict resolution strategies. This involves

active listening, empathy, and the ability to communicate clearly and assertively. The parties involved need to be willing to share their needs, interests, and concerns openly and honestly.

3. Identify the root causes: To effectively implement conflict resolution strategies, it is essential to identify the root causes of the conflict. This involves exploring the underlying issues and understanding the perspectives of all parties involved.

4. Brainstorm possible solutions: Once the root causes of the conflict have been identified, the parties involved can begin to brainstorm possible solutions. This involves exploring different options and considering the potential benefits and drawbacks of each.

5. Choose the best approach: After considering the different options, the parties involved can choose the best approach for resolving the conflict. This involves selecting the approach that is most likely to lead to a mutually acceptable solution.

6. Implement the chosen approach: Once the approach has been chosen, the parties involved can begin to implement it. This involves working together to find a solution that meets the needs and interests of all parties involved.

7. Evaluate the outcome: After implementing the chosen approach, it is important to evaluate the outcome. This involves assessing whether the conflict has been effectively resolved and whether the desired outcome has been achieved.

Overall, implementing conflict resolution strategies requires effective communication, active listening, and the ability to identify the root causes of the conflict. By working together to find a mutually acceptable solution, individuals and groups can resolve conflicts effectively and build stronger relationships.

## THE BENEFITS OF EFFECTIVE CONFLICT RESOLUTION

Effective conflict resolution can have several benefits for individuals and organizations. The following are some key benefits of effective conflict resolution:

a. Improved relationships: Effective conflict resolution can lead to improved relationships between individuals and groups. By resolving conflicts in a constructive and respectful manner, individuals and groups can build stronger relationships based on trust, mutual respect, and understanding.

b. Increased productivity: Unresolved conflicts can lead to stress, reduced motivation, and decreased productivity. By resolving conflicts effectively, individuals and groups can focus on their work and achieve their goals more efficiently.

c. Better decision-making: Effective conflict resolution can lead to better decision-making. By exploring different perspectives and considering different options, individuals and groups can make more informed and objective decisions.

d. Improved communication: Effective conflict resolution can improve communication between individuals and groups. By actively listening and communicating openly and honestly, individuals and groups can establish clear expectations and avoid misunderstandings.

e. Increased creativity: Effective conflict resolution can lead to increased creativity. By exploring different options and considering different perspectives, individuals and groups can generate new ideas and solutions.

f. Reduced stress: Unresolved conflicts can lead to stress and anxiety. By resolving conflicts effectively, individuals and groups can reduce stress and create a more positive and supportive work environment.

g. Strengthened organizational culture: Effective conflict resolution can strengthen organizational culture by promoting values such as respect, collaboration, and transparency. By resolving conflicts constructively, organizations can create a culture that supports positive relationships and effective teamwork.

Overall, effective conflict resolution can have several benefits for individuals and organizations. By resolving conflicts in a constructive and respectful manner, individuals and groups can build stronger relationships, increase productivity, and make better decisions. Effective conflict resolution can also improve communication, increase creativity, reduce stress, and strengthen organizational culture.

# 4.6 THE ART OF NEGOTIATION: PLANNING AND CONDUCTING SUCCESSFUL NEGOTIATIONS

Negotiation is a process of communication between two or more parties with the aim of reaching an agreement on a particular issue or dispute. Negotiation skills are essential in both personal and professional settings, and they require careful planning and execution. To become a successful negotiator, you need to understand the basics of the negotiation process, including the different stages involved, the roles and responsibilities of the parties involved, and the various strategies that can be used to achieve a successful outcome.

The negotiation process typically involves the following stages:

1. Preparation: This is the stage where you identify the issues to be negotiated, gather relevant information, set goals and objectives, and decide on the approach and strategy to be used.

2. Opening: This is the stage where the parties involved introduce themselves and their positions, and state their initial proposals.

3. Bargaining: This is the stage where the parties exchange offers and counteroffers and attempt to find a mutually acceptable agreement.

4. Closing: This is the stage where the parties finalize the agreement, including the terms and conditions, and any follow-up actions that may be required.

In addition to the stages, it is important to understand the roles and responsibilities of the parties involved in a negotiation. The primary parties are the negotiators, who are responsible for representing the interests of their respective parties, and the decision-makers, who have the authority to approve or reject any agreement reached. Other parties may include advisers, experts, and mediators, who can provide guidance and support throughout the negotiation process.

Finally, it is essential to be familiar with the various strategies that can be used to achieve a successful negotiation outcome. These include distributive bargaining, where the parties focus on maximizing their share of the available resources, and integrative bargaining, where the parties collaborate to find a mutually beneficial solution that meets the interests of both parties. By understanding these basics, you can plan and conduct effective negotiations that achieve positive results for all parties involved.

## PREPARING FOR A NEGOTIATION: SETTING GOALS AND OBJECTIVES

The preparation stage is one of the most important stages in the negotiation process as it lays the foundation for the entire negotiation. A well-prepared negotiator has a better chance of achieving a successful outcome. The key to effective preparation is to set clear goals and objectives. These goals should be specific, measurable, achievable, relevant, and time bound. Setting clear goals and objectives can help you to focus on the issues that matter, and to develop a strategy that is tailored to your specific situation.

Here are some steps to help you set clear goals and objectives for your negotiation:

1. Identify the issues: Identify the key issues that need to be addressed in the negotiation. This could include the price, delivery schedule, quality, or other terms and conditions.

2. Determine your priorities: Determine what is most important to you and your organization. This will help you to identify your priorities and to focus on the issues that matter most.

3. Define your BATNA: Determine your Best Alternative to a Negotiated Agreement (BATNA). This is the course of action you will take if you cannot reach an agreement with the other party. Knowing your BATNA can help you to set realistic goals and objectives.

4. Research the other party: Research the other party to gain an understanding of their interests, goals, and priorities. This can help you to develop a strategy that is tailored to their specific situation.

5. Develop a strategy: Based on your research and analysis, develop a negotiation strategy that is designed to achieve your goals and objectives. This strategy should take into account the other party's interests and priorities, as well as your own.

6. Prepare for the negotiation: Finally, prepare for the negotiation by organizing your thoughts, practicing your negotiation skills, and anticipating potential objections or challenges that may arise during the negotiation.

By setting clear goals and objectives and developing a well-thought-out negotiation strategy, you can increase your chances of achieving a successful outcome.

## THE IMPORTANCE OF KNOWING YOUR ZOPA AND BATNA

In negotiation, the Zone of Possible Agreement (ZOPA) and Best Alternative to a Negotiated Agreement (BATNA) are two critical concepts that can help you to achieve a successful outcome.

The ZOPA is the range of outcomes that are possible and acceptable to both parties in a negotiation. It represents the overlap between the negotiator's interests and the other party's interests. Knowing your ZOPA can help you to identify the potential areas of agreement and to develop a negotiation strategy that maximizes the value of the agreement for both parties.

Here are some tips for identifying your ZOPA:

1. Analyse the issues: Analyse the key issues that need to be addressed in the negotiation and identify the areas where there is potential for agreement.

2. Determine your priorities: Determine what is most important to you and your organization, and identify the issues that are most critical to achieving your goals and objectives.

3. Research the other party: Research the other party to gain an understanding of their interests, goals, and priorities. This can help you to identify potential areas of agreement and to develop a strategy that is tailored to their specific situation.

4. Evaluate the alternatives: Evaluate the alternatives that are available to both parties, and identify the range of outcomes that are possible and acceptable to both parties.

5. Consider the context: Consider the context of the negotiation, including any external factors that may impact the negotiation, such as market conditions, regulatory requirements, or political considerations.

In addition to knowing your ZOPA, it is also important to have a clear understanding of your BATNA. Your BATNA is the course of action you will take if you cannot reach an agreement with the other party. Knowing your BATNA can help you to set realistic goals and objectives, and to develop a negotiation strategy that maximizes your leverage in the negotiation.

Here are some tips for identifying your BATNA:

1. Consider your options: Consider the alternatives that are available to you if you cannot reach an agreement with the other party.

2. Evaluate the costs and benefits: Evaluate the costs and benefits of each alternative, including the risks, time, and resources required to pursue each option.

3. Establish your bottom line: Establish your bottom line, which is the minimum acceptable outcome for you in the negotiation.

4. Prepare for the worst-case scenario: Prepare for the worst-case scenario by developing a plan of action in case the negotiation fails to reach an agreement.

By knowing your ZOPA and BATNA, you can develop a negotiation strategy that is tailored to your specific situation, and that maximizes your chances of achieving a successful outcome.

## STRATEGIES FOR ACHIEVING A WIN-WIN OUTCOME

One of the most important goals of negotiation is to achieve a win-win outcome, where both parties benefit from the agreement. This type of outcome is based on the principle of mutual gain, where the parties collaborate to find a solution that meets the interests of both parties. Achieving a win-win outcome requires effective communication, active listening, and a willingness to explore creative solutions.

Here are some strategies that can help you to achieve a win-win outcome in negotiation:

a. Focus on interests, not positions: Instead of focusing on positions, focus on the underlying interests that are driving each party's position. By understanding each other's interests, you can identify potential areas of agreement and develop a solution that meets the interests of both parties.

b. Explore creative solutions: Look for creative solutions that meet the interests of both parties. This may involve brainstorming new ideas or exploring unconventional approaches.

c. Build relationships: Building relationships with the other party can help to establish trust and rapport, which can lead to more effective communication and a greater willingness to collaborate.

d. Use objective criteria: Use objective criteria to establish the value of the agreement. This can help to avoid positional bargaining and create a more objective basis for the negotiation.

e. Communicate effectively: Effective communication is essential for achieving a win-win outcome. This includes active listening, clarifying misunderstandings, and expressing your needs and interests clearly and respectfully.

f. Be flexible: Be flexible and willing to make concessions in order to achieve a mutually beneficial outcome.

g. Keep the focus on the future: Keep the focus on the future and the potential benefits of the agreement, rather than dwelling on past disputes or conflicts.

By using these strategies, you can create a collaborative environment that fosters a win-win outcome. This type of outcome can lead to stronger relationships, greater trust, and a more positive outcome for both parties.

## CONDUCTING THE NEGOTIATION: EFFECTIVE COMMUNICATION AND ACTIVE LISTENING

Effective communication and active listening are key skills in conducting successful negotiations. Communication is the process of exchanging information, ideas, and opinions between two or more parties, while active listening involves paying close attention to what the other party is saying and responding in a way that shows you understand their perspective.

Here are some tips for effective communication and active listening in negotiation:

a. Establish rapport: Establishing rapport with the other party can help to create a more positive and productive negotiation environment. This can involve finding common ground, sharing personal stories or experiences, or simply being friendly and approachable.

b. Use clear and concise language: Use clear and concise language when communicating your position or proposals. Avoid using technical jargon or complex language that may be difficult for the other party to understand.

c. Ask open-ended questions: Ask open-ended questions that encourage the other party to share their perspective and ideas. This can help to build trust and rapport, and can lead to a more productive negotiation.

d. Avoid making assumptions: Avoid making assumptions about the other party's position or interests. Instead, ask clarifying questions to ensure that you understand their perspective.

e. Show empathy: Show empathy by acknowledging the other party's perspective and expressing understanding of their interests and concerns.

f. Listen actively: Listen actively to the other party by paying close attention to what they are saying, asking clarifying questions, and summarizing their position to ensure that you understand their perspective.

g. Use non-verbal communication: Use non-verbal communication, such as nodding or maintaining eye contact, to show that you are actively listening and engaged in the conversation.

h. Respond constructively: Respond constructively to the other party's position or proposals by acknowledging their perspective, expressing your own interests, and exploring potential areas of agreement.

By using effective communication and active listening skills in negotiation, you can create a more collaborative and productive environment that is focused on finding a mutually beneficial outcome. These skills can help to build trust, foster understanding, and lead to a more positive outcome for both parties.

## Dealing with Challenges and Conflicts during Negotiations

Challenges and conflicts are an inevitable part of the negotiation process. These can arise from differences in goals, values, or interests, or from misunderstandings or miscommunications. Dealing with challenges and conflicts effectively is essential for achieving a successful negotiation outcome.

Here are some tips for dealing with challenges and conflicts during negotiations:

a. Stay calm: It is important to stay calm and focused when faced with challenges or conflicts during a negotiation. This can help you to maintain control of the situation and to respond in a constructive and professional manner.

b. Understand the other party's perspective: Try to understand the other party's perspective by asking clarifying questions and actively listening to their responses. This can help to identify the underlying interests and concerns that are driving their position.

c. Identify areas of agreement: Look for areas of agreement between your position and the other party's position. This can help to build trust and rapport, and can create a foundation for further negotiation.

d. Be open to compromise: Be willing to make concessions or compromise on certain issues in order to achieve a mutually beneficial outcome. This may involve finding creative solutions or exploring alternative options.

e. Use objective criteria: Use objective criteria to evaluate the value of the agreement and to avoid positional bargaining. This can help to create a more objective basis for negotiation and can reduce the impact of subjective or emotional factors.

f. Maintain a professional demeanour: Maintain a professional demeanour throughout the negotiation process, even in the face of challenges or conflicts. This can help to establish credibility and trust, and can create a more positive negotiation environment.

g. Take a break if needed: If the negotiation becomes too tense or difficult, take a break to allow both parties to regroup and refocus. This can help to prevent the situation from escalating and can provide an opportunity for both parties to re-evaluate their position and strategy.

By dealing with challenges and conflicts effectively, you can increase your chances of achieving a successful negotiation outcome. These tips can help to build trust, maintain control, and create a more positive negotiation environment, even in the face of difficult or challenging situations.

## CLOSING THE DEAL: FINALIZING AGREEMENTS AND FOLLOW-UP ACTIONS

The final stage of a negotiation is closing the deal, which involves finalizing the agreement and establishing any necessary follow-up actions. This stage is crucial for ensuring that both parties are satisfied with the outcome and that the terms of the agreement are clear and enforceable.

Here are some tips for closing the deal and finalizing the agreement:

a. Document the agreement: Document the agreement in writing to ensure that both parties have a clear understanding of the terms and conditions. This should include all relevant details, such as the scope of work, timelines, payment terms, and any other important considerations.

b. Review and revise: Review and revise the agreement as needed to ensure that it accurately reflects the negotiated terms and conditions. This may involve making changes or clarifications to the original agreement.

c. Obtain signatures: Obtain signatures from both parties to indicate their agreement and commitment to the terms of the agreement.

d. Follow-up actions: Establish any necessary follow-up actions, such as delivery dates, payments, or other milestones. This can help to ensure that the agreement is implemented effectively and that both parties are accountable for their commitments.

e. Establish a dispute resolution process: Establish a dispute resolution process in case any issues or disputes arise after the agreement is finalized. This can help to prevent conflicts and ensure that any issues are resolved in a fair and timely manner.

f. Celebrate the agreement: Celebrate the agreement and acknowledge the hard work and effort that went into achieving a successful outcome. This can help to build goodwill and establish a positive relationship between the parties.

By following these tips, you can ensure that the agreement is finalized effectively and that both parties are satisfied with the outcome. This can help to build trust and establish a positive relationship, and can lay the foundation for future successful negotiations.

## CONTINUOUS IMPROVEMENT: LEARNING FROM PAST NEGOTIATIONS AND REFINING YOUR SKILLS

Continuous improvement is an important aspect of developing effective negotiation skills. By reflecting on past negotiations and refining your skills, you can become a more effective negotiator and achieve better outcomes in future negotiations.

Here are some tips for continuous improvement in negotiation:

a. Reflect on past negotiations: Reflect on past negotiations to identify what went well and what could have been improved. Consider the outcomes, the process, and the strategies used.

b. Analyse the results: Analyse the results of past negotiations to identify any patterns or trends. Look for areas of success and areas where improvements could be made.

c. Seek feedback: Seek feedback from colleagues, mentors, or other professionals to gain insight into your negotiation style and areas for improvement.

d. Develop a plan: Develop a plan for improving your negotiation skills based on your reflections and analysis. This may involve setting specific goals, practicing new strategies, or seeking additional training or education.

e. Practice: Practice your negotiation skills in a variety of settings, such as mock negotiations or role-playing exercises. This can help you to refine your skills and build confidence in your abilities.

f. Evaluate your progress: Evaluate your progress regularly to track your development and to identify areas where further improvement is needed.

g. Stay up-to-date: Stay up-to-date with current trends and best practices in negotiation by reading books, attending seminars or workshops, or engaging with industry experts.

By continuously improving your negotiation skills, you can become a more effective negotiator and achieve better outcomes in future negotiations. This can help you to build stronger relationships, establish trust, and create a more positive negotiation environment.

# CHAPTER FIVE

## *LEADERSHIP AND TEAMWORK PRINCIPLES FOR PROJECT SUCCESS*

# 5.1 The Impact of Leadership on Team Performance and Motivation: Insights from Maslow, Herzberg, and McGregor Models

Effective leadership is crucial to the success of any team, organization or business. Leaders provide direction, motivation, and guidance to their teams in order to achieve their goals and objectives. In order for a team to perform at its best, it needs a strong leader who can communicate effectively, make decisions, and create a positive and motivating work environment.

Leadership has a direct impact on the performance of a team. A good leader can inspire their team to work hard and achieve their goals, while a poor leader can demotivate and disengage their team, leading to poor performance and low morale.

Effective leadership involves a range of skills and qualities, including communication, vision, integrity, adaptability, and emotional intelligence. Leaders must also be able to understand and respond to the needs of their team members, and create a culture of trust, respect, and collaboration.

In this section, we will explore how different leadership models, such as Maslow's Hierarchy of Needs, Herzberg's Two-Factor Theory, and McGregor's Theory X and Theory Y, can impact team performance and motivation. We will also provide insights into best practices for leaders to motivate and improve team performance.

## MASLOW'S HIERARCHY OF NEEDS AND ITS APPLICATION IN TEAM MOTIVATION

Maslow's Hierarchy of Needs is a popular motivational model that was developed by psychologist Abraham Maslow. According to this model, human needs are arranged in a hierarchical order, with physiological needs at the bottom, followed by safety needs, social needs, esteem needs, and self-actualization needs at the top.

In the context of team motivation, Maslow's model suggests that leaders should focus on meeting the basic needs of their team members before moving on to higher level needs. For example, leaders can ensure that team members have a safe and comfortable work environment, and access to basic resources like food and water.

Once basic needs are met, leaders can focus on addressing higher level needs, such as social needs by fostering a sense of community and teamwork among team members, and esteem needs by recognizing and rewarding their contributions.

Leaders who understand and apply Maslow's Hierarchy of Needs can create a more motivating work environment and help their team members reach their full potential. However, it's important to note that not all team members will have the same needs or priorities, so leaders must also be able to adapt their leadership style and approach to meet the needs of different individuals.

Overall, Maslow's Hierarchy of Needs is a valuable model for leaders who want to create a work environment that promotes team motivation and performance.

## HERZBERG'S TWO-FACTOR THEORY AND ITS EFFECT ON TEAM PERFORMANCE

Herzberg's Two-Factor Theory, also known as the Motivation-Hygiene Theory, is another popular model that explores the factors that contribute to employee motivation and job satisfaction. According to this theory, there are two types of factors that affect job satisfaction and motivation: hygiene factors and motivators.

Hygiene factors are basic needs that must be met for employees to feel satisfied with their jobs, but their presence alone does not necessarily lead to increased motivation or performance. Examples of hygiene factors include pay, working conditions, job security, and organizational policies.

On the other hand, motivators are factors that contribute to job satisfaction and motivation, and are directly related to the work itself. Examples of motivators include challenging work, opportunities for growth and development, recognition, and achievement.

In the context of team performance, Herzberg's Two-Factor Theory suggests that leaders should focus on both hygiene factors and motivators in order to create a motivating work environment. Leaders can ensure that hygiene factors are met by providing fair compensation, safe and comfortable working conditions, and clear policies and procedures. Additionally, leaders can focus on providing opportunities for growth and development, recognizing and rewarding team members' achievements, and challenging team members with interesting and meaningful work.

By understanding and applying Herzberg's Two-Factor Theory, leaders can create a work environment that promotes team motivation, satisfaction, and ultimately, improved performance.

## MCGREGOR'S THEORY X AND THEORY Y AND THEIR INFLUENCE ON LEADERSHIP STYLE

McGregor's Theory X and Theory Y are two contrasting management styles that describe how leaders view their employees and the work they do. According to Theory X, employees are inherently lazy and require constant supervision and motivation to get work done. In contrast, Theory Y assumes that employees are self-motivated and capable of taking responsibility for their work.

In the context of team performance, McGregor's Theory X and Theory Y can influence a leader's management style and approach. Leaders who adhere to Theory X may use a more authoritarian leadership style, closely monitoring their team members and providing strict rules and guidelines to ensure work is completed on time. Leaders who adhere to Theory Y, on the other hand, may use a more participative leadership style, encouraging team members to take responsibility for their work and contribute to decision-making.

While neither Theory X nor Theory Y is inherently good or bad, leaders who understand the strengths and weaknesses of each approach can choose a leadership style that is best suited to their team and organizational goals. For example, a Theory X leadership style may be appropriate for a team working on a high-risk project where strict guidelines are necessary to ensure safety, while a Theory Y leadership style may be more effective for a creative team where individual contributions and autonomy are important.

Ultimately, understanding McGregor's Theory X and Theory Y can help leaders tailor their leadership style to the needs of their team and improve team performance.

## How Different Leadership Styles Affect Team Performance and Motivation

There are several different leadership styles that can impact team performance and motivation in different ways. Some of the most common leadership styles include:

a. Autocratic Leadership - An autocratic leader makes decisions independently without involving their team members. This style can be effective in situations where quick decisions are necessary, but it can also lead to low morale and poor motivation among team members who feel excluded from the decision-making process.

b. Democratic Leadership - A democratic leader involves their team members in the decision-making process and encourages collaboration and communication. This style can lead to higher motivation and better team performance, but it can also be time-consuming and may not be effective in situations where quick decisions are necessary.

c. Transformational Leadership - A transformational leader inspires and motivates their team members to reach their full potential by providing a clear vision and supporting their growth and development. This style can lead to high levels of motivation and improved performance, but it may also be demanding and require a high level of commitment from team members.

d. Laissez-faire Leadership - A laissez-faire leader delegates responsibility to their team members and allows them to make decisions independently. This style can be effective for highly skilled and motivated teams, but it can also lead to a lack of direction and low performance if team members are not adequately supported or motivated.

Overall, different leadership styles can impact team performance and motivation in different ways, and the most effective leadership style will depend on the needs and goals of the team. Leaders who are able to adapt their leadership style to different situations and team members can create a more motivating work environment and improve team performance.

## BEST PRACTICES FOR LEADERS TO MOTIVATE AND IMPROVE TEAM PERFORMANCE

While there is no one-size-fits-all approach to motivating and improving team performance, there are several best practices that leaders can follow to create a more positive and motivating work environment. Some of these practices include:

a. Setting clear expectations and goals - Leaders should communicate clear expectations and goals to their team members, and ensure that everyone is aligned and working towards the same objectives.

b. Providing constructive feedback - Leaders should provide regular feedback to their team members, highlighting areas of strength and opportunities for improvement. This can help team members feel valued and motivated to improve their performance.

c. Creating a culture of trust and respect - Leaders should foster a culture of trust and respect by listening to their team members' opinions and ideas, and encouraging open communication and collaboration.

d. Recognizing and rewarding achievements - Leaders should recognize and reward team members' achievements, whether through public recognition, bonuses, or promotions. This can help team members feel valued and motivated to continue performing well.

e. Providing opportunities for growth and development - Leaders should provide opportunities for team members to grow and develop their skills and knowledge, whether through training, mentoring, or job rotations. This can help team members feel valued and motivated to continue learning and improving.

f. Adapting leadership style to individual team members - Leaders should be able to adapt their leadership style to individual team members, taking into account their strengths, weaknesses, and motivations. This can help ensure that each team member feels supported and motivated to perform their best.

By following these best practices, leaders can create a work environment that promotes team motivation and performance, and ultimately, helps the team achieve its goals and objectives.

## CONCLUSION: KEY TAKEAWAYS ON LEADERSHIP AND ITS IMPACT ON TEAM PERFORMANCE AND MOTIVATION

Effective leadership plays a critical role in the performance and motivation of a team. Leaders who are able to inspire, guide, and motivate their team members can create a positive work environment and improve team performance. In this section, we explored several leadership models, including Maslow's Hierarchy of Needs, Herzberg's Two-Factor Theory, and McGregor's Theory X and Theory Y, and how they can be applied to motivate and improve team performance.

Maslow's Hierarchy of Needs emphasizes the importance of meeting basic needs before moving on to higher level needs, while Herzberg's Two-Factor Theory focuses on hygiene factors and motivators to create a motivating work environment. McGregor's Theory X and Theory Y highlight the importance of understanding different management styles and adapting them to individual team members.

Leaders who follow best practices such as setting clear expectations, providing constructive feedback, creating a culture of trust and respect, recognizing achievements, providing opportunities for growth and development, and adapting leadership style to individual team members, can create a more positive and motivating work environment and improve team performance.

In conclusion, effective leadership is crucial for team performance and motivation. By understanding and applying different leadership models and best practices, leaders can create a work environment that promotes teamwork, innovation, and high performance, leading to greater success for the organization as a whole.

# 5.2 THE IMPORTANCE OF ADAPTING LEADERSHIP STYLES FOR EFFECTIVE PROJECT MANAGEMENT

Leadership style refers to the manner in which a leader provides direction, motivation, and guidance to a team or organization. There are various leadership styles, and each one has its own strengths and weaknesses. Some leadership styles are more effective in certain situations, while others may not be suitable.

The most common leadership styles are autocratic, democratic, laissez-faire, transformational, and transactional. Autocratic leaders make all the decisions and provide little opportunity for input from their team. Democratic leaders encourage participation and collaboration from team members. Laissez-faire leaders provide little direction and allow team members to make most of the decisions. Transformational leaders inspire and motivate their team to achieve a common goal. Transactional leaders focus on rewards and punishments to motivate their team.

Understanding different leadership styles is important because each style can have a significant impact on the success of a project. The right leadership style can motivate team members, encourage collaboration, and foster a positive work environment. In contrast, the wrong leadership style can lead to conflicts, low morale, and poor project outcomes. As such, it is important for project managers to recognize the importance of adapting their leadership styles to effectively manage their teams and achieve project success.

## PROJECT MANAGEMENT AND LEADERSHIP STYLES

Project management involves planning, organizing, and executing tasks and resources to achieve specific goals and objectives within a set timeframe. Effective project management requires strong leadership skills to motivate and guide team members throughout the project lifecycle.

The leadership style used in project management can have a significant impact on project outcomes. For example, a laissez-faire leadership style may work well when managing a team of experienced professionals who are self-motivated and require minimal supervision. However, a democratic leadership style may be more effective when managing a diverse team with varying levels of experience and skills.

Different stages of a project may also require different leadership styles. For example, during the definition phase, a transformational leadership style may be effective in inspiring the team to develop creative solutions and set ambitious goals. During the deployment phase, a transactional leadership style may be more effective in providing clear direction and ensuring that team members are meeting their targets.

Project managers must also consider the organizational culture and values when selecting a leadership style. For example, a company with a culture of innovation and risk-taking may require a transformational leadership style that encourages experimentation and creativity. On the other hand, a company with a culture of stability and risk aversion may require a more conservative leadership style that emphasizes careful planning and risk mitigation.

Overall, effective project management requires an understanding of different leadership styles and how they can be adapted to meet the specific needs of a project and team.

# REASONS FOR CHANGING LEADERSHIP STYLES IN PROJECT MANAGEMENT

There are several reasons why project managers may need to change their leadership style to effectively manage a project. These reasons can include changes in team dynamics, project scope, and project goals.

One reason for changing leadership styles is a change in team dynamics. For example, if new team members are added to the project, the project manager may need to adjust their leadership style to account for the new team members' skills and experience. Similarly, if team members leave the project, the project manager may need to adapt their leadership style to account for the loss of expertise and knowledge.

Another reason for changing leadership styles is a change in project scope. If the scope of the project changes significantly, the project manager may need to adjust their leadership style to ensure that team members are focused on the new priorities and goals. For example, if the project is expanded to include additional deliverables, the project manager may need to shift to a more democratic leadership style to encourage collaboration and involvement from all team members.

A change in project goals can also require a change in leadership style. For example, if the project goals shift from a focus on efficiency to a focus on innovation, the project manager may need to adopt a transformational leadership style that encourages creative thinking and risk-taking.

External factors, such as changes in market conditions or technological advancements, can also require a change in leadership style. For example, if a new competitor enters the market, the project manager may need to adopt a more autocratic leadership style to quickly pivot the project strategy and maintain a competitive advantage.

Overall, changing leadership styles in project management is essential to effectively manage a project and adapt to changing circumstances. Project managers must be flexible and willing to adapt their leadership style to meet the needs of the project and team.

## THE IMPACT OF LEADERSHIP STYLE ON PROJECT SUCCESS

The leadership style used in project management can have a significant impact on project success. A leadership style that is well-matched to the project's needs can motivate team members, encourage collaboration, and foster a positive work environment, leading to improved project outcomes. In contrast, a leadership style that is poorly matched to the project's needs can lead to conflicts, low morale, and poor project outcomes.

For example, a transformational leadership style may be effective in motivating team members to go above and beyond their usual efforts, leading to improved project outcomes. A transactional leadership style may be effective in ensuring that team members meet their targets and adhere to project timelines. However, an autocratic leadership style that provides little opportunity for team input and collaboration may lead to low morale and decreased motivation among team members, which can negatively impact project outcomes.

Research has shown that there is no one "best" leadership style for all projects, as the effectiveness of a leadership style depends on various factors, including project goals, team dynamics, and organizational culture. Project managers must be able to identify the leadership style that is most appropriate for the specific project they are managing and be able to adapt their leadership style as needed throughout the project lifecycle.

Overall, the impact of leadership style on project success cannot be overstated. The right leadership style can inspire and motivate team members to achieve their best work, while the wrong leadership style can hinder team performance and result in suboptimal project outcomes. Project managers must therefore carefully consider their leadership style and adapt it to meet the unique needs of their project and team.

## HOW TO IDENTIFY THE NEED FOR CHANGING LEADERSHIP STYLES IN PROJECT MANAGEMENT

Identifying the need for changing leadership styles in project management requires careful observation and evaluation of the project and team dynamics. Some common indicators that may suggest the need for changing leadership styles include:

a. Low team morale: If team members are expressing dissatisfaction or disengagement with the project, it may be an indication that the current leadership style is not motivating or inspiring them effectively.

b. Lack of collaboration: If team members are not working together effectively, it may be an indication that the current leadership style is not encouraging collaboration or providing sufficient opportunities for team input.

c. Missed project milestones or deadlines: If the project is not meeting its targets or is falling behind schedule, it may be an indication that the current leadership style is not providing sufficient direction or motivation for the team.

d. Changes in project scope or goals: If the project scope or goals change significantly, it may be necessary to adjust the leadership style to align with the new priorities and objectives.

e. Changes in team dynamics: If there are changes in the team composition, such as the addition or departure of team members, it may be necessary to adjust the leadership style to account for the new team dynamics.

f. External factors: Changes in market conditions or technological advancements may require a shift in leadership style to remain competitive or adapt to new challenges.

Project managers must be vigilant in monitoring these indicators and identifying when changes in leadership styles are necessary. They must also be able to accurately diagnose the underlying issues and select the appropriate leadership style to address them effectively.

Overall, identifying the need for changing leadership styles in project management is crucial to ensuring project success. Project managers must be proactive in observing team dynamics and project progress and be willing to adapt their leadership style to meet the evolving needs of the project and team.

## BEST PRACTICES FOR ADAPTING LEADERSHIP STYLES IN PROJECT MANAGEMENT

Adapting leadership styles in project management requires a combination of self-awareness, flexibility, and effective communication. Here are some best practices for adapting leadership styles in project management:

a. Develop self-awareness: Project managers must have a clear understanding of their own leadership style and how it impacts their team. This requires self-reflection, feedback from team members, and a willingness to learn and adapt.

b. Understand team dynamics: Project managers must also have a deep understanding of their team members' skills, motivations, and communication styles. This understanding can help project managers select the most effective leadership style for each team member and ensure that the team is working together effectively.

c. Identify the appropriate leadership style: Once project managers have a clear understanding of their own leadership style and their team's dynamics, they must be able to identify the appropriate leadership style for the project and adapt their approach as needed. This may require a combination of leadership styles, depending on the project's goals and the team's needs.

PMQ Exam Prep Essays

d. Communicate effectively: Effective communication is essential to adapting leadership styles in project management. Project managers must be able to clearly communicate their expectations, goals, and vision for the project, as well as provide feedback and support to team members.

e. Provide opportunities for feedback: Project managers must provide regular opportunities for team members to provide feedback on the leadership style and the project's progress. This feedback can help project managers adjust their leadership style and make course corrections as needed.

f. Continuously evaluate and adapt: Adapting leadership styles in project management is an ongoing process that requires continuous evaluation and adaptation. Project managers must be willing to make changes as necessary and continuously improve their leadership skills to ensure project success.

Overall, adapting leadership styles in project management requires a combination of self-awareness, effective communication, and a willingness to learn and adapt. Project managers who follow these best practices can create a positive work environment, motivate team members, and achieve project success.

## OVERCOMING CHALLENGES IN CHANGING LEADERSHIP STYLES FOR PROJECT SUCCESS

Adapting leadership styles in project management is not always easy and can present challenges for project managers. Here are some common challenges that project managers may face when changing leadership styles and how to overcome them:

a. Resistance from team members: When changing leadership styles, team members may feel uncomfortable or resistant to the new approach. To overcome this challenge, project managers must clearly communicate the reasons for the change, provide training and support to help team members adjust to the new approach, and emphasize the benefits of the new approach.

b. Lack of self-awareness: Project managers who lack self-awareness may struggle to identify the most effective leadership style for the project and team. To overcome this challenge, project managers should seek feedback from team members and work on developing their self-awareness through self-reflection, coaching, and training.

c. Inflexibility: Project managers who are inflexible in their leadership style may struggle to adapt to changing project needs and team dynamics. To overcome this challenge, project managers should work on developing their flexibility by being open to feedback, seeking new perspectives, and continuously learning and improving their leadership skills.

d. Lack of communication: Changing leadership styles requires effective communication with team members. Project managers who struggle with communication may face challenges in implementing changes. To overcome this challenge, project managers should prioritize communication, provide regular updates to team members, and create opportunities for feedback and collaboration.

e. Limited resources: Project managers who lack the resources or support necessary to make changes in leadership styles may struggle to implement changes effectively. To overcome this challenge, project managers should work on building support from stakeholders, advocating for necessary resources, and prioritizing the changes that will have the biggest impact on project success.

Overall, overcoming challenges in changing leadership styles for project success requires a combination of self-awareness, flexibility, effective communication, and support from stakeholders. Project managers who can navigate these challenges can create a positive work environment, motivate team members, and achieve project success.

# 5.3 THE CHARACTERISTICS AND BENEFITS OF EFFECTIVE TEAMS AND TEAMWORK

Effective teams and teamwork are essential for achieving success in any organization, whether it be a business, sports team, or community group. A team is a group of individuals who work together towards a common goal or objective. Teamwork, on the other hand, is the collaborative effort of a group of people to achieve a common goal.

Effective teams are those that are able to work together seamlessly to achieve their goals. They possess certain characteristics that set them apart from other teams that may not be as effective. Effective teams are essential in today's fast-paced and ever-changing work environment, where complex problems require multiple perspectives and skillsets to solve.

This section will delve into the characteristics and benefits of effective teams and teamwork, as well as explore strategies for building and improving teamwork. We will also discuss common challenges that teams may face and offer solutions for overcoming them. By the end of this section, you will have a better understanding of what it takes to create and maintain effective teams and how they can benefit your organization.

## CHARACTERISTICS OF EFFECTIVE TEAMS

Effective teams share certain key characteristics that set them apart from less effective teams. These characteristics include:

a. Clear Goals and Objectives: Effective teams have clear goals and objectives that are specific, measurable, achievable, relevant, and time bound. Each team member understands the team's purpose

257

and how their individual contributions support the team's overall objectives.

b. Strong Communication: Communication is essential for effective teamwork. Effective teams communicate regularly and openly, sharing information, ideas, and feedback. They actively listen to one another and respect each other's opinions and perspectives.

c. Collaboration: Effective teams collaborate and work together towards a common goal. They recognize that each team member brings unique skills, knowledge, and experience to the table and leverage each other's strengths to achieve their objectives.

d. Trust: Trust is essential for effective teamwork. Effective teams trust each other to do their best, respect each other's opinions, and follow through on commitments. They create a safe and supportive environment where team members feel comfortable sharing their ideas and concerns.

e. Accountability: Effective teams hold themselves accountable for their actions and outcomes. They take ownership of their work and hold each other accountable for meeting deadlines and achieving goals.

f. Diversity: Effective teams embrace diversity and recognize the value of different perspectives, backgrounds, and experiences. They create an inclusive environment where all team members feel valued and respected.

g. Continuous Learning: Effective teams are committed to continuous learning and improvement. They reflect on their successes and failures, identify areas for improvement, and seek out opportunities for growth and development.

By embodying these characteristics, effective teams are able to work together seamlessly to achieve their goals, deliver high-quality work, and drive success for their organization.

## BENEFITS OF EFFECTIVE TEAMS AND TEAMWORK

Effective teams and teamwork offer numerous benefits for organizations. These benefits include:

a. Increased Productivity: Effective teams are able to work together efficiently and collaboratively, which leads to increased productivity. By leveraging each other's strengths, sharing knowledge and expertise, and working towards a common goal, effective teams are able to produce high-quality work in less time.

b. Improved Quality: Effective teams are able to produce high-quality work by sharing knowledge and expertise, reviewing each other's work, and providing feedback. They are able to identify and address potential issues early on, which leads to better outcomes.

c. Innovation: Effective teams are able to generate new ideas and approaches through collaboration and brainstorming. They are able to leverage the diverse skills and experiences of their team members to come up with innovative solutions to complex problems.

d. Employee Engagement: Effective teams promote employee engagement by creating a supportive and collaborative work environment. When employees feel valued, respected, and part of a team, they are more likely to be engaged in their work, which leads to higher job satisfaction and retention.

e. Improved Decision Making: Effective teams are able to make better decisions by leveraging the diverse perspectives and expertise of their team members. They are able to consider multiple viewpoints and weigh the pros and cons of different options, which leads to better outcomes.

f. Increased Accountability: Effective teams hold each other accountable for their actions and outcomes, which leads to greater responsibility and ownership. When team members know that their contributions are important to the team's success, they are more likely to take their work seriously and deliver high-quality results.

Overall, effective teams and teamwork are essential for achieving success in today's fast-paced and competitive work environment. By promoting collaboration, innovation, and employee engagement, effective teams are able to drive organizational success and achieve their goals.

## BUILDING EFFECTIVE TEAMS

Building an effective team requires careful planning and consideration of several key factors. These factors include:

a. Clear Objectives: Before building a team, it's important to have clear objectives and goals in mind. Knowing what the team is trying to achieve will help guide the selection of team members and the development of the team's structure and processes.

b. Team Composition: The composition of a team is critical to its success. The team should be composed of individuals with complementary skills and experiences who are able to work well together. It's important to consider factors such as personality, work style, and communication skills when selecting team members.

c. Team Roles and Responsibilities: Each team member should have clearly defined roles and responsibilities. This ensures that everyone knows what they are responsible for and what is expected of them, which promotes accountability and teamwork.

d. Team Processes: Effective teams have clear processes in place for decision making, communication, and conflict resolution. These processes should be established early on and regularly reviewed to ensure that they are effective and efficient.

e. Leadership: Effective teams require strong leadership. A good team leader is able to inspire and motivate team members, facilitate communication and collaboration, and ensure that the team is working towards its goals.

f.  Training and Development: Ongoing training and development is essential for building and maintaining an effective team. Team members should be given opportunities to develop new skills, learn about new technologies and processes, and receive feedback on their performance.

By considering these factors and implementing strategies to address them, organizations can build effective teams that are able to achieve their goals and drive success.

## STRATEGIES FOR IMPROVING TEAMWORK

Improving teamwork requires ongoing effort and attention. Here are some strategies that can be implemented to improve teamwork within an organization:

a.  Encourage Communication: Communication is essential for effective teamwork. Encouraging open and honest communication among team members is crucial. This can be achieved by creating an environment where team members feel comfortable sharing their ideas and concerns, and by providing opportunities for regular team meetings and check-ins.

b.  Build Trust: Trust is essential for effective teamwork. Team members should be encouraged to build relationships and get to know each other on a personal level. Activities such as team building exercises and social events can help to build trust and improve relationships among team members.

c.  Clarify Roles and Responsibilities: Each team member should have a clear understanding of their role and responsibilities within the team. This helps to promote accountability and ensures that everyone is working towards the same goals.

d.  Encourage Collaboration: Collaboration is key to effective teamwork. Team members should be encouraged to work together to achieve their goals. This can be achieved by creating opportunities for brainstorming and idea-sharing, and by providing tools and resources that facilitate collaboration.

e. Provide Feedback: Regular feedback is important for improving teamwork. Team members should be encouraged to provide feedback to each other, both positive and constructive. This helps to promote continuous learning and improvement.

f. Recognize Achievements: Recognizing team achievements is important for promoting morale and teamwork. Celebrating successes, big or small, can help to boost team spirit and motivation.

These strategies can be implemented to improve teamwork within an organization. By promoting communication, trust, collaboration, accountability, and recognition, organizations can build effective teams that are able to achieve their goals and drive success.

## COMMON CHALLENGES AND HOW TO OVERCOME THEM

Despite the many benefits of effective teamwork, there are also common challenges that teams may face. These challenges include:

a. Communication Breakdowns: Communication breakdowns can occur when team members don't communicate effectively or when there is a lack of clarity about roles, responsibilities, and expectations. To overcome communication breakdowns, it's important to establish clear channels of communication and encourage team members to speak up if they have questions or concerns.

b. Conflicts: Conflicts can arise when team members have different ideas, opinions, or work styles. To overcome conflicts, it's important to encourage open communication, establish clear processes for conflict resolution, and ensure that team members feel heard and respected.

c. Lack of Trust: A lack of trust among team members can undermine teamwork and lead to a lack of engagement and motivation. To build trust, it's important to encourage team members to get to know each other on a personal level, establish clear expectations and boundaries, and promote transparency and honesty.

d. Limited Resources: Limited resources can create challenges for teams, such as time constraints, budget constraints, or lack of expertise. To overcome limited resources, it's important to establish priorities and focus on the most important tasks. This may also involve seeking out external resources or expertise when necessary.

To overcome these challenges, it's important to establish clear processes and procedures for communication, conflict resolution, and decision-making. Teams should also regularly assess their progress and identify areas for improvement. By addressing these challenges head-on and promoting a culture of continuous improvement, teams can overcome obstacles and achieve their goals.

## CONCLUSION: THE IMPORTANCE OF EFFECTIVE TEAMS AND TEAMWORK

Effective teams and teamwork are essential for achieving success in today's fast-paced and competitive work environment. By promoting collaboration, innovation, and employee engagement, effective teams are able to drive organizational success and achieve their goals.

To build effective teams, it's important to establish clear goals and objectives, select team members with complementary skills and experiences, define roles and responsibilities, and establish clear processes and procedures for communication, decision-making, and conflict resolution. Ongoing training and development is also essential for building and maintaining effective teams.

Despite the many benefits of effective teamwork, teams may face challenges such as communication breakdowns, conflicts, lack of trust, and limited resources. To overcome these challenges, it's important to establish clear processes and procedures for communication, conflict resolution, and decision-making, and to promote a culture of continuous improvement.

In conclusion, effective teams and teamwork are essential for achieving success in today's complex and dynamic work environment. By embodying the characteristics of effective teams and addressing common challenges, organizations can build teams that are able to achieve their goals, drive success, and make a positive impact on their communities and society as a whole.

# 5.4 NAVIGATING THE CHALLENGES OF LEADING VIRTUAL TEAMS: FACTORS AND IMPACT

Leading a virtual team requires a different set of skills and strategies compared to leading an in-person team. Virtual teams are comprised of individuals who work remotely, often across different locations and time zones, using technology to communicate and collaborate. This means that there is less face-to-face interaction and a greater reliance on technology to bridge the gap.

One of the primary challenges of leading virtual teams is the lack of physical presence, which can lead to a sense of disconnection and isolation among team members. As a leader, it's important to understand the dynamics of virtual teams and to be aware of the unique challenges they face in order to build a cohesive and productive team.

Effective communication is key in virtual teams. Leaders must establish clear communication channels, expectations, and guidelines for interactions. They should encourage open communication among team members and foster a sense of community and collaboration.

In addition, leaders must be able to adapt to different communication styles and preferences, as team members may come from different cultures and backgrounds. They should also be aware of potential language barriers and take steps to ensure that all team members are able to communicate effectively.

Overall, understanding the nature of virtual teams is critical for effective leadership. Leaders must be able to navigate the unique challenges of virtual work and create a supportive and productive environment for their team members.

## COMMUNICATION AND COLLABORATION TOOLS

In virtual teams, communication and collaboration tools are essential for enabling team members to work together effectively. Without these tools, virtual teams may struggle to stay connected and may experience difficulties with information sharing and collaboration.

As a leader of a virtual team, it's important to select the right communication and collaboration tools to support your team's work. This may include video conferencing software, messaging apps, project management tools, and document sharing platforms.

It's also important to establish guidelines and expectations for how these tools should be used. Leaders should ensure that team members are trained in the use of these tools and are familiar with the organization's policies around their use.

Effective communication is critical in virtual teams, and leaders must work to create an environment that supports open and transparent communication. They should establish regular check-ins and meetings to ensure that team members are staying connected and aligned with the team's goals.

In addition, collaboration tools can help virtual teams to work together more effectively. Leaders should encourage team members to share their ideas and contributions, and to collaborate on projects and tasks. Collaboration tools can also help to streamline workflows and reduce duplication of effort.

Overall, effective communication and collaboration tools are essential for virtual teams. Leaders must select the right tools and establish clear guidelines for their use in order to support team communication, collaboration, and productivity.

## CULTURAL AND LANGUAGE DIFFERENCES

Virtual teams often bring together individuals from different cultures and backgrounds, which can present unique challenges for leaders. Cultural and language differences can impact communication, collaboration, and teamwork, and may lead to misunderstandings or conflict if not managed effectively.

As a leader of a virtual team, it's important to be aware of these differences and to take steps to ensure that they are not barriers to effective communication and collaboration. This may include providing training on cultural awareness and sensitivity, and developing strategies for managing language barriers.

One approach to managing cultural differences is to encourage team members to share their cultural perspectives and to build a culture of respect and understanding. Leaders can facilitate this by setting clear expectations around behaviour and communication, and by modelling inclusive behaviour themselves.

Language barriers can be managed through the use of translation tools, such as automated translation software or professional translation services. Leaders should also be aware of the impact of language differences on communication, and should ensure that all team members have the opportunity to participate in discussions and decision-making processes.

In addition to these strategies, leaders should also be aware of the impact of cultural and language differences on team dynamics and performance. They should monitor team performance and be alert to signs of conflict or disengagement, and take steps to address these issues as they arise.

Overall, managing cultural and language differences is an important aspect of leading virtual teams. Leaders must be aware of these differences and be proactive in developing strategies to support effective communication and collaboration across cultures and languages.

## Time Zone and Work-life Balance

Virtual teams often work across different time zones, which can make scheduling meetings and collaboration challenging. Time zone differences can also impact work-life balance, as team members may need to work outside of traditional business hours to accommodate colleagues in other time zones.

As a leader of a virtual team, it's important to be aware of these challenges and to take steps to manage them effectively. This may include establishing clear expectations around working hours and availability, and developing strategies for scheduling meetings and collaboration across time zones.

One approach to managing time zone differences is to establish core working hours that overlap across different time zones. This can help to ensure that team members have dedicated time to collaborate and communicate with their colleagues. Leaders should also be aware of the impact of time zone differences on work-life balance, and should encourage team members to prioritize self-care and work-life balance in their work schedules.

In addition, leaders should be aware of the potential for burnout among virtual team members, who may feel pressure to be constantly available and connected. They should establish clear guidelines around work expectations and encourage team members to take breaks and prioritize their well-being.

Overall, managing time zone and work-life balance is a critical aspect of leading virtual teams. Leaders must be aware of the challenges and take proactive steps to manage these effectively, while also prioritizing the well-being and work-life balance of their team members.

## BUILDING TRUST AND ACCOUNTABILITY

Building trust and accountability is critical in virtual teams, where team members may be working remotely and have limited face-to-face interaction. Without trust and accountability, virtual teams may struggle to collaborate effectively and achieve their goals.

As a leader of a virtual team, it's important to establish trust and accountability among team members. This may include setting clear expectations around roles and responsibilities, and ensuring that team members have the necessary resources and support to do their jobs effectively.

Effective communication is also key to building trust and accountability. Leaders should establish clear communication channels and encourage open and transparent communication among team members. They should also be available to answer questions and provide guidance as needed.

In addition, leaders can build trust by demonstrating their own commitment to the team's goals and by modelling the behaviour they expect from their team members. This may include setting a positive tone and demonstrating empathy and understanding towards team members.

Accountability can be fostered through the use of performance metrics and regular check-ins. Leaders should establish clear performance metrics and communicate these effectively to team members. They should also provide regular feedback and recognition for team members who are performing well, and take corrective action when performance falls short.

Overall, building trust and accountability is essential in virtual teams. Leaders must be proactive in establishing clear expectations and communication channels, and in providing the support and resources necessary for team members to do their jobs effectively. By building trust and accountability, virtual teams can achieve their goals and work together effectively.

## MANAGING PERFORMANCE AND PRODUCTIVITY

Managing performance and productivity is an essential aspect of leading virtual teams. Without regular check-ins and performance management, virtual teams may struggle to achieve their goals and maintain high levels of productivity.

As a leader of a virtual team, it's important to establish clear performance metrics and to communicate these effectively to team members. This may include setting individual and team goals, and providing regular feedback and recognition for team members who are performing well.

Effective communication is also key to managing performance and productivity in virtual teams. Leaders should establish regular check-ins and meetings with team members to review progress and identify any challenges or roadblocks. They should also be available to answer questions and provide guidance as needed.

In addition, leaders can foster productivity by establishing clear workflows and processes. This may include developing project management tools and templates, and providing training on these tools to team members. Leaders should also be aware of the impact of time zone differences and workloads on productivity, and take steps to manage these effectively.

Finally, it's important for leaders to recognize the contributions of individual team members and to foster a culture of recognition and appreciation. Leaders can do this by providing regular feedback and recognition for team members who are performing well, and by celebrating team successes.

Overall, managing performance and productivity is a critical aspect of leading virtual teams. Leaders must establish clear performance metrics, communicate effectively with team members, and foster a culture of recognition and appreciation in order to achieve their goals and maintain high levels of productivity.

## DEVELOPING LEADERSHIP SKILLS FOR VIRTUAL TEAMS

Leading virtual teams requires a different set of skills and strategies compared to leading in-person teams. As a result, it's important for leaders to develop the necessary leadership skills to effectively manage virtual teams.

One important skill for virtual team leaders is effective communication. Leaders must be able to communicate effectively across different communication channels, including email, messaging apps, video conferencing, and other collaboration tools. They must also be able to adapt their communication style to different cultural and language preferences, and be sensitive to potential language barriers.

Another important skill is the ability to build trust and accountability among team members. Leaders must establish clear expectations and communication channels, and provide the necessary support and resources for team members to do their jobs effectively. They must also model the behaviour they expect from their team members, and recognize and reward performance and contributions.

Time management and organization skills are also critical for virtual team leaders. Leaders must be able to manage their own time effectively and prioritize their work, while also ensuring that team members have the necessary support and resources to do their jobs effectively. This may include establishing workflows and processes, and providing training and support for team members as needed.

Finally, virtual team leaders must be able to adapt to changing circumstances and navigate uncertainty effectively. They must be able to anticipate and manage risks, and make informed decisions in a dynamic and evolving environment.

Overall, developing leadership skills for virtual teams is critical for effective management and success. Leaders must be able to communicate effectively, build trust and accountability, manage time and resources effectively, and navigate uncertainty and change. By developing these skills, leaders can effectively manage their virtual teams and achieve their goals.

## OVERCOMING CHALLENGES AND ACHIEVING SUCCESS

Leading virtual teams can present a number of challenges, including communication barriers, cultural differences, time zone challenges, and work-life balance issues. In order to overcome these challenges and achieve success, virtual team leaders must be proactive in developing strategies to support effective communication, collaboration, and performance.

One approach to overcoming challenges in virtual teams is to establish clear goals and expectations for the team. This may include setting individual and team goals, and providing regular feedback and recognition for team members who are performing well. Leaders should also establish clear workflows and processes, and provide training and support for team members as needed.

Another approach is to foster a culture of communication and collaboration. Leaders should establish regular check-ins and meetings with team members to review progress and identify any challenges or roadblocks. They should also encourage open and transparent communication among team members, and be available to answer questions and provide guidance as needed.

In addition, leaders can manage time zone differences and work-life balance issues by establishing core working hours that overlap across different time zones. They should also encourage team members to prioritize self-care and work-life balance in their work schedules.

Finally, it's important for leaders to celebrate successes and recognize individual and team contributions. Leaders can do this by providing regular feedback and recognition for team members who are performing well, and by celebrating team successes.

Overall, virtual team leaders must be proactive in developing strategies to overcome challenges and achieve success. By establishing clear goals and expectations, fostering a culture of communication and collaboration, managing time zone differences and work-life balance issues, and recognizing individual and team contributions, leaders can effectively manage their virtual teams and achieve their goals.

# 5.5 Understanding Factors Influencing Team Creation, Development and Leadership

Teams are an essential part of any organization, and their success is critical to achieving organizational goals. Teams are formed for different purposes, such as problem-solving, decision-making, and task completion, and they can vary in size and composition.

Effective team dynamics involve a wide range of factors that determine team performance, including communication, leadership, conflict management, diversity, and team culture. It is essential to understand these factors to build and sustain high-performing teams.

Team dynamics also play a crucial role in promoting employee engagement and job satisfaction. When employees feel valued and included in a team, they are more likely to be motivated, committed, and productive. In contrast, teams that lack cohesion, communication, and trust can result in low morale, high turnover rates, and reduced productivity.

Therefore, it is vital for organizations to invest in team development and leadership to create a positive team environment that fosters collaboration, innovation, and excellence. By understanding the different models and factors that influence team dynamics, organizations can enhance team performance and achieve their goals effectively.

# BELBIN TEAM ROLE MODEL AND ITS SIGNIFICANCE IN BUILDING TEAMS

The Belbin Team Role Model is a widely recognized model used to identify and understand team member strengths and weaknesses. It was developed by Dr. Meredith Belbin in the 1970s and is based on nine team roles that individuals naturally adopt when working in a team.

According to the model, every team requires a balance of different roles to be successful. The nine team roles include Plant, Resource Investigator, Coordinator, Monitor Evaluator, Teamworker, Implementer, Completer Finisher, Specialist, and Shaper.

Each role has its unique characteristics, and individuals tend to excel in some roles and struggle in others. Understanding these roles can help teams build a more balanced and effective team. For example, a Plant is creative and innovative but may lack practicality, while an Implementer is dependable and efficient but may struggle with adapting to new ideas.

Using the Belbin model, teams can identify their strengths and weaknesses and allocate tasks and responsibilities accordingly. A team with a good balance of roles is likely to be more productive and creative, as each member can contribute their unique skills and perspectives.

In summary, the Belbin Team Role Model is an important tool for team building as it helps individuals understand their strengths and weaknesses and work together more effectively as a team. By creating a balanced team, organizations can achieve their goals and objectives more efficiently.

## Margerison-McCann Team Management Profile and Its Application in Team Development

The Margerison-McCann Team Management Profile is a model that helps individuals and teams understand their preferred management styles and how they contribute to team effectiveness. The model was developed by Dr. Meredith Belbin in collaboration with Dr. Marjorie Margerison and Dr. Dick McCann in the 1980s.

The model classifies management styles into four types, including the Analyzer, the Driver, the Creator, and the Integrator. Each management style is characterized by different preferences for activities, such as problem-solving, decision-making, planning, and communicating.

The Analyzer, for example, is detail-oriented, logical, and prefers to analyse information before making decisions. The Driver is goal-oriented, decisive, and likes to take charge of situations. The Creator is innovative, imaginative, and enjoys generating new ideas. The Integrator is empathetic, supportive, and skilled at bringing people together to work towards a common goal.

Understanding these management styles can help teams improve their communication, problem-solving, and decision-making processes. For example, a team may struggle with decision-making if all team members are Analysers and tend to overanalyse information, leading to slow decision-making. In this case, it may be helpful to involve a Driver to make a quick decision.

The Margerison-McCann Team Management Profile can also help teams identify areas where they may need additional training or development. For example, a team with mostly Drivers may need to improve their listening skills and consider other perspectives to ensure that all team members feel heard.

In conclusion, the Margerison-McCann Team Management Profile is a valuable tool for team development as it helps teams understand their management styles and how they contribute to team effectiveness. By using this model, teams can improve their communication, decision-making, and problem-solving processes, and work towards achieving their goals more efficiently.

## MYERS-BRIGGS TYPE INDICATOR AND ITS ROLE IN TEAM BUILDING

The Myers-Briggs Type Indicator (MBTI) is a personality assessment tool that is widely used to identify individual preferences and behaviours. It was developed by Katherine Briggs and her daughter Isabel Myers in the early 1900s, based on the theory of Swiss psychiatrist Carl Jung.

The MBTI assesses personality based on four dichotomies: Extraversion vs. Introversion, Sensing vs. Intuition, Thinking vs. Feeling, and Judging vs. Perceiving. Each dichotomy measures a different aspect of personality, and individuals are classified into one of 16 personality types based on their results.

The MBTI can be used in team building to identify individual strengths and preferences and help team members understand each other better. For example, individuals with a preference for extraversion tend to be outgoing and social, while those with a preference for introversion tend to be more reserved and reflective. Understanding these differences can help team members communicate more effectively and avoid misunderstandings.

The MBTI can also be used to identify areas where team members may need additional support or development. For example, an individual with a preference for intuition may struggle with details and may benefit from additional support in this area.

In summary, the MBTI can be a valuable tool for team building as it helps individuals understand their strengths and preferences and how they fit into a team. By understanding each other's personalities, team members can communicate more effectively and work together more efficiently towards a common goal.

## HACKMAN'S FIVE FACTORS MODEL FOR EFFECTIVE TEAM LEADERSHIP

Richard Hackman, a Harvard University professor, developed the Five Factors Model for Effective Team Leadership, which is a framework for understanding the leadership behaviours that can contribute to team effectiveness. Hackman's model emphasizes the importance of creating a supportive environment and providing the necessary resources for team success.

The five factors in Hackman's model include:

1. Team Design: Effective team design involves structuring the team around a clear and compelling task, defining team member roles and responsibilities, and providing adequate resources and support.

2. Supportive Context: The team leader must provide a supportive context that enables team members to collaborate effectively and focus on the task at hand. This can include establishing clear goals, providing feedback, and creating a positive team culture.

3. Clear Norms and Expectations: The team leader must establish clear norms and expectations that govern team behaviour and ensure that all team members understand what is expected of them. This can include setting standards for communication, decision-making, and problem-solving.

4. Adequate Training: Team members need to have the necessary skills and knowledge to perform their roles effectively. The team

leader must provide adequate training and support to ensure that team members are prepared to contribute to the team's success.

5. Appropriate Rewards and Recognition: Effective team leadership involves providing appropriate rewards and recognition to team members who contribute to the team's success. This can include public recognition, financial incentives, or other forms of reward that are meaningful to team members.

By focusing on these five factors, team leaders can create a supportive environment that enables team members to collaborate effectively and achieve their goals. The model emphasizes the importance of providing adequate resources and support, establishing clear expectations, and recognizing the contributions of team members. When these factors are present, teams are more likely to be successful and achieve their objectives.

## TUCKMAN'S TEAM DEVELOPMENT MODEL AND ITS RELEVANCE IN MODERN ORGANIZATIONS

Tuckman's Team Development Model, also known as Tuckman's stages of group development, was developed by Bruce Tuckman in 1965. The model describes the process that teams go through as they form, mature, and eventually disband. The four stages of Tuckman's model include forming, storming, norming, and performing.

1. Forming: In the forming stage, team members are getting to know each other, and the team is just beginning to take shape. There is typically a lot of uncertainty and confusion during this stage, as team members are trying to understand each other's roles and responsibilities.

2. Storming: The storming stage is characterized by conflict and disagreement as team members begin to voice their opinions and ideas. This stage is critical for team development, as team

members must learn to resolve conflicts and work together effectively.

3. Norming: In the norming stage, team members begin to work together more effectively, and they establish clear roles and responsibilities. This stage is characterized by a growing sense of teamwork and collaboration.

4. Performing: In the performing stage, the team is working at its highest level of effectiveness, and team members are working together seamlessly towards a common goal. The focus is on achieving the team's objectives and delivering high-quality results.

The relevance of Tuckman's Team Development Model in modern organizations lies in its ability to provide a roadmap for team development. The model helps team members understand the process of team development and the challenges that they will encounter along the way. By understanding the stages of team development, team members can be more effective in their roles and work towards creating a high-performing team.

Moreover, modern organizations are complex, and teams need to work together effectively to achieve their objectives. The Tuckman model can help teams build the necessary skills and processes to work together effectively. It provides a framework for team members to communicate effectively, manage conflict, establish norms and expectations, and focus on achieving the team's objectives.

In conclusion, Tuckman's Team Development Model provides a valuable framework for team development in modern organizations. By understanding the stages of team development and the challenges that teams will encounter along the way, teams can work together more effectively and achieve their objectives more efficiently.

# KATZENBACH AND SMITH'S MODEL OF HIGH-PERFORMING TEAMS

Jon Katzenbach and Douglas Smith's model of high-performing teams focuses on the characteristics of successful teams and how organizations can develop these teams. Their model emphasizes the importance of leadership, accountability, and a strong team culture.

Katzenbach and Smith's model of high-performing teams includes the following characteristics:

a. Common Purpose: Successful teams have a clear and compelling purpose that motivates team members to work towards a common goal.

b. Clear Roles and Responsibilities: Team members understand their roles and responsibilities, and they are accountable for their individual contributions to the team.

c. Effective Processes: Successful teams have effective processes in place for communication, decision-making, and problem-solving.

d. Skilled Members: Team members have the necessary skills and knowledge to perform their roles effectively, and they are continually developing their skills.

e. Mutual Trust: Successful teams have a strong sense of trust among team members, which enables effective collaboration and decision-making.

f. Shared Leadership: High-performing teams have shared leadership, where all team members take responsibility for leading the team towards its goals.

g. Strong Team Identity: Successful teams have a strong team culture and identity, which fosters a sense of belonging and pride among team members.

By focusing on these characteristics, organizations can develop high-performing teams that are motivated, accountable, and effective in achieving their objectives. Leaders can facilitate the development of high-performing teams by establishing a clear purpose, defining roles and responsibilities, and promoting trust and collaboration among team members.

In conclusion, Katzenbach and Smith's model of high-performing teams provides a valuable framework for organizations to develop effective teams. By focusing on the characteristics of successful teams, organizations can create a culture of excellence and achieve their goals more efficiently.

## FACTORS AFFECTING TEAM SUCCESS AND SUSTENANCE

The success and sustenance of a team depend on various factors, including communication, leadership, trust, collaboration, and accountability. Organizations must understand these factors to develop and maintain high-performing teams that achieve their goals effectively.

a. Communication: Effective communication is critical to the success of any team. Team members must be able to communicate openly and honestly, share their ideas and opinions, and listen to each other's feedback. Communication should be frequent, clear, and respectful to avoid misunderstandings and conflicts.

b. Leadership: Team leadership is essential for establishing a clear vision and direction, setting expectations, and motivating team members to achieve their objectives. Effective leaders must be able to communicate effectively, delegate tasks, provide support, and hold team members accountable for their contributions.

c. Trust: Building trust among team members is critical to the success of a team. Trust enables team members to work together effectively, share their ideas and opinions, and take risks without fear of judgment or criticism. Organizations can promote trust by creating a culture of openness and transparency, encouraging collaboration, and recognizing team members' contributions.

d. Collaboration: Collaboration is essential to effective team performance. Team members must be able to work together, share responsibilities, and support each other to achieve their objectives. Organizations can promote collaboration by establishing clear roles and responsibilities, facilitating communication, and promoting a sense of shared purpose.

e. Accountability: Team members must be accountable for their contributions to the team's success. This includes taking responsibility for their actions, meeting deadlines, and delivering high-quality work. Organizations can promote accountability by setting clear expectations, establishing performance metrics, and providing feedback and recognition for team members' contributions.

By focusing on these factors, organizations can develop and maintain high-performing teams that are motivated, accountable, and effective in achieving their objectives. Leaders can facilitate the development of these teams by promoting a culture of openness, trust, and collaboration, and by providing effective communication, leadership, and accountability structures.

## STRATEGIES FOR ENHANCING TEAM PERFORMANCE

Organizations can employ various strategies to enhance team performance, including training, feedback and recognition, and creating a supportive team environment. These strategies can help teams improve their communication, problem-solving, decision-making, and overall effectiveness.

a. Training: Providing training and development opportunities for team members can enhance their skills and knowledge and improve team performance. Training can be focused on specific areas, such as communication, leadership, problem-solving, or team building. It can be delivered through workshops, coaching, or online learning platforms.

b. Feedback and Recognition: Providing regular feedback and recognition to team members can help them stay motivated and engaged. Feedback can be focused on individual performance, team performance, or specific projects. Recognition can be provided in various forms, such as public acknowledgment, financial incentives, or promotions.

c. Supportive Team Environment: Creating a supportive team environment can foster trust, collaboration, and innovation. Organizations can promote a supportive team environment by establishing clear expectations, providing resources and support, encouraging open communication, and promoting a culture of respect and trust.

d. Effective Communication: Effective communication is critical to team performance. Organizations can promote effective communication by establishing clear communication channels, providing feedback and recognition, and promoting active listening and constructive feedback.

e. Performance Metrics: Establishing performance metrics can help teams track their progress and identify areas for improvement. Performance metrics can be focused on individual performance, team performance, or specific projects. Organizations can use performance metrics to provide feedback, recognize achievements, and identify areas for improvement.

By employing these strategies, organizations can enhance team performance, promote a culture of excellence, and achieve their objectives more efficiently. Effective team development and leadership are critical to organizational success, and these strategies can help organizations build and maintain high-performing teams.

## OVERCOMING COMMON TEAM CHALLENGES

Despite the best efforts of organizations to develop high-performing teams, teams can still face common challenges that can hinder their effectiveness. These challenges include lack of trust, poor communication, conflict, lack of motivation, and unclear goals. Here are some strategies for overcoming these challenges:

a. Lack of Trust: Building trust among team members is essential to effective team performance. To overcome a lack of trust, organizations can promote transparency and honesty, encourage open communication, and establish clear expectations and guidelines for behavior.

b. Poor Communication: Effective communication is critical to team performance. To overcome poor communication, organizations can establish clear communication channels, encourage active listening, and promote regular check-ins to ensure that team members are aligned and working towards the same goals.

c. Conflict: Conflict can arise in any team, and it is important to address it quickly to avoid escalating tensions. Organizations can overcome conflict by encouraging open communication, promoting active listening, and establishing clear conflict resolution processes.

d. Lack of Motivation: Team members can lose motivation when they feel that their contributions are not valued or that their goals are not aligned with the team's objectives. To overcome a lack of motivation, organizations can provide regular feedback and recognition, establish clear goals and expectations, and create opportunities for team members to learn and grow.

e. Unclear Goals: Team members can become disengaged when goals are unclear or when they are not aligned with the team's objectives. To overcome unclear goals, organizations can establish clear goals and objectives, communicate them effectively, and ensure that team members understand their roles and responsibilities.

By overcoming these common team challenges, organizations can develop and maintain high-performing teams that are motivated, accountable, and effective in achieving their objectives. Effective team leadership, communication, and collaboration are critical to addressing these challenges, and organizations must be proactive in addressing them to ensure team success.

## DIVERSITY AND INCLUSION IN TEAMS

Diversity and inclusion are critical to effective team performance. Teams that are diverse in terms of backgrounds, experiences, and perspectives are more likely to be innovative, creative, and effective in solving problems. However, diversity and inclusion can also present challenges that must be addressed for teams to work effectively together.

To promote diversity and inclusion in teams, organizations can take several steps:

a. Establish a culture of inclusiveness: Organizations can establish a culture of inclusiveness by promoting respect, open communication, and diversity of perspectives. This can be achieved by providing training on diversity and inclusion, creating opportunities for team members to learn from one another, and celebrating diversity and differences.

b. Recognize and value differences: Organizations must recognize and value the differences among team members to promote a diverse and inclusive team environment. This can be achieved by creating opportunities for team members to share their unique perspectives and experiences, encouraging open communication, and actively seeking out diverse perspectives.

c. Address unconscious bias: Unconscious bias can hinder team performance and limit diversity and inclusion. Organizations can address unconscious bias by providing training on unconscious bias, promoting self-awareness among team members, and actively seeking out diverse perspectives.

d. Create opportunities for team members to connect: Creating opportunities for team members to connect outside of work can foster a sense of belonging and promote a diverse and inclusive team environment. This can be achieved by organizing team-building activities, promoting social events, and encouraging team members to connect on a personal level.

e. Foster a culture of respect: Organizations can foster a culture of respect by promoting positive communication, setting clear expectations and guidelines for behavior, and addressing any behavior that violates the organization's values.

By promoting diversity and inclusion in teams, organizations can create a more innovative and effective team environment that can lead to improved performance and better outcomes. Effective team leadership, communication, and collaboration are critical to promoting diversity and inclusion, and organizations must be proactive in addressing these issues to ensure team success.

# CHAPTER SIX

## *PLANNING FOR SUCCESS: AN OVERVIEW OF PROJECT PLANNING*

# 6.1 THE IMPORTANCE OF A BUSINESS CASE THROUGHOUT THE PROJECT LIFE CYCLE

A business case is a document that outlines the justification for undertaking a project. It presents the reasons for the project, the expected outcomes, the costs and benefits, and the risks and challenges associated with the project. A business case helps stakeholders make informed decisions about whether to proceed with the project or not. It is an essential tool that guides the project team throughout the project life cycle.

A business case is typically developed during the project concept phase and is reviewed and updated periodically throughout the project. It serves as a reference point for all project decisions, ensuring that the project aligns with the organization's strategic goals and objectives.

The business case should provide a clear and concise description of the project's purpose and objectives, the expected benefits and outcomes, the cost estimates, and the risks and challenges associated with the project. It should also outline the project's feasibility and how it aligns with the organization's priorities and resources.

In summary, a business case is a critical document that ensures that the project is worthwhile, feasible, and aligned with the organization's strategic goals and objectives.

## BENEFITS OF HAVING A BUSINESS CASE

There are numerous benefits to having a business case throughout the project life cycle. Some of these benefits include:

a. Provides a Clear Understanding of the Project: A business case ensures that all stakeholders have a clear understanding of the project's purpose, objectives, and expected outcomes. It helps stakeholders make informed decisions about the project, ensuring that the project aligns with the organization's strategic goals and objectives.

b. Helps Identify Risks and Challenges: A business case helps identify potential risks and challenges associated with the project. By identifying potential risks early in the project life cycle, the project team can take steps to mitigate them and ensure that the project is delivered on time, within budget, and with the desired outcomes.

c. Ensures Stakeholder Buy-In: A well-developed business case can help secure stakeholder buy-in and support for the project. By clearly outlining the project's benefits and outcomes, stakeholders can see the value of the project and the impact it will have on the organization.

d. Helps Manage Project Costs: A business case outlines the project's estimated costs and benefits, enabling the project team to manage project costs effectively. The business case provides a framework for tracking project expenses, ensuring that the project is delivered within budget.

e. Guides Project Decisions: A business case guides project decisions throughout the project life cycle. It ensures that all project decisions align with the project's objectives and goals, minimizing the risk of scope creep and ensuring that the project remains on track.

In conclusion, having a well-developed business case provides numerous benefits to the project team and stakeholders. It ensures that the project is feasible, worthwhile, and aligned with the organization's strategic goals and objectives. It helps identify potential risks and challenges, secures stakeholder buy-in, manages project costs, and guides project decisions throughout the project life cycle.

## How the Business Case Guides Project Decisions

A business case is an essential tool that guides project decisions throughout the project life cycle. The business case sets out the project's objectives, scope, and expected outcomes, providing a framework for all project decisions. Here are some ways in which the business case guides project decisions:

a. Defines Project Scope: The business case defines the project scope and outlines the project's objectives and goals. This ensures that all project decisions are aligned with the project's scope and objectives, minimizing the risk of scope creep and ensuring that the project remains on track.

b. Guides Resource Allocation: The business case outlines the estimated costs and benefits of the project, providing a framework for resource allocation. The project team can use the business case to allocate resources effectively, ensuring that the project is delivered within budget and with the desired outcomes.

c. Guides Project Prioritization: The business case helps prioritize project activities and tasks, ensuring that the most critical tasks are completed first. This ensures that the project progresses efficiently and that the desired outcomes are achieved.

d. Identifies Risks and Mitigation Strategies: The business case helps identify potential risks and challenges associated with the project. The project team can use the business case to develop mitigation strategies that minimize the impact of these risks on the project's outcomes.

e. Facilitates Communication: The business case serves as a communication tool for the project team and stakeholders. It helps stakeholders understand the project's purpose, objectives, and expected outcomes, facilitating communication and collaboration throughout the project life cycle.

In conclusion, the business case is a critical tool that guides project decisions throughout the project life cycle. It provides a framework for all project decisions, ensuring that they align with the project's objectives and goals. It guides resource allocation, project prioritization, identifies risks and mitigation strategies, and facilitates communication among the project team and stakeholders.

## MONITORING AND UPDATING THE BUSINESS CASE

Developing a business case is not a one-time task but an ongoing process that requires regular monitoring and updating throughout the project life cycle. The business case should be reviewed periodically to ensure that the project remains aligned with the organization's strategic goals and objectives. Here are some ways in which monitoring and updating the business case is important:

a. Ensures Project Alignment with Strategic Goals: The business case outlines the project's alignment with the organization's strategic goals and objectives. By monitoring and updating the business case, the project team can ensure that the project remains aligned with the organization's strategic goals and objectives throughout the project life cycle.

b. Keeps Project on Track: Monitoring and updating the business case helps keep the project on track by ensuring that it remains aligned with the project's scope and objectives. This helps minimize the risk of scope creep and ensures that the project remains focused on delivering the desired outcomes.

c. Facilitates Resource Allocation: Monitoring and updating the business case helps the project team allocate resources effectively. The business case outlines the estimated costs and benefits of the project, providing a framework for resource allocation. By monitoring and updating the business case, the project team can ensure that resources are allocated effectively throughout the project life cycle.

d. Identifies Changes in Project Environment: Monitoring and updating the business case helps the project team identify changes in the project environment. The business case outlines potential risks and challenges associated with the project. By monitoring and updating the business case, the project team can identify new risks and challenges and develop mitigation strategies to minimize their impact on the project's outcomes.

e. Guides Decision Making: The business case guides project decision making throughout the project life cycle. By monitoring and updating the business case, the project team can ensure that all project decisions align with the project's scope and objectives, minimizing the risk of scope creep and ensuring that the project remains on track.

In conclusion, monitoring and updating the business case is an essential task that ensures project alignment with the organization's strategic goals and objectives, keeps the project on track, facilitates resource allocation, identifies changes in the project environment, and guides decision making throughout the project life cycle.

## RISKS OF IGNORING THE BUSINESS CASE

Ignoring the business case can have severe consequences for a project. Failing to develop a business case or not updating it regularly throughout the project life cycle can lead to the following risks:

a. Scope Creep: Ignoring the business case can lead to scope creep, where the project's scope expands beyond its original objectives. This can result in the project taking longer, costing more, and delivering outcomes that do not align with the organization's strategic goals and objectives.

b. Misaligned Objectives: Ignoring the business case can result in the project being misaligned with the organization's strategic goals and objectives. This can lead to the project delivering outcomes that do not align with the organization's priorities, resulting in a waste of resources.

c. Resource Misallocation: Failing to develop or update the business case can lead to ineffective resource allocation. This can result in the project not having the resources it needs to achieve its objectives, leading to delays and cost overruns.

d. Inadequate Risk Management: Ignoring the business case can lead to inadequate risk management. Without a business case, the project team may fail to identify potential risks and challenges, which can have a significant impact on the project's outcomes.

e. Lack of Stakeholder Buy-in: Failing to develop a business case or not updating it regularly can result in a lack of stakeholder buy-in. Stakeholders may not see the value of the project or understand its purpose, leading to a lack of support for the project.

In conclusion, ignoring the business case can have severe consequences for a project. It can result in scope creep, misaligned objectives, resource misallocation, inadequate risk management, and a lack of stakeholder buy-in. To mitigate these risks, it is essential to develop a well-defined business case and update it regularly throughout the project life cycle.

## EXAMPLES OF SUCCESSFUL BUSINESS CASES

There are numerous examples of successful business cases that have guided projects to success. Here are some examples:

1. Apple iPhone: The development of the Apple iPhone is a classic example of a successful business case. The business case outlined the potential market for the product, the expected costs and benefits, and the risks and challenges associated with the project. The business case helped secure stakeholder buy-in and guided project decisions throughout the project life cycle, resulting in one of the most successful products in history.

2. London Olympics 2012: The London Olympics 2012 is another example of a successful business case. The business case outlined the expected benefits of the project, including economic benefits, job creation, and infrastructure improvements. The business case helped secure stakeholder buy-in, guided project decisions, and

ensured that the project was delivered on time, within budget, and with the desired outcomes.

3. Boeing 787 Dreamliner: The development of the Boeing 787 Dreamliner is another example of a successful business case. The business case outlined the potential market for the product, the expected costs and benefits, and the risks and challenges associated with the project. The business case guided project decisions, resulting in the successful development and launch of the Boeing 787 Dreamliner.

4. Disney World: The development of Disney World is another example of a successful business case. The business case outlined the expected benefits of the project, including economic benefits, job creation, and tourism revenue. The business case helped secure stakeholder buy-in, guided project decisions, and ensured that the project was delivered on time, within budget, and with the desired outcomes.

In conclusion, there are numerous examples of successful business cases that have guided projects to success. These business cases outlined the potential benefits and outcomes of the project, identified potential risks and challenges, guided project decisions, and ensured that the project was delivered on time, within budget, and with the desired outcomes. By developing a well-defined business case and updating it regularly throughout the project life cycle, project teams can increase the chances of project success.

## CONCLUSION AND FINAL THOUGHTS

A business case is a critical tool that guides project decisions throughout the project life cycle. It outlines the project's purpose, objectives, expected outcomes, costs and benefits, and potential risks and challenges. A well-developed business case ensures that the project is worthwhile, feasible, and aligned with the organization's strategic goals and objectives.

The benefits of having a business case throughout the project life cycle are numerous. It provides a clear understanding of the project, helps identify potential risks and challenges, ensures stakeholder buy-in, guides project decisions, and helps manage project costs. Monitoring and updating the business case is also essential to ensure that the project remains aligned with the organization's strategic goals and objectives, keeps the project on track, facilitates resource allocation, identifies changes in the project environment, and guides decision making throughout the project life cycle.

Ignoring the business case can have severe consequences for a project. It can result in scope creep, misaligned objectives, resource misallocation, inadequate risk management, and a lack of stakeholder buy-in. To mitigate these risks, it is essential to develop a well-defined business case and update it regularly throughout the project life cycle.

In conclusion, a well-developed and regularly updated business case is essential for project success. It ensures that the project is aligned with the organization's strategic goals and objectives, guides project decisions, and helps manage project costs and risks. By prioritizing the development and monitoring of the business case, project teams can increase the chances of project success and deliver the desired outcomes.

## 6.2 UNDERSTANDING BENEFITS MANAGEMENT: FROM IDENTIFICATION TO REALIZATION

Benefits management is a structured approach that helps organizations maximize the value they obtain from their projects and programs. It involves identifying, defining, planning, tracking, and realizing the benefits that a project or program is intended to deliver. Benefits management aims to ensure that projects and programs deliver the expected outcomes, benefits, and value, and that they are aligned with the organization's strategic objectives.

Effective benefits management starts with the recognition that the primary objective of any project or program is to deliver benefits, rather than simply delivering outputs or completing tasks. Benefits can be tangible or intangible, and they can be financial or non-financial. Tangible benefits are usually easier to quantify and measure, while intangible benefits can be more challenging to define and assess. Non-financial benefits can include improved customer satisfaction, increased employee morale, or enhanced reputation, while financial benefits can include increased revenue, reduced costs, or improved profitability.

Benefits management involves a continuous process of identifying, assessing, and managing the benefits throughout the lifecycle of a project or program. It starts with the identification of potential benefits and the development of a benefits management plan that outlines how the benefits will be defined, tracked, and realized. Benefits management requires the involvement of stakeholders throughout the process, including senior management, project managers, project teams, and business users.

Effective benefits management can help organizations to make better investment decisions, optimize resources, and increase the likelihood of project success. It provides a framework for measuring the value of projects and programs, and for ensuring that they deliver the expected outcomes and benefits. By adopting a structured approach to benefits management, organizations can enhance their ability to achieve their strategic objectives and realize their vision.

## IDENTIFICATION: THE FIRST STEP IN BENEFITS MANAGEMENT

The first step in benefits management is identifying the potential benefits that a project or program is expected to deliver. This involves understanding the strategic objectives of the organization, and determining how the project or program will contribute to those objectives. It is essential to involve stakeholders in the identification process to ensure that all perspectives are considered.

The identification of benefits should be based on a thorough analysis of the business case for the project or program. This involves examining the costs and benefits of the proposed initiative, and determining whether the benefits justify the investment. The identification of benefits should also take into account any risks and uncertainties that may affect the delivery of the benefits.

Benefits can be categorized as direct or indirect, and primary or secondary. Direct benefits are those that are directly attributable to the project or program, such as increased revenue or reduced costs. Indirect benefits are those that are not directly attributable to the project or program, but are still expected to result from the initiative, such as improved customer satisfaction or increased employee morale. Primary benefits are the primary reason for undertaking the project or program, while secondary benefits are those that arise as a result of the primary benefits.

Once the potential benefits have been identified, it is important to prioritize them based on their importance and feasibility. The prioritization of benefits should take into account factors such as the strategic importance of the benefits, the risks and uncertainties associated with their delivery, and the resources required to achieve them.

The identification of benefits should be an ongoing process throughout the lifecycle of the project or program. As the project progresses, it may become necessary to revise the benefits that have been identified, and to identify new benefits that were not initially anticipated. This requires a flexible and iterative approach to benefits management, with regular reviews and updates to the benefits management plan.

In summary, the identification of potential benefits is the first step in benefits management, and is essential to ensuring that the project or program delivers the expected outcomes and value. It involves a thorough analysis of the business case, the involvement of stakeholders, and the prioritization of benefits based on their importance and feasibility. The identification of benefits is an ongoing process that requires a flexible and iterative approach throughout the lifecycle of the project or program.

## DEFINITION: DEFINING THE SCOPE OF BENEFITS

Once the potential benefits have been identified, the next step in benefits management is to define the scope of the benefits. This involves developing a clear and concise definition of each benefit, and establishing how it will be measured and tracked throughout the lifecycle of the project or program.

The definition of benefits should be based on a detailed understanding of the benefits and their relationship to the project or program objectives. The benefits should be defined in terms of their expected outcomes, such as the level of improvement that is expected in a particular area, and the timeframe in which the benefit is expected to be realized.

It is important to involve stakeholders in the definition of benefits to ensure that the benefits are aligned with their needs and expectations. Stakeholders should be consulted to determine their expectations of the benefits, and to identify any factors that may impact their ability to achieve the benefits.

The definition of benefits should also take into account the level of effort required to achieve the benefits. This involves identifying the resources required to deliver the benefits, such as the level of investment required, the skills and expertise needed, and the timeframe for delivery.

Once the benefits have been defined, it is important to establish how they will be measured and tracked throughout the lifecycle of the project or program. This involves establishing a set of metrics or indicators that will be used to measure the progress of the project or program, and to track the delivery of the benefits.

The metrics or indicators should be aligned with the definition of benefits, and should be regularly reviewed and updated throughout the lifecycle of the project or program. They should be used to monitor progress, identify any issues or risks that may impact the delivery of the benefits, and to determine whether the benefits have been achieved.

In summary, the definition of benefits is a critical step in benefits management, and involves developing a clear and concise definition of each benefit, and establishing how it will be measured and tracked throughout the lifecycle of the project or program. The definition of benefits should be based on a detailed understanding of the benefits and their relationship to the project or program objectives, and should involve the input of stakeholders. The establishment of metrics or indicators is essential to monitor progress and track the delivery of the benefits.

## PLANNING: STRATEGIZING FOR EFFECTIVE BENEFITS MANAGEMENT

After the identification and definition of benefits, the next step in benefits management is planning. Planning involves developing a benefits management plan that outlines how the benefits will be achieved, tracked, and realized. The benefits management plan should be developed in alignment with the project or program plan, and should be integrated into the overall project management approach.

The benefits management plan should include a detailed description of each benefit, and a plan for achieving it. The plan should identify the specific activities that are required to deliver the benefits, as well as the resources needed, the timelines, and the risks and uncertainties associated with the delivery of the benefits.

The benefits management plan should also include a description of the metrics or indicators that will be used to track progress and measure the achievement of the benefits. The metrics or indicators should be aligned with the definition of benefits, and should be regularly reviewed and updated throughout the lifecycle of the project or program.

The benefits management plan should also identify the roles and responsibilities of the stakeholders involved in benefits management. This includes the project or program manager, the benefits owner, and the business owner. The benefits owner is responsible for ensuring that the benefits are delivered, and that the metrics or indicators are being tracked and reported. The business owner is responsible for providing the resources and support needed to achieve the benefits.

The benefits management plan should be regularly reviewed and updated throughout the lifecycle of the project or program. This includes regular reviews of progress against the metrics or indicators, as well as reviews of the risks and uncertainties associated with the delivery of the benefits. Any changes to the benefits management plan should be communicated to all stakeholders, and should be reflected in the overall project or program plan.

In summary, planning is a critical step in benefits management, and involves developing a benefits management plan that outlines how the benefits will be achieved, tracked, and realized. The benefits management plan should be aligned with the project or program plan, and should include a detailed description of each benefit, a plan for achieving it, metrics or indicators for tracking progress, and roles and responsibilities for stakeholders involved in benefits management. The benefits management plan should be regularly reviewed and updated throughout the lifecycle of the project or program.

## TRACKING: MONITORING AND MEASURING BENEFITS

Once the benefits management plan has been developed and implemented, the next step in benefits management is tracking. Tracking involves monitoring and measuring the progress of the project or program against the metrics or indicators that were established in the benefits management plan.

The tracking process should be ongoing throughout the lifecycle of the project or program. This involves regular reviews of progress against the metrics or indicators, as well as reviews of the risks and uncertainties associated with the delivery of the benefits.

The tracking process should also involve regular communication with stakeholders to ensure that they are aware of progress and any issues or risks that may impact the delivery of the benefits. This includes regular reporting to senior management, project teams, and business users.

The tracking process should also involve the identification of any issues or risks that may impact the delivery of the benefits. This includes identifying any changes in the business environment, changes in the project scope, or changes in the availability of resources. Any issues or risks should be addressed promptly to minimize their impact on the delivery of the benefits.

In addition to monitoring progress, tracking also involves measuring the achievement of the benefits. This involves measuring the actual outcomes and benefits that have been achieved, and comparing them to the expected outcomes and benefits that were defined in the benefits management plan. Any variances between the actual and expected outcomes and benefits should be analysed, and appropriate action taken to address any discrepancies.

The tracking process should also include regular reviews of the benefits management plan. Any changes to the benefits management plan should be reflected in the overall project or program plan, and communicated to all stakeholders.

In summary, tracking is a critical step in benefits management, and involves monitoring and measuring the progress of the project or program against the metrics or indicators that were established in the benefits management plan. The tracking process should be ongoing throughout the lifecycle of the project or program, and should involve regular communication with stakeholders, the identification of any issues or risks, and the measurement of the actual outcomes and benefits achieved. The benefits management plan should be regularly reviewed and updated based on the results of the tracking process.

## REALIZATION: ACHIEVING THE EXPECTED BENEFITS

The final step in benefits management is the realization of the expected benefits. Realization involves ensuring that the project or program delivers the expected outcomes, benefits, and value, and that the benefits are aligned with the organization's strategic objectives.

To achieve the expected benefits, it is important to ensure that the project or program is implemented effectively, and that any issues or risks are addressed promptly. This requires a strong focus on project management, with regular reviews of progress against the benefits management plan, and the identification of any issues or risks that may impact the delivery of the benefits.

The realization of benefits also requires effective stakeholder management. This includes regular communication with stakeholders to ensure that they are aware of progress and any issues or risks that may impact the delivery of the benefits. It also includes the involvement of stakeholders in the implementation of the project or program, to ensure that their needs and expectations are being met.

The realization of benefits also requires effective change management. This includes managing the impact of the project or program on the organization, and ensuring that the organization is ready to accept and adopt the changes that are being introduced. It also involves providing the necessary training and support to ensure that the organization is able to utilize the new processes, systems, or technologies effectively.

Finally, the realization of benefits requires a focus on continuous improvement. This involves regular reviews of the benefits management plan, and the identification of opportunities to improve the delivery of benefits. It also involves the implementation of best practices and lessons learned from previous projects or programs.

In summary, the realization of benefits is a critical step in benefits management, and involves ensuring that the project or program delivers the expected outcomes, benefits, and value, and that the benefits are aligned with the organization's strategic objectives. This requires effective project management, stakeholder management, and change management, as well as a focus on continuous improvement.

The realization of benefits is an ongoing process, and requires a long-term commitment to the successful delivery of benefits.

## BENEFITS MANAGEMENT BEST PRACTICES

Effective benefits management involves a range of best practices that can help organizations to maximize the value they obtain from their projects and programs. Some of the key best practices in benefits management include:

a. Early and Ongoing Engagement of Stakeholders: Effective benefits management requires the early and ongoing engagement of stakeholders throughout the lifecycle of the project or program. This includes senior management, project teams, business users, and other stakeholders who may be impacted by the project or program.

b. Clear and Concise Definition of Benefits: The definition of benefits should be clear, concise, and based on a thorough understanding of the benefits and their relationship to the project or program objectives. The benefits should be defined in terms of their expected outcomes, and the timeframe in which they are expected to be realized.

c. Integration with Project or Program Management: Benefits management should be integrated with project or program management, and should be reflected in the overall project or program plan. This ensures that benefits management is aligned with the overall objectives of the project or program, and that the necessary resources and support are provided.

d. Regular Review and Update of the Benefits Management Plan: The benefits management plan should be regularly reviewed and updated throughout the lifecycle of the project or program, based on the results of tracking and monitoring activities. This ensures that the benefits management plan remains aligned with the project or program objectives, and that any issues or risks are addressed promptly.

e. Robust Metrics and Indicators: The metrics and indicators used to track and measure the delivery of benefits should be robust and aligned with the definition of benefits. They should be regularly reviewed and updated based on the results of tracking and monitoring activities, and should be used to identify any issues or risks that may impact the delivery of the benefits.

f. Focus on Continuous Improvement: Benefits management should be seen as an ongoing process of continuous improvement, rather than a one-time activity. Lessons learned from previous projects or programs should be incorporated into the benefits management approach, and best practices should be identified and implemented to enhance the delivery of benefits.

In summary, effective benefits management requires the early and ongoing engagement of stakeholders, a clear and concise definition of benefits, integration with project or program management, regular review and update of the benefits management plan, robust metrics and indicators, and a focus on continuous improvement. By adopting these best practices, organizations can maximize the value they obtain from their projects and programs, and achieve their strategic objectives.

## BENEFITS MANAGEMENT TOOLS AND TECHNIQUES

There are several tools and techniques that can be used to support benefits management. These tools and techniques can help organizations to identify, define, plan, track, and realize the benefits of their projects and programs. Some of the key benefits management tools and techniques include:

a. Benefits Mapping: Benefits mapping is a tool that helps organizations to identify and define the benefits of a project or program. It involves creating a visual representation of the expected outcomes and benefits, and their relationship to the project or program objectives.

b. Benefit Profiles: Benefit profiles are a tool that helps organizations to define the scope of each benefit, and to establish how it will be measured and tracked. Benefit profiles typically include a description of the benefit, the metrics or indicators that will be used to measure it, and the timeframe for delivery.

c. Benefits Dependency Network: A benefits dependency network is a tool that helps organizations to understand the dependencies between different benefits. It involves identifying the relationships between the benefits, and the impact that changes to one benefit may have on other benefits.

d. Benefits Realization Plan: A benefits realization plan is a tool that outlines how the benefits will be achieved, tracked, and realized. It includes a detailed description of each benefit, a plan for achieving it, metrics or indicators for tracking progress, and roles and responsibilities for stakeholders involved in benefits management.

e. Benefits Register: A benefits register is a tool that tracks the progress of each benefit, and compares the actual outcomes and benefits achieved to the expected outcomes and benefits defined in the benefits management plan.

f. Risk Management: Effective risk management is an essential tool for benefits management. It involves identifying and assessing risks that may impact the delivery of benefits, and developing strategies to mitigate or manage those risks.

g. Stakeholder Management: Effective stakeholder management is another essential tool for benefits management. It involves identifying and engaging with stakeholders, understanding their needs and expectations, and ensuring that they are involved in the delivery of the benefits.

In summary, benefits management tools and techniques can help organizations to identify, define, plan, track, and realize the benefits of their projects and programs. Benefits mapping, benefit profiles, benefits dependency networks, benefits realization plans, benefits registers, risk management, and stakeholder management are all key tools and techniques that can be used to support effective benefits management.

## CHALLENGES IN BENEFITS MANAGEMENT

While benefits management is an essential component of project and program management, there are several challenges that organizations may face when trying to implement a benefits management approach. Some of the key challenges in benefits management include:

a. Lack of Clarity and Consensus: One of the biggest challenges in benefits management is a lack of clarity and consensus around the expected outcomes and benefits of a project or program. This can lead to confusion and disagreement about the scope and measurement of benefits, and can make it difficult to track and realize the expected benefits.

b. Insufficient Resources: Another challenge in benefits management is insufficient resources to support the delivery of benefits. This can include a lack of funding, staff, or technology needed to achieve the benefits, and can result in delays or failure to deliver the expected benefits.

c. Unrealistic Expectations: Unrealistic expectations can also be a challenge in benefits management. This can occur when the benefits are overestimated or when the project or program is not properly aligned with the organization's strategic objectives.

Unrealistic expectations can lead to disappointment and failure to achieve the expected benefits.

d. Resistance to Change: Resistance to change can also be a challenge in benefits management. This can occur when stakeholders are not involved in the process, or when the changes introduced by the project or program are perceived as threatening or disruptive. Resistance to change can impede the realization of the expected benefits.

e. Inadequate Metrics and Indicators: Inadequate metrics and indicators can also be a challenge in benefits management. If the metrics or indicators used to track and measure the benefits are not aligned with the definition of benefits or are not robust, it can be difficult to track progress and measure the achievement of benefits.

f. Lack of Continuous Improvement: Finally, a lack of continuous improvement can be a challenge in benefits management. If organizations do not regularly review and update their benefits management approach, they may miss opportunities to improve the delivery of benefits and may fail to achieve their strategic objectives.

In summary, benefits management can face several challenges, including a lack of clarity and consensus, insufficient resources, unrealistic expectations, resistance to change, inadequate metrics and indicators, and a lack of continuous improvement. Organizations should be aware of these challenges and work to address them to maximize the value they obtain from their projects and programs.

## BENEFITS MANAGEMENT AND ORGANIZATIONAL STRATEGY

Benefits management is closely tied to an organization's strategic objectives. Effective benefits management helps to ensure that the benefits of a project or program are aligned with the organization's strategic objectives, and that the organization realizes the expected value from its investments. By aligning benefits management with organizational strategy, organizations can ensure that they are investing their resources in the right projects and programs, and that they are achieving their strategic objectives.

There are several ways in which benefits management can support organizational strategy:

a. Identification of Strategic Objectives: Benefits management can help to identify the strategic objectives of an organization. By understanding the strategic objectives, the organization can determine which projects or programs will contribute to the achievement of those objectives, and can prioritize its investments accordingly.

b. Alignment of Benefits with Strategic Objectives: Effective benefits management ensures that the benefits of a project or program are aligned with the organization's strategic objectives. This alignment ensures that the organization is investing its resources in projects and programs that will contribute to the achievement of its strategic objectives.

c. Prioritization of Investments: Benefits management can help to prioritize investments based on their expected benefits and their alignment with the organization's strategic objectives. By prioritizing investments in this way, organizations can ensure that they are investing their resources in the projects and programs that will have the greatest impact on their strategic objectives.

d. Evaluation of Investment Decisions: Benefits management can help to evaluate the success of investment decisions by tracking the progress of the projects or programs and measuring their actual benefits against the expected benefits. This evaluation provides feedback that can be used to improve future investment decisions.

e. Communication of Results: Effective benefits management requires regular communication with stakeholders, including senior management, project teams, and business users. By communicating the results of benefits management activities, organizations can ensure that all stakeholders are aware of progress and any issues or risks that may impact the delivery of the benefits. This communication also helps to ensure that stakeholders understand how the projects or programs contribute to the organization's strategic objectives.

In summary, benefits management is closely tied to organizational strategy. By aligning benefits management with organizational strategy, organizations can ensure that they are investing their resources in the right projects and programs, and that they are achieving their strategic objectives. Benefits management supports the identification of strategic objectives, alignment of benefits with strategic objectives, prioritization of investments, evaluation of investment decisions, and communication of results.

# 6.3 INVESTMENT APPRAISAL TECHNIQUES FOR PROJECT MANAGERS

Investment appraisal is a critical process that project managers use to evaluate the feasibility of a potential investment or project. It is an essential decision-making tool that helps managers to determine whether to invest in a project or not by analysing its expected returns, risks, and costs. The investment appraisal process involves identifying and analysing the various costs and benefits associated with a project and then selecting the most appropriate investment option based on the analysis.

The primary objective of investment appraisal is to ensure that the project or investment generates a positive return on investment (ROI) and adds value to the organization. By using investment appraisal techniques, project managers can assess the potential risks and rewards of a project and make informed decisions that align with the organization's strategic goals.

Investment appraisal techniques typically involve calculating key financial metrics such as internal rate of return (IRR), net present value (NPV), payback period, and profitability index. These metrics help project managers to compare and evaluate different investment opportunities and select the most profitable one.

In this section, we will focus on two of the most commonly used investment appraisal techniques: Internal Rate of Return (IRR) and Net Present Value (NPV). We will discuss the concepts, calculations, and applications of these techniques in project management.

## INTERNAL RATE OF RETURN (IRR):

Internal Rate of Return (IRR) is a popular investment appraisal technique that project managers use to evaluate the profitability of an investment. It measures the rate of return that an investment is expected to generate over its lifespan, and it is expressed as a percentage. The IRR is the discount rate that makes the net present value (NPV) of a project equal to zero.

The IRR calculation involves estimating the expected cash inflows and outflows of a project and then finding the discount rate that equates the present value of the cash inflows to the present value of the cash outflows. If the IRR is greater than the required rate of return or hurdle rate, the investment is deemed to be profitable and vice versa.

One of the advantages of IRR is that it considers the time value of money and provides a more accurate measure of profitability compared to other methods like payback period. IRR also allows project managers to compare different investment opportunities with different cash flow profiles and select the most attractive one.

However, IRR has some limitations that project managers need to be aware of. For example, it assumes that cash inflows are reinvested at the same rate as the IRR, which may not be realistic in practice. Also, IRR may give conflicting results when evaluating mutually exclusive projects that have different cash flow patterns.

In summary, IRR is a useful investment appraisal technique that project managers use to assess the profitability of an investment. It considers the time value of money and allows for comparison of different investment opportunities. However, it has some limitations that project managers need to be aware of when using it for decision making.

# NET PRESENT VALUE (NPV):

Net Present Value (NPV) is another popular investment appraisal technique used by project managers to evaluate the profitability of an investment. It measures the present value of the expected cash inflows of a project minus the present value of the expected cash outflows. A positive NPV indicates that the investment is profitable, while a negative NPV indicates that the investment is not profitable.

The NPV calculation involves discounting the future cash flows of a project back to their present values using a discount rate. The discount rate represents the required rate of return or the cost of capital of the investment. The NPV formula is as follows:

$$NPV = CF1/(1+r)^1 + CF2/(1+r)^2 + ... + CFn/(1+r)^n - \text{Initial Investment}$$

Where CF1, CF2, CFn are the expected cash inflows of the project for each year, r is the discount rate, n is the lifespan of the project in years, and Initial Investment is the initial cost of the investment.

NPV has several advantages over other investment appraisal techniques. First, it considers the time value of money, which means that it takes into account the fact that a dollar received in the future is worth less than a dollar received today due to inflation and the opportunity cost of capital. Second, it allows project managers to account for the risk of the investment by adjusting the discount rate accordingly. Finally, it enables project managers to compare different investment opportunities and select the most profitable one.

However, like IRR, NPV also has some limitations. One limitation is that it assumes that cash inflows can be reinvested at the required rate of return, which may not be possible in practice. Another limitation is that it does not consider the size of the investment or the scale of the project. Therefore, project managers should use NPV in conjunction with other investment appraisal techniques to get a more comprehensive evaluation of the investment opportunity.

In conclusion, NPV is a valuable investment appraisal technique used by project managers to evaluate the profitability of an investment. It considers the time value of money, allows for risk adjustment, and enables comparison of different investment opportunities. However, project managers need to be aware of its limitations and use it in conjunction with other techniques to make informed investment decisions.

## COMPARISON OF IRR AND NPV:

While IRR and NPV are both widely used investment appraisal techniques, they have some significant differences that project managers need to understand to make informed investment decisions.

IRR focuses on the rate of return of the investment, while NPV focuses on the total value generated by the investment. IRR measures the discount rate at which the net present value of the project's cash flows equals zero, while NPV measures the total present value of the project's cash inflows minus the total present value of the project's cash outflows, discounted at a specific rate.

One advantage of IRR is that it provides a straightforward measure of the profitability of an investment, expressed as a percentage, which makes it easy to compare different investment opportunities. However, IRR assumes that cash inflows are reinvested at the same rate, which may not be realistic in practice. In addition, IRR may give conflicting results when evaluating mutually exclusive projects that have different cash flow profiles.

On the other hand, NPV considers the time value of money and allows project managers to account for the risk of the investment by adjusting the discount rate. NPV also allows for a more accurate comparison of different investment opportunities and provides a clearer picture of the total value generated by the investment. However, NPV requires a specific discount rate to be chosen, which may be subjective and can impact the outcome of the analysis.

In practice, project managers often use both IRR and NPV to evaluate investment opportunities. If the IRR and NPV of an investment are both positive, then the investment is deemed profitable, and the project manager can consider investing in it. If the IRR and NPV are both negative, then the investment should be rejected. However, if the IRR and NPV yield different results, project managers should carefully consider other factors, such as the size and scale of the project, the level of risk, and the availability of funding, before making a decision.

In conclusion, both IRR and NPV are valuable investment appraisal techniques that project managers can use to evaluate the profitability of an investment. While they have some differences, they are often used together to provide a more comprehensive analysis of an investment opportunity.

## FACTORS AFFECTING INVESTMENT APPRAISAL:

Several factors can affect the investment appraisal process and the results of the analysis. Project managers should consider these factors when using investment appraisal techniques to evaluate investment opportunities. The following are some of the key factors that can impact investment appraisal:

a. Cost of capital: The cost of capital is the minimum rate of return that investors expect from an investment to compensate them for the risk and opportunity cost of capital. The cost of capital is a critical factor in investment appraisal as it determines the discount rate used in NPV calculations. A higher cost of capital results in a higher discount rate, which lowers the present value of future cash flows and decreases the NPV.

b. Timing of cash flows: The timing of cash flows can impact the results of investment appraisal techniques. In particular, a delay in cash inflows can decrease the IRR and NPV, while an acceleration of cash inflows can increase the IRR and NPV. Project managers should consider the timing of cash flows when evaluating investment opportunities.

c.  Risk and uncertainty: Investment appraisal is subject to risks and uncertainties that can impact the results of the analysis. Project managers should consider the level of risk associated with an investment and adjust the discount rate accordingly. They should also consider the level of uncertainty in cash flow projections and account for it in their analysis.

d.  Scale and size of the project: The scale and size of the project can impact the results of investment appraisal. Larger projects may require more investment, which can impact the cash flows and the NPV. Project managers should consider the size and scale of the project when using investment appraisal techniques.

e.  Taxes and inflation: Taxes and inflation can impact the results of investment appraisal techniques. Project managers should consider the impact of taxes on cash flows and adjust their analysis accordingly. They should also account for inflation when discounting future cash flows.

In summary, investment appraisal is subject to several factors that can impact the results of the analysis. Project managers should consider these factors when using investment appraisal techniques and adjust their analysis accordingly. By accounting for these factors, project managers can make informed investment decisions that align with their organization's strategic goals.

## CONCLUSION AND RECOMMENDATIONS:

Investment appraisal is a critical process that project managers use to evaluate the feasibility and profitability of an investment. Through investment appraisal, project managers can determine the expected returns, risks, and costs associated with a potential investment opportunity and make informed decisions that align with their organization's strategic goals.

The two most commonly used investment appraisal techniques are Internal Rate of Return (IRR) and Net Present Value (NPV). IRR measures the rate of return of an investment, while NPV measures the total value generated by the investment. While both techniques have their advantages and disadvantages, project managers often use them together to provide a more comprehensive analysis of an investment opportunity.

Project managers should also be aware of other investment appraisal techniques, such as payback period, profitability index, accounting rate of return, modified internal rate of return, and real options analysis. Each technique has its strengths and weaknesses, and project managers should choose the appropriate technique based on the specific characteristics of the investment opportunity.

Several factors can impact investment appraisal, including the cost of capital, timing of cash flows, risk and uncertainty, scale and size of the project, and taxes and inflation. Project managers should consider these factors when using investment appraisal techniques and adjust their analysis accordingly.

In conclusion, investment appraisal is a critical process that project managers should use to evaluate potential investment opportunities. By using investment appraisal techniques, project managers can make informed decisions that align with their organization's strategic goals and generate positive returns on investment.

# 6.4 UNDERSTANDING THE INFORMATION MANAGEMENT PROCESS: FROM COLLECTION TO DESTRUCTION

Information management is a process that involves collecting, storing, organizing, maintaining, disseminating, archiving, and eventually destroying information. This process helps to ensure that information is accessible, accurate, reliable, and secure. It is an essential part of modern business operations, and it plays a critical role in the success of many organizations.

The information management process can be complex and multifaceted, involving a range of different activities and technologies. Effective information management requires a clear understanding of the organization's information needs and goals, as well as an ability to apply best practices and tools to manage information effectively.

At its core, information management is about creating and maintaining an organized system for managing data and other forms of information. It involves a range of activities, including data analysis, data storage and retrieval, content management, document management, and knowledge management.

In today's fast-paced digital age, information management is more critical than ever before. The amount of data that organizations collect and generate is growing exponentially, and effective information management is crucial to making sense of this data and using it to drive business success.

## THE IMPORTANCE OF COLLECTION AND STORAGE

The first step in the information management process is collecting and storing data and other forms of information. This step is essential because it lays the foundation for all other activities in the information management process. Without accurate and reliable data, it is impossible to make informed decisions or take appropriate actions.

Effective collection and storage of information require careful planning and consideration. It is essential to define the types of data and information that are relevant to the organization and to establish processes for collecting and storing this information. This may involve the use of various tools and technologies, including databases, file servers, and cloud-based storage solutions.

Data collection should be systematic, consistent, and timely to ensure that the information is up-to-date and accurate. In addition, data quality must be monitored regularly to identify and address any issues or errors that may arise.

Data storage is equally important. Effective storage solutions should be designed to ensure that information is easily accessible, secure, and protected against loss or corruption. Organizations may use a range of storage solutions, including on-premises servers, cloud-based storage solutions, and other types of storage media.

In addition to ensuring that data is collected and stored effectively, it is important to establish clear policies and procedures for accessing and using the information. This includes implementing appropriate security measures to protect sensitive data, such as passwords, encryption, and firewalls.

In summary, effective collection and storage of data and information are crucial components of the information management process. It lays the foundation for all other activities in the process and is essential for making informed decisions and taking appropriate actions.

Organizations must implement best practices and tools to collect and store information effectively and to ensure that it is easily accessible, secure, and protected against loss or corruption.

## CURATION: ORGANIZING AND MAINTAINING INFORMATION

Curation is the process of organizing and maintaining information to ensure that it is accurate, up-to-date, and easily accessible. It involves activities such as data cleaning, data integration, metadata management, and taxonomy development.

Effective curation of information is essential for ensuring that the data and information are relevant, useful, and meaningful. Curation helps to eliminate redundant, outdated, or inaccurate information, making it easier to find and use the information when needed.

One of the primary goals of curation is to ensure that information is organized in a way that is easy to navigate and search. This may involve the development of taxonomies or classification systems to categorize information and make it easier to find. Metadata, such as descriptive tags or keywords, can also be added to information to help users find what they need more easily.

Data cleaning is another critical aspect of curation. This involves identifying and correcting errors, inconsistencies, or inaccuracies in the data. Common data cleaning techniques include standardization, normalization, and validation. This helps to ensure that the data is accurate and reliable, making it more useful for decision-making and other activities.

Data integration is also an essential aspect of curation. This involves combining data from multiple sources to create a unified view of the information. This can be challenging, as data from different sources may be stored in different formats or have different levels of quality. Effective data integration requires careful planning, clear processes, and appropriate tools and technologies.

Overall, effective curation of information is essential for ensuring that data and information are accurate, up-to-date, and easily accessible. It helps to eliminate redundancies and inaccuracies, making it easier to find and use the information when needed. Organizations must implement best practices and tools for curation to ensure that their data and information are effectively organized and maintained.

## DISSEMINATION: SHARING INFORMATION EFFECTIVELY

Dissemination is the process of sharing information with the intended audience. Effective dissemination ensures that the right information is delivered to the right people at the right time and in the right format. It helps to ensure that the information is accessible, understandable, and usable by those who need it.

Dissemination can take many forms, including reports, dashboards, presentations, emails, or newsletters. The choice of format depends on the nature of the information, the intended audience, and the purpose of the communication.

Effective dissemination requires a clear understanding of the audience and their needs. This involves identifying who the information is intended for and what they need to know. It is also essential to consider how the information will be used and to present it in a way that is understandable and meaningful to the audience.

Another important aspect of dissemination is the use of technology. Advances in technology have made it easier than ever to share information across different platforms and channels. For example, organizations may use social media, video conferencing, or collaboration tools to disseminate information to a wider audience.

It is also important to ensure that the information is secure and protected against unauthorized access. This involves implementing appropriate security measures, such as encryption, firewalls, or access controls.

Finally, dissemination should be evaluated to ensure that it is effective. This involves assessing whether the information is reaching the intended audience, whether it is being used as intended, and whether it is having the desired impact.

In summary, effective dissemination of information is critical for ensuring that the right information is delivered to the right people at the right time and in the right format. It requires a clear understanding of the audience and their needs, the use of appropriate technology, and the implementation of appropriate security measures. Dissemination should also be evaluated to ensure that it is effective in achieving its intended purpose.

## ARCHIVING: PRESERVING INFORMATION FOR THE FUTURE

Archiving is the process of preserving information for long-term use. It involves the selection, preservation, and management of records that have long-term value for the organization. Effective archiving helps to ensure that important records are preserved and accessible for future use.

Archiving involves several key activities, including appraisal, retention, and disposal. Appraisal involves identifying records that have long-term value and should be preserved. Retention involves determining how long records should be kept and in what format. Disposal involves the secure and responsible destruction of records that are no longer needed.

One of the primary goals of archiving is to ensure that records are preserved in a way that ensures their authenticity, integrity, and accessibility. This requires the use of appropriate storage conditions, such as temperature and humidity controls, and the use of appropriate preservation techniques, such as digitization or microfilming.

Another key aspect of archiving is the use of metadata to describe the records and make them easier to find and use. Metadata may include information about the content of the records, their creator, their date of creation, and their format.

Effective archiving requires careful planning and consideration. It is essential to establish clear policies and procedures for archiving, including the selection criteria for records to be archived, the retention schedule, and the disposal process. It is also important to ensure that the archiving process is secure and that records are protected against unauthorized access, loss, or destruction.

Overall, effective archiving is critical for preserving important records and ensuring that they are accessible for future use. It involves several key activities, including appraisal, retention, and disposal, as well as the use of appropriate storage conditions and preservation techniques. Organizations must implement best practices and policies for archiving to ensure that their records are effectively managed and preserved.

## THE IMPORTANCE OF SECURE DESTRUCTION

Secure destruction is the process of destroying information that is no longer needed in a way that ensures that it cannot be accessed or retrieved by unauthorized parties. This is an essential aspect of information management because it helps to protect sensitive information from being accessed by individuals who should not have access to it.

Secure destruction can take many forms, depending on the nature of the information and the medium in which it is stored. For paper documents, secure destruction may involve shredding or incineration. For electronic information, secure destruction may involve degaussing, wiping, or physically destroying the storage media.

Secure destruction is essential for protecting sensitive information, such as personal data, financial information, or trade secrets. It helps to ensure that this information cannot be accessed or used by unauthorized individuals, reducing the risk of identity theft, fraud, or other types of cybercrime.

Secure destruction is also necessary to comply with legal and regulatory requirements. Many industries, such as healthcare or finance, have strict rules regarding the destruction of sensitive information. Failure to comply with these rules can result in significant fines or legal consequences.

Effective secure destruction requires a clear understanding of the information that needs to be destroyed and the risks associated with its retention. It is essential to establish clear policies and procedures for secure destruction, including the types of information that should be destroyed, the method of destruction, and the frequency of destruction.

It is also important to ensure that the destruction process is secure and that information is protected against unauthorized access or retrieval. This may involve implementing appropriate security measures, such as access controls, encryption, or physical security measures.

In summary, secure destruction is an essential aspect of information management. It helps to protect sensitive information from being accessed or used by unauthorized individuals, reduces the risk of identity theft or fraud, and ensures compliance with legal and regulatory requirements. Effective secure destruction requires clear policies and procedures, appropriate security measures, and a clear understanding of the risks associated with retaining sensitive information.

## BEST PRACTICES FOR INFORMATION MANAGEMENT

Effective information management requires the implementation of best practices to ensure that data and information are collected, stored, organized, maintained, disseminated, archived, and destroyed effectively. Here are some best practices for information management:

a. Establish Clear Policies and Procedures: Establishing clear policies and procedures is essential for effective information management. It helps to ensure that everyone in the organization understands the expectations and requirements for managing information.

b. Use Technology Effectively: Technology plays a critical role in information management. Organizations must use technology effectively to collect, store, organize, maintain, disseminate, archive, and destroy information. This may involve using tools such as databases, content management systems, and archiving solutions.

c. Ensure Data Quality: Effective information management requires accurate and reliable data. Organizations must implement processes for ensuring data quality, including data cleaning, data integration, and data validation.

d. Protect Sensitive Information: Protecting sensitive information is crucial for effective information management. Organizations must implement appropriate security measures, such as encryption, access controls, and firewalls, to protect sensitive information from unauthorized access or retrieval.

e. Plan for Disaster Recovery: Organizations must plan for disaster recovery to ensure that information can be restored in the event of a disaster or system failure. This involves backing up data regularly and implementing appropriate recovery procedures.

f. Establish Clear Retention Policies: Establishing clear retention policies is essential for effective information management. It helps to ensure that information is retained for the appropriate length of time and in the appropriate format.

g. Provide Training and Support: Providing training and support to employees is crucial for effective information management. This ensures that everyone in the organization understands the importance of managing information and knows how to do so effectively.

Overall, effective information management requires the implementation of best practices to ensure that data and information are collected, stored, organized, maintained, disseminated, archived, and destroyed effectively. By following these best practices, organizations can ensure that their information management processes are effective, efficient, and secure.

# 6.5 KEY FACTORS FOR SUCCESSFUL PROJECT OUTCOMES

Defining what constitutes project success is crucial in ensuring successful project outcomes. Without a clear understanding of what the project is expected to achieve, it is difficult to measure its success. Typically, project success is measured in terms of achieving project objectives, completing the project within budget, meeting the project timeline, and meeting quality standards.

Project objectives should be SMART (specific, measurable, achievable, relevant, and time-bound) and should align with the organization's strategic goals. It is important to involve stakeholders in defining project success criteria to ensure that everyone has a clear understanding of what is expected.

Once project success criteria are defined, they should be communicated to the project team and regularly reviewed to ensure that the project is on track. Having a shared understanding of project success criteria helps to keep the project team focused and motivated, and helps to ensure that project outcomes are aligned with organizational objectives.

## IMPORTANCE OF REPORTING PROJECT FACTORS:

Reporting project factors is critical to ensuring successful project outcomes. It allows project managers and stakeholders to monitor progress, identify potential issues, and make informed decisions to keep the project on track.

Project reporting should be timely, accurate, and concise, and should provide a clear and comprehensive picture of project status. The information reported should be relevant and actionable, and should help stakeholders understand how the project is progressing towards achieving its objectives.

Regular project reporting helps to build trust and transparency with stakeholders and helps to manage expectations. It also helps to identify potential risks and issues before they become major problems. For example, if a project is behind schedule or over budget, project reporting can highlight this issue early on, allowing stakeholders to make informed decisions to mitigate the impact.

In addition to regular project reporting, it is important to establish a project governance framework to ensure that project reporting is effective. This includes defining roles and responsibilities, setting up communication channels, and establishing a process for escalating issues. Effective project governance helps to ensure that project reporting is aligned with organizational objectives and that project outcomes are achieved on time, within budget, and to the expected quality standards.

## PROJECT PLANNING:

Project planning is a critical factor in ensuring successful project outcomes. A well-planned project sets the foundation for successful project delivery and helps to manage project risks and uncertainties. Project planning involves developing a project management plan, defining project scope, identifying project objectives, and developing a project schedule and budget.

The project management plan outlines how the project will be executed, monitored, and controlled. It includes information on the project scope, objectives, stakeholders, project schedule, budget, risk management, communication plan, and quality management plan. The project management plan is a living document that should be regularly reviewed and updated throughout the project lifecycle.

Defining project scope involves identifying the boundaries of the project, including what is included and what is excluded from the project. This helps to manage stakeholder expectations and ensures that the project team is working towards a common goal.

Identifying project objectives involves defining what the project is expected to achieve, and how success will be measured. Project objectives should be SMART, and should align with the organization's strategic goals.

Developing a project schedule and budget involves breaking down the project scope into manageable tasks and estimating the time and resources required to complete each task. The project schedule and budget should be realistic and achievable, and should be regularly reviewed and updated as the project progresses.

Overall, effective project planning helps to ensure that project objectives are clearly defined, resources are allocated appropriately, and risks are managed effectively, resulting in successful project outcomes.

## STAKEHOLDER MANAGEMENT:

Stakeholder management is a critical factor in ensuring successful project outcomes. Effective stakeholder management involves identifying stakeholders, understanding their needs and expectations, and developing strategies to engage and communicate with them throughout the project lifecycle.

Stakeholders are individuals or groups who have an interest in the project, or who may be affected by the project outcomes. Stakeholders can include project sponsors, project team members, customers, suppliers, regulators, and the wider community.

Understanding stakeholder needs and expectations is key to managing stakeholder relationships. This involves engaging with stakeholders to understand their interests, concerns, and expectations, and developing strategies to address them. Effective stakeholder engagement helps to build trust, manage expectations, and minimize project risks.

Developing a stakeholder engagement plan is an important part of stakeholder management. The stakeholder engagement plan outlines how stakeholders will be engaged, what information will be communicated, and how feedback will be gathered and acted upon. The stakeholder engagement plan should be regularly reviewed and updated to ensure that stakeholder needs and expectations are being met.

Overall, effective stakeholder management helps to ensure that project outcomes are aligned with stakeholder needs and expectations, and that project risks are minimized. By engaging stakeholders throughout the project lifecycle, project managers can build trust and credibility, manage stakeholder expectations, and deliver successful project outcomes.

## RISK MANAGEMENT:

Risk management is an essential factor in ensuring successful project outcomes. Risk management involves identifying potential risks, assessing their likelihood and impact, and developing strategies to mitigate or manage them. Effective risk management helps to minimize project uncertainties and ensure that project outcomes are achieved on time, within budget, and to the expected quality standards.

Risk identification involves identifying potential risks that may impact the project, such as resource constraints, technical issues, regulatory changes, or changes in customer needs. Risk assessment involves evaluating the likelihood and impact of each identified risk and prioritizing them based on their significance.

Risk mitigation involves developing strategies to reduce the likelihood and impact of identified risks. This may involve developing contingency plans, identifying alternative approaches, or implementing risk management measures. Risk management plans should be regularly reviewed and updated throughout the project lifecycle to ensure that new risks are identified and managed effectively.

Effective risk management also involves managing opportunities. Opportunities are events or situations that could have a positive impact on the project. Identifying and managing opportunities can help to maximize project benefits and ensure that project outcomes are achieved to the best possible standard.

Overall, effective risk management helps to minimize project uncertainties, improve project outcomes, and build stakeholder confidence. By identifying and managing risks and opportunities, project managers can ensure that project outcomes are achieved on time, within budget, and to the expected quality standards.

## PROJECT COMMUNICATION:

Project communication is a key factor in ensuring successful project outcomes. Effective communication helps to build trust, manage expectations, and ensure that project goals and objectives are clearly understood by all stakeholders.

Project communication involves the exchange of information between project stakeholders, including the project team, project sponsors, customers, suppliers, and other interested parties. Effective project communication should be timely, accurate, and targeted to the needs of each stakeholder.

Developing a project communication plan is an important part of project communication. The communication plan outlines how project information will be communicated, who will be responsible for communicating it, and how often it will be communicated. The communication plan should also include contingency plans for managing unexpected issues or changes in project status.

Communication channels should be established to ensure that project information is shared in a timely and effective manner. Communication channels can include project meetings, status reports, email, phone calls, and social media. The choice of communication channel should be based on the needs of each stakeholder and the type of information being communicated.

Effective project communication also involves listening to stakeholder feedback and responding to their concerns. Feedback should be actively sought from stakeholders throughout the project lifecycle, and actions should be taken to address any concerns or issues that are raised.

Overall, effective project communication helps to build trust and credibility, manage expectations, and ensure that project goals and objectives are clearly understood by all stakeholders. By communicating project information effectively, project managers can minimize project risks, improve project outcomes, and build stakeholder confidence.

## RESOURCE MANAGEMENT:

Resource management is a crucial factor in ensuring successful project outcomes. Resource management involves identifying, allocating, and managing the resources required to complete the project. Resources can include people, equipment, materials, and facilities.

Effective resource management requires a thorough understanding of project requirements and the availability of resources. The project team should have the necessary skills and experience to complete the project, and resources should be allocated in a way that maximizes their efficiency and effectiveness.

Resource allocation should be based on project priorities and should take into account the availability of resources, the project schedule, and the needs of each project task. Resource allocation should also be reviewed regularly to ensure that resources are being used effectively and efficiently.

Effective resource management also involves managing project dependencies. Project dependencies are tasks or activities that must be completed before other tasks can be started. Identifying and managing project dependencies helps to ensure that project tasks are completed in the correct order, minimizing project delays and improving project outcomes.

Overall, effective resource management helps to ensure that project tasks are completed on time, within budget, and to the expected quality standards. By identifying and allocating resources effectively, project managers can maximize the efficiency and effectiveness of the project team, minimize project risks, and deliver successful project outcomes.

## Project Monitoring and Control:

Project monitoring and control is an important factor in ensuring successful project outcomes. Project monitoring involves tracking project progress, identifying issues and risks, and reporting project status to stakeholders. Project control involves taking corrective actions to keep the project on track and managing project changes.

Effective project monitoring and control requires regular project status updates and a thorough understanding of project risks and issues. Project progress should be tracked against project plans, and any deviations should be identified and addressed promptly. Project managers should also regularly review project risks and issues and take corrective actions to minimize their impact.

Project changes should be managed using a change management process. The change management process should include a change control board or committee, which is responsible for reviewing and approving project changes. Changes should be documented, and their impact on the project schedule, budget, and scope should be assessed before they are approved.

Effective project monitoring and control also involves establishing project metrics and key performance indicators (KPIs). Project metrics and KPIs should be aligned with project objectives and should be regularly monitored and reported to stakeholders. This helps to ensure that project outcomes are achieved on time, within budget, and to the expected quality standards.

Overall, effective project monitoring and control helps to ensure that project outcomes are achieved on time, within budget, and to the expected quality standards. By monitoring project progress, identifying risks and issues, and taking corrective actions, project managers can minimize project risks, improve project outcomes, and build stakeholder confidence.

## CONTINUOUS IMPROVEMENT:

Continuous improvement is an important factor in ensuring successful project outcomes. Continuous improvement involves identifying areas for improvement, developing strategies to address them, and implementing changes to improve project processes and outcomes.

Continuous improvement requires a culture of learning and feedback within the project team. Project team members should be encouraged to share their experiences and ideas for improvement, and feedback should be sought from stakeholders throughout the project lifecycle.

Effective continuous improvement also involves the use of project retrospectives. Project retrospectives are a structured review process that allows project teams to reflect on project successes and challenges, identify opportunities for improvement, and develop strategies to address them.

Project retrospectives should be conducted regularly, and their outcomes should be used to inform future project planning and decision-making. The insights gained from project retrospectives can be used to improve project processes, identify best practices, and minimize project risks.

Overall, effective continuous improvement helps to ensure that project outcomes are continuously improved, and that project processes are optimized to deliver successful project outcomes. By encouraging a culture of learning and feedback, and using project retrospectives to inform project planning and decision-making, project managers can improve project outcomes, minimize project risks, and build stakeholder confidence.

## LESSONS LEARNED AND POST-PROJECT EVALUATION:

Lessons learned and post-project evaluation are important factors in ensuring successful project outcomes. Lessons learned involve capturing and documenting project experiences and identifying areas for improvement. Post-project evaluation involves reviewing the project outcomes and assessing the project's success against project objectives.

Lessons learned involve capturing both positive and negative project experiences. This includes what worked well and what did not work well during the project. Capturing these experiences allows project managers to identify areas for improvement and implement changes in future projects.

Lessons learned should be captured throughout the project lifecycle and should be documented in a lessons learned repository. The lessons learned repository should be regularly reviewed and updated to ensure that new lessons learned are captured and shared with the project team.

Post-project evaluation involves assessing the project outcomes and determining the success of the project. This includes reviewing the project objectives, schedule, budget, and quality standards, and assessing how well they were achieved.

Post-project evaluation should be conducted after the project has been completed and should involve all project stakeholders. The outcomes of the post-project evaluation should be documented and shared with the project team, stakeholders, and senior management.

Overall, effective lessons learned and post-project evaluation helps to ensure that project outcomes are continuously improved, and that project processes are optimized to deliver successful project outcomes. By capturing and documenting project experiences, and assessing project outcomes against project objectives, project managers can improve project outcomes, minimize project risks, and build stakeholder confidence.

# 6.6 The Relationship Between Deployment Baseline and Project Management Plan in Linear and Iterative Life Cycles

Deployment baseline is an essential aspect of project management that defines the end state of a project. It refers to a specific point in time where a project reaches a stable and reliable state, where all critical functions are met, and the project is ready for deployment or release. The deployment baseline includes all the necessary requirements, features, and functionalities agreed upon by stakeholders, ensuring that the project meets all the necessary criteria.

The deployment baseline acts as a reference point for the project team, providing clarity on the end goal and a measure of progress. It helps to align the project team's efforts and activities towards achieving the project's objectives, ensuring that they are all working towards a common goal. The deployment baseline is particularly important for projects that involve multiple teams, stakeholders, and suppliers, as it provides a shared understanding of the project's goals and objectives.

The development of a project management plan must take into account the deployment baseline. The plan should define the activities, timelines, and resources required to achieve the deployment baseline, ensuring that all necessary steps are taken to reach the end state. The plan should also outline the quality assurance measures and testing protocols required to ensure that the deployment baseline is met.

In linear and iterative life cycles, the deployment baseline plays a critical role in determining the project's progress and success. In linear life cycles, the deployment baseline represents the final deliverable, which is usually a product or service. In iterative life cycles, the deployment baseline represents the current state of the project, with each iteration aiming to achieve the deployment baseline.

## DEVELOPING A PROJECT MANAGEMENT PLAN IN LINEAR LIFE CYCLES

In linear life cycles, also known as waterfall models, the project progresses in a linear, sequential manner from concept to transition. The development of a project management plan in linear life cycles requires a structured approach that ensures that the project meets its objectives and achieves the deployment baseline.

The project management plan in linear life cycles is typically developed during the definition phase, where the project team defines the project's scope, objectives, and requirements. The plan should also identify the necessary resources, timelines, and milestones required to achieve the project's goals. The project management plan should also outline the quality assurance measures and testing protocols required to ensure that the deployment baseline is met.

In linear life cycles, the project team follows a predefined set of steps or phases, each building on the previous one. The project management plan should outline the specific deliverables required at each stage of the project and identify the critical path for achieving the deployment baseline. The critical path refers to the sequence of activities that must be completed on time to ensure that the project meets its objectives and achieves the deployment baseline.

The project management plan in linear life cycles should also identify potential risks and develop risk mitigation strategies to minimize the impact of any unforeseen issues. The plan should also define the communication and reporting protocols required to keep stakeholders informed of the project's progress and any changes in scope or timelines.

Overall, the development of a project management plan in linear life cycles requires a structured approach that ensures that the project meets its objectives and achieves the deployment baseline within the defined timelines and resources.

## THE ROLE OF DEPLOYMENT BASELINE IN LINEAR LIFE CYCLES

In linear life cycles, the deployment baseline represents the final deliverable of the project, which is typically a product or service. The deployment baseline serves as a reference point for the project team, providing clarity on the end goal and a measure of progress.

The deployment baseline plays a critical role in determining the project's success in linear life cycles. The project team must ensure that all requirements are met, and the product or service is of high quality and meets stakeholders' expectations. The deployment baseline also helps to ensure that the project is delivered on time and within budget.

The deployment baseline in linear life cycles is typically established during the definition phase and refined during the deployment phase. The project team should continuously monitor the project's progress and make any necessary adjustments to ensure that the deployment baseline is met.

The deployment baseline in linear life cycles also helps to ensure that the project meets regulatory and compliance requirements. It serves as a reference point for quality assurance and testing protocols, ensuring that the product or service meets all necessary criteria.

Overall, the deployment baseline in linear life cycles plays a critical role in determining the project's success. It provides a reference point for the project team and stakeholders, ensuring that the project meets its objectives, is of high quality, and is delivered on time and within budget.

## DEVELOPING A PROJECT MANAGEMENT PLAN IN ITERATIVE LIFE CYCLES

In iterative life cycles, also known as agile models, the project progresses through a series of iterations, with each iteration building on the previous one. The development of a project management plan in iterative life cycles requires a flexible and adaptive approach that enables the project team to respond to changing requirements and feedback from stakeholders.

The project management plan in iterative life cycles is typically developed during the definition phase, where the project team defines the project's scope, objectives, and requirements. The plan should also identify the necessary resources, timelines, and milestones required to achieve the project's goals. However, unlike linear life cycles, the plan in iterative life cycles is not fixed and can be modified as the project progresses.

The project management plan in iterative life cycles should outline the specific deliverables required for each iteration and identify the critical path for achieving the deployment baseline. The plan should also define the quality assurance measures and testing protocols required to ensure that the deployment baseline is met for each iteration.

In iterative life cycles, the project team follows an iterative approach that involves developing a minimum viable product (MVP) and then refining it through a series of iterations. Each iteration involves feedback from stakeholders, which is then used to refine the MVP and ensure that it meets the necessary requirements and achieves the deployment baseline.

The project management plan in iterative life cycles should also identify potential risks and develop risk mitigation strategies to minimize the impact of any unforeseen issues. The plan should also define the communication and reporting protocols required to keep stakeholders informed of the project's progress and any changes in scope or timelines.

Overall, the development of a project management plan in iterative life cycles requires a flexible and adaptive approach that enables the project team to respond to changing requirements and feedback from stakeholders. The plan should outline the specific deliverables required for each iteration and identify the critical path for achieving the deployment baseline, while also allowing for modifications as the project progresses.

## THE ROLE OF DEPLOYMENT BASELINE IN ITERATIVE LIFE CYCLES

In iterative life cycles, the deployment baseline represents the current state of the project, with each iteration aiming to achieve the deployment baseline. The deployment baseline serves as a reference point for the project team, providing clarity on the end goal and a measure of progress.

The deployment baseline plays a critical role in determining the project's success in iterative life cycles. Each iteration aims to refine the MVP and ensure that it meets the necessary requirements and achieves the deployment baseline. The deployment baseline helps to ensure that the project is delivered on time, within budget, and meets stakeholder expectations.

The deployment baseline in iterative life cycles is typically established during the definition phase and refined through a series of iterations. The project team should continuously monitor the project's progress and make any necessary adjustments to ensure that the deployment baseline is met for each iteration.

The deployment baseline in iterative life cycles also helps to ensure that the project is responsive to changing requirements and feedback from stakeholders. It serves as a reference point for quality assurance

343

and testing protocols, ensuring that the product or service meets all necessary criteria and achieves the deployment baseline for each iteration.

Overall, the deployment baseline in iterative life cycles plays a critical role in determining the project's success. It provides a reference point for the project team and stakeholders, ensuring that the project meets its objectives, is of high quality, and is delivered on time and within budget. The deployment baseline also enables the project to be responsive to changing requirements and feedback from stakeholders, ensuring that the project meets their needs and expectations.

## COMPARING THE RELATIONSHIP BETWEEN DEPLOYMENT BASELINE AND PROJECT MANAGEMENT PLAN IN LINEAR AND ITERATIVE LIFE CYCLES

The relationship between deployment baseline and project management plan in linear and iterative life cycles differs significantly. In linear life cycles, the deployment baseline represents the final deliverable, while in iterative life cycles, the deployment baseline represents the current state of the project.

In linear life cycles, the project management plan is typically developed during the definition phase and outlines the specific steps required to achieve the deployment baseline. The plan is often fixed and does not allow for significant modifications as the project progresses. The project team follows a predefined set of steps or phases, with each phase building on the previous one towards the final deliverable.

In contrast, the project management plan in iterative life cycles is typically more flexible and adaptive. The plan is developed during the definition phase but is designed to be modified as the project progresses. The project team follows an iterative approach, with each iteration building on the previous one towards achieving the deployment baseline. The plan outlines the specific deliverables required for each iteration, allowing the team to respond to changing requirements and feedback from stakeholders.

The deployment baseline in linear life cycles serves as a reference point for the project team and stakeholders, providing clarity on the end goal and a measure of progress. The deployment baseline is typically established during the definition phase and refined during the deployment phase, with the project team ensuring that all requirements are met, and the product or service is of high quality and meets stakeholders' expectations.

In contrast, the deployment baseline in iterative life cycles represents the current state of the project, with each iteration aiming to achieve the deployment baseline. The deployment baseline helps to ensure that the project is delivered on time, within budget, and meets stakeholder expectations. The deployment baseline is continuously refined through a series of iterations, with each iteration building on the previous one towards achieving the final product or service.

Overall, the relationship between deployment baseline and project management plan in linear and iterative life cycles differs significantly. While both approaches aim to achieve the deployment baseline, linear life cycles follow a more structured and fixed approach, while iterative life cycles follow a more flexible and adaptive approach. The choice of approach depends on the project's nature, scope, and requirements, as well as the stakeholders' expectations and project team's capabilities.

## BEST PRACTICES FOR INCORPORATING DEPLOYMENT BASELINE IN PROJECT MANAGEMENT PLANNING

Incorporating deployment baseline in project management planning is critical to ensuring that the project meets its objectives, is of high quality, and is delivered on time and within budget. Here are some best practices for incorporating deployment baseline in project management planning:

a. Define clear and specific requirements: Clearly defining the project requirements ensures that the project team has a clear understanding of the project goals and objectives. The requirements should be measurable, achievable, relevant, and time-bound, making it easier to track progress towards achieving the deployment baseline.

b. Develop a comprehensive project management plan: A comprehensive project management plan outlines the specific steps required to achieve the deployment baseline, including timelines, milestones, and resource requirements. The plan should also define quality assurance measures and testing protocols required to ensure that the deployment baseline is met.

c. Use an iterative approach: Using an iterative approach enables the project team to respond to changing requirements and feedback from stakeholders, ensuring that the project meets their needs and expectations. Each iteration should aim to achieve the deployment baseline, with the deployment baseline continuously refined through a series of iterations.

d. Monitor progress and adjust as necessary: Monitoring the project's progress enables the project team to identify any issues or challenges that may impact the project's ability to achieve the deployment baseline. The team should adjust the project management plan as necessary, making changes to ensure that the deployment baseline is met.

e. Incorporate risk management: Risk management is critical to minimizing the impact of unforeseen issues on the project's ability to achieve the deployment baseline. The project team should identify potential risks and develop risk mitigation strategies to ensure that the project stays on track towards achieving the deployment baseline.

f. Foster effective communication and collaboration: Effective communication and collaboration are critical to ensuring that the project team and stakeholders are aligned towards achieving the deployment baseline. The project team should define communication protocols and foster a collaborative environment to ensure that all stakeholders are informed and engaged throughout the project's lifecycle.

g. Continuously evaluate and improve: Continuous evaluation and improvement are critical to ensuring that the project meets its objectives and achieves the deployment baseline. The project team should continuously evaluate the project's progress and adjust the project management plan as necessary, making changes to ensure that the deployment baseline is met. The team should also identify lessons learned and best practices to improve future projects.

Overall, incorporating deployment baseline in project management planning requires a structured and flexible approach that ensures that the project meets its objectives, is of high quality, and is delivered on time and within budget. By following these best practices, the project team can ensure that the deployment baseline is achieved, and the project meets stakeholders' needs and expectations.

# 6.7 THE SIGNIFICANCE OF DEVELOPING A PROJECT MANAGEMENT PLAN

A project management plan is a comprehensive document that outlines the strategy and approach for managing a project from start to finish. It defines the goals, objectives, timelines, resources, and constraints of the project and serves as a roadmap for the project team. Developing a project management plan is a critical step in any project because it lays the foundation for success.

The purpose of a project management plan is to provide a structured approach to project management that ensures all aspects of the project are coordinated and controlled. It serves as a blueprint that guides the project team through the definition and deployment phases of the project. The plan outlines the roles and responsibilities of team members, identifies potential risks and opportunities, and provides a framework for making decisions throughout the project lifecycle.

Without a project management plan, it is difficult to ensure that all aspects of the project are aligned and that everyone is working towards the same goals. It can also lead to confusion, delays, and cost overruns if the project is not managed effectively. Therefore, it is important to develop a project management plan before starting any project to ensure that it is successful and delivers the desired outcomes.

## PROVIDES A CLEAR SCOPE AND OBJECTIVES

One of the most critical aspects of a project management plan is defining the scope and objectives of the project. The scope outlines what the project will deliver, and the objectives define what the project aims to achieve. Without a clear understanding of the scope and objectives, the project team may waste time and resources working on tasks that are not essential or fail to deliver the desired outcomes.

The project management plan helps define the scope and objectives by providing a clear understanding of the project's goals and what needs to be accomplished to achieve those goals. It outlines the deliverables and milestones that need to be completed and identifies any constraints or limitations that may impact the project's success. It also provides a framework for managing changes to the project scope and objectives throughout the project's lifecycle.

By having a well-defined project scope and objectives, the project team can focus their efforts on completing the essential tasks, ensuring that the project is completed on time, within budget, and with the desired outcomes. A clear scope and objectives also help manage stakeholder expectations and promote alignment among team members, stakeholders, and sponsors.

## HELPS TO DEFINE ROLES AND RESPONSIBILITIES

A project management plan helps to define the roles and responsibilities of each team member involved in the project. By defining the responsibilities of each team member, the plan ensures that everyone knows what is expected of them and what their specific contributions to the project are. It also helps to avoid confusion, duplication of effort, and potential conflicts by establishing clear lines of authority and accountability.

The project management plan outlines the roles and responsibilities of the project manager, project team members, stakeholders, sponsors, and other parties involved in the project. It provides a clear understanding of who is responsible for what tasks, what decisions they are authorized to make, and how they will be held accountable for their actions.

Defining roles and responsibilities through the project management plan helps to ensure that everyone is on the same page and working towards the same goals. This leads to better collaboration, improved communication, and higher levels of engagement from team members. It also helps to reduce the risk of misunderstandings, errors, and omissions that could lead to project delays, cost overruns, or failure to meet project objectives.

## ENSURES EFFECTIVE RESOURCE ALLOCATION

Effective resource allocation is crucial to the success of any project. A project management plan helps to ensure that the resources needed to complete the project are identified, allocated, and utilized efficiently. Resources may include personnel, equipment, materials, and financial resources.

The project management plan outlines the resource requirements for the project, including the number and types of personnel needed, the equipment required, and the materials necessary to complete the project. It also outlines the budget for the project and how it will be managed throughout the project's lifecycle.

By ensuring effective resource allocation, the project management plan helps to minimize waste and maximize efficiency. It ensures that resources are used where they are needed most and that they are not wasted on tasks that are not critical to the project's success. This leads to cost savings and helps to ensure that the project is completed on time and within budget.

Additionally, effective resource allocation helps to improve team morale by ensuring that team members have the resources they need to complete their tasks effectively. It also helps to manage stakeholder expectations by ensuring that the project is completed on time and within budget.

## Establishes Communication Protocols and Reporting Procedures

Effective communication is essential for the success of any project. A project management plan helps to establish communication protocols and reporting procedures, ensuring that information is communicated effectively and efficiently throughout the project lifecycle.

The project management plan outlines the communication channels that will be used for various aspects of the project, including regular team meetings, progress updates, and status reports. It also establishes the frequency and format of communication, ensuring that all stakeholders are kept informed of the project's progress.

Effective communication protocols and reporting procedures help to manage stakeholder expectations, build trust, and promote transparency. They also help to identify and resolve issues early, reducing the risk of project delays and cost overruns. By ensuring that all stakeholders are informed, the project management plan helps to ensure that decisions are made with the best available information.

Furthermore, communication protocols and reporting procedures ensure that the project team is aligned with the project's objectives and goals. This helps to keep the team motivated, engaged, and focused on the tasks at hand. It also helps to promote collaboration, coordination, and cooperation among team members and stakeholders.

## Mitigates Risks and Anticipates Contingencies

Every project involves risks, and the project management plan helps to identify potential risks, evaluate their impact, and develop strategies to mitigate them. The project management plan also includes contingency plans, which are strategies put in place to address unexpected events that may arise during the project's lifecycle.

The project management plan outlines the risk management strategy for the project, which includes risk identification, risk analysis, risk response planning, and risk monitoring and control. It also includes contingency plans for possible risks that may impact the project's timeline, budget, or outcome.

By identifying and addressing risks early in the project lifecycle, the project management plan helps to mitigate the potential impact of those risks. This helps to ensure that the project is completed on time and within budget, even if unexpected events occur.

Contingency plans included in the project management plan help to prepare the project team for unexpected events and ensure that they are ready to respond quickly and effectively. This helps to reduce the impact of unexpected events, minimizing delays, and additional costs.

Furthermore, by anticipating contingencies, the project management plan helps to build stakeholder confidence by demonstrating that the project team is proactive in managing risks and is prepared to deal with unexpected events. It also helps to maintain the project team's focus on project objectives, even in the face of unexpected events.

## FACILITATES MONITORING AND CONTROL

A project management plan helps to monitor and control project progress, ensuring that the project is on track and that issues are identified and addressed promptly. The project management plan outlines the monitoring and control strategy for the project, which includes tracking progress against the plan, identifying and managing issues, and taking corrective action when necessary.

The project management plan also defines the metrics and performance indicators that will be used to measure progress against the plan. This helps the project team to identify trends and patterns, evaluate the effectiveness of project management processes, and make data-driven decisions.

Monitoring and control also help to manage stakeholder expectations by providing timely updates on the project's progress. It helps to build stakeholder confidence by demonstrating that the project team is actively managing the project and is committed to delivering the project objectives.

By facilitating monitoring and control, the project management plan also helps to identify potential risks and issues early, allowing the project team to take corrective action before they become major problems. This helps to reduce the risk of project delays and cost overruns and ensures that the project is completed on time and within budget.

Moreover, monitoring and control provide feedback to the project team, enabling them to adjust their approach as necessary to achieve the project objectives. This helps to ensure that the project is delivering the desired outcomes and that it is meeting the expectations of stakeholders.

## PROMOTES ACCOUNTABILITY AND TRANSPARENCY

A project management plan helps to promote accountability and transparency by establishing clear roles and responsibilities, outlining communication protocols, and defining metrics for measuring progress. The project management plan also promotes accountability by setting performance targets and expectations for team members and stakeholders.

By promoting accountability, the project management plan helps to ensure that team members are responsible for their actions and that they are held accountable for their performance. This helps to create a culture of ownership and responsibility, where team members are motivated to deliver their best work.

Transparency is also promoted through the project management plan by providing regular updates to stakeholders on the project's progress.

This includes information on project milestones, budget, and any issues or risks that have been identified. This helps to build trust among stakeholders by demonstrating that the project team is open and honest about the project's progress.

The project management plan also promotes transparency by establishing decision-making processes and providing guidelines for managing changes to the project scope, objectives, or budget. This helps to ensure that decisions are made transparently and that all stakeholders are aware of the rationale behind those decisions.

Moreover, by promoting accountability and transparency, the project management plan helps to reduce the risk of misunderstandings, conflicts, and delays. It creates a culture of trust and collaboration, where team members and stakeholders work together towards the common goal of delivering a successful project.

## CONCLUSION: BENEFITS OF DEVELOPING A PROJECT MANAGEMENT PLAN

In conclusion, developing a project management plan is essential for the success of any project. It helps to provide a structured approach to project management, ensuring that all aspects of the project are coordinated and controlled. By developing a project management plan, the project team can:

a. Provide a clear scope and objectives for the project

b. Define roles and responsibilities for team members

c. Ensure effective resource allocation

d. Establish communication protocols and reporting procedures

e. Mitigate risks and anticipate contingencies

f. Facilitate monitoring and control

g. Promote accountability and transparency

Developing a project management plan also helps to manage stakeholder expectations, reduce the risk of project delays and cost overruns, and ensure that the project is completed on time, within budget, and with the desired outcomes. It also promotes collaboration, coordination, and cooperation among team members and stakeholders, leading to a more efficient and effective project management process.

In summary, developing a project management plan is a critical step in ensuring the success of any project. It is a comprehensive document that provides a roadmap for the project team, outlining the strategy and approach for managing the project from start to finish. By investing time and resources in developing a project management plan, the project team can ensure that the project is completed successfully and delivers the desired outcomes.

# 6.8 ESSENTIAL COMPONENTS OF A PROJECT MANAGEMENT PLAN

The introduction section of a project management plan provides an overview of the project and sets the context for the plan. It outlines the purpose of the project, its goals and objectives, the scope of the project, and the key stakeholders involved. The introduction also provides a brief background of the project, including any relevant history or context that informs the project's goals and objectives.

The introduction should also explain the structure of the project management plan, describing the sections that follow and how they relate to one another. This section is important because it provides a roadmap for the reader, helping them to navigate the plan and understand the project as a whole. Finally, the introduction should highlight the importance of the project and why it matters to the organization or stakeholders involved.

## PROJECT SCOPE AND OBJECTIVES

This section of the project management plan outlines the project's scope, objectives, and deliverables. It provides a clear description of what the project is intended to accomplish, and what specifically will be delivered at the end of the project.

The scope of the project describes the boundaries of the project, including what is included and excluded from the project. This section also outlines the project objectives, which describe the specific goals that the project is intended to achieve. These objectives should be specific, measurable, achievable, relevant, and time-bound (SMART).

The deliverables section describes the tangible outcomes of the project. This includes any products, services, or results that will be produced by the project. It is important to list all the deliverables that are expected from the project so that stakeholders can have a clear understanding of what they should expect from the project.

This section should also outline any assumptions or constraints that may affect the project's scope or objectives. This can include factors such as time, budget, or available resources. By defining the scope, objectives, and deliverables of the project, this section provides a clear roadmap for the project team to follow throughout the project lifecycle.

## PROJECT DELIVERABLES

The project deliverables section of the project management plan outlines the specific outputs that will be produced by the project. These can include products, services, reports, or other tangible results that will be delivered to stakeholders. It is important to clearly define the deliverables so that stakeholders have a clear understanding of what they can expect from the project.

In this section, the project manager should describe the purpose of each deliverable, how it will be produced, and who will be responsible for producing it. The deliverables should be broken down into specific tasks or activities that can be easily tracked and managed throughout the project lifecycle.

The deliverables should also be prioritized and sequenced according to their importance and dependencies. This will help the project team to focus their efforts on the most critical tasks and ensure that the project is delivered on time and within budget.

Finally, this section should also describe the criteria for measuring the success of each deliverable. This can include metrics such as quality, timeliness, and cost. By setting clear criteria for success, the project team can ensure that the deliverables meet the expectations of stakeholders and contribute to the overall success of the project.

## PROJECT SCHEDULE AND TIMELINE

The project schedule and timeline section of the project management plan outlines the specific activities and tasks that need to be completed in order to achieve the project objectives. This section should include a detailed project schedule and timeline that identifies all of the tasks, activities, and milestones required to complete the project.

The schedule should be organized in a logical sequence, and should take into account any dependencies or constraints that may affect the project timeline. It should also include information on the duration of each activity, the resources required, and any milestones or deliverables associated with each activity.

The timeline should include specific start and end dates for each activity, as well as any critical dates or deadlines that must be met. It should also take into account any potential risks or issues that may impact the project schedule, and include contingency plans to address these risks.

The project schedule and timeline is an essential tool for managing the project, and should be updated regularly to reflect any changes or adjustments that may be required. By monitoring the project schedule and timeline, the project manager can ensure that the project is on track and that all activities are being completed in a timely and efficient manner.

## PROJECT BUDGET AND RESOURCES

The project budget and resources section of the project management plan outlines the financial and resource requirements needed to complete the project successfully. This section should include a detailed budget that outlines all the costs associated with the project, including labour, materials, equipment, and other expenses.

The budget should be organized in a logical way and should be based on the project schedule and timeline. It should also include contingencies for unexpected expenses or changes to the project scope. The project manager should work closely with the finance team to ensure that the budget is accurate and realistic.

In addition to the budget, this section should also include information on the resources needed to complete the project, including personnel, equipment, and materials. The project manager should identify the specific resources required for each activity and ensure that they are available when needed.

This section should also describe how the project team will manage and monitor expenses throughout the project lifecycle. This may include setting up a budget tracking system, establishing spending thresholds, and conducting regular budget reviews.

By developing a detailed budget and resource plan, the project manager can ensure that the project is completed within budget and that all necessary resources are available to support the project team throughout the project lifecycle.

## RISK MANAGEMENT PLAN

The risk management plan section of the project management plan outlines the approach that the project team will take to identify, assess, and manage risks that may impact the project's success. This section should describe the processes and procedures that will be used to identify potential risks, assess their likelihood and impact, and develop strategies to mitigate or manage those risks.

The risk management plan should begin with a risk assessment, which involves identifying and analysing potential risks that could affect the project's success. The project manager should work with the project team and stakeholders to identify risks related to the project scope, objectives, timeline, budget, resources, and other areas.

Once the risks have been identified, the project manager should assess their likelihood and potential impact on the project. This will help to prioritize the risks and determine which risks require immediate attention.

The risk management plan should also include a risk mitigation or management strategy for each identified risk. This may involve developing contingency plans, implementing risk avoidance measures, or transferring the risk to a third party. The plan should also outline the responsibilities of the project team members for managing and monitoring risks.

Finally, the risk management plan should be reviewed and updated regularly throughout the project lifecycle. This will ensure that new risks are identified and that the risk management strategies remain effective. By proactively managing project risks, the project manager can reduce the likelihood of negative impacts on the project's success.

## QUALITY ASSURANCE PLAN

The quality assurance plan section of the project management plan outlines the processes and procedures that will be used to ensure that the project's deliverables meet the required quality standards. This section should describe the approach that the project team will take to monitor, control, and improve the quality of the project's deliverables.

The quality assurance plan should begin with a description of the quality standards that the project team will be expected to meet. This may include industry standards, regulatory requirements, or the organization's own quality standards. The plan should also identify the quality criteria that will be used to assess the project's deliverables.

The quality assurance plan should also describe the processes and procedures that will be used to monitor and control the quality of the project's deliverables. This may include quality reviews, testing, inspections, or audits. The plan should also outline the roles and responsibilities of the project team members for ensuring that the project's deliverables meet the required quality standards.

In addition to monitoring and controlling quality, the quality assurance plan should also describe how the project team will improve the quality of the project's deliverables over time. This may involve implementing continuous improvement processes, conducting regular quality reviews, or providing training and support to project team members.

Finally, the quality assurance plan should be reviewed and updated regularly throughout the project lifecycle. This will ensure that the quality assurance processes and procedures remain effective and that the project's deliverables meet the required quality standards. By proactively managing project quality, the project manager can ensure that the project's deliverables meet or exceed stakeholders' expectations.

## COMMUNICATION PLAN

The communication plan section of the project management plan outlines the approach that the project team will take to communicate with stakeholders throughout the project lifecycle. This section should describe the methods and channels that will be used to share project information, as well as the roles and responsibilities of the project team members for managing project communication.

The communication plan should begin with a stakeholder analysis, which involves identifying all of the stakeholders who will be impacted by the project. This may include project sponsors, customers, team members, vendors, or other stakeholders. The plan should also identify the communication needs of each stakeholder group.

The communication plan should also describe the methods and channels that will be used to communicate project information to stakeholders. This may include regular status reports, progress updates, project meetings, or other communication methods. The plan should also identify the frequency and timing of each communication method.

In addition to identifying communication methods, the communication plan should also outline the roles and responsibilities of the project team members for managing project communication. This may include identifying a single point of contact for each stakeholder group or establishing a communication team to manage all project communication.

Finally, the communication plan should be reviewed and updated regularly throughout the project lifecycle. This will ensure that project information is communicated effectively and that stakeholders are kept informed about the project's progress. By proactively managing project communication, the project manager can ensure that stakeholders are engaged and supportive of the project's objectives.

## STAKEHOLDER MANAGEMENT PLAN

The stakeholder management plan section of the project management plan outlines the approach that the project team will take to identify, engage, and manage stakeholders throughout the project lifecycle. This section should describe the processes and procedures that will be used to identify stakeholders, understand their needs and expectations, and ensure that their concerns are addressed.

The stakeholder management plan should begin with a stakeholder analysis, which involves identifying all of the stakeholders who will be impacted by the project. The plan should also identify the level of influence that each stakeholder has on the project and the level of interest they have in the project's success.

Once the stakeholders have been identified, the stakeholder management plan should describe the approach that will be used to engage and communicate with each stakeholder group. This may include regular project updates, meetings, or other communication methods.

The stakeholder management plan should also outline the processes and procedures that will be used to manage stakeholder expectations and concerns. This may include establishing a process for addressing stakeholder issues or concerns, as well as identifying the roles and responsibilities of the project team members for managing stakeholder relationships.

In addition to managing stakeholder relationships, the stakeholder management plan should also describe how the project team will use stakeholder feedback to inform project decisions. This may involve establishing a process for gathering stakeholder feedback, analysing the feedback, and using it to make informed project decisions.

Finally, the stakeholder management plan should be reviewed and updated regularly throughout the project lifecycle. This will ensure that stakeholder needs and expectations are addressed throughout the project and that stakeholders remain engaged and supportive of the project's objectives. By proactively managing stakeholder relationships, the project manager can ensure that the project's objectives are met, and that stakeholder satisfaction is achieved.

## CHANGE MANAGEMENT PLAN

The change management plan section of the project management plan outlines the approach that the project team will take to manage changes to the project scope, schedule, budget, or other aspects of the project. This section should describe the processes and procedures that will be used to identify, evaluate, and implement changes to the project.

The change management plan should begin with a description of the change management process, which outlines the steps that must be taken to request, evaluate, and approve changes to the project. This may include a change request form, a change review board, or other change management procedures.

The change management plan should also describe the roles and responsibilities of the project team members for managing changes to the project. This may include identifying a change manager or change control board to oversee the change management process.

In addition to the change management process, the change management plan should also describe the approach that will be used to assess the impact of changes on the project. This may include evaluating the impact on the project scope, schedule, budget, resources, or other aspects of the project.

The change management plan should also outline the communication approach that will be used to inform stakeholders of any changes to the project. This may include regular updates or reports on the status of the project and any changes that have been approved.

Finally, the change management plan should be reviewed and updated regularly throughout the project lifecycle. This will ensure that changes to the project are managed effectively and that stakeholders are informed of any changes that may impact the project. By proactively managing changes to the project, the project manager can ensure that the project remains on track and that stakeholders remain engaged and supportive of the project's objectives.

## PROCUREMENT MANAGEMENT PLAN

The procurement management plan section of the project management plan outlines the approach that the project team will take to procure goods and services necessary for the project's success. This section should describe the processes and procedures that will be used to identify, evaluate, and select vendors and suppliers.

The procurement management plan should begin with a description of the procurement process, which outlines the steps that must be taken to identify, evaluate, and select vendors and suppliers. This may include identifying the goods and services required for the project, identifying potential vendors, and evaluating their proposals.

The procurement management plan should also describe the roles and responsibilities of the project team members for managing the procurement process. This may include identifying a procurement manager or procurement team to oversee the procurement process.

In addition to the procurement process, the procurement management plan should also describe the approach that will be used to manage vendor relationships throughout the project lifecycle. This may include establishing vendor performance metrics, conducting regular vendor performance reviews, and addressing any issues that arise during the project.

The procurement management plan should also outline the communication approach that will be used to inform stakeholders of any procurement-related activities. This may include regular updates or reports on the status of procurement activities and any issues that arise.

Finally, the procurement management plan should be reviewed and updated regularly throughout the project lifecycle. This will ensure that the procurement process is managed effectively and that stakeholders are informed of any procurement-related activities that may impact the project. By proactively managing procurement activities, the project manager can ensure that the project remains on track and that stakeholders remain engaged and supportive of the project's objectives.

## PROJECT CLOSURE PLAN

The project closure plan section of the project management plan outlines the approach that the project team will take to close out the project and transfer the project deliverables to the stakeholders. This section should describe the processes and procedures that will be used to close out the project and ensure that all project objectives have been met.

The project closure plan should begin with a description of the criteria that must be met in order to close out the project. This may include completion of all project activities, acceptance of all project deliverables by stakeholders, and approval of the final project report.

The project closure plan should also outline the steps that must be taken to transfer the project deliverables to the stakeholders. This may include identifying the stakeholders who will receive the project deliverables, ensuring that the deliverables are complete and accurate, and providing training or support to stakeholders as needed.

In addition to the transfer of project deliverables, the project closure plan should also describe the steps that must be taken to close out project contracts or agreements, and to release project resources. This may include returning equipment, releasing team members from the project, or closing out any financial accounts associated with the project.

The project closure plan should also outline the steps that will be taken to conduct a final project review, which may include an evaluation of project success, lessons learned, and recommendations for future projects.

Finally, the project closure plan should be reviewed and updated regularly throughout the project lifecycle. This will ensure that all project closure activities are planned and executed effectively, and that the project is successfully closed out in a timely manner. By proactively managing the project closure process, the project manager can ensure that all project objectives are met and that stakeholders are satisfied with the project outcomes.

# 6.9 EXPLORING APPROACHES TO PRODUCING ESTIMATES

Estimates are crucial for decision-making in a variety of fields, including business, engineering, and science. Estimates are approximations of future costs, resources, or outcomes based on available information, assumptions, and expert judgment. They can help to inform decisions about project scope, budget, schedule, and risk management.

In order to produce accurate and reliable estimates, it is important to use a structured and systematic approach. There are several approaches to producing estimates, each with its own strengths and weaknesses. In this section, we will provide an overview of the four main approaches: parametric, analogous, analytical, and Delphi.

By understanding the different approaches, their benefits, and limitations, you can choose the most appropriate approach for your specific needs and increase the accuracy and reliability of your estimates. Let's dive deeper into each approach.

## PARAMETRIC APPROACH

The parametric approach is a statistical method of estimating the cost, duration, or other characteristics of a project based on historical data and mathematical formulas. This approach assumes that there is a linear relationship between the project variables and uses historical data to establish the parameters of the relationship.

The process of parametric estimating involves identifying the variables that are most relevant to the project, collecting data on these variables from previous projects, and using regression analysis to develop a mathematical model that relates these variables to the project outcome.

This model is then used to estimate the expected outcome for the current project.

The advantages of the parametric approach include its speed, accuracy, and ability to incorporate a large amount of data. However, the approach assumes that the historical data is relevant to the current project and that the relationship between variables is linear. If these assumptions are not valid, the estimates produced by the parametric approach may be inaccurate.

An example of the parametric approach would be estimating the cost of a construction project based on the square footage of the building, the cost per square foot for similar buildings in the area, and the expected inflation rate. The mathematical model developed would be used to estimate the cost of the current project based on these variables.

In conclusion, the parametric approach can be a useful tool for estimating project outcomes when the assumptions of the approach are valid and relevant data is available.

## ANALOGOUS APPROACH

The analogous approach, also known as the top-down approach, involves using information from similar projects as a basis for estimating the cost, duration, or other characteristics of the current project. This approach assumes that the current project is similar in nature to previous projects and uses the experience gained from those projects to estimate the current project.

The process of analogous estimating involves identifying similar projects, analysing their characteristics, and using this information to estimate the expected outcome for the current project. The analysis may consider factors such as project scope, complexity, geographic location, size, and other relevant variables.

The advantages of the analogous approach include its simplicity and ease of use, especially when there is limited data available for the current project. The approach also allows for the incorporation of expert judgment and knowledge gained from previous projects. However, the approach may not be accurate if the current project is significantly different from the previous projects used as a basis for estimation.

An example of the analogous approach would be estimating the cost of a software development project based on the cost of a similar project completed by the same team in the past. The characteristics of the previous project, such as the number of lines of code and the complexity of the software, would be analysed and used to estimate the expected cost for the current project.

In conclusion, the analogous approach can be a useful tool for estimating project outcomes when there is limited data available and the current project is similar to previous projects. However, the approach should be used with caution and expert judgment when the current project is significantly different from previous projects.

## ANALYTICAL APPROACH

The analytical approach, also known as the bottom-up approach, involves breaking down the project into smaller components and estimating the cost, duration, or other characteristics of each component. The estimates for each component are then aggregated to provide an overall estimate for the project.

The process of analytical estimating involves identifying the work required for each component, estimating the time and resources required to complete the work, and aggregating the estimates to provide an overall estimate for the project. This approach requires a detailed understanding of the project scope and the ability to break down the project into manageable components.

The advantages of the analytical approach include its accuracy and ability to incorporate detailed information about the project. The approach also allows for the identification of potential risks and opportunities associated with each component of the project. However, the approach can be time-consuming and may not be appropriate for projects with a high level of uncertainty.

An example of the analytical approach would be estimating the cost of a building construction project by breaking down the project into smaller components such as foundation, structure, electrical, plumbing, and HVAC systems. The time and resources required for each component would be estimated, and the estimates would be aggregated to provide an overall estimate for the project.

In conclusion, the analytical approach can be a useful tool for estimating project outcomes when a detailed understanding of the project scope is available and the project can be broken down into manageable components. However, the approach may not be appropriate for projects with a high level of uncertainty or when there is limited information available about the project.

## DELPHI APPROACH

The Delphi approach is a method of estimating that involves seeking the opinions and judgments of a panel of experts. This approach is particularly useful when there is a high level of uncertainty about the project and when a consensus view is desired.

The process of Delphi estimating involves identifying a panel of experts, providing them with information about the project, and asking them to provide estimates or opinions about the project. The responses are collected and summarized, and the experts are provided with feedback and the opportunity to revise their estimates. This process is repeated until a consensus view is reached.

The advantages of the Delphi approach include the ability to incorporate expert judgment, the ability to reduce bias and subjectivity, and the ability to reach a consensus view. The approach also allows for the identification of potential risks and opportunities associated with the project. However, the approach can be time-consuming and may not be appropriate for projects with a short timeline.

An example of the Delphi approach would be estimating the market potential for a new product by gathering opinions and estimates from a panel of experts such as industry analysts, marketing professionals, and product development experts. The opinions and estimates would be summarized and feedback provided to the experts. The process would be repeated until a consensus view is reached.

In conclusion, the Delphi approach can be a useful tool for estimating project outcomes when a high level of uncertainty is present, and expert judgment is required. However, the approach may not be appropriate for projects with a short timeline or when a consensus view is not necessary.

## COMPARISON OF APPROACHES

Each of the four approaches to producing estimates - parametric, analogous, analytical, and Delphi - has its own strengths and weaknesses, and choosing the right approach depends on the specific requirements of the project. Here is a brief comparison of the four approaches:

  a. The parametric approach is a statistical method that relies on historical data to estimate project outcomes. It is useful when there is a large amount of relevant data available, and the relationship between project variables is linear. However, the approach may not be accurate if the assumptions are not valid or if there is limited data available.

b. The analogous approach is a top-down method that relies on the experience gained from similar projects to estimate project outcomes. It is useful when there is limited data available for the current project and when the current project is similar to previous projects. However, the approach may not be accurate if the current project is significantly different from the previous projects used as a basis for estimation.

c. The analytical approach is a bottom-up method that involves breaking down the project into smaller components and estimating the cost, duration, or other characteristics of each component. It is useful when a detailed understanding of the project scope is available, and the project can be broken down into manageable components. However, the approach may not be appropriate for projects with a high level of uncertainty or when there is limited information available about the project.

d. The Delphi approach is a method that involves seeking the opinions and judgments of a panel of experts. It is useful when there is a high level of uncertainty about the project and when a consensus view is desired. However, the approach can be time-consuming and may not be appropriate for projects with a short timeline.

Choosing the right approach to producing estimates depends on several factors, including the level of uncertainty, the availability of data, and the complexity of the project. It is also important to consider the strengths and weaknesses of each approach and to use expert judgment when selecting an approach.

In conclusion, selecting the most appropriate approach to producing estimates is essential for accurate and reliable project planning and decision-making. Understanding the advantages and limitations of each approach can help project managers and decision-makers to choose the most appropriate approach for their specific needs.

## CONCLUSION

Producing accurate and reliable estimates is crucial for successful project management and decision-making. The four approaches to producing estimates - parametric, analogous, analytical, and Delphi - offer different advantages and limitations, and the choice of approach depends on the specific requirements of the project.

The parametric approach is useful when there is a large amount of relevant data available, and the relationship between project variables is linear. The analogous approach is useful when there is limited data available for the current project and when the current project is similar to previous projects. The analytical approach is useful when a detailed understanding of the project scope is available, and the project can be broken down into manageable components. The Delphi approach is useful when there is a high level of uncertainty about the project and when a consensus view is desired.

In selecting an approach, project managers and decision-makers should consider the level of uncertainty, the availability of data, and the complexity of the project. It is also important to use expert judgment when selecting an approach.

In conclusion, understanding the different approaches to producing estimates and selecting the most appropriate approach is essential for accurate and reliable project planning and decision-making. By selecting the most appropriate approach, project managers and decision-makers can increase the accuracy and reliability of their estimates and improve the success of their projects.

# 6.10 THE IMPORTANCE OF RE-ESTIMATING THROUGHOUT THE PROJECT LIFE CYCLE

Re-estimating is an essential practice in project management that involves revising the initial project estimates and making necessary adjustments throughout the project life cycle. Project estimates are often based on assumptions, constraints, and uncertainties that may change as the project progresses. Therefore, it is essential to monitor and update project estimates regularly to ensure that they remain accurate and realistic.

There are several reasons why re-estimating is necessary in project management. First, it allows project managers to identify potential problems and risks that may affect the project's progress, budget, and timeline. By re-estimating, project managers can identify areas where the project is over or underestimating costs, resources, or time, and make adjustments accordingly.

Second, re-estimating enables project managers to keep stakeholders informed of project progress and changes. Stakeholders, including clients, team members, and management, need to be aware of any changes in project estimates, as this can affect project goals, expectations, and decisions.

Third, re-estimating helps project managers to improve the accuracy and reliability of project estimates. By regularly reviewing and updating project estimates, project managers can learn from past mistakes, refine their estimation techniques, and improve their ability to predict project outcomes.

Overall, re-estimating is a critical practice in project management that can help ensure project success by providing accurate and up-to-date information about project progress, risks, and opportunities.

## BENEFITS OF RE-ESTIMATING DURING THE PROJECT LIFE CYCLE

Re-estimating provides several benefits throughout the project life cycle. Here are some of the key benefits:

a. Improved Project Planning: Re-estimating can help project managers to better plan and allocate project resources. As project details become clearer and uncertainties are reduced, re-estimating can help project managers to refine their planning and scheduling, ensuring that resources are allocated effectively.

b. Increased Accuracy of Estimates: Re-estimating helps project managers to improve the accuracy of project estimates. As the project progresses, project managers can revise estimates based on actual data, which increases the accuracy of future estimates.

c. Better Decision Making: Re-estimating provides project managers with up-to-date information that can help them make better decisions. By re-estimating, project managers can identify potential problems and risks that may impact project progress, enabling them to make informed decisions to mitigate those risks.

d. Improved Communication: Re-estimating allows project managers to communicate more effectively with stakeholders. By providing stakeholders with accurate and up-to-date project estimates, project managers can manage stakeholder expectations and ensure that everyone is aware of any changes that may impact the project.

e. Better Resource Management: Re-estimating helps project managers to optimize the use of project resources. As project estimates become more accurate, project managers can adjust resource allocation to ensure that resources are being used efficiently and effectively.

f. Increased Project Success: Re-estimating can increase the likelihood of project success. By providing project managers with accurate and up-to-date information, they can make informed decisions, manage risks and resources more effectively, and ultimately ensure that the project is completed on time, within budget, and to the satisfaction of stakeholders.

Overall, re-estimating provides many benefits to project managers throughout the project life cycle. By improving project planning, increasing the accuracy of estimates, enabling better decision making, improving communication, optimizing resource management, and increasing project success, re-estimating is an essential practice in project management.

## KEY FACTORS TO CONSIDER WHEN RE-ESTIMATING

Re-estimating is a critical practice in project management, but it is important to consider some key factors before doing so. Here are some of the key factors to consider when re-estimating:

a. Project Scope: The project scope defines the work that needs to be completed to achieve project objectives. Re-estimating should consider any changes to the project scope, as this can affect the project's cost, time, and resource requirements.

b. Project Schedule: The project schedule outlines the timeline for completing project activities. Re-estimating should consider any changes to the project schedule, such as delays or acceleration, as this can affect project estimates.

c. Project Budget: The project budget outlines the financial resources allocated to the project. Re-estimating should consider any changes to the project budget, such as funding reductions or increases, as this can affect project estimates.

d. Risks and Uncertainties: Re-estimating should consider any risks and uncertainties that may impact the project's progress, costs, or resource requirements. Risks and uncertainties may arise from changes to project scope, schedule, or budget, or external factors such as market conditions, regulatory requirements, or natural disasters.

e. Stakeholder Expectations: Re-estimating should consider the expectations of stakeholders, including clients, team members, and management. Stakeholder expectations may change over time, and re-estimating should ensure that stakeholders are informed of any changes and that their expectations are managed effectively.

f. Estimation Techniques: Re-estimating should consider the estimation techniques used to develop initial project estimates. Different estimation techniques have varying levels of accuracy and reliability, and re-estimating should ensure that the most appropriate estimation techniques are used to revise project estimates.

Overall, re-estimating should consider a range of factors, including project scope, schedule, budget, risks, uncertainties, stakeholder expectations, and estimation techniques. By considering these factors, project managers can ensure that re-estimating is done effectively and that project estimates remain accurate and realistic throughout the project life cycle.

## BEST PRACTICES FOR RE-ESTIMATING TO IMPROVE PROJECT SUCCESS

Re-estimating is a critical practice in project management, and there are several best practices that project managers can follow to ensure that re-estimating is done effectively. Here are some of the best practices for re-estimating:

a. Regularly Review Project Estimates: Project managers should regularly review project estimates to ensure that they remain accurate and up to date. Re-estimating should be done at key milestones in the project life cycle, such as the end of each project phase or after significant changes to project scope, schedule, or budget.

b. Use Actual Data: Re-estimating should be based on actual data rather than assumptions or guesswork. Actual data can be used to refine estimates and improve the accuracy of future estimates.

c. Involve the Project Team: Re-estimating should involve the project team, including subject matter experts and stakeholders. The project team can provide valuable insights into the project's progress, risks, and opportunities, which can be used to refine project estimates.

d. Use Multiple Estimation Techniques: Re-estimating should use multiple estimation techniques to ensure that estimates are as accurate and reliable as possible. Different estimation techniques have varying levels of accuracy and reliability, and using multiple techniques can help project managers to develop more accurate estimates.

e. Communicate Changes to Stakeholders: Re-estimating should be communicated to stakeholders, including clients, team members, and management. Stakeholders need to be informed of any changes to project estimates, as this can affect project goals, expectations, and decisions.

f. Document Changes and Reasons: Re-estimating should be documented, including any changes made to project estimates and the reasons for those changes. Documentation can help project managers to track the evolution of project estimates, learn from past mistakes, and improve their estimation techniques.

Overall, re-estimating should follow best practices that involve regularly reviewing project estimates, using actual data, involving the project team, using multiple estimation techniques, communicating changes to stakeholders, and documenting changes and reasons. By following these best practices, project managers can ensure that re-estimating is done effectively and that project estimates remain accurate and realistic throughout the project life cycle, leading to improved project success.

## CHALLENGES AND RISKS ASSOCIATED WITH RE-ESTIMATING

While re-estimating is an essential practice in project management, it is not without its challenges and risks. Here are some of the key challenges and risks associated with re-estimating:

a. Time Constraints: Re-estimating can be time-consuming, particularly if multiple estimation techniques are used. Time constraints can make it difficult for project managers to conduct re-estimating regularly or to involve the project team adequately.

b. Data Availability: Re-estimating relies on actual data, and sometimes, data may not be readily available or reliable. Insufficient or inaccurate data can lead to incorrect re-estimates, which can affect project goals, expectations, and decisions.

c. Resistance to Change: Re-estimating may be met with resistance from stakeholders, particularly if they are not aware of the need for re-estimating or if they believe that re-estimating will lead to delays or additional costs.

d. Over-Optimism Bias: Re-estimating may be influenced by over-optimism bias, where project managers are overly optimistic about project progress or outcomes. Over-optimism bias can lead to underestimating the time, cost, or resource requirements of the project, leading to delays or additional costs.

e. Scope Creep: Re-estimating may be affected by scope creep, where the project scope expands beyond its original boundaries. Scope creep can lead to additional costs, resource requirements, and time, which can affect project estimates.

f. Communication Challenges: Re-estimating requires effective communication with stakeholders, including clients, team members, and management. Communication challenges, such as miscommunication or lack of communication, can lead to misunderstandings and incorrect re-estimates.

Overall, re-estimating is not without its challenges and risks. Time constraints, data availability, resistance to change, over-optimism bias, scope creep, and communication challenges are some of the key challenges and risks associated with re-estimating. However, by understanding and addressing these challenges and risks, project managers can ensure that re-estimating is done effectively and that project estimates remain accurate and realistic throughout the project life cycle.

## EXAMPLES OF SUCCESSFUL RE-ESTIMATING IN PROJECT MANAGEMENT

Re-estimating is a critical practice in project management that can lead to improved project success. Here are some examples of successful re-estimating in project management:

1. NASA's Mars Rover Project: NASA's Mars Rover Project is a successful example of re-estimating. The project involved developing and launching several robotic rovers to explore the surface of Mars. Re-estimating was done regularly throughout the project, and adjustments were made to project estimates based on actual data. This led to more accurate project estimates, improved resource management, and successful project outcomes.

2. Software Development Projects: Software development projects often involve re-estimating, particularly if the project scope or requirements change over time. Successful software development projects use agile development methodologies, which involve re-estimating at the end of each sprint or iteration. This enables project managers to adjust project estimates based on actual progress and to deliver projects on time and within budget.

3. Construction Projects: Construction projects also involve re-estimating, particularly if the project scope or requirements change over time. Successful construction projects use lean construction methodologies, which involve continuous improvement and re-estimating throughout the project life cycle.

This enables project managers to adjust project estimates based on actual progress and to optimize resource utilization.

4. Healthcare Projects: Healthcare projects, such as clinical trials, often involve re-estimating, particularly if patient enrollment or protocol adherence changes over time. Successful healthcare projects use adaptive trial designs, which involve re-estimating at predefined interim analyses. This enables project managers to adjust project estimates based on actual progress and to optimize trial design.

Overall, successful re-estimating in project management involves regularly reviewing project estimates, using actual data, involving the project team, using multiple estimation techniques, communicating changes to stakeholders, and documenting changes and reasons. By following these best practices, project managers can ensure that re-estimating is done effectively and that project estimates remain accurate and realistic throughout the project life cycle, leading to improved project success.

# 6.11 Understanding the Relationship between Stakeholder Analysis, Influence, and Engagement

Stakeholder analysis is a crucial tool used by organizations to identify and analyse the individuals, groups, and organizations that can significantly impact or be impacted by the decisions and actions of the organization. This analysis enables the organization to identify the needs, interests, and expectations of its stakeholders, understand their potential influence, and develop effective strategies to engage with them.

Stakeholder analysis involves several steps, including identifying the stakeholders, assessing their power, interest, and influence, mapping their relationships with the organization, and developing engagement strategies. This process enables organizations to make informed decisions that consider the perspectives and interests of their stakeholders while mitigating potential conflicts.

Stakeholder analysis is critical for any organization, whether it is a business, government agency, non-profit organization, or community group. It helps organizations to understand the complex web of relationships that they must navigate to achieve their goals while balancing the interests of their stakeholders. By conducting a stakeholder analysis, organizations can identify potential opportunities and risks, enhance their decision-making processes, and build positive relationships with their stakeholders.

## IDENTIFYING STAKEHOLDERS AND THEIR INFLUENCE

The first step in stakeholder analysis is to identify the individuals, groups, and organizations that can significantly impact or be impacted by the decisions and actions of the organization. This includes both internal stakeholders, such as employees and shareholders, and external stakeholders, such as customers, suppliers, regulatory agencies, and community groups.

Once stakeholders have been identified, the next step is to assess their influence and level of interest in the organization's activities. This involves considering factors such as their level of involvement, their ability to influence decision-making, and their level of support or opposition to the organization's goals.

Stakeholders can be categorized based on their level of influence and interest in the organization. High-influence, high-interest stakeholders are those who have a significant impact on the organization and are highly invested in its activities. Low-influence, low-interest stakeholders are those who have minimal impact on the organization and are not highly invested in its activities.

By identifying stakeholders and assessing their influence and interest, organizations can prioritize their engagement efforts and focus on building positive relationships with those stakeholders who have the most significant impact on their activities.

It is essential to note that stakeholder analysis is an ongoing process, and stakeholder priorities can change over time. Organizations must continuously monitor and update their stakeholder analysis to ensure they remain relevant and effective.

# MAPPING STAKEHOLDER RELATIONSHIPS AND POWER DYNAMICS

Once stakeholders have been identified and their influence and interest assessed, the next step in stakeholder analysis is to map their relationships with the organization and with each other. This involves understanding the power dynamics and the level of collaboration or conflict that exists between stakeholders.

Mapping stakeholder relationships is critical because it helps organizations understand the complex web of relationships that exist within their stakeholder network. By mapping these relationships, organizations can identify potential conflicts or opportunities for collaboration and develop strategies to mitigate conflicts and build positive relationships.

Power dynamics are an essential element of stakeholder analysis. Stakeholders with more power have a greater ability to influence decision-making and outcomes. Identifying the power dynamics within stakeholder relationships can help organizations develop strategies to manage conflicts, build alliances, and address power imbalances.

One way to map stakeholder relationships is through a stakeholder mapping tool, such as a power-interest grid. A power-interest grid plots stakeholders based on their level of power and their level of interest in the organization's activities. Stakeholders with high power and high interest are placed in the top-right quadrant of the grid, while those with low power and low interest are placed in the bottom-left quadrant.

By using a stakeholder mapping tool, organizations can prioritize their engagement efforts and develop targeted strategies for building positive relationships with their most important stakeholders. This can help to reduce conflicts, increase stakeholder support, and enhance the organization's overall reputation and performance.

## ENGAGING STAKEHOLDERS FOR EFFECTIVE DECISION MAKING

Engaging stakeholders is a critical aspect of stakeholder analysis. Effective stakeholder engagement involves building positive relationships with stakeholders, listening to their concerns and perspectives, and incorporating their feedback into decision-making processes.

Stakeholder engagement should be an ongoing process that begins early in the decision-making process and continues throughout the project's lifecycle. It is essential to involve stakeholders in meaningful ways, such as through focus groups, surveys, town hall meetings, or other forms of consultation. This helps to build trust and credibility with stakeholders and demonstrates the organization's commitment to transparency and accountability.

Engaging stakeholders can also help organizations to identify potential risks and opportunities that may not have been considered otherwise. By involving stakeholders in the decision-making process, organizations can gain a better understanding of the potential impacts of their decisions and develop more effective strategies for managing risks and maximizing opportunities.

It is important to note that effective stakeholder engagement is not a one-size-fits-all approach. Different stakeholders may have different needs, interests, and preferences, and organizations must tailor their engagement strategies to meet these diverse needs.

Overall, effective stakeholder engagement is critical for ensuring that organizations make informed decisions that consider the perspectives and interests of all stakeholders. By involving stakeholders in the decision-making process and building positive relationships with them, organizations can improve their performance, enhance their reputation, and create value for all stakeholders.

## STRATEGIES FOR BUILDING POSITIVE STAKEHOLDER RELATIONSHIPS

Building positive relationships with stakeholders is crucial for the success of any organization. Positive relationships can help to build trust and credibility, increase stakeholder support, and mitigate potential conflicts. Here are some strategies that organizations can use to build positive stakeholder relationships:

a. Communication: Effective communication is essential for building positive relationships with stakeholders. Organizations should communicate clearly, honestly, and frequently with stakeholders, providing them with information about the organization's activities, plans, and progress.

b. Collaboration: Collaboration is an effective way to build positive relationships with stakeholders. Organizations can work with stakeholders to develop mutually beneficial solutions that meet their needs and expectations.

c. Involvement: Involving stakeholders in decision-making processes is a powerful way to build positive relationships. By involving stakeholders, organizations can demonstrate their commitment to transparency and accountability and show that they value stakeholders' input.

d. Responsiveness: Organizations should be responsive to stakeholders' concerns and needs. This involves listening to their feedback and taking action to address their concerns in a timely and effective manner.

e. Relationship-building activities: Organizations can also engage in relationship-building activities, such as community outreach, social events, and volunteer activities. These activities can help to build rapport with stakeholders and demonstrate the organization's commitment to the community.

f. Proactive engagement: Rather than waiting for stakeholders to reach out, organizations can proactively engage with stakeholders to build positive relationships. This involves identifying potential stakeholders, reaching out to them, and developing strategies to engage with them effectively.

By implementing these strategies, organizations can build positive relationships with stakeholders, which can help to improve their performance, enhance their reputation, and create value for all stakeholders.

## MEASURING AND EVALUATING STAKEHOLDER ENGAGEMENT

Measuring and evaluating stakeholder engagement is critical for determining the effectiveness of engagement strategies and identifying areas for improvement. Here are some approaches that organizations can use to measure and evaluate stakeholder engagement:

a. Surveys: Surveys can be used to measure stakeholders' perceptions of the organization and its engagement efforts. Surveys can provide valuable insights into stakeholder needs and preferences, as well as the effectiveness of engagement strategies.

b. Metrics: Organizations can use metrics to track and measure stakeholder engagement, such as the number of stakeholders engaged, the frequency of engagement, and the level of satisfaction with engagement efforts.

c. Feedback mechanisms: Organizations can use feedback mechanisms, such as suggestion boxes or online forums, to gather feedback from stakeholders about their engagement experiences.

d. Stakeholder participation: Organizations can evaluate stakeholder participation in engagement efforts, such as the number of stakeholders who attend events or participate in focus groups.

e. Impact on decision-making: Organizations can evaluate the impact of stakeholder engagement on decision-making processes, such as the extent to which stakeholder feedback is incorporated into decision-making.

f. Continuous improvement: Organizations should continuously evaluate and improve their stakeholder engagement strategies to ensure that they remain effective and relevant.

By measuring and evaluating stakeholder engagement, organizations can identify areas for improvement, enhance their engagement efforts, and build stronger relationships with stakeholders. This can help to improve organizational performance, enhance reputation, and create value for all stakeholders.

# 6.12 THE IMPORTANCE OF MANAGING STAKEHOLDER EXPECTATIONS FOR PROJECT SUCCESS

Effective stakeholder management starts with understanding the expectations of those who have a stake in the project. Stakeholders can include customers, team members, project sponsors, investors, vendors, government agencies, and community groups. Each stakeholder group may have different expectations, needs, and priorities related to the project.

It's important to identify and prioritize stakeholder groups, and then engage with each group to understand their expectations, concerns, and goals related to the project. This may involve conducting surveys, holding focus groups, or conducting one-on-one interviews to gain insights into stakeholder perspectives.

Once you have a clear understanding of stakeholder expectations, you can develop a plan to manage those expectations effectively. This plan may involve setting realistic project goals and timelines, communicating regularly with stakeholders, and managing stakeholder feedback throughout the project lifecycle.

## THE IMPACT OF UNMANAGED STAKEHOLDER EXPECTATIONS

Failing to manage stakeholder expectations can have a significant impact on project success. Unmet or unrealistic expectations can lead to confusion, frustration, and even conflict among stakeholders. This can result in delays, budget overruns, and a lack of support for the project.

When stakeholders feel like their needs are not being addressed or their expectations are not being met, they may lose confidence in the project team and withdraw their support. This can lead to negative publicity, reduced stakeholder buy-in, and even project failure.

Additionally, unmanaged stakeholder expectations can lead to scope creep, where the project expands beyond its original goals and budget. This can result in project delays, budget overruns, and decreased stakeholder satisfaction.

In short, failing to manage stakeholder expectations can have a significant impact on project success. It's important to identify and prioritize stakeholder groups, engage with them early and often, and develop a plan to manage their expectations throughout the project lifecycle.

## THE BENEFITS OF MANAGING STAKEHOLDER EXPECTATIONS

Effective stakeholder management, including managing stakeholder expectations, offers numerous benefits to the success of a project.

Firstly, managing stakeholder expectations helps ensure that the project is aligned with stakeholder needs and goals. By understanding and addressing stakeholder expectations, the project team can create a project plan that meets stakeholder needs and minimizes potential conflicts.

Secondly, managing stakeholder expectations helps to reduce risk. By engaging with stakeholders early and often, the project team can identify potential risks and develop a plan to mitigate those risks. This can help ensure that the project stays on track and on budget, reducing the likelihood of delays, cost overruns, and scope creep.

Thirdly, effective stakeholder management helps to build stakeholder buy-in and support for the project. When stakeholders feel like their needs and expectations are being addressed, they are more likely to support the project and advocate for its success. This can help the project team secure necessary resources and funding, as well as generate positive publicity for the project.

Overall, managing stakeholder expectations is crucial to the success of a project. It helps to ensure that the project is aligned with stakeholder needs and goals, reduces risk, and builds stakeholder buy-in and support. By prioritizing stakeholder engagement and communication throughout the project lifecycle, project teams can increase the likelihood of project success.

## STRATEGIES FOR MANAGING STAKEHOLDER EXPECTATIONS

There are several strategies that project teams can use to manage stakeholder expectations effectively.

Firstly, it's important to establish clear and realistic project goals and timelines. This can help set stakeholder expectations early on in the project and provide a roadmap for success. The project team should work with stakeholders to set goals and timelines that are achievable, while also taking into account stakeholder needs and priorities.

Secondly, effective communication is key to managing stakeholder expectations. Project teams should communicate regularly with stakeholders to provide updates on project progress, identify potential risks, and gather feedback. This can help stakeholders feel informed and involved in the project, reducing the likelihood of surprises or misunderstandings.

Thirdly, it's important to manage stakeholder feedback effectively. Project teams should establish a process for gathering and addressing stakeholder feedback throughout the project lifecycle. This can help ensure that stakeholder concerns are addressed in a timely and effective manner, reducing the likelihood of conflict or delays.

Fourthly, the project team should identify and prioritize stakeholder groups, and develop tailored communication and engagement plans for each group. This can help ensure that each stakeholder group's needs and expectations are addressed effectively, and reduce the likelihood of conflicts arising.

Finally, it's important to be transparent and honest with stakeholders throughout the project lifecycle. This can help build trust and credibility with stakeholders, and reduce the likelihood of misunderstandings or miscommunications.

By using these strategies to manage stakeholder expectations effectively, project teams can increase the likelihood of project success and build strong relationships with stakeholders.

## BEST PRACTICES FOR EFFECTIVE STAKEHOLDER MANAGEMENT

Effective stakeholder management involves a range of activities and strategies, but there are some best practices that can help project teams to manage stakeholder expectations effectively.

Firstly, it's important to involve stakeholders early and often in the project planning and decision-making process. This can help ensure that stakeholder needs and expectations are incorporated into the project plan, reducing the likelihood of conflicts arising later in the project lifecycle.

Secondly, project teams should communicate regularly and transparently with stakeholders. This can involve providing regular project updates, sharing information on project progress, and being responsive to stakeholder feedback and concerns.

Thirdly, the project team should take a proactive approach to managing stakeholder expectations, anticipating potential conflicts or concerns and developing plans to address them before they become problems.

Fourthly, it's important to establish clear roles and responsibilities for stakeholder engagement and management. This can help ensure that each team member understands their role in managing stakeholder expectations, reducing the likelihood of miscommunications or misunderstandings.

Fifthly, project teams should use a range of communication channels and methods to engage with stakeholders. This can include in-person meetings, virtual meetings, email communication, and social media channels. By using a range of channels, the project team can reach a wider audience and ensure that stakeholders have multiple opportunities to provide feedback and input.

Finally, project teams should regularly evaluate their stakeholder engagement and management strategies, and make adjustments as needed. This can involve gathering feedback from stakeholders on their experience with the project team, and using that feedback to improve future stakeholder engagement and management efforts.

By following these best practices for effective stakeholder management, project teams can increase the likelihood of project success, build strong relationships with stakeholders, and mitigate potential risks and conflicts.

## MEASURING THE SUCCESS OF STAKEHOLDER MANAGEMENT

Measuring the success of stakeholder management is an important aspect of effective project management. There are several metrics that project teams can use to assess the success of their stakeholder management efforts.

Firstly, stakeholder satisfaction is a key metric for measuring the success of stakeholder management. This can involve gathering feedback from stakeholders on their experience with the project team, including their level of engagement, the quality of communication, and their overall satisfaction with the project.

Secondly, project teams can measure stakeholder engagement and participation, such as the number of stakeholders who attended project meetings or provided feedback on project documents.

Thirdly, project teams can measure the effectiveness of their stakeholder communication efforts, such as the number of communication channels used, the frequency of communication, and the quality of communication.

Fourthly, the project team can measure the impact of stakeholder management on project outcomes, such as whether stakeholder needs and expectations were met, and whether the project was completed on time and within budget.

Finally, project teams can assess the level of stakeholder support for the project, such as the number of stakeholders who advocate for the project, provide funding, or offer other types of support.

By measuring these metrics, project teams can identify areas for improvement in their stakeholder management efforts, and make adjustments to ensure that stakeholder needs and expectations are effectively managed throughout the project lifecycle. This can help ensure project success, build strong relationships with stakeholders, and mitigate potential risks and conflicts.

# 6.13 UNDERSTANDING EARNED VALUE MANAGEMENT AND ITS BENEFITS FOR PROJECT MANAGERS

Earned Value Management (EVM) is a project management technique used to measure the progress and performance of a project against its planned objectives. It provides a comprehensive and objective way to measure the actual work completed, the time taken to complete it, and the cost incurred in the process.

EVM is a critical tool for project managers as it provides a clear and accurate picture of project performance at any given time. With EVM, project managers can track project performance in real-time and take corrective actions whenever necessary to ensure the project stays on track.

EVM is particularly useful for large and complex projects with multiple stakeholders, significant financial investment, and tight deadlines. By implementing EVM, project managers can ensure that their projects are completed within budget, on time, and to the required quality standards.

## HOW EARNED VALUE MANAGEMENT HELPS PROJECT MANAGERS:

EVM provides project managers with a range of benefits, including:

a. Accurate Progress Tracking: EVM provides a standardized method for tracking the progress of a project against the planned objectives. It helps project managers to identify any variances between the actual performance and the planned performance. By monitoring these variances, project managers can take corrective actions to keep the project on track.

b. Early Warning System: EVM is an early warning system that alerts project managers to any potential issues or risks. By using EVM, project managers can quickly identify any deviations from the planned performance and take timely corrective actions to address them.

c. Resource Allocation: EVM helps project managers to allocate resources effectively. By monitoring the progress of the project against the planned objectives, project managers can identify any resource constraints and allocate resources accordingly.

d. Improved Communication: EVM provides project managers with a standardized method for reporting project performance to stakeholders. It helps project managers to communicate the progress of the project in a clear and concise manner, which improves stakeholder engagement and buy-in.

e. Cost Control: EVM provides project managers with a clear and accurate picture of the cost performance of the project. By monitoring the cost performance of the project, project managers can identify any cost overruns and take corrective actions to control costs.

Overall, EVM helps project managers to deliver projects on time, within budget, and to the required quality standards. It provides project managers with a comprehensive and objective way to measure project performance and identify any potential issues or risks.

## BENEFITS OF EARNED VALUE MANAGEMENT:

The benefits of EVM for project managers are numerous, including:

a. Improved Decision Making: EVM provides project managers with real-time and accurate data on project performance, which enables them to make informed decisions. This helps project managers to prioritize tasks, allocate resources, and identify any issues or risks that may impact project performance.

b. Early Detection of Problems: EVM provides an early warning system that allows project managers to detect problems and issues before they escalate. This enables project managers to take timely corrective actions to keep the project on track and avoid any delays or cost overruns.

c. Improved Forecasting: EVM provides project managers with a clear and accurate picture of project performance, which helps them to forecast project completion dates and costs. This enables project managers to make more accurate and reliable predictions, which improves stakeholder confidence and trust.

d. Better Resource Management: EVM helps project managers to manage project resources more effectively. By monitoring project performance against planned objectives, project managers can identify any resource constraints and allocate resources accordingly.

e. Enhanced Stakeholder Engagement: EVM provides project managers with a standardized method for reporting project performance to stakeholders. This helps to improve stakeholder engagement and buy-in, which is essential for project success.

Overall, EVM is a valuable tool for project managers as it provides a comprehensive and objective way to measure project performance. It helps project managers to make informed decisions, detect problems early, forecast project completion dates and costs accurately, manage resources effectively, and engage stakeholders more effectively.

## THE THREE KEY METRICS IN EARNED VALUE MANAGEMENT:

EVM relies on three key metrics to measure project performance:

- Planned Value (PV): This is the budgeted cost of work scheduled (BCWS), which is the budgeted cost for the work that was planned to be completed during a specific period. PV represents the planned value of the work that is scheduled to be completed at a given point in time.

- Earned Value (EV): This is the budgeted cost of work performed (BCWP), which is the value of the work that has been completed up to a specific point in time. EV represents the value of the work that has been completed at a given point in time.

- Actual Cost (AC): This is the actual cost of work performed (ACWP), which is the actual cost incurred to complete the work up to a specific point in time. AC represents the actual cost of the work that has been completed at a given point in time.

By using these three key metrics, project managers can calculate a range of performance indicators that help to measure the project's progress and performance. These performance indicators include:

- Schedule Variance (SV): SV measures the difference between the earned value (EV) and the planned value (PV). If SV is positive, it means that the project is ahead of schedule. If SV is negative, it means that the project is behind schedule.

- Cost Variance (CV): CV measures the difference between the earned value (EV) and the actual cost (AC). If CV is positive, it means that the project is under budget. If CV is negative, it means that the project is over budget.

- Schedule Performance Index (SPI): SPI measures the project's efficiency in terms of schedule performance. SPI is calculated by dividing the earned value (EV) by the planned value (PV). If SPI is greater than 1, it means that the project is ahead of schedule. If SPI is less than 1, it means that the project is behind schedule.

- Cost Performance Index (CPI): CPI measures the project's efficiency in terms of cost performance. CPI is calculated by dividing the earned value (EV) by the actual cost (AC). If CPI is greater than 1, it means that the project is under budget. If CPI is less than 1, it means that the project is over budget.

Overall, these key metrics help project managers to measure project performance, identify any variances between planned and actual performance, and take timely corrective actions to keep the project on track.

## THE EARNED VALUE MANAGEMENT PROCESS:

The EVM process involves several steps that project managers must follow to implement EVM effectively:

1. Define the Work Breakdown Structure (WBS): The WBS is a hierarchical decomposition of the project scope into smaller, more manageable components. The WBS forms the basis for identifying the project tasks and activities that will be measured using EVM.

2. Determine the Planned Value (PV): The planned value is the budgeted cost of work scheduled (BCWS) for the project tasks and activities. The PV is calculated by assigning a cost estimate to each task or activity in the WBS.

3. Determine the Earned Value (EV): The earned value is the budgeted cost of work performed (BCWP) for the project tasks and activities. The EV is calculated by measuring the progress of each task or activity against the project schedule.

4. Determine the Actual Cost (AC): The actual cost is the actual cost of work performed (ACWP) for the project tasks and activities. The AC is calculated by tracking the actual costs incurred for each task or activity.

5. Calculate the Performance Indicators: The performance indicators, such as the Schedule Variance (SV), Cost Variance (CV), Schedule Performance Index (SPI), and Cost Performance Index (CPI), are calculated using the PV, EV, and AC data.

6. Analyse the Performance Indicators: The project manager analyses the performance indicators to identify any variances between the planned and actual project performance. The project manager then takes corrective actions to address any variances and keep the project on track.

7. Report on the Project Performance: The project manager reports on the project performance to stakeholders using the performance indicators and other EVM data. The project manager communicates any variances, corrective actions, and progress towards project objectives.

8. Monitor and Control: The project manager continues to monitor and control the project performance using EVM throughout the project lifecycle to ensure that the project stays on track.

Overall, the EVM process provides project managers with a standardized method for measuring project performance, identifying any variances between planned and actual performance, and taking timely corrective actions to keep the project on track. By implementing EVM, project managers can deliver projects on time, within budget, and to the required quality standards.

## CHALLENGES AND LIMITATIONS OF EARNED VALUE MANAGEMENT:

While EVM is a valuable tool for project managers, there are several challenges and limitations that project managers should be aware of:

a. Complex and Time-Consuming: EVM is a complex and time-consuming process that requires a significant amount of effort to implement effectively. Project managers must be willing to invest the necessary time and resources to ensure the success of EVM.

b. Requires Accurate Data: EVM relies on accurate data to measure project performance. Any inaccuracies in the data can result in inaccurate performance indicators and mislead project managers in their decision-making process.

c. Assumes Linear Progress: EVM assumes that progress on a project will be linear and consistent over time. However, in reality, progress can be non-linear, and project managers must be aware of this limitation and make necessary adjustments to the EVM process.

d. Limited Application: EVM may not be suitable for all types of projects. Small and straightforward projects may not require the level of detail and analysis provided by EVM.

e. Costly to Implement: EVM may require the implementation of new processes and tools, which can be costly for organizations. Additionally, EVM may require specialized training for project managers and team members, which can also be expensive.

f. Limited Insight into Non-Financial Metrics: EVM primarily focuses on financial metrics, such as cost and schedule performance. However, it may not provide insight into non-financial metrics, such as customer satisfaction or employee morale.

Despite these challenges and limitations, EVM remains a valuable tool for project managers to measure project performance and identify any potential issues or risks. Project managers must carefully consider the application of EVM and make necessary adjustments to the process to ensure its success.

## CONCLUSION AND KEY TAKEAWAYS:

Earned Value Management (EVM) is a valuable tool for project managers to measure project performance, identify variances between planned and actual performance, and take timely corrective actions to keep the project on track. By using EVM, project managers can deliver projects on time, within budget, and to the required quality standards.

EVM relies on three key metrics: Planned Value (PV), Earned Value (EV), and Actual Cost (AC), which are used to calculate a range of performance indicators. These performance indicators, such as Schedule Variance (SV), Cost Variance (CV), Schedule Performance Index (SPI), and Cost Performance Index (CPI), provide project managers with a standardized method for measuring project performance.

However, there are several challenges and limitations associated with EVM, including its complexity, time-consuming nature, reliance on accurate data, limited application, and cost to implement. Despite these challenges, EVM remains a valuable tool for project managers, provided that it is applied appropriately and adjusted to suit the project's specific needs.

Key takeaways for project managers using EVM include:

a. Establish a clear and accurate baseline plan for the project.

b. Ensure that accurate data is collected and used for calculating the EVM metrics.

c. Regularly monitor project performance using EVM and take corrective actions whenever necessary.

d. Communicate project performance to stakeholders using EVM data and performance indicators.

e. Adjust the EVM process to suit the project's specific needs and limitations.

Overall, EVM is an effective tool for project managers to measure project performance and ensure the success of their projects. By understanding its benefits, limitations, and implementation process, project managers can use EVM to deliver successful projects.

# 6.14 UNDERSTANDING EARNED VALUE DATA: ANALYSING VARIANCES AND PERFORMANCE INDEXES

Effective project management involves monitoring and controlling project performance to ensure that it is on track and within budget. Earned Value Management (EVM) is a powerful project management technique that enables project managers to track project performance, measure progress, and forecast the project's final cost and schedule. By analysing earned value data, project managers can make informed decisions, identify potential problems, and take corrective actions to keep the project on track.

In this guide, we will explore how to interpret earned value data, including variances and performance indexes. We will begin by defining EVM and discussing its importance in project management. We will then review the key concepts of EVM, including Planned Value (PV), Earned Value (EV), and Actual Cost (AC).

Next, we will delve into the topic of variances in EVM, which provide project managers with information on how the project is performing compared to the baseline plan. We will explain the two primary types of variances - Schedule Variance (SV) and Cost Variance (CV) - and explore how to analyse them.

Following this, we will look at EVM performance indexes, which provide insight into project performance in terms of cost and schedule. We will discuss the two primary indexes - Schedule Performance Index (SPI) and Cost Performance Index (CPI) - and explain how to analyse them.

In the next section, we will focus on interpreting EVM data. We will explore how to interpret variances and performance indexes, identify potential problems, and develop corrective actions to address them.

Finally, we will discuss the benefits of EVM analysis, including improved project performance, better decision-making, and increased stakeholder satisfaction. We will conclude by summarizing the key points of this guide and emphasizing the importance of ongoing EVM analysis to ensure project success.

## KEY CONCEPTS OF EVM

Earned Value Management (EVM) is a project management methodology that integrates scope, time, and cost into one performance measurement system. EVM provides a quantitative measurement of project performance by comparing the planned value (PV) of work scheduled to be completed with the earned value (EV) of work actually completed, and the actual cost (AC) of work completed. By comparing these values, EVM provides project managers with a way to monitor project performance and forecast project cost and schedule.

PV, also known as Budgeted Cost of Work Scheduled (BCWS), is the value of work scheduled to be completed on a project. PV is calculated by multiplying the planned percentage of work completed by the total project budget. For example, if a project has a total budget of £100,000 and 50% of the work is scheduled to be completed by a certain date, the PV for that date would be £50,000.

EV, also known as Budgeted Cost of Work Performed (BCWP), is the value of work actually completed on a project. EV is calculated by multiplying the percentage of work completed by the total project budget. For example, if a project has a total budget of £100,000 and 40% of the work is actually completed by a certain date, the EV for that date would be £40,000.

405

AC, also known as Actual Cost of Work Performed (ACWP), is the actual cost of work completed on a project. AC is the sum of all costs incurred for completed work, including labour, materials, and equipment. AC provides a measure of the actual cost of the work performed and is used to calculate the Cost Variance (CV) and Cost Performance Index (CPI).

EVM provides a snapshot of project performance at a specific point in time. By analysing EVM data, project managers can identify whether the project is on track, behind schedule, or over budget. EVM data can also be used to forecast the final cost and schedule of the project, enabling project managers to take corrective actions to keep the project on track.

## VARIANCES IN EVM

Variances in EVM compare the planned and actual performance of the project. There are two primary types of variances in EVM: Schedule Variance (SV) and Cost Variance (CV).

Schedule Variance (SV) measures the difference between the earned value (EV) and planned value (PV) of work scheduled to be completed at a specific point in time. SV is calculated as EV minus PV. A positive SV indicates that the project is ahead of schedule, while a negative SV indicates that the project is behind schedule. For example, if the PV for a project is £50,000 and the EV for the same period is £40,000, the SV would be -£10,000, indicating that the project is behind schedule.

Cost Variance (CV) measures the difference between the earned value (EV) and actual cost (AC) of work completed at a specific point in time. CV is calculated as EV minus AC. A positive CV indicates that the project is under budget, while a negative CV indicates that the project is over budget. For example, if the AC for a project is £60,000 and the EV for the same period is £70,000, the CV would be £10,000, indicating that the project is under budget.

Analysing SV and CV is crucial to understanding project performance. By comparing the planned and actual performance, project managers can identify whether the project is on track or whether corrective actions are required to bring the project back on track. For example, if the project is behind schedule (negative SV), the project manager can investigate the causes of the delay and take corrective actions to bring the project back on schedule.

Project managers can also calculate the Schedule Performance Index (SPI) and Cost Performance Index (CPI) to provide further insight into project performance.

IV. EVM Performance Indexes

The Schedule Performance Index (SPI) measures the efficiency of the project in terms of schedule performance. SPI is calculated as EV divided by PV. An SPI of greater than one indicates that the project is ahead of schedule, while an SPI of less than one indicates that the project is behind schedule. For example, if the PV for a project is £50,000 and the EV for the same period is £60,000, the SPI would be 1.2, indicating that the project is ahead of schedule.

The Cost Performance Index (CPI) measures the efficiency of the project in terms of cost performance. CPI is calculated as EV divided by AC. A CPI of greater than one indicates that the project is under budget, while a CPI of less than one indicates that the project is over budget. For example, if the AC for a project is £60,000 and the EV for the same period is £70,000, the CPI would be 1.17, indicating that the project is under budget.

Analysing SPI and CPI is critical to understanding project performance. These indexes provide project managers with a measure of the efficiency of the project in terms of schedule and cost performance. By monitoring SPI and CPI, project managers can identify potential problems and take corrective actions to keep the project on track.

In summary, analysing variances and performance indexes in EVM provides project managers with a comprehensive understanding of project performance. By comparing planned and actual performance, project managers can identify potential problems and take corrective actions to keep the project on track.

## EVM PERFORMANCE INDEXES

In addition to analysing variances, EVM provides project managers with performance indexes that measure the efficiency of the project in terms of schedule and cost performance. The two primary EVM performance indexes are the Schedule Performance Index (SPI) and the Cost Performance Index (CPI).

The Schedule Performance Index (SPI) measures the efficiency of the project in terms of schedule performance. It is calculated by dividing the earned value (EV) by the planned value (PV). An SPI of greater than one indicates that the project is ahead of schedule, while an SPI of less than one indicates that the project is behind schedule.

For example, if a project has a PV of £50,000 and an EV of £60,000, the SPI would be 1.2. This indicates that the project is ahead of schedule, with 20% more work completed than planned.

The Cost Performance Index (CPI) measures the efficiency of the project in terms of cost performance. It is calculated by dividing the earned value (EV) by the actual cost (AC). A CPI of greater than one indicates that the project is under budget, while a CPI of less than one indicates that the project is over budget.

For example, if a project has an AC of £80,000 and an EV of £90,000, the CPI would be 1.125. This indicates that the project is under budget, with the project team completing 12.5% more work than the actual cost incurred.

Analysing SPI and CPI can provide valuable insights into project performance. For instance, a high SPI and CPI indicate that the project is on track and performing efficiently. However, a low SPI or CPI suggests that the project is facing potential issues, and corrective actions may be necessary.

Moreover, SPI and CPI can be used together to forecast the project's final cost and schedule. By using these indexes, project managers can predict if the project will complete within the budget and schedule constraints.

In conclusion, analysing EVM performance indexes, such as SPI and CPI, provides project managers with critical information to measure the efficiency of their projects. By keeping track of these indexes, project managers can identify potential problems early on and take corrective actions to keep the project on track.

## INTERPRETING EVM DATA

Interpreting EVM data is a critical aspect of project management. Analysing earned value data, variances, and performance indexes can help project managers identify potential problems, track project performance, and make informed decisions to keep the project on track.

Here are some steps for interpreting EVM data:

1. Interpret variances: Analysing variances provides project managers with an understanding of how the project is performing compared to the baseline plan. A negative Schedule Variance (SV) indicates that the project is behind schedule, while a negative Cost Variance (CV) suggests that the project is over budget. Project managers should investigate the causes of negative variances and take corrective actions to bring the project back on track.

2. Analyse performance indexes: SPI and CPI provide project managers with a measure of the efficiency of the project in terms of schedule and cost performance. A high SPI and CPI indicate that the project is on track and performing efficiently. Project managers should monitor these indexes regularly to identify potential issues early on and take corrective actions.

3. Identify potential problems: Analysing variances and performance indexes can help project managers identify potential problems, such as schedule delays, cost overruns, or scope creep. Identifying these issues early on can help project managers take corrective actions to mitigate their impact on the project.

4. Develop corrective actions: Based on the analysis of EVM data, project managers should develop corrective actions to address potential problems. These corrective actions should be specific, measurable, achievable, relevant, and time-bound (SMART). For instance, if the project is behind schedule, the corrective action could be to increase the pace of work or reallocate resources to ensure that the project is completed on time.

5. Monitor progress: After implementing corrective actions, project managers should monitor the project's progress to ensure that it is back on track. Regular monitoring of variances and performance indexes can help project managers determine if the corrective actions have been effective or if further actions are necessary.

In summary, interpreting EVM data is a critical aspect of project management. By analysing variances, performance indexes, and potential problems, project managers can make informed decisions, take corrective actions, and keep the project on track. Regular monitoring of EVM data can provide project managers with a real-time view of project performance and enable them to make timely decisions to ensure project success.

## CONCLUSION

In conclusion, understanding earned value data, including variances and performance indexes, is crucial for project managers to monitor and control project performance effectively. EVM analysis provides a quantitative measure of project performance that can inform decision-making, identify potential issues, and provide project managers with the ability to forecast project performance in terms of cost and schedule.

By interpreting EVM data, project managers can identify potential problems, develop corrective actions, and keep the project on track. Regular monitoring of EVM data can provide project managers with a real-time view of project performance and enable them to make timely decisions to ensure project success.

The benefits of EVM analysis include improved project performance, better decision-making, increased stakeholder satisfaction, improved resource management, and increased predictability. By using EVM analysis, project managers can optimize project performance, reduce risks, and improve stakeholder confidence.

Overall, EVM is a powerful project management methodology that enables project managers to monitor and control project performance effectively. Understanding and interpreting earned value data, including variances and performance indexes, is critical to the success of any project. By following the steps outlined in this guide, project managers can use EVM analysis to improve project performance, make informed decisions, and ensure project success.

# 6.15 THE BENEFITS OF INTERPRETING EARNED VALUE DATA FOR PROJECT MANAGEMENT

Earned Value Management (EVM) is a project management methodology that enables the measurement of project performance and progress in terms of cost and schedule. It uses specific metrics to track the actual progress of a project against the planned progress, providing valuable insight into whether a project is on track or not.

EVM helps project managers gain a better understanding of the status of their project by measuring three key components: planned value (PV), actual cost (AC), and earned value (EV). Planned value represents the total planned cost of a project, while actual cost represents the actual amount of money spent on the project to date. Earned value is the value of the work that has been completed to date, and is calculated by multiplying the percentage of the work completed by the total planned value.

By analysing these metrics, project managers can identify if a project is running over budget, behind schedule, or if there are any variances in performance. EVM also provides a standardized way of measuring project performance, making it easier to compare the performance of different projects or phases within a project.

Overall, understanding EVM and the metrics used to measure project performance can help project managers make more informed decisions about how to allocate resources, adjust project timelines, and make other critical project management decisions.

## IMPROVING PROJECT FORECASTING

One of the primary benefits of interpreting earned value data is that it helps project managers improve their project forecasting. By using EVM metrics, project managers can assess the current status of a project and predict how it will perform in the future, providing valuable insights into potential issues before they become major problems.

For example, if a project is currently behind schedule or over budget, project managers can use EVM metrics to determine if the current performance trend is likely to continue or if the project is likely to recover. This helps project managers make informed decisions about how to adjust the project plan, such as allocating additional resources or changing project timelines.

Moreover, EVM metrics also help project managers forecast the estimated completion date and final project cost. By comparing the actual progress to the planned progress, project managers can determine if the project is ahead or behind schedule and make adjustments accordingly. Additionally, project managers can use EVM to estimate the final project cost by extrapolating the project's current cost performance index (CPI) or schedule performance index (SPI).

Overall, interpreting earned value data helps project managers improve their project forecasting by providing them with accurate and reliable metrics to measure project performance and make informed decisions about project planning, resource allocation, and other critical project management decisions.

## IDENTIFYING PROJECT VARIANCE AND DEVIATIONS

Interpreting earned value data can help project managers identify project variances and deviations from the planned project performance. By comparing the actual project performance to the planned performance, project managers can easily identify any areas where the project is falling behind schedule or over budget.

For example, if the actual cost of the project is higher than the planned cost, or if the earned value is lower than the planned value, then it indicates that the project is running behind schedule or over budget. By identifying these variances, project managers can take corrective action to get the project back on track.

Moreover, EVM metrics also help project managers identify the root cause of the variance. For instance, if the project is running over budget, the project manager can analyse the EVM data to identify which specific tasks or activities are responsible for the cost overrun. This information can be used to adjust project plans, allocate additional resources, or take other corrective measures to bring the project back on track.

By using EVM metrics to identify project variances and deviations, project managers can proactively manage project risks and take corrective action before the project goes too far off course. This helps to ensure that the project stays on track and is completed within the planned budget and schedule.

## BETTER RESOURCE ALLOCATION

Interpreting earned value data can also help project managers make better decisions about resource allocation. By analysing the EVM metrics, project managers can identify which specific tasks or activities are using more resources than planned or which tasks are behind schedule.

This information can be used to make adjustments to the project plan or to allocate additional resources to specific tasks or activities to bring the project back on track. By allocating resources more effectively, project managers can optimize the project's progress and ensure that it is completed within the planned budget and schedule.

Moreover, EVM metrics also help project managers identify the optimal level of resources required to complete the project. By comparing the planned value to the earned value and actual cost, project managers can calculate the cost performance index (CPI) and determine the project's efficiency in using its resources.

This information can be used to make informed decisions about resource allocation, such as determining whether additional resources are required to complete the project on time or whether the project can be completed with the current resources.

By using EVM metrics to optimize resource allocation, project managers can ensure that they are making the most effective use of the available resources and help the project team deliver a successful project.

## ENHANCED PROJECT COMMUNICATION AND REPORTING

Interpreting earned value data can also improve project communication and reporting. EVM metrics provide a standardized way of measuring project performance that can be easily communicated to stakeholders, team members, and executives.

By using EVM metrics in project reporting, project managers can provide accurate and timely information on the status of the project, including its progress, cost, and schedule. This information can be communicated in various formats, including reports, graphs, and dashboards, providing stakeholders with a clear understanding of the project's status.

Moreover, EVM metrics can help project managers identify any potential issues or concerns, allowing them to communicate these issues to stakeholders in a timely manner. This can help build trust and confidence among stakeholders by demonstrating that the project is being managed effectively.

Furthermore, EVM metrics can also help project managers identify areas where the project is performing well, providing an opportunity to showcase successes and accomplishments to stakeholders. This can help motivate team members and promote a positive project culture.

By using EVM metrics to enhance project communication and reporting, project managers can ensure that stakeholders are informed about the project's status and progress, promote transparency, and facilitate collaboration among team members.

## FACILITATING TIMELY DECISION MAKING

Interpreting earned value data can also facilitate timely decision-making. By analysing EVM metrics, project managers can identify project variances and deviations, and make informed decisions about how to address them.

For instance, if the EVM data indicates that the project is behind schedule or over budget, project managers can take immediate corrective action to bring the project back on track. This can include adjusting the project plan, reallocating resources, or changing project timelines.

Moreover, EVM metrics can also help project managers anticipate potential risks or issues, enabling them to take proactive measures to mitigate these risks before they impact the project. This can help minimize the impact of risks and reduce the likelihood of project delays or cost overruns.

Furthermore, EVM metrics can also help project managers make informed decisions about whether to continue with a project or terminate it. If the EVM data indicates that the project is not likely to meet its objectives or that the cost of continuing the project exceeds the benefits, project managers can make the decision to terminate the project and allocate resources to other projects that offer better prospects for success.

By using EVM metrics to facilitate timely decision-making, project managers can ensure that they are making informed decisions based on accurate and reliable data. This can help prevent project delays and cost overruns, and increase the likelihood of project success.

## ACHIEVING PROJECT SUCCESS WITH EVM

Interpreting earned value data is a critical component of achieving project success. By using EVM metrics to measure project performance, project managers can ensure that the project is progressing according to plan and identify any potential issues that could impact project success.

EVM metrics provide project managers with a standardized way of measuring project performance, enabling them to compare the performance of different projects or phases within a project. This helps project managers identify best practices and areas for improvement, which can be applied to future projects.

Moreover, EVM metrics can help project managers ensure that the project is completed within the planned budget and schedule. By analysing the EVM data, project managers can identify any areas where the project is falling behind schedule or over budget and take corrective action to get the project back on track.

Furthermore, EVM metrics can also help project managers identify potential risks or issues, enabling them to take proactive measures to mitigate these risks before they impact the project. This can help minimize the impact of risks and reduce the likelihood of project delays or cost overruns.

Overall, by interpreting earned value data, project managers can ensure that the project is completed within the planned budget and schedule and meets its objectives. This can help build a reputation for delivering successful projects, which can be invaluable in securing future projects and funding.

# 6.16 The Importance of Contingency Planning in Projects: Mitigating Risks and Maximizing Success

Contingency planning is the process of creating a plan B or backup plan to address potential risks or uncertainties that may arise during the course of a project. It involves identifying and analysing potential risks and developing strategies to mitigate or avoid them. The goal of contingency planning is to ensure that a project can continue even if unforeseen events occur, and to minimize the impact of those events on the project's timeline, budget, and overall success.

In project management, contingency planning is an essential component of risk management. It involves anticipating potential risks and developing plans to respond to them, should they occur. Contingency plans can include alternative approaches, workarounds, and fallback strategies that allow a project to continue even when the unexpected happens. By planning for contingencies, project managers can minimize the impact of risks and uncertainties and ensure that the project stays on track towards its goals.

## Understanding the Need for Contingency Planning

In any project, there are many potential risks and uncertainties that can arise, including changes in scope, unexpected delays, budget overruns, equipment failures, and personnel issues. These risks can derail a project and cause it to fail, resulting in wasted time, money, and resources.

Contingency planning is needed because it allows project managers to identify potential risks and develop strategies to mitigate them before they happen. By planning for contingencies, project managers can minimize the impact of risks and uncertainties and ensure that the project stays on track towards its goals.

Additionally, contingency planning helps project managers anticipate and prepare for unexpected events. It allows them to be proactive rather than reactive, which can save time, money, and resources in the long run. By having contingency plans in place, project managers can quickly respond to unexpected events and minimize their impact on the project.

Overall, contingency planning is essential to project success because it helps project managers stay ahead of potential risks and uncertainties and ensures that the project stays on track towards its goals. Without contingency planning, projects are more vulnerable to unexpected events and may not be able to recover from them.

## THE BENEFITS OF CONTINGENCY PLANNING

Contingency planning provides several benefits to project managers and their teams.

First, it helps to reduce project risk. By identifying potential risks and developing contingency plans to address them, project managers can minimize the likelihood and impact of negative events. This can help to reduce project costs, improve project timelines, and enhance overall project quality.

Second, contingency planning helps project managers to be more proactive in managing risks. Instead of waiting for negative events to occur and reacting to them, project managers can anticipate potential risks and put measures in place to address them proactively. This can help to save time, money, and resources by avoiding the negative impacts of potential risks.

Third, contingency planning provides a sense of security and confidence to project teams. Knowing that there are contingency plans in place to address potential risks and uncertainties can help team members to feel more secure in their roles and responsibilities. This can boost team morale and motivation, which can ultimately lead to better project outcomes.

Fourth, contingency planning can help project managers to stay within budget and timeline constraints. By anticipating potential risks and developing contingency plans to address them, project managers can avoid unexpected delays and costs that can lead to project overruns. This can help to ensure that the project stays within budget and timeline constraints and is completed on time and within budget.

Overall, contingency planning is an essential part of project management that provides several benefits to project managers and their teams. It helps to reduce project risk, improve project quality, boost team morale, and ensure that the project stays within budget and timeline constraints.

## THE PROCESS OF CONTINGENCY PLANNING

The process of contingency planning involves several steps, which include:

1. Risk Identification: The first step in contingency planning is to identify potential risks that could impact the project. This can be done through brainstorming sessions, risk assessments, and other techniques that help to identify potential risks.

2. Risk Analysis: Once potential risks have been identified, the next step is to analyse them. This involves assessing the likelihood and potential impact of each risk on the project, as well as identifying any interdependencies or connections between risks.

3. Contingency Plan Development: Based on the results of the risk analysis, contingency plans are developed. These plans should include specific strategies and actions that can be taken to address each potential risk.

4. Contingency Plan Testing: Contingency plans should be tested to ensure that they are effective and can be implemented in the event of a risk occurring. Testing can be done through simulations, tabletop exercises, and other techniques that allow project teams to practice implementing the contingency plans.

5. Contingency Plan Implementation: In the event that a risk occurs, contingency plans are implemented to address the risk and minimize its impact on the project. This may involve executing specific actions, using alternative approaches, or implementing fallback strategies that allow the project to continue.

6. Contingency Plan Evaluation: After a risk has been addressed, it's important to evaluate the effectiveness of the contingency plan. This can help project managers to identify any areas for improvement and refine the contingency plan for future use.

Overall, the process of contingency planning involves identifying potential risks, analysing their impact, developing specific plans to address them, testing those plans, and implementing them in the event of a risk occurring. By following this process, project managers can be more proactive in managing risks and ensuring the success of their projects.

## EXAMPLES OF CONTINGENCY PLANNING IN REAL-LIFE PROJECTS

Contingency planning is a critical part of project management, and it is used in many real-life projects across different industries. Here are some examples of contingency planning in action:

1. Construction Projects: In construction projects, contingency planning is used to address potential delays, cost overruns, and unforeseen site conditions. For example, if a construction crew uncovers unexpected underground utilities during excavation,

the project manager may have a contingency plan in place to reroute the utilities or adjust the project timeline to accommodate the delay.

2. Information Technology Projects: In IT projects, contingency planning is used to address potential software bugs, data breaches, and system failures. For example, if a company's data is compromised due to a cyber attack, the project manager may have a contingency plan in place to restore the data from backups or implement security protocols to prevent further breaches.

3. Event Planning: In event planning, contingency planning is used to address potential weather-related issues, vendor cancellations, and attendee issues. For example, if an outdoor event is threatened by rain, the event planner may have a contingency plan in place to move the event indoors or provide shelter for attendees.

4. Product Development: In product development, contingency planning is used to address potential manufacturing issues, supply chain disruptions, and design flaws. For example, if a product is found to have a design flaw during testing, the project manager may have a contingency plan in place to modify the design or halt production until the issue is resolved.

Overall, contingency planning is used in many real-life projects to address potential risks and uncertainties. By having contingency plans in place, project managers can ensure that their projects stay on track towards their goals and can minimize the impact of unexpected events.

## CHALLENGES AND LIMITATIONS OF CONTINGENCY PLANNING

While contingency planning is a critical part of project management, there are also challenges and limitations that project managers should be aware of. Some of the challenges and limitations of contingency planning include:

a. Resource Constraints: Developing and implementing contingency plans requires additional resources, including time, money, and personnel. Project managers may need to balance the need for contingency planning with available resources and project constraints.

b. Over-reliance on Contingency Plans: Project managers may become over-reliant on contingency plans, which can lead to complacency and a lack of proactive risk management. It's important for project managers to continue to identify and analyze potential risks even after contingency plans are developed and implemented.

c. Unforeseeable Risks: Despite thorough risk analysis, there may be unforeseeable risks that cannot be addressed through contingency planning. Project managers must be prepared to adapt to these risks and develop new contingency plans as needed.

d. Lack of Buy-In: Contingency plans may not be effective if project team members do not understand or support them. Project managers must ensure that all team members understand the importance of contingency planning and are committed to implementing the plans.

e. Limited Effectiveness: Contingency plans may not always be effective in addressing risks. There may be instances where a contingency plan is not sufficient to mitigate the impact of a risk, or where a risk occurs that was not identified during the risk analysis phase.

Overall, contingency planning is an important part of project management, but it is not without its challenges and limitations. Project managers must be aware of these challenges and limitations and develop strategies to address them in order to ensure the effectiveness of their contingency plans.

## INCORPORATING CONTINGENCY PLANNING INTO PROJECT MANAGEMENT BEST PRACTICES

Contingency planning is an essential part of project management, and it is important for project managers to incorporate it into their best practices. Here are some strategies for incorporating contingency planning into project management:

1. Develop a Risk Management Plan: A risk management plan is an essential component of contingency planning. It involves identifying potential risks, analysing their impact, and developing strategies to mitigate or avoid them. Project managers should develop a risk management plan at the outset of a project and continue to update it throughout the project lifecycle.

2. Create a Contingency Budget: Project managers should consider creating a contingency budget as part of their overall project budget. This budget should include funds set aside specifically for addressing potential risks and uncertainties.

3. Assign Responsibility for Contingency Planning: Project managers should assign responsibility for contingency planning to specific team members. This can include risk management, developing contingency plans, and implementing them in the event of a risk occurring.

4. Test and Refine Contingency Plans: Contingency plans should be tested and refined on an ongoing basis to ensure their effectiveness. This can involve running simulations, tabletop exercises, and other techniques that allow project teams to practice implementing the contingency plans.

5. Communicate Contingency Plans to Stakeholders: It's important for project managers to communicate contingency plans to stakeholders, including clients, team members, and other

relevant parties. This can help to build confidence in the project and demonstrate the project manager's proactive approach to risk management.

6. Continuously Monitor and Update Contingency Plans: Contingency plans should be monitored and updated throughout the project lifecycle to ensure their ongoing effectiveness. This can involve revisiting the risk management plan, reviewing the contingency budget, and revising the contingency plans themselves based on new information.

Overall, incorporating contingency planning into project management best practices involves developing a risk management plan, creating a contingency budget, assigning responsibility for contingency planning, testing and refining contingency plans, communicating contingency plans to stakeholders, and continuously monitoring and updating contingency plans. By following these strategies, project managers can be more proactive in managing risks and ensuring the success of their projects.

## Conclusion: The Critical Role of Contingency Planning in Project Success

Contingency planning is a critical component of project management that involves identifying potential risks and developing strategies to mitigate or avoid them. It is essential for ensuring project success and minimizing the impact of unexpected events on project timelines, budgets, and outcomes.

The process of contingency planning involves several steps, including risk identification, risk analysis, contingency plan development, contingency plan testing, contingency plan implementation, and contingency plan evaluation. By following this process, project managers can be more proactive in managing risks and ensuring the success of their projects.

Contingency planning provides several benefits, including reducing project risk, improving project quality, boosting team morale, and ensuring that the project stays within budget and timeline constraints. However, there are also challenges and limitations associated with contingency planning, including resource constraints, over-reliance on contingency plans, unforeseeable risks, lack of buy-in, and limited effectiveness.

To incorporate contingency planning into project management best practices, project managers should develop a risk management plan, create a contingency budget, assign responsibility for contingency planning, test and refine contingency plans, communicate contingency plans to stakeholders, and continuously monitor and update contingency plans.

In conclusion, contingency planning is a critical part of project management that can help to ensure project success in the face of potential risks and uncertainties. By implementing effective contingency planning strategies, project managers can minimize the impact of unexpected events on their projects and ensure that they stay on track towards their goals.

# CHAPTER SEVEN

## *ESSENTIALS OF PROJECT SCOPE MANAGEMENT*

# 7.1 DEFINING SCOPE IN TERMS OF OUTPUTS, OUTCOMES, AND BENEFITS

When it comes to project management, defining scope is a crucial step that helps set the foundation for project success. The scope outlines what the project aims to achieve and what it will include or exclude. It provides a clear understanding of the project's boundaries and defines what is expected to be delivered by the end of the project.

Scope can be defined in different ways, but one of the most effective methods is through outputs, outcomes, and benefits. By focusing on these three aspects, you can ensure that the project is aligned with the organization's goals and that it delivers the intended value.

In this section, we will discuss how to define scope in terms of outputs, outcomes, and benefits, and how product breakdown structures, cost breakdown structures, and work breakdown structures can be used to achieve this. We will also provide tips for defining scope effectively and ensuring that it remains on track throughout the project.

## UNDERSTANDING THE CONCEPTS OF OUTPUTS, OUTCOMES, AND BENEFITS:

Before diving into the details of defining scope through outputs, outcomes, and benefits, it is essential to understand these concepts.

Outputs refer to the tangible deliverables or products of the project. These can be physical or digital, such as reports, software, equipment, or infrastructure. Outputs are the measurable results of the project and are typically defined in terms of quality, quantity, and timeliness.

Outcomes, on the other hand, refer to the broader impact of the project. They represent the changes that the project is expected to bring about, either in the short or long term. Outcomes are often intangible and can be difficult to measure, but they are critical to the success of the project. Examples of outcomes include increased customer satisfaction, improved employee morale, or enhanced operational efficiency.

Benefits are the positive results that the project is expected to bring to the organization or its stakeholders. Benefits are closely linked to outcomes, but they focus on the value that the project creates. Benefits can be measured in terms of financial returns, increased market share, or improved public perception, among others.

In defining scope, it is essential to consider all three of these concepts and ensure that they are aligned with the organization's overall goals and objectives.

## THE IMPORTANCE OF DEFINING SCOPE:

Defining scope is crucial to the success of any project, as it sets the foundation for everything that follows. When the scope is not clearly defined, it can lead to confusion, delays, and unexpected costs. This is why it is important to define scope early on in the project and to ensure that it is reviewed and updated regularly.

Defining scope in terms of outputs, outcomes, and benefits is particularly important, as it ensures that the project is focused on delivering value to the organization and its stakeholders. By considering all three of these concepts, you can ensure that the project is aligned with the organization's overall goals and that it creates the intended impact.

Additionally, defining scope through outputs, outcomes, and benefits helps to provide clarity and direction to the project team. It helps to ensure that everyone understands what is expected of them and what they are working towards. This, in turn, can improve communication, collaboration, and overall project performance.

Overall, defining scope is critical to the success of any project, and doing so in terms of outputs, outcomes, and benefits can help ensure that the project delivers the intended value to the organization and its stakeholders.

## DEFINING SCOPE THROUGH PRODUCT BREAKDOWN STRUCTURES (PBS):

One way to define scope in terms of outputs is through the use of a Product Breakdown Structure (PBS). A PBS is a hierarchical diagram that breaks down the project deliverables into smaller, more manageable components. Each component is then broken down further until a clear and concise description of the project deliverables is achieved.

The PBS can help the project team understand the scope of the project by providing a visual representation of the project deliverables. It can also be used to identify the different tasks required to complete each deliverable, the resources needed, and the dependencies between tasks.

To create a PBS, start by listing the major deliverables of the project. Then, break down each deliverable into its component parts. Continue breaking down each component until you have a clear and concise description of the project deliverables.

Defining scope through a PBS can help ensure that the project team is focused on the deliverables and the specific outputs that need to be produced. It can also help to identify any gaps or overlaps in the project scope, which can be addressed before they become issues.

Overall, using a PBS to define scope in terms of outputs can help to provide a clear understanding of the project deliverables, reduce confusion and misunderstandings, and ensure that the project team is aligned on the project objectives.

## DEFINING SCOPE THROUGH COST BREAKDOWN STRUCTURES (CBS):

Another way to define scope is through the use of a Cost Breakdown Structure (CBS). A CBS is a hierarchical diagram that breaks down the project costs into smaller, more manageable components. Each component is then broken down further until a clear and concise description of the project costs is achieved.

The CBS can help the project team understand the scope of the project by providing a visual representation of the project costs. It can also be used to identify the different tasks required to complete each cost component, the resources needed, and the dependencies between tasks.

To create a CBS, start by listing the major cost components of the project. Then, break down each cost component into its smaller parts. Continue breaking down each component until you have a clear and concise description of the project costs.

Defining scope through a CBS can help ensure that the project team is focused on the costs and the specific resources needed to complete the project. It can also help to identify any cost overruns or underestimations, which can be addressed before they become issues.

Overall, using a CBS to define scope in terms of costs can help to provide a clear understanding of the project budget, reduce confusion and misunderstandings, and ensure that the project team is aligned on the project budget and resource requirements.

## DEFINING SCOPE THROUGH WORK BREAKDOWN STRUCTURES (WBS):

Another way to define scope is through the use of a Work Breakdown Structure (WBS). A WBS is a hierarchical diagram that breaks down the project into smaller, more manageable tasks. Each task is then broken down further until a clear and concise description of the project activities is achieved.

The WBS can help the project team understand the scope of the project by providing a visual representation of the project activities. It can also be used to identify the different tasks required to complete each deliverable, the resources needed, and the dependencies between tasks.

To create a WBS, start by listing the major deliverables of the project. Then, break down each deliverable into its component parts. For each component, identify the tasks required to complete it, the resources needed, and the dependencies between tasks. Continue breaking down each task until you have a clear and concise description of the project activities.

Defining scope through a WBS can help ensure that the project team is focused on the specific activities needed to complete the project. It can also help to identify any potential delays or issues, which can be addressed before they become problems.

Overall, using a WBS to define scope in terms of activities can help to provide a clear understanding of the project tasks, reduce confusion and misunderstandings, and ensure that the project team is aligned on the project activities and requirements.

## TIPS FOR DEFINING SCOPE EFFECTIVELY:

Defining scope is a critical step in project management, and it requires careful planning and execution to ensure that it is done effectively. Here are some tips for defining scope:

a. Start Early: It is essential to define scope early in the project to ensure that everyone is aligned on the project objectives. This can help to avoid any potential delays or issues down the line.

b. Involve Stakeholders: It is important to involve stakeholders in the scope definition process to ensure that their expectations and requirements are taken into account. This can help to ensure that the project is aligned with the organization's overall goals and objectives.

c. Use Clear and Concise Language: When defining scope, use clear and concise language to ensure that everyone understands what is expected. Avoid using technical jargon or ambiguous terms that can lead to confusion.

d. Review and Update Regularly: Scope can change over the course of a project, so it is important to review and update it regularly. This can help to ensure that the project stays on track and that everyone is aligned on the project objectives.

e. Use Visual Aids: Visual aids, such as diagrams or charts, can be helpful in defining scope. They can help to provide a clear and concise representation of the project deliverables, costs, and activities.

f. Focus on Outputs, Outcomes, and Benefits: When defining scope, it is important to focus on the outputs, outcomes, and benefits of the project. This can help to ensure that the project is aligned with the organization's overall goals and that it delivers the intended value.

g. Seek Expertise: Defining scope can be complex, and it may be necessary to seek the expertise of a project management professional. This can help to ensure that scope is defined effectively and that the project is set up for success.

Overall, defining scope is a critical step in project management, and it requires careful planning and execution to ensure that it is done effectively. By following these tips, you can ensure that scope is defined clearly and concisely, and that the project is set up for success.

## CONCLUSION:

Defining scope is a critical step in project management, and it requires careful planning and execution to ensure that it is done effectively. By defining scope in terms of outputs, outcomes, and benefits, and using product breakdown structures, cost breakdown structures, and work breakdown structures, you can ensure that the project is aligned with the organization's overall goals and objectives.

When defining scope, it is important to involve stakeholders, use clear and concise language, review and update regularly, use visual aids, focus on outputs, outcomes, and benefits, and seek expertise when necessary. By following these tips, you can ensure that scope is defined clearly and effectively, and that the project is set up for success.

Overall, defining scope is a critical step in project management, and it requires careful planning and execution to ensure that it is done effectively. By defining scope in terms of outputs, outcomes, and benefits, you can ensure that the project delivers the intended value and is aligned with the organization's overall goals and objectives.

# 7.2 ESTABLISHING SCOPE THROUGH EFFECTIVE REQUIREMENTS MANAGEMENT PROCESSES

Requirements management is a critical process that ensures project success by clearly defining the scope of the project. Establishing project scope involves defining what work is included and excluded from the project and setting clear expectations for what will be delivered. By defining the scope of a project through effective requirements management, project teams can ensure that they are delivering the right product, on time, and within budget.

The requirements management process involves gathering, analysing, justifying, and baselining requirements to ensure that they align with business objectives and meet the needs of stakeholders. Effective requirements management enables project teams to avoid costly rework, project delays, and scope creep, which can result in project failure.

In this section, we will discuss the key processes involved in requirements management and how they can be used to establish project scope. We will cover techniques for gathering requirements, analysing requirements, justifying requirements, and baselining requirements. By the end of this section, you will have a better understanding of how to manage requirements effectively and establish a solid foundation for project success.

## GATHERING REQUIREMENTS

Gathering requirements is the first step in the requirements management process. It involves identifying and understanding the needs and goals of stakeholders who will be impacted by the project. Stakeholders can include customers, end-users, business owners, project sponsors, and other project team members.

To gather requirements effectively, it is important to use a variety of techniques that will enable you to capture all of the necessary information. Some common techniques include interviews, surveys, focus groups, and observation. It is also important to involve stakeholders throughout the gathering process to ensure that their needs are being addressed.

Once requirements have been gathered, they should be documented and organized in a clear and concise manner. This can be done using a requirements document, which should include information such as the requirement's priority, description, acceptance criteria, and any associated risks. Organizing requirements in a structured manner can help to identify inconsistencies and ensure that all requirements are addressed throughout the project lifecycle.

By effectively gathering and documenting requirements, project teams can ensure that they have a clear understanding of the project's scope and are able to deliver a product that meets the needs of stakeholders.

## ANALYSING REQUIREMENTS

After requirements have been gathered, the next step in the requirements management process is to analyse them to ensure that they are complete, consistent, and achievable. Analysing requirements involves identifying any inconsistencies, conflicts, or gaps in requirements and addressing them to ensure that all requirements are aligned with project goals.

One common technique for analysing requirements is to conduct a requirements traceability matrix. This matrix tracks each requirement through the project lifecycle, enabling project teams to easily identify inconsistencies and ensure that all requirements have been addressed.

Once requirements have been analysed, it is important to prioritize them to ensure that the most important requirements are addressed first. Prioritization can be based on a variety of factors, including stakeholder needs, project goals, and risk.

In addition to prioritization, it is important to define functional and non-functional requirements. Functional requirements describe what the product should do, while non-functional requirements describe how the product should perform. Examples of non-functional requirements include performance, reliability, and security.

By analysing requirements and prioritizing them, project teams can ensure that they are delivering a product that meets the needs of stakeholders and aligns with project goals. Defining functional and non-functional requirements can help to ensure that the product meets performance and usability standards.

## JUSTIFYING REQUIREMENTS

Once requirements have been analysed and prioritized, the next step in the requirements management process is to justify them. Justifying requirements involves evaluating their feasibility, ensuring they align with business objectives, and communicating their benefits to stakeholders.

One important aspect of justifying requirements is evaluating their feasibility. This involves determining whether the requirements are achievable given the project's constraints, such as time, budget, and resources. It is important to identify any potential risks associated with each requirement and assess their impact on the project's success.

In addition to evaluating feasibility, it is important to ensure that requirements align with business objectives. This involves ensuring that the requirements support the overall goals of the project and provide value to stakeholders. Requirements that do not align with business objectives should be re-evaluated or removed from the project scope.

Finally, communicating the benefits of each requirement to stakeholders is crucial to ensuring buy-in and support for the project. This involves clearly articulating the benefits of each requirement in terms of how it supports project goals, improves performance, or meets stakeholder needs. It is important to communicate the benefits in a way that is clear and understandable to stakeholders, using language that is tailored to their needs.

By justifying requirements, project teams can ensure that they are delivering a product that aligns with business objectives, is feasible given project constraints, and provides value to stakeholders. Communicating the benefits of each requirement can help to ensure that stakeholders are supportive and engaged throughout the project lifecycle.

## BASELINING NEEDS

Establishing a baseline for requirements is an important step in the requirements management process. Baseline requirements represent a snapshot of the project scope at a particular point in time, and provide a reference point for managing changes to requirements throughout the project lifecycle.

To establish a baseline for requirements, it is important to ensure that all requirements have been documented, analysed, and justified. Once the requirements have been baselined, it is important to manage changes to requirements to ensure that they remain aligned with project goals.

Managing changes to requirements involves evaluating each proposed change to determine its impact on the project's scope, schedule, and budget. Changes that are approved should be documented and incorporated into the project plan, while changes that are rejected should be communicated to stakeholders and removed from the project scope.

Throughout the project lifecycle, it is important to track requirements to ensure that they are being addressed and to identify any changes that need to be made. This can be done using a requirements management tool, which enables project teams to track the status of each requirement and ensure that it is being addressed.

By establishing a baseline for requirements, managing changes to requirements, and tracking requirements throughout the project lifecycle, project teams can ensure that they are delivering a product that meets stakeholder needs and aligns with project goals. The ability to manage changes to requirements effectively can help to avoid costly rework and ensure that the project remains on track.

## CONCLUSION

In conclusion, establishing scope through effective requirements management processes is critical to project success. By gathering, analysing, justifying, and baselining requirements, project teams can ensure that they are delivering a product that meets stakeholder needs and aligns with project goals.

Key points to remember when establishing scope through requirements management include the importance of understanding stakeholder needs and goals, using a variety of techniques to gather requirements, analysing and prioritizing requirements to ensure alignment with project goals, and justifying requirements based on feasibility and alignment with business objectives. It is also crucial to establish a baseline for requirements, manage changes to requirements, and track requirements throughout the project lifecycle.

It is important to note that requirements management is an ongoing process that must be maintained throughout the project lifecycle. As project goals, stakeholder needs, and project constraints change, it is important to evaluate and adjust requirements accordingly. By maintaining ongoing requirements management, project teams can ensure that they are delivering a product that meets stakeholder needs and aligns with project goals, and avoid costly rework, project delays, and scope creep.

# 7.3 MANAGING PROJECT SCOPE THROUGH CONFIGURATION MANAGEMENT PROCESSES

Configuration Management (CM) is a systematic approach to identifying, organizing, and controlling the changes made to a system, product, or service. It is an essential aspect of project management and is critical in ensuring that the project objectives are met within the defined scope, schedule, and budget.

Configuration Management Processes are the set of activities that are carried out to manage the configuration of a product or system throughout its life cycle. It includes planning, identification, control, status accounting, and verification audit. These processes enable project teams to effectively manage the changes made to the project scope and minimize the risk of scope creep.

Effective configuration management processes enable project teams to track the status of changes made to the project scope and ensure that all stakeholders are informed and updated on the progress of the project. The processes also enable project teams to identify potential risks early on and take appropriate measures to mitigate them.

In this section, we will discuss the key processes involved in configuration management and how they can be used to manage the project scope effectively. We will also discuss the benefits of effective configuration management and best practices for implementing it in a project.

## PLANNING FOR CONFIGURATION MANAGEMENT

The definition phase of configuration management is essential in ensuring that the project team has a clear understanding of the scope of the project and the configuration items that need to be managed.

The planning process involves defining the scope of the project, identifying the configuration items, and establishing the procedures and tools required to manage them.

The first step in planning for configuration management is to define the scope of the project. This involves identifying the products, services, or systems that need to be delivered as part of the project and defining their boundaries. This information is used to identify the configuration items that need to be managed throughout the project life cycle.

Once the configuration items have been identified, the next step is to establish the procedures and tools required to manage them. This involves defining the processes for managing changes to the configuration items, establishing the roles and responsibilities of the project team members, and identifying the tools and resources required to support the configuration management processes.

During the definition phase, the project team should also develop a configuration management plan that outlines the processes and procedures to be followed throughout the project life cycle. This plan should include details on how changes to the configuration items will be managed, how the status of the configuration items will be tracked, and how the configuration items will be verified and audited.

Effective planning for configuration management ensures that the project team has a clear understanding of the scope of the project and the configuration items that need to be managed. It also enables the project team to establish the procedures and tools required to manage the configuration items effectively.

## IDENTIFICATION OF CONFIGURATION ITEMS

The identification process is critical in configuration management as it involves identifying all the configuration items that need to be managed throughout the project life cycle. Configuration items are any tangible or intangible items that are part of the project and that need to be controlled and managed.

Examples of configuration items include project documents, software code, hardware components, project plans, and test cases. These items are typically identified during the definition phase of the project and are recorded in a configuration management plan.

The identification process involves establishing a naming convention for the configuration items and assigning unique identifiers to them. This ensures that the configuration items can be easily tracked and managed throughout the project life cycle.

The project team should also establish a process for managing changes to the configuration items. This involves defining the procedures for requesting, reviewing, and approving changes to the configuration items. The process should also include a mechanism for tracking the status of the changes and ensuring that all stakeholders are informed of any changes made to the configuration items.

Effective identification of configuration items ensures that all project deliverables are accounted for and that they are managed throughout the project life cycle. It also enables the project team to effectively manage changes to the configuration items, minimizing the risk of scope creep and ensuring that project objectives are met within the defined scope, schedule, and budget.

## CONTROL OF CONFIGURATION ITEMS

Control of configuration items involves managing changes to the configuration items identified in the project. The control process ensures that any changes made to the configuration items are authorized, tracked, and implemented in a controlled manner.

The control process begins with the identification of the change. This can come from a variety of sources, including project stakeholders, team members, or other sources. Once a change has been identified, it is reviewed to determine its impact on the project scope, schedule, and budget.

If the change is approved, it is documented and implemented using a defined change management process. This process typically includes documentation of the change, testing of the change, approval of the change, and implementation of the change.

Changes that are not approved are documented and communicated to the appropriate stakeholders. The reasons for rejecting the change should be clearly documented, and any impacts on the project scope, schedule, and budget should be communicated to the appropriate stakeholders.

Effective control of configuration items ensures that any changes made to the project are managed in a controlled manner, minimizing the risk of scope creep and ensuring that project objectives are met within the defined scope, schedule, and budget. It also enables the project team to track the status of changes made to the configuration items and ensures that all stakeholders are informed of any changes made to the project.

## STATUS ACCOUNTING OF CONFIGURATION ITEMS

Status accounting is the process of tracking the status of configuration items throughout the project life cycle. This involves documenting the current status of the configuration items, including any changes that have been made to them, and communicating this information to the appropriate stakeholders.

The status accounting process involves recording the current status of each configuration item, including its current version number, its status (e.g., approved, in review, under development, etc.), and any other relevant information. This information is typically stored in a centralized configuration management database, which can be accessed by all members of the project team.

The status accounting process also involves tracking changes made to the configuration items. This includes documenting the date and time of the change, the person who made the change, and any other relevant information. This information is used to track the progress of the project and to ensure that all stakeholders are informed of any changes made to the project.

Effective status accounting ensures that all stakeholders are informed of the current status of the project and that any changes made to the project are tracked and managed in a controlled manner. It also enables the project team to monitor the progress of the project and to identify any potential risks or issues early on.

## VERIFICATION AUDIT OF CONFIGURATION ITEMS

Verification audit is the process of reviewing the configuration items to ensure that they meet the project requirements and that they are consistent with the project plans and specifications. The verification audit process is typically carried out at predefined stages of the project, such as at the end of each phase or at the completion of the project.

The verification audit process involves reviewing the configuration items to ensure that they meet the quality standards and requirements defined in the project plans and specifications. This includes verifying that the configuration items have been developed and tested according to the project requirements and that they are consistent with the project plans and specifications.

The verification audit process also involves verifying that any changes made to the configuration items have been authorized, documented, and implemented in a controlled manner. This includes reviewing the documentation of the change, the testing of the change, and the approval of the change.

The results of the verification audit are typically documented in a report, which is used to communicate the findings to the appropriate stakeholders. If any issues or defects are identified during the verification audit, they are documented, and corrective actions are taken to address them.

Effective verification audit ensures that the project deliverables meet the quality standards and requirements defined in the project plans and specifications. It also ensures that any changes made to the project are authorized, documented, and implemented in a controlled manner, minimizing the risk of scope creep and ensuring that project objectives are met within the defined scope, schedule, and budget.

## INTEGRATING CONFIGURATION MANAGEMENT WITH PROJECT MANAGEMENT

Integrating configuration management with project management is critical in ensuring that the project scope is effectively managed throughout the project life cycle. Configuration management provides the framework for managing changes to the project scope, while project management provides the framework for managing the project schedule, cost, and resources.

The integration of configuration management with project management involves aligning the configuration management processes with the project management processes. This includes integrating the planning, identification, control, status accounting, and verification audit processes with the project management processes.

During the definition phase, the project team should establish a configuration management plan that outlines the processes and procedures to be followed throughout the project life cycle. The configuration management plan should be integrated with the project management plan to ensure that both plans are aligned and that the project team has a clear understanding of the project scope, schedule, and budget.

During the implementation phase, the project team should ensure that the configuration management processes are followed consistently and that any changes made to the project are managed in a controlled manner. The project team should also ensure that the status of the configuration items is tracked and communicated to the appropriate stakeholders.

During the deployment phase, the project team should monitor the progress of the project and identify any potential risks or issues early on. This includes monitoring the status of the configuration items and ensuring that any changes made to the project are managed in a controlled manner.

Effective integration of configuration management with project management ensures that the project scope is effectively managed throughout the project life cycle. It also ensures that the project objectives are met within the defined scope, schedule, and budget, minimizing the risk of scope creep and ensuring that the project delivers the desired results.

## BENEFITS OF EFFECTIVE CONFIGURATION MANAGEMENT

Effective configuration management provides several benefits to the project team and the organization as a whole. Some of the key benefits of effective configuration management are:

   a. Better control over the project scope: Effective configuration management enables project teams to track the status of changes made to the project scope and ensures that all stakeholders are informed of any changes made to the project. This minimizes the risk of scope creep and ensures that the project objectives are met within the defined scope, schedule, and budget.

b. Improved quality and consistency of project deliverables: Effective configuration management ensures that project deliverables meet the quality standards and requirements defined in the project plans and specifications. This improves the consistency and reliability of the project deliverables and enhances the reputation of the organization.

c. Improved collaboration and communication among project stakeholders: Configuration management processes provide a framework for communication and collaboration among project stakeholders. This ensures that all stakeholders are informed of the progress of the project and that any issues or concerns are addressed in a timely manner.

d. Reduced risk of errors and defects: Effective configuration management ensures that any changes made to the project are authorized, documented, and implemented in a controlled manner. This reduces the risk of errors and defects and ensures that the project deliverables meet the quality standards and requirements defined in the project plans and specifications.

e. Improved project visibility and decision-making: Configuration management provides project teams with a centralized repository of project data, including the status of the configuration items and the progress of the project. This improves project visibility and enables project teams to make informed decisions based on accurate and up-to-date information.

In summary, effective configuration management provides several benefits to the project team and the organization as a whole. It enables project teams to manage the project scope effectively, improve the quality and consistency of project deliverables, enhance collaboration and communication among project stakeholders, reduce the risk of errors and defects, and improve project visibility and decision-making.

## CONCLUSION AND BEST PRACTICES FOR MANAGING SCOPE WITH CONFIGURATION MANAGEMENT PROCESSES

Configuration management processes are essential for managing changes to the project scope and ensuring that project objectives are met within the defined scope, schedule, and budget. The key processes involved in configuration management include planning, identification, control, status accounting, and verification audit.

To effectively manage the project scope with configuration management processes, project teams should follow some best practices, including:

1. Define the project scope clearly: The project team should define the scope of the project clearly and ensure that all stakeholders have a clear understanding of the project objectives.

2. Establish a configuration management plan: The project team should establish a configuration management plan that outlines the processes and procedures to be followed throughout the project life cycle. The configuration management plan should be integrated with the project management plan to ensure that both plans are aligned.

3. Identify all configuration items: The project team should identify all configuration items that need to be managed throughout the project life cycle and assign unique identifiers to them.

4. Establish procedures for managing changes: The project team should establish procedures for managing changes to the configuration items, including requesting, reviewing, and approving changes.

5. Track the status of configuration items: The project team should track the status of the configuration items throughout the project life cycle and ensure that any changes made to the configuration items are managed in a controlled manner.

6. Conduct verification audits: The project team should conduct verification audits at predefined stages of the project to ensure that the configuration items meet the project requirements and that they are consistent with the project plans and specifications.

7. Use a centralized repository for project data: The project team should use a centralized repository for project data, including the status of the configuration items and the progress of the project. This improves project visibility and enables project teams to make informed decisions based on accurate and up-to-date information.

In conclusion, managing the project scope effectively is critical in ensuring that project objectives are met within the defined scope, schedule, and budget. Configuration management processes provide the framework for managing changes to the project scope and ensuring that project objectives are met. By following best practices for managing scope with configuration management processes, project teams can minimize the risk of scope creep and ensure the successful delivery of the project.

# 7.4 Understanding the Stages of a Typical Change Control Process

## Request: The First Step in a Change Control Process

The request stage is the starting point of any change control process. At this stage, the person or team who wants to implement the change submits a request to the relevant authority or department. The request should contain information such as the reason for the change, the scope of the change, the potential impact of the change, and any other relevant details.

The request is usually accompanied by a formal document or form, which is specific to the organization's change control process. This form helps to ensure that all necessary information is provided, and the change control process can be initiated effectively.

Once the request is received, it is typically assigned a unique identification number, and the change control process moves to the next stage: initial evaluation.

## Initial Evaluation: Assessing the Impact of the Proposed Change

During the initial evaluation stage, the proposed change is assessed to determine its impact on the organization's processes, resources, and stakeholders. The evaluation is typically conducted by a team of experts who have the relevant knowledge and expertise to evaluate the proposed change.

The team will review the request document and assess the potential impact of the change on the organization. This evaluation includes assessing the feasibility of the change, identifying any potential risks, and evaluating the resources required to implement the change.

The team may also consult with stakeholders who are likely to be affected by the proposed change. This may include individuals or teams from different departments, suppliers, and customers. The objective of this consultation is to gain insight into the potential impact of the change on these stakeholders and to identify any additional concerns or risks that were not identified during the initial assessment.

Based on the initial evaluation, the team will provide a preliminary assessment of the proposed change, which includes a recommendation on whether to proceed with the change or not. If the decision is made to proceed, the change control process moves to the next stage: detailed evaluation.

## DETAILED EVALUATION: EXAMINING THE PROPOSED CHANGE IN DEPTH

The detailed evaluation stage involves a more thorough examination of the proposed change. This stage is critical as it helps to identify potential risks and challenges that were not identified during the initial evaluation.

During this stage, the change control team will conduct a more detailed analysis of the proposed change. This analysis may include a detailed review of the technical requirements of the change, an assessment of the potential impact on the organization's processes and systems, and a review of the financial implications of the change.

The team may also conduct a risk assessment to identify any potential risks associated with the proposed change. This may include an evaluation of the impact of the change on existing processes and systems, the potential impact on customers and suppliers, and any regulatory or compliance requirements that may need to be considered.

The detailed evaluation stage also involves consultation with stakeholders. This may include individuals or teams from different departments, suppliers, and customers. The objective of this consultation is to gain insight into the potential impact of the change on these stakeholders and to identify any additional concerns or risks that were not identified during the initial evaluation.

Based on the detailed evaluation, the team will provide a recommendation on whether to proceed with the change or not. If the decision is made to proceed, the change control process moves to the next stage: recommendation.

## RECOMMENDATION: MAKING A DECISION BASED ON THE EVALUATIONS

The recommendation stage involves making a final decision on whether to proceed with the proposed change or not. This decision is based on the findings from the initial and detailed evaluations, as well as feedback from stakeholders.

The change control team will review the findings from the initial and detailed evaluations, as well as any feedback from stakeholders, to make an informed decision on whether to proceed with the proposed change or not. The team will consider factors such as the feasibility of the change, the potential risks and challenges associated with the change, and the potential impact of the change on the organization and its stakeholders.

If the decision is made to proceed with the change, the team will provide recommendations on how to implement the change effectively. This may include recommendations on the resources required, the timeline for implementation, and any training or communication that may be necessary.

If the decision is made not to proceed with the change, the team will provide feedback on why the change was rejected and any alternative solutions that may be explored.

Once the final decision has been made, the change control process moves to the next stage: update plans.

## UPDATE PLANS: PREPARING FOR THE IMPLEMENTATION OF THE CHANGE

The update plans stage involves preparing for the implementation of the approved change. This stage is critical to ensure that the change is implemented effectively and efficiently, with minimal disruption to the organization's operations.

During this stage, the change control team will develop a detailed plan for implementing the change. This plan will outline the specific steps that need to be taken to implement the change, the resources required, and the timeline for implementation.

The team will also identify any potential risks or challenges that may arise during the implementation process and develop contingency plans to mitigate these risks.

The update plans may also include communication plans to ensure that all stakeholders are informed about the change and any potential impacts on their work. This may include training plans to ensure that employees have the necessary skills and knowledge to implement the change effectively.

The update plans stage may involve testing the proposed change in a controlled environment before rolling it out to the entire organization. This helps to identify any potential issues or challenges that may arise during the implementation process and provides an opportunity to address them before the change is implemented.

Once the update plans have been developed and tested, the change control process moves to the final stage: implement.

## IMPLEMENT: PUTTING THE CHANGE INTO ACTION

The implementation stage is the final stage of the change control process. This stage involves putting the approved change into action, based on the update plans developed in the previous stage.

During this stage, the change control team will implement the change according to the update plans. This may involve updating systems, processes, or procedures, and training employees on the new way of doing things.

The team will closely monitor the implementation process to ensure that the change is being implemented effectively and efficiently, with minimal disruption to the organization's operations. Any issues or challenges that arise during the implementation process will be addressed promptly to minimize the impact on the organization.

Once the change has been successfully implemented, the change control team will conduct a post-implementation review to evaluate the effectiveness of the change and identify any areas for improvement. This review will provide valuable feedback for future change control processes and help to improve the organization's overall change management capabilities.

The final step in the implementation stage is to close out the change control process. This involves documenting the results of the post-implementation review, updating any relevant documentation or procedures, and archiving the change control records.

In conclusion, the change control process is a critical process that ensures that changes are made effectively and efficiently, with minimal disruption to the organization's operations. The process involves several stages, including request, initial evaluation, detailed evaluation, recommendation, update plans, and implementation. By following a structured change control process, organizations can improve their ability to manage change and reduce the risks associated with change implementation.

# CHAPTER EIGHT

## *OPTIMIZING PROJECT SCHEDULE AND RESOURCE MANAGEMENT*

# 8.1 EFFECTIVE STRATEGIES FOR CREATING AND MAINTAINING A SCHEDULE

Scheduling is a fundamental aspect of effective time management. Whether you are a student, a professional, or a business owner, having a well-planned schedule is essential for staying organized, meeting deadlines, and achieving your goals. Scheduling allows you to allocate time for important tasks, prioritize your work, and maintain a healthy work-life balance.

Creating a schedule can also help you identify potential roadblocks or obstacles that may impede your progress. By setting realistic timelines and deadlines, you can stay on track and avoid procrastination or last-minute rush. Moreover, scheduling enables you to measure your progress and make adjustments as necessary to stay focused and productive.

In summary, scheduling is a vital tool for effective time management, helping you to stay organized, prioritize tasks, and achieve your goals.

## TECHNIQUES FOR CREATING A SCHEDULE

There are several techniques that you can use to create an effective schedule. These include:

a. Identify Tasks: The first step in creating a schedule is to identify all the tasks that need to be completed. Make a list of everything you need to do, no matter how small or insignificant it may seem.

b. Prioritize Tasks: Once you have identified all your tasks, prioritize them based on their level of importance and urgency.

Use a ranking system, such as high, medium, or low, to categorize each task.

c. Estimate Time: Estimate the amount of time required to complete each task. This will help you to allocate the appropriate amount of time and avoid overcommitting yourself.

d. Break Down Tasks: If a task seems too overwhelming, break it down into smaller, more manageable tasks. This will help you to stay focused and avoid getting overwhelmed.

e. Consider Dependencies: Some tasks may be dependent on others, meaning that they cannot be started until a previous task is completed. Consider these dependencies when creating your schedule.

f. Allocate Time: Once you have prioritized your tasks and estimated the time required for each task, allocate time for each task in your schedule. Make sure to leave some buffer time for unexpected events or delays.

g. Review and Adjust: Regularly review and adjust your schedule as necessary to ensure that you stay on track and meet your goals.

By using these techniques, you can create an effective schedule that allows you to stay organized, prioritize your tasks, and achieve your goals.

## CRITICAL PATH METHOD

The Critical Path Method (CPM) is a project management technique that is commonly used to create schedules for complex projects. It involves identifying the critical path, which is the sequence of tasks that must be completed on time for the project to be completed within the desired timeframe.

The first step in using the CPM is to identify all the tasks required to complete the project. Next, estimate the time required for each task and identify any dependencies between tasks. Once you have this information, you can create a network diagram that shows the sequence of tasks and the dependencies between them.

Using the network diagram, you can identify the critical path, which is the sequence of tasks that has the longest duration and must be completed on time for the project to be completed within the desired timeframe. By focusing on the critical path, you can ensure that you allocate sufficient time and resources to these tasks and avoid delays that could impact the overall project schedule.

One of the key advantages of using the CPM is that it allows you to identify potential scheduling conflicts and delays before they occur. By regularly reviewing and updating the project schedule, you can stay on top of any changes or issues that may impact the project timeline.

Overall, the CPM is a powerful tool for creating schedules for complex projects, helping you to identify the critical path, allocate resources effectively, and stay on track to meet your project goals.

## GANTT CHARTS

A Gantt chart is a popular tool for creating and visualizing project schedules. It is a bar chart that displays the timeline of a project, with tasks represented as horizontal bars on the chart. The length of each bar represents the duration of the task, and the bars are arranged in chronological order.

Gantt charts allow you to visualize the timeline of your project and the dependencies between tasks. You can use colour coding to differentiate between different types of tasks or to highlight critical tasks that require special attention.

One of the key advantages of using a Gantt chart is that it allows you to easily identify potential scheduling conflicts and delays. By visually representing the timeline of your project, you can quickly see where tasks overlap or where there are gaps in the schedule that may need to be addressed.

Gantt charts also allow you to track progress and adjust the schedule as necessary. You can use the chart to monitor the completion of tasks and adjust the timeline as needed to ensure that you stay on track to meet your project goals.

Finally, Gantt charts are a useful communication tool for sharing project timelines with stakeholders. By creating a visual representation of the project schedule, you can easily share information about the project timeline and progress with others.

Overall, Gantt charts are a powerful tool for creating and maintaining schedules, helping you to visualize the timeline of your project, identify potential scheduling conflicts and delays, and track progress towards your goals.

## INTEGRATING SCHEDULING TOOLS

There are many software and online tools available that can help you create and maintain a schedule. Integrating these tools into your scheduling process can help streamline the process and make it more efficient.

One example of a scheduling tool is project management software, such as Microsoft Project or Asana. These tools allow you to create and manage project schedules, assign tasks to team members, and track progress towards project goals. They often include features such as Gantt charts and critical path analysis, making it easier to identify potential scheduling conflicts and adjust the schedule as necessary.

Another example of a scheduling tool is time tracking software, such as Toggl or Harvest. These tools allow you to track the time you spend on different tasks, making it easier to accurately estimate the time required for each task and allocate resources effectively.

461

Calendar and scheduling apps, such as Google Calendar or Outlook, can also be useful tools for maintaining a schedule. These tools allow you to schedule appointments and deadlines, set reminders, and share your schedule with others.

When integrating scheduling tools into your process, it's important to choose tools that are compatible with your existing workflows and processes. It's also important to ensure that all team members are trained on how to use the tools effectively.

Overall, integrating scheduling tools into your process can help you create and maintain an effective schedule, streamline the scheduling process, and improve collaboration and communication among team members.

## Tips for Maintaining a Schedule

Creating a schedule is only half the battle - the other half is maintaining it. Here are some tips for maintaining a schedule:

a. Regularly Review and Update: Review your schedule regularly and update it as necessary. This will help you to stay on track and adjust the schedule to reflect any changes or unforeseen events that may impact your progress.

b. Prioritize Tasks: Focus on completing the most important tasks first. This will help you to stay on track and avoid getting bogged down in less important tasks.

c. Set Realistic Deadlines: Be realistic when setting deadlines for tasks. Avoid overcommitting yourself or setting deadlines that are too aggressive. This can lead to burnout and frustration, and may impact the overall project timeline.

d. Allocate Time for Unexpected Events: Build in some buffer time in your schedule for unexpected events or delays. This will help you to stay on track even if unforeseen events arise.

e. Communicate with Team Members: Communicate regularly with team members to ensure that everyone is on the same page and that the project is progressing as planned.

f. Use Scheduling Tools: Use scheduling tools such as reminders, alarms, and notifications to help you stay on track and remind you of important deadlines.

g. Avoid Multitasking: Multitasking can be tempting, but it can actually reduce productivity and lead to delays. Focus on one task at a time and complete it before moving on to the next.

By following these tips, you can maintain an effective schedule, stay on track, and achieve your goals. Remember, maintaining a schedule requires discipline and commitment, but the rewards are worth it in the end.

## COMMON SCHEDULING MISTAKES AND HOW TO AVOID THEM

Despite our best efforts, scheduling mistakes can still occur. Here are some common scheduling mistakes and how to avoid them:

a. Overcommitting: One of the most common scheduling mistakes is overcommitting yourself. Avoid taking on too many tasks or setting unrealistic deadlines that you cannot meet.

b. Underestimating Time Required: Another common mistake is underestimating the time required for a task. This can lead to delays and impact the overall project timeline. Be realistic when estimating the time required for a task, and build in some buffer time to account for unexpected events or delays.

c. Not Prioritizing Tasks: Failing to prioritize tasks can also lead to delays and impact the overall project timeline. Focus on completing the most important tasks first, and avoid getting bogged down in less important tasks.

d.    Ignoring Dependencies: Tasks are often dependent on other tasks, meaning that they cannot be started until a previous task is completed. Failing to account for dependencies can lead to delays and impact the overall project timeline. Be sure to identify dependencies when creating your schedule and adjust the timeline accordingly.

e.    Not Reviewing and Updating the Schedule: Schedules can quickly become outdated if they are not regularly reviewed and updated. Be sure to review your schedule regularly and adjust it as necessary to reflect any changes or unforeseen events that may impact your progress.

f.    Not Communicating with Team Members: Communication is key to maintaining an effective schedule. Failing to communicate with team members can lead to misunderstandings and delays. Regularly communicate with team members to ensure that everyone is on the same page and that the project is progressing as planned.

By avoiding these common scheduling mistakes, you can maintain an effective schedule, stay on track, and achieve your goals. Remember, scheduling requires discipline and commitment, but the rewards are worth it in the end.

## BENEFITS OF EFFECTIVE SCHEDULING

Maintaining an effective schedule offers numerous benefits, including:

a.    Increased Productivity: An effective schedule allows you to allocate your time efficiently and avoid wasting time on less important tasks. By prioritizing tasks and focusing on the most important ones, you can increase your productivity and achieve more in less time.

b.   Improved Time Management: Scheduling helps you to manage your time effectively, making it easier to balance work and personal commitments. It allows you to allocate sufficient time for important tasks, avoid overcommitting yourself, and reduce stress and burnout.

c.   Better Planning and Coordination: An effective schedule helps you to plan and coordinate tasks more effectively, ensuring that everyone is on the same page and working towards the same goals. This can lead to improved collaboration, better communication, and more successful outcomes.

d.   Enhanced Accountability: Scheduling provides a clear roadmap for completing tasks, making it easier to track progress and ensure accountability. By regularly reviewing and updating the schedule, you can ensure that everyone is meeting their deadlines and working towards the same goals.

e.   Reduced Stress: Maintaining an effective schedule can help to reduce stress and improve overall well-being. It allows you to avoid last-minute rush and procrastination, giving you more time to focus on the things that matter most.

Overall, effective scheduling is an essential tool for achieving success in both personal and professional settings. It helps you to allocate time efficiently, prioritize tasks, and achieve your goals while reducing stress and burnout. By embracing scheduling as a key part of your time management strategy, you can achieve more in less time and enjoy greater success and fulfilment.

# 8.2 CRITICAL PATH VS. CRITICAL CHAIN: A COMPARISON OF SCHEDULING TECHNIQUES

Project management is a complex process that involves various steps such as planning, execution, monitoring, and control. One of the most critical aspects of project management is scheduling. Scheduling involves the process of determining the start and end dates of activities and tasks that are required to complete a project.

Two commonly used techniques for scheduling projects are Critical Path Method (CPM) and Critical Chain Method (CCM). While both techniques are used for scheduling, they differ in their approach and methodology. Understanding the differences between CPM and CCM can help project managers choose the best technique for their projects.

In this section, we will explain the characteristics, steps, advantages, and limitations of CPM and CCM. We will also compare the two techniques to help project managers understand the differences and choose the most appropriate technique for their projects.

## UNDERSTANDING CRITICAL PATH SCHEDULING TECHNIQUE

The Critical Path Method (CPM) is a scheduling technique used to determine the critical path of a project. The critical path is the longest sequence of tasks that must be completed to finish a project. This sequence determines the minimum time required to complete the project.

A. Definition and Characteristics of Critical Path Method (CPM)

The Critical Path Method (CPM) is a mathematical technique that uses a network diagram to identify the critical path of a project. The network diagram is a graphical representation of the project activities, which shows the dependencies between tasks. CPM assumes that all activities have a fixed duration, and there is no variability in the time required to complete them.

The characteristics of CPM include:

a. CPM is a deterministic method of scheduling that assumes all activities have a fixed duration.

b. CPM assumes that there is no variability in the time required to complete each activity.

c. CPM identifies the critical path, which is the longest sequence of activities that must be completed to finish the project.

d. The critical path determines the minimum time required to complete the project.

e. CPM can be used to identify the earliest start and finish times for each activity, as well as the total project duration.

B. Steps Involved in Critical Path Analysis

The steps involved in critical path analysis include:

1. Identify all the activities required to complete the project.

2. Determine the sequence of activities and the dependencies between them.

3. Create a network diagram to represent the project activities and their dependencies.

4. Estimate the duration of each activity.

5. Calculate the earliest start and finish times for each activity.

6. Calculate the latest start and finish times for each activity.

7. Identify the critical path, which is the longest sequence of activities that must be completed to finish the project.

8. Calculate the total project duration.

C. Advantages and Limitations of CPM

The advantages of CPM include:

a. CPM helps project managers to identify the critical path and the minimum time required to complete a project.

b. CPM can be used to estimate the earliest start and finish times for each activity, as well as the total project duration.

c. CPM helps project managers to identify the activities that can be delayed without affecting the project completion date.

The limitations of CPM include:

a. CPM assumes that all activities have a fixed duration, which may not be realistic in some projects.

b. CPM does not account for the variability in the time required to complete each activity.

c. CPM does not consider the availability of resources and the resource constraints, which can affect the project schedule.

## UNDERSTANDING CRITICAL CHAIN SCHEDULING TECHNIQUE

The Critical Chain Method (CCM) is a scheduling technique that was developed to address the limitations of the Critical Path Method (CPM). CCM focuses on the management of project resources, and it assumes that the duration of tasks is not fixed, but rather, it is influenced by the availability of resources.

A. Definition and Characteristics of Critical Chain Method (CCM)

The Critical Chain Method (CCM) is a project scheduling technique that focuses on resource management. CCM assumes that the duration of tasks is not fixed, but it is influenced by the availability of resources. CCM uses buffers to manage uncertainties and variations in the project schedule.

The characteristics of CCM include:

a. CCM is a probabilistic method of scheduling that considers the availability of resources.

b. CCM assumes that tasks have variable durations that are influenced by the availability of resources.

c. CCM uses buffers to manage uncertainties and variations in the project schedule.

d. CCM identifies the critical chain, which is the sequence of tasks that determines the minimum time required to complete the project.

e. CCM considers the availability of resources and the resource constraints when scheduling tasks.

B. Steps Involved in Critical Chain Analysis

The steps involved in critical chain analysis include:

1. Identify all the activities required to complete the project.

2. Determine the sequence of activities and the dependencies between them.

3. Estimate the duration of each activity, taking into account the availability of resources.

4. Create a network diagram to represent the project activities and their dependencies.

5. Identify the critical chain, which is the sequence of tasks that determines the minimum time required to complete the project.

6. Add resource buffers to the critical chain to manage uncertainties and variations in the project schedule.

7. Identify project buffers to manage overall project uncertainties.

C. Advantages and Limitations of CCM

The advantages of CCM include:

- CCM considers the availability of resources and resource constraints when scheduling tasks, which makes it more realistic than CPM.

- CCM uses buffers to manage uncertainties and variations in the project schedule, which makes it more flexible than CPM.

- CCM helps project managers to manage project resources effectively.

The limitations of CCM include:

- CCM is a probabilistic method of scheduling that considers the availability of resources, which can be challenging to estimate accurately.

- CCM requires more effort and resources to manage buffers effectively.

- CCM may not be suitable for small projects with simple schedules.

## COMPARISON OF CRITICAL PATH AND CRITICAL CHAIN TECHNIQUES

A. Differences in Approach and Methodology

The Critical Path Method (CPM) and Critical Chain Method (CCM) differ in their approach and methodology. CPM assumes that all activities have a fixed duration and no variability, while CCM considers the availability of resources and the variability in the duration of tasks.

CPM focuses on identifying the critical path, which is the longest sequence of tasks that must be completed to finish the project. CCM, on the other hand, focuses on the critical chain, which is the sequence of tasks that determines the minimum time required to complete the project.

CPM uses forward and backward pass calculations to determine the earliest and latest start and finish times for each activity. CCM uses resource buffers and project buffers to manage uncertainties and variations in the project schedule.

B. Differences in Time and Resource Management

CPM and CCM also differ in their approach to time and resource management. CPM assumes that all activities have a fixed duration and no variability, while CCM considers the availability of resources and the variability in the duration of tasks.

CPM uses float to identify the activities that can be delayed without affecting the project completion date. CCM uses buffers to manage uncertainties and variations in the project schedule.

CPM does not consider the availability of resources and the resource constraints, which can affect the project schedule. CCM considers the availability of resources and resource constraints when scheduling tasks.

C. Advantages and Disadvantages of Each Technique

The advantages of CPM include:

- CPM helps project managers to identify the critical path and the minimum time required to complete a project.

- CPM can be used to estimate the earliest start and finish times for each activity, as well as the total project duration.

- CPM helps project managers to identify the activities that can be delayed without affecting the project completion date.

The disadvantages of CPM include:

- CPM assumes that all activities have a fixed duration, which may not be realistic in some projects.

- CPM does not account for the variability in the time required to complete each activity.

- CPM does not consider the availability of resources and the resource constraints, which can affect the project schedule.

The advantages of CCM include:

- CCM considers the availability of resources and resource constraints when scheduling tasks, which makes it more realistic than CPM.

- CCM uses buffers to manage uncertainties and variations in the project schedule, which makes it more flexible than CPM.

- CCM helps project managers to manage project resources effectively.

The disadvantages of CCM include:

- CCM is a probabilistic method of scheduling that considers the availability of resources, which can be challenging to estimate accurately.

- CCM requires more effort and resources to manage buffers effectively.

- CCM may not be suitable for small projects with simple schedules.

D. Conclusion: Which Technique is Right for Your Project?

The choice between CPM and CCM depends on the specific requirements of a project. If the project has a simple schedule and does not involve many resources, CPM may be more appropriate. However, if the project is complex and involves multiple resources, CCM may be more suitable.

Project managers should consider the advantages and limitations of both techniques before choosing the most appropriate technique for their projects. It is also important to ensure that the chosen technique aligns with the project goals and objectives, as well as the organizational culture and values.

## CONCLUSION: WHICH TECHNIQUE IS RIGHT FOR YOUR PROJECT?

When it comes to selecting the most appropriate scheduling technique for your project, it is important to consider the specific requirements of the project. As we have seen, the Critical Path Method (CPM) and Critical Chain Method (CCM) have their advantages and limitations. Therefore, project managers must weigh the pros and cons of each technique to determine the best fit for their projects.

For simple projects with a straightforward schedule and limited resources, CPM is an ideal technique. CPM is easy to implement and provides a clear understanding of the critical path of the project. However, if the project is complex and involves multiple resources, CCM may be more appropriate. CCM helps project managers to manage resources effectively, and it provides more flexibility than CPM in dealing with uncertainties and variations in the project schedule.

Regardless of the technique chosen, project managers must be aware of the limitations of each technique and make adjustments where necessary. For example, in CPM, project managers can use buffers to manage uncertainties and variations in the project schedule. In CCM, project managers can use a resource levelling technique to ensure that resources are utilized efficiently.

In conclusion, the choice between CPM and CCM depends on the specific requirements of the project. Both techniques have their advantages and limitations, and project managers must choose the most appropriate technique for their projects based on their project goals, objectives, and constraints. Ultimately, the success of a project depends on effective scheduling and resource management, regardless of the technique chosen.

# 8.3 Resource Categorization and Allocation in a Linear Life Cycle Schedule

The linear life cycle schedule is a project management methodology that involves a sequential and straightforward approach to project management. In this methodology, the project progresses through a series of phases that are completed one after the other, in a linear fashion. Each phase builds on the previous one and leads to the completion of the project.

The phases in a linear life cycle schedule typically include concept, definition, deployment, monitoring and control, and transition. During each phase, specific deliverables are produced, which are reviewed and approved before moving to the next phase. This methodology is best suited for projects with a clear and well-defined scope, limited changes, and a fixed budget and timeline.

Effective resource management is crucial for the success of a project managed using a linear life cycle schedule. The categorization and allocation of resources are essential components of resource management in this methodology. By categorizing resources and allocating them appropriately, project managers can ensure that resources are used efficiently, and the project is completed on time and within budget.

## Types of Resources in the Linear Life Cycle Schedule:

There are several types of resources required for successful project completion in a linear life cycle schedule. These resources include:

a. Human Resources: These are the people involved in the project, including the project team members, project manager, stakeholders, and subject matter experts.

b. Material Resources: These are the physical resources required for the project, such as equipment, tools, and supplies.

c. Financial Resources: These are the funds needed to finance the project, including the budget for each phase, contingency funds, and reserve funds.

d. Time Resources: These are the time constraints and deadlines set for the project, including project duration, milestones, and critical paths.

e. Information Resources: These are the knowledge and data required for the project, including project documentation, project plans, and project reports.

f. Infrastructure Resources: These are the resources required for the project's physical infrastructure, such as office space, power, and connectivity.

Identifying and categorizing these resources is crucial for effective resource management in a linear life cycle schedule. Each resource type requires a different management approach, and project managers must allocate resources efficiently to ensure timely completion of the project.

## CATEGORIZING RESOURCES IN THE LINEAR LIFE CYCLE SCHEDULE:

Categorizing resources is a crucial step in managing resources in a linear life cycle schedule. Resource categorization involves grouping resources based on their characteristics, requirements, and availability. This process helps project managers to allocate resources efficiently, avoid duplication, and identify potential bottlenecks in resource allocation.

Here are some common ways of categorizing resources in the linear life cycle schedule:

a.  Critical and non-critical resources: Critical resources are those that are essential for the successful completion of the project, while non-critical resources are those that are less important or can be replaced. Identifying critical resources helps project managers to allocate them first and ensures that the project moves forward smoothly.

b.  Internal and external resources: Internal resources are those within the organization, such as staff and equipment, while external resources are those outside the organization, such as contractors and vendors. Categorizing resources based on their origin helps project managers to manage them effectively and negotiate better rates and terms with external resources.

c.  Available and unavailable resources: Available resources are those that are readily accessible and can be used immediately, while unavailable resources are those that are in high demand or being used by other projects. Categorizing resources based on their availability helps project managers to plan ahead and avoid delays in resource allocation.

d.  Fixed and variable resources: Fixed resources are those with a fixed quantity, such as equipment or office space, while variable resources are those that can be adjusted based on project needs, such as staff and funds. Categorizing resources based on their flexibility helps project managers to manage them effectively and make adjustments as necessary.

By categorizing resources in a linear life cycle schedule, project managers can identify potential issues in resource allocation and ensure that resources are used effectively and efficiently.

## Resource Allocation in the Linear Life Cycle Schedule:

Resource allocation involves assigning resources to specific tasks and activities in the project plan. In a linear life cycle schedule, resource allocation is typically done during the definition phase, based on the project's needs and requirements.

Here are some steps involved in resource allocation in the linear life cycle schedule:

1. Resource requirement identification: The project manager must identify the types and quantities of resources required for each phase of the project. This involves reviewing the project plan, determining the tasks and activities required for each phase, and identifying the resources needed to complete them.

2. Resource availability assessment: The project manager must determine the availability of each resource type and the quantity available for allocation. This involves reviewing the current resources in use, assessing the availability of external resources, and identifying potential constraints in resource allocation.

3. Resource allocation planning: Based on the resource requirement identification and availability assessment, the project manager develops a resource allocation plan that assigns resources to specific tasks and activities in the project plan. The plan must take into account the criticality of each resource, the availability of resources, and any potential risks or bottlenecks in resource allocation.

4. Resource allocation execution: The project manager allocates resources according to the resource allocation plan. This involves communicating resource assignments to team members, ensuring that resources are available when needed, and resolving any conflicts or issues that arise during resource allocation.

5. Resource monitoring and control: The project manager must monitor resource usage during each phase of the project, assess

whether the resources are being used efficiently, and adjust the resource allocation plan as necessary. This involves tracking resource usage, assessing the impact of changes to the project plan on resource allocation, and ensuring that the project stays within budget and timeline constraints.

By following these steps, project managers can ensure that resources are allocated effectively and efficiently in a linear life cycle schedule, leading to successful project completion.

## CHALLENGES AND BEST PRACTICES IN RESOURCE MANAGEMENT FOR LINEAR LIFE CYCLE SCHEDULE:

Resource management in a linear life cycle schedule presents several challenges, which project managers must address to ensure successful project completion. Here are some of the challenges and best practices for managing resources in a linear life cycle schedule:

a. Limited flexibility: In a linear life cycle schedule, changes to the project plan can be challenging, and resources allocated to specific tasks or activities may not be easily transferable. To address this challenge, project managers must plan ahead, anticipate potential changes, and build in flexibility where possible.

b. Resource conflicts: As resources are allocated to specific tasks and activities, conflicts may arise between competing demands for resources. To address this challenge, project managers must prioritize resource allocation based on criticality and establish a clear process for resolving conflicts.

c. Resource availability: In a linear life cycle schedule, resources may be in high demand or limited availability, leading to delays in resource allocation. To address this challenge, project managers must identify potential resource constraints early in the definition phase and develop contingency plans to ensure that critical resources are available when needed.

d. Resource tracking and monitoring: In a linear life cycle schedule, resources must be tracked and monitored throughout the project's duration to ensure efficient resource usage. To address this challenge, project managers must establish a clear process for tracking and reporting resource usage, ensuring that resources are used efficiently and identifying potential issues early.

e. Communication: Effective communication is crucial for successful resource management in a linear life cycle schedule. Project managers must establish clear lines of communication with team members, stakeholders, and external resources to ensure that everyone is aware of the resource allocation plan, potential conflicts or issues, and any changes to the project plan.

Best practices for managing resources in a linear life cycle schedule include:

- Prioritizing resource allocation based on criticality

- Planning ahead and anticipating potential changes

- Establishing a clear process for resolving conflicts

- Identifying potential resource constraints early in the definition phase

- Tracking and monitoring resource usage throughout the project's duration

- Establishing clear lines of communication with team members, stakeholders, and external resources.

By addressing these challenges and following best practices, project managers can effectively manage resources in a linear life cycle schedule, leading to successful project completion within budget and timeline constraints.

# 8.4 RESOURCE CATEGORIZATION AND ALLOCATION IN ITERATIVE LIFE CYCLE SCHEDULES

Iterative life cycle schedules are an approach to software development that involves a cyclic process of planning, designing, building, testing, and evaluating software products. This approach is characterized by short development cycles or iterations, which allow for constant feedback and adaptation to changing requirements.

Iterative life cycle schedules are typically used in agile software development methodologies, such as Scrum or Extreme Programming (XP), where teams work in sprints of two to four weeks. These sprints are designed to deliver a working product increment at the end of each cycle. This approach allows teams to quickly respond to changes in requirements, address issues as they arise, and deliver a high-quality product within a shorter timeframe.

In an iterative life cycle schedule, resources such as time, money, and people are critical to the success of the project. Effective resource management is essential to ensure that each iteration is completed on time, within budget, and to the desired quality standards. Therefore, resource categorization and allocation play a crucial role in the success of an iterative life cycle schedule.

## RESOURCE CATEGORIZATION AND ITS IMPORTANCE IN ITERATIVE LIFE CYCLE SCHEDULES

Resource categorization involves classifying the resources required for the project into different categories, such as human resources, material resources, financial resources, and time resources. This process is essential to effectively manage and allocate resources throughout the project's lifecycle.

Effective resource categorization helps project managers to determine the types of resources required for each iteration and ensure that they are available when needed. It also helps them to allocate resources in a way that maximizes their utilization and efficiency, while minimizing waste.

The importance of resource categorization in iterative life cycle schedules cannot be overstated. Poor resource management can result in missed deadlines, increased costs, and reduced quality. It can also lead to burnout and demotivation among team members, which can have a significant impact on the project's success.

By categorizing resources and allocating them effectively, project managers can ensure that each iteration is completed on time, within budget, and to the desired quality standards. It also enables them to optimize resource usage, prevent resource conflicts, and ensure that the right resources are available at the right time.

Overall, resource categorization is a critical step in the success of an iterative life cycle schedule. It helps project managers to effectively manage resources and ensure that each iteration is completed efficiently and effectively.

## THE DIFFERENT TYPES OF RESOURCES USED IN ITERATIVE LIFE CYCLE SCHEDULES

Iterative life cycle schedules require various types of resources to ensure that each iteration is completed successfully. These resources can be broadly categorized into four main types: human resources, material resources, financial resources, and time resources.

Human resources: Human resources refer to the people involved in the project, including project managers, developers, testers, and other team members. These resources are essential to the success of the project, as they are responsible for planning, designing, building, and testing the software product. Human resources are typically the most significant expense in an iterative life cycle schedule, and their allocation and management are critical to the project's success.

Material resources: Material resources include any physical equipment, tools, or software required to complete the project. Examples of material resources used in iterative life cycle schedules include computers, servers, software licenses, and testing equipment. These resources are necessary to ensure that the software product is developed and tested efficiently and effectively.

Financial resources: Financial resources refer to the funds required to complete the project. These resources are typically used to pay for human and material resources, as well as other expenses such as office space, utilities, and travel expenses. Financial resources are critical to ensure that the project is completed within the allocated budget.

Time resources: Time resources refer to the time required to complete each iteration of the project. Time resources are critical in iterative life cycle schedules as each iteration has a set duration, typically ranging from two to four weeks. Efficient time management is essential to ensure that each iteration is completed within the allocated time, and the project progresses as planned.

Overall, effective management and allocation of these four types of resources are essential to the success of an iterative life cycle schedule. Project managers must prioritize the allocation of resources to ensure that each iteration is completed efficiently and effectively within the allocated budget and timeline.

## RESOURCE ALLOCATION STRATEGIES IN ITERATIVE LIFE CYCLE SCHEDULES

Resource allocation in iterative life cycle schedules involves determining how resources will be allocated to each iteration of the project. Effective resource allocation ensures that each iteration is completed efficiently and effectively, within the allocated budget and timeline.

There are several resource allocation strategies that project managers can use in iterative life cycle schedules. These include:

a. Time-boxing: Time-boxing involves setting a fixed duration for each iteration. This strategy ensures that the team focuses on completing the most important tasks within the allocated time, which helps to prevent scope creep.

b. Capacity planning: Capacity planning involves analyzing the available resources and determining the amount of work that can be completed in each iteration. This strategy helps to ensure that the team has enough resources to complete the tasks within the allocated time and budget.

c. Resource leveling: Resource leveling involves balancing the workload across the team to prevent resource conflicts. This strategy ensures that team members are not overburdened and that resources are allocated efficiently.

d. Prioritization: Prioritization involves identifying the most critical tasks and allocating resources accordingly. This strategy ensures that the most important tasks are completed first, which helps to prevent delays and ensure that the project progresses as planned.

e. Agile estimation: Agile estimation involves using techniques such as story points and planning poker to estimate the effort required for each task. This strategy helps to ensure that the team has a clear understanding of the work required and can allocate resources accordingly.

Overall, effective resource allocation in iterative life cycle schedules requires a combination of these strategies. Project managers must prioritize the allocation of resources to ensure that each iteration is completed efficiently and effectively within the allocated budget and timeline.

## CHALLENGES AND SOLUTIONS IN RESOURCE ALLOCATION FOR ITERATIVE LIFE CYCLE SCHEDULES

Resource allocation in iterative life cycle schedules can be challenging, especially when dealing with multiple iterations and changing requirements. Some of the common challenges faced by project managers in resource allocation include:

a. Unclear requirements: Unclear or changing requirements can make it challenging to allocate resources effectively. Project managers must ensure that they have a clear understanding of the requirements and allocate resources accordingly.

b. Resource conflicts: Resource conflicts can arise when team members are allocated to multiple tasks or iterations simultaneously. This can result in delays and reduced productivity. Project managers must balance the workload across the team and ensure that resources are allocated efficiently.

c. Inadequate resources: Inadequate resources, such as a shortage of skilled personnel or insufficient budget, can hinder the project's progress. Project managers must ensure that they have sufficient resources to complete each iteration effectively.

d. Unrealistic timelines: Unrealistic timelines can make it challenging to allocate resources effectively. Project managers must ensure that the allocated time for each iteration is realistic and achievable.

To address these challenges, project managers can adopt various solutions, including:

a. Effective communication: Effective communication with stakeholders and team members is essential to ensure that the project's requirements are clear and that resources are allocated accordingly.

b. Continuous planning: Continuous planning involves regular review and adaptation of the project plan to ensure that it remains aligned with the project's objectives and requirements.

c. Flexibility: Flexibility in resource allocation involves the ability to adapt quickly to changing requirements and priorities. Project managers must be willing to adjust the allocation of resources as needed to ensure that the project progresses as planned.

d. Risk management: Risk management involves identifying potential risks that could affect resource allocation and developing strategies to mitigate them. Project managers must have a clear understanding of the project's risks and develop contingency plans to minimize their impact.

Overall, effective resource allocation in iterative life cycle schedules requires a proactive and adaptive approach. Project managers must be prepared to address challenges as they arise and ensure that resources are allocated efficiently to ensure the project's success.

## MONITORING AND CONTROLLING RESOURCE USAGE IN ITERATIVE LIFE CYCLE SCHEDULES

Monitoring and controlling resource usage in iterative life cycle schedules is essential to ensure that resources are allocated effectively and efficiently. This involves tracking resource usage, identifying any deviations from the planned usage, and taking corrective action as needed.

Effective monitoring and control of resource usage in iterative life cycle schedules involves the following steps:

1. Defining metrics: Project managers must define metrics for measuring resource usage, such as the amount of time spent on

each task or iteration, the amount of money spent on resources, and the utilization of each team member.

2. Tracking resource usage: Project managers must track the actual usage of resources against the planned usage, using the defined metrics. This helps to identify any deviations from the plan and allows project managers to take corrective action as needed.

3. Analysing resource usage: Project managers must analyse resource usage data to identify any trends or patterns that could affect resource allocation. This analysis helps to identify potential bottlenecks or areas of inefficiency that could be addressed to improve resource allocation.

4. Taking corrective action: Based on the analysis of resource usage data, project managers must take corrective action as needed to ensure that resources are allocated efficiently. This may involve reallocating resources, adjusting timelines or priorities, or addressing any inefficiencies identified in the analysis.

5. Continuous improvement: Project managers must continually review and improve the resource allocation process to ensure that it remains effective and efficient. This involves incorporating feedback from team members and stakeholders and making adjustments to the resource allocation process as needed.

Overall, effective monitoring and control of resource usage in iterative life cycle schedules is critical to ensure that resources are allocated efficiently and effectively. Project managers must be proactive in identifying any deviations from the plan and taking corrective action as needed to ensure the project's success.

## BEST PRACTICES FOR EFFECTIVE RESOURCE MANAGEMENT IN ITERATIVE LIFE CYCLE SCHEDULES

Effective resource management is critical to the success of an iterative life cycle schedule. To ensure that resources are allocated efficiently and effectively, project managers can adopt various best practices. These best practices include:

a. Prioritizing requirements: Prioritizing requirements involves identifying the most critical tasks and allocating resources accordingly. This helps to ensure that the most important tasks are completed first, which helps to prevent delays and ensure that the project progresses as planned.

b. Agile estimation: Agile estimation involves using techniques such as story points and planning poker to estimate the effort required for each task. This helps to ensure that the team has a clear understanding of the work required and can allocate resources accordingly.

c. Capacity planning: Capacity planning involves analyzing the available resources and determining the amount of work that can be completed in each iteration. This helps to ensure that the team has enough resources to complete the tasks within the allocated time and budget.

d. Effective communication: Effective communication with stakeholders and team members is essential to ensure that the project's requirements are clear and that resources are allocated accordingly.

e. Flexibility: Flexibility in resource allocation involves the ability to adapt quickly to changing requirements and priorities. Project managers must be willing to adjust the allocation of resources as needed to ensure that the project progresses as planned.

f. Continuous planning: Continuous planning involves regular review and adaptation of the project plan to ensure that it remains aligned with the project's objectives and requirements.

g. Monitoring and control: Monitoring and control of resource usage involves tracking resource usage, identifying any deviations from the planned usage, and taking corrective action as needed.

By adopting these best practices, project managers can ensure that resources are allocated effectively and efficiently, and that each iteration is completed on time, within budget, and to the desired quality standards. These practices also help to ensure that the project progresses as planned and that stakeholders are satisfied with the final product.

# 8.5 Understanding Resource Smoothing and Resource Levelling in Project Management

Resource management is an essential aspect of project management that involves allocating and optimizing resources to achieve project goals within a given timeline and budget. Resource levelling and resource smoothing are two popular techniques used in project management to manage resources effectively.

Resource smoothing is a technique used to balance resource utilization by adjusting the start and end dates of project activities without changing the total project duration. The goal of resource smoothing is to minimize the peaks and valleys in resource demand and ensure that the resources are optimally utilized. Resource smoothing is typically used when the availability of resources is limited, and the priority is to maintain a constant utilization rate of resources throughout the project.

On the other hand, resource levelling is a technique used to balance resource utilization by adjusting the project schedule and duration to meet resource constraints. The goal of resource levelling is to eliminate resource overloads and ensure that the resources are optimally utilized without compromising project objectives. Resource levelling is typically used when the priority is to complete the project within a specific time frame, and the availability of resources is flexible.

While resource smoothing and resource levelling are similar in their aim to balance resource utilization, they differ in their approach and the outcome they produce. Understanding the difference between resource smoothing and resource levelling is crucial in selecting the most appropriate technique for effective resource management.

## RESOURCE SMOOTHING: DEFINITION AND PROCESS

Resource smoothing is a technique used to balance resource utilization by adjusting the start and end dates of project activities without changing the total project duration. The goal of resource smoothing is to minimize the peaks and valleys in resource demand and ensure that the resources are optimally utilized.

The process of resource smoothing involves several steps, including:

1. Identifying Resource Constraints: The first step in resource smoothing is to identify the resources that are limited or have constrained availability. This may include personnel, equipment, or materials.

2. Analysing Resource Utilization: The next step is to analyse the utilization of resources across the project timeline. This involves identifying the activities that require the most resources and the periods of high and low resource demand.

3. Adjusting Activity Start and End Dates: Based on the analysis of resource utilization, the project manager can adjust the start and end dates of activities to balance resource demand. This involves delaying or accelerating the start or end date of an activity to smooth out the resource demand curve.

4. Re-evaluating Resource Utilization: After adjusting activity start and end dates, the project manager must re-evaluate resource utilization to ensure that the changes have balanced resource demand and minimized resource constraints.

5. Monitoring Resource Utilization: Throughout the project, the project manager must continuously monitor resource utilization to ensure that resource smoothing is effective and that resources are optimally utilized.

Resource smoothing is typically used when the availability of resources is limited, and the priority is to maintain a constant utilization rate of resources throughout the project. However, it is important to note that resource smoothing may result in increased project duration and may not be appropriate for projects with strict timelines.

## RESOURCE LEVELLING: DEFINITION AND PROCESS

Resource levelling is a technique used to balance resource utilization by adjusting the project schedule and duration to meet resource constraints. The goal of resource levelling is to eliminate resource overloads and ensure that the resources are optimally utilized without compromising project objectives.

The process of resource levelling involves several steps, including:

1. Identifying Resource Constraints: The first step in resource levelling is to identify the resources that are limited or have constrained availability. This may include personnel, equipment, or materials.

2. Analysing Resource Utilization: The next step is to analyse the utilization of resources across the project timeline. This involves identifying the activities that require the most resources and the periods of high and low resource demand.

3. Adjusting Activity Durations: Based on the analysis of resource utilization, the project manager can adjust the duration of activities to balance resource demand. This involves extending or reducing the duration of an activity to eliminate resource overloads.

4. Re-evaluating Project Schedule: After adjusting activity durations, the project manager must re-evaluate the project

schedule to ensure that the changes have balanced resource demand and optimized resource utilization.

5. Monitoring Resource Utilization: Throughout the project, the project manager must continuously monitor resource utilization to ensure that resource levelling is effective and that resources are optimally utilized.

Resource levelling is typically used when the priority is to complete the project within a specific time frame, and the availability of resources is flexible. However, it is important to note that resource levelling may result in changes to project activities and dependencies, and may not be appropriate for projects with strict scope or quality requirements.

In summary, resource levelling aims to balance resource demand by adjusting the project schedule and duration to meet resource constraints, while resource smoothing aims to balance resource demand by adjusting activity start and end dates without changing the project duration. The selection of the appropriate technique depends on the project's requirements and constraints.

## KEY DIFFERENCES BETWEEN RESOURCE SMOOTHING AND RESOURCE LEVELLING

Resource smoothing and resource levelling are two popular techniques used in project management to manage resources effectively. While these techniques share similarities in their goal to balance resource utilization, they differ in their approach and the outcome they produce.

Here are some key differences between resource smoothing and resource levelling:

a. Focus: Resource smoothing focuses on balancing resource utilization by adjusting the start and end dates of activities without changing the project duration. Resource leveling focuses on balancing resource utilization by adjusting the project schedule and duration to meet resource constraints.

b. Effect on Project Duration: Resource smoothing does not change the project duration, while resource leveling may result in changes to the project duration.

c. Resource Allocation: Resource smoothing aims to maintain a constant utilization rate of resources throughout the project, while resource leveling aims to optimize resource utilization without compromising project objectives.

d. Impact on Project Activities: Resource smoothing may result in changes to project activities and their dependencies, while resource leveling may result in changes to the project schedule and duration.

e. Applicability: Resource smoothing is typically used when the availability of resources is limited, and the priority is to maintain a constant utilization rate of resources throughout the project. Resource leveling is typically used when the priority is to complete the project within a specific time frame, and the availability of resources is flexible.

Understanding these key differences is crucial in selecting the most appropriate technique for effective resource management. The selection of the appropriate technique depends on the project's requirements and constraints, such as time, budget, scope, and quality.

## FACTORS TO CONSIDER WHEN CHOOSING BETWEEN RESOURCE SMOOTHING AND RESOURCE LEVELLING

The selection of the appropriate technique for effective resource management depends on the project's requirements and constraints, such as time, budget, scope, and quality. Here are some factors to consider when choosing between resource smoothing and resource levelling:

a. Resource Availability: The availability of resources is a critical factor in determining the appropriate technique to use. If the availability of resources is limited, resource smoothing may be more appropriate to ensure a constant utilization rate of resources. If the availability of resources is flexible, resource leveling may be more appropriate to optimize resource utilization.

b. Project Timeline: The project timeline is another important factor in selecting the appropriate technique. If the project has a strict timeline and the priority is to complete the project within a specific timeframe, resource leveling may be more appropriate to ensure that resource constraints are met without compromising project objectives. If the project timeline is more flexible, resource smoothing may be more appropriate to balance resource demand.

c. Impact on Project Activities: The impact of resource management techniques on project activities is another important factor to consider. Resource smoothing may result in changes to project activities and their dependencies, while resource leveling may result in changes to the project schedule and duration. Therefore, it is essential to consider the impact on project activities when selecting the appropriate technique.

d. Project Budget: The project budget is another factor to consider when selecting the appropriate technique. Resource smoothing may result in increased project duration and may impact the project budget. Resource leveling may also result in changes to the project schedule and duration, which may impact the project budget. Therefore, it is essential to consider the impact on the project budget when selecting the appropriate technique.

e. Project Quality: The quality of the project deliverables is another factor to consider when selecting the appropriate technique. Resource smoothing may result in compromised project quality if resources are not allocated optimally. Resource leveling may also result in compromised project quality if the project schedule and duration are not adjusted optimally. Therefore, it is essential to consider the impact on project quality when selecting the appropriate technique.

In conclusion, selecting the appropriate resource management technique depends on the project's requirements and constraints. Considering factors such as resource availability, project timeline, impact on project activities, project budget, and project quality can help project managers make an informed decision on the appropriate technique to use.

## EXAMPLES OF RESOURCE SMOOTHING AND RESOURCE LEVELLING IN PRACTICE

To understand the practical applications of resource smoothing and resource levelling, let's consider two examples:

Example 1: Software Development Project

A software development project has a limited number of programmers who are skilled in a particular programming language. The project has a fixed timeline, and the priority is to maintain a constant utilization rate of resources throughout the project. In this case, resource smoothing is the appropriate technique to use.

The project manager can adjust the start and end dates of activities to balance resource demand. For example, if two programming tasks require a high level of resources in the same period, one task can be delayed or accelerated to balance the resource demand. The project manager must continuously monitor resource utilization to ensure that the changes have balanced resource demand and minimized resource constraints.

Example 2: Construction Project

A construction project has a flexible timeline, and the availability of resources is flexible. The project has a fixed budget, and the priority is to complete the project within the budget while optimizing resource utilization. In this case, resource levelling is the appropriate technique to use.

The project manager can adjust the project schedule and duration to balance resource demand. For example, if a construction task requires a high level of resources, the project manager can extend the duration of the task to balance the resource demand. The project manager must continuously monitor resource utilization to ensure that resource levelling is effective and that resources are optimally utilized.

In summary, the selection of the appropriate resource management technique depends on the project's requirements and constraints. Examples of practical applications of resource smoothing and resource levelling demonstrate the application of these techniques in real-world scenarios. Project managers must carefully consider the project's specific requirements and constraints to make an informed decision on the appropriate technique to use.

## CONCLUSION AND RECOMMENDATIONS FOR EFFECTIVE RESOURCE MANAGEMENT

Effective resource management is crucial for project success. Resource smoothing and resource levelling are two popular techniques used in project management to manage resources effectively. While these techniques share similarities in their goal to balance resource utilization, they differ in their approach and the outcome they produce.

Resource smoothing focuses on balancing resource utilization by adjusting the start and end dates of activities without changing the project duration. Resource levelling focuses on balancing resource utilization by adjusting the project schedule and duration to meet resource constraints.

To select the appropriate technique, project managers must consider factors such as resource availability, project timeline, impact on project activities, project budget, and project quality. Practical examples of resource smoothing and resource levelling demonstrate the application of these techniques in real-world scenarios.

To effectively manage resources, project managers must continuously monitor resource utilization to ensure that the selected technique is effective and that resources are optimally utilized. Project managers must also communicate effectively with team members and stakeholders to ensure that resource management decisions are understood and supported.

In conclusion, effective resource management is crucial for project success. The selection of the appropriate resource management technique depends on the project's requirements and constraints. Project managers must carefully consider these factors and continuously monitor resource utilization to ensure effective resource management.

# 8.6 Cost Planning in Iterative vs Linear Life Cycles

Iterative and linear life cycles are two different approaches to project management. A linear life cycle, also known as a waterfall model, is a traditional project management methodology that consists of a series of sequential phases, with each phase building upon the previous one. In a linear life cycle, the project progresses through distinct stages, including concept, definition, deployment, monitoring, and transition. The linear life cycle assumes that all requirements can be gathered upfront and that the project can be completed in a single, sequential effort.

On the other hand, an iterative life cycle is a more flexible approach to project management that involves a cyclical process of planning, executing, and evaluating each iteration. Iterative life cycles are often used in projects where requirements are not fully understood or where the project's end-state is subject to change. In an iterative life cycle, the project progresses through a series of iterations or cycles, each of which produces a deliverable or prototype that is evaluated by stakeholders. The feedback from each iteration is used to inform the next iteration, allowing the project to evolve over time.

Understanding the differences between iterative and linear life cycles is essential for cost planning, as each approach requires a different cost planning strategy. In the following subheadings, we will explore the key differences between iterative and linear life cycles and how they impact cost planning.

## KEY DIFFERENCES BETWEEN ITERATIVE AND LINEAR LIFE CYCLES

The primary difference between iterative and linear life cycles is their approach to project management. Linear life cycles follow a strict sequence of steps, with each phase building upon the previous one. The project moves forward in a linear fashion, and changes to the project scope or requirements are typically difficult to accommodate once the project has progressed beyond a particular phase. Iterative life cycles, on the other hand, involve a cyclical process of planning, executing, and evaluating each iteration. Each iteration builds upon the previous one, and the project evolves over time in response to stakeholder feedback.

This fundamental difference in approach has significant implications for cost planning. In a linear life cycle, cost planning typically occurs at the beginning of the project, during the definition phase. The project's budget and timeline are estimated based on the project requirements gathered at that time, and any changes to the project scope or requirements are likely to result in cost overruns or delays. In contrast, iterative life cycles require a more flexible approach to cost planning. Cost planning occurs at the beginning of each iteration, based on the requirements and scope of that iteration. As each iteration produces a deliverable or prototype, stakeholders evaluate it, providing feedback that can impact subsequent iterations' requirements and scope. This feedback loop allows the project team to adjust the project's budget and timeline as necessary, responding to changes in the project's scope or requirements.

Another key difference between iterative and linear life cycles is the level of stakeholder involvement. In a linear life cycle, stakeholders typically provide input during the definition phase and are less involved in the deployment phase. In contrast, iterative life cycles involve frequent stakeholder involvement, as stakeholders evaluate each iteration and provide feedback that guides subsequent iterations.

This increased stakeholder involvement can have a significant impact on the project's budget and timeline, as stakeholders may request changes or modifications to the project's scope or requirements based on their evaluation of each iteration.

Overall, the key differences between iterative and linear life cycles impact the project's approach to cost planning. In the following subheadings, we will explore cost planning strategies for iterative and linear life cycles in more detail.

## COST PLANNING FOR ITERATIVE LIFE CYCLES

Cost planning for iterative life cycles requires a more flexible approach than linear life cycles. Instead of creating a single budget and timeline for the entire project, cost planning occurs at the beginning of each iteration, based on the iteration's requirements and scope. The project team must estimate the resources required for each iteration, including labour, materials, and equipment, as well as any external costs, such as consulting or vendor fees. The cost estimates for each iteration are then used to create a budget for that iteration.

As each iteration produces a deliverable or prototype, stakeholders evaluate it and provide feedback that can impact subsequent iterations' requirements and scope. This feedback loop allows the project team to adjust the project's budget and timeline as necessary, responding to changes in the project's scope or requirements. The project team should also track the actual costs incurred during each iteration and compare them to the estimated costs to ensure that the project remains on track.

One challenge of cost planning for iterative life cycles is the difficulty in estimating costs accurately, especially if the project scope or requirements are subject to change. The project team must ensure that the cost estimates are based on realistic assumptions and account for any potential risks or uncertainties that may impact the project's budget or timeline.

To mitigate these challenges, the project team may choose to use agile project management methodologies, which are designed specifically for iterative life cycles. Agile methodologies emphasize close collaboration between stakeholders and the project team, frequent iterations, and a flexible approach to project management, making them well-suited for projects with evolving requirements or uncertain outcomes.

Overall, cost planning for iterative life cycles requires a more flexible approach than linear life cycles. Cost estimates must be based on realistic assumptions, and the project team must be prepared to adjust the project's budget and timeline in response to stakeholder feedback and changes in the project's scope or requirements.

## COST PLANNING FOR LINEAR LIFE CYCLES

Cost planning for linear life cycles typically occurs at the beginning of the project, during the definition phase. The project team must estimate the resources required for each phase of the project, including labour, materials, and equipment, as well as any external costs, such as consulting or vendor fees. The cost estimates for each phase are then used to create a budget for the entire project.

In a linear life cycle, the project progresses through distinct stages, with each phase building upon the previous one. Once a phase is complete, the project team moves on to the next phase, and changes to the project scope or requirements are typically difficult to accommodate. As a result, cost planning for linear life cycles requires a detailed and comprehensive understanding of the project's requirements and scope.

One challenge of cost planning for linear life cycles is the difficulty in estimating costs accurately, especially if the project's requirements or scope are subject to change. The project team must ensure that the cost estimates are based on realistic assumptions and account for any potential risks or uncertainties that may impact the project's budget or timeline.

To mitigate these challenges, the project team may choose to use project management tools and techniques, such as earned value management (EVM) or critical path analysis (CPA), which can help track project progress and identify potential cost overruns or delays. EVM involves measuring the project's performance against the project plan, allowing the project team to identify variances between actual and planned costs and take corrective action as necessary. CPA involves identifying the critical path, or the sequence of activities that must be completed on time to ensure the project is completed on schedule, allowing the project team to prioritize activities and allocate resources accordingly.

Overall, cost planning for linear life cycles requires a detailed and comprehensive understanding of the project's requirements and scope. Cost estimates must be based on realistic assumptions, and the project team must be prepared to track progress and identify potential cost overruns or delays using project management tools and techniques.

## CHALLENGES IN COST PLANNING FOR ITERATIVE AND LINEAR LIFE CYCLES

Both iterative and linear life cycles present unique challenges in cost planning. In iterative life cycles, the primary challenge is accurately estimating costs for each iteration, especially if the project's requirements or scope are subject to change. The project team must be prepared to adjust the project's budget and timeline in response to stakeholder feedback and changes in the project's scope or requirements. Additionally, the project team must ensure that the cost estimates are based on realistic assumptions and account for any potential risks or uncertainties that may impact the project's budget or timeline.

In linear life cycles, the primary challenge is identifying potential cost overruns or delays early in the project's lifecycle. Once a phase is complete, the project team moves on to the next phase, and changes to the project scope or requirements are typically difficult to accommodate. As a result, cost planning for linear life cycles requires a detailed and comprehensive understanding of the project's requirements and scope. The project team must ensure that the cost estimates are based on realistic assumptions and account for any potential risks or uncertainties that may impact the project's budget or timeline.

Another challenge in cost planning for both iterative and linear life cycles is managing stakeholder expectations. In iterative life cycles, frequent stakeholder involvement can result in changes to the project's scope or requirements, which can impact the project's budget or timeline. In linear life cycles, changes to the project's scope or requirements may be difficult to accommodate once the project has progressed beyond a particular phase, which can lead to cost overruns or delays. Managing stakeholder expectations requires effective communication and collaboration between stakeholders and the project team, as well as a flexible approach to project management.

To mitigate these challenges, project teams may choose to use project management tools and techniques, such as EVM or CPA, which can help track project progress and identify potential cost overruns or delays. Additionally, project teams may choose to use agile project management methodologies, which are designed specifically for iterative life cycles and emphasize close collaboration between stakeholders and the project team, frequent iterations, and a flexible approach to project management.

Overall, the challenges in cost planning for iterative and linear life cycles require project teams to adopt a proactive and flexible approach to project management. The project team must be prepared to adjust the project's budget and timeline in response to stakeholder feedback and changes in the project's scope or requirements, while also ensuring that cost estimates are based on realistic assumptions and account for any potential risks or uncertainties that may impact the project's budget or timeline. Effective communication and collaboration between stakeholders and the project team are also essential to managing stakeholder expectations and ensuring project success.

## BEST PRACTICES FOR COST PLANNING IN ITERATIVE AND LINEAR LIFE CYCLES

Cost planning is an essential component of project management, whether using an iterative or linear life cycle approach. To ensure project success, project teams should adopt the following best practices when planning and managing project costs:

a. Involve stakeholders in the cost planning process: In both iterative and linear life cycles, stakeholders play a critical role in defining the project's scope and requirements. By involving stakeholders in the cost planning process, project teams can ensure that cost estimates are based on realistic assumptions and account for potential risks or uncertainties.

b. Use historical data to inform cost estimates: Historical data, such as past project budgets, can be a valuable resource for cost planning. By analyzing past project budgets, project teams can identify patterns and trends that can inform cost estimates for future projects.

c. Regularly review and adjust cost estimates: In iterative life cycles, cost estimates should be reviewed and adjusted at the beginning of each iteration, based on the iteration's requirements and scope. In linear life cycles, cost estimates should be reviewed regularly throughout the project's lifecycle to ensure they remain accurate and up-to-date.

d. Use project management tools and techniques: Project management tools and techniques, such as EVM and CPA, can help track project progress and identify potential cost overruns or delays. Project teams should choose the tools and techniques that best suit their project's needs and objectives.

e. Monitor and manage project risks: Project risks, such as scope creep or unexpected delays, can have a significant impact on project costs. Project teams should identify and assess potential risks early in the project's lifecycle and develop strategies to mitigate or manage them.

f. Communicate and collaborate effectively: Effective communication and collaboration between stakeholders and the project team are essential to managing stakeholder expectations and ensuring project success. Project teams should establish clear communication channels and regularly update stakeholders on project progress and cost status.

Overall, adopting these best practices can help project teams successfully plan and manage project costs in both iterative and linear life cycles. By involving stakeholders in the cost planning process, using historical data to inform cost estimates, regularly reviewing and adjusting cost estimates, using project management tools and techniques, monitoring and managing project risks, and communicating and collaborating effectively, project teams can ensure that their projects are completed on time and within budget.

# CHAPTER NINE

## *DEMYSTIFYING PROJECT PROCUREMENT*

# 9.1 Understanding the Importance of a Procurement Strategy

A procurement strategy is a detailed plan that outlines how a business will acquire the goods and services it needs to operate efficiently and effectively. The purpose of a procurement strategy is to ensure that a business can source the right products or services, from the right suppliers, at the right price, and at the right time.

A procurement strategy helps businesses to manage their procurement process effectively by providing a framework for decision-making, risk management, and supplier relationship management. It enables businesses to identify potential risks and opportunities in the procurement process, and to put in place measures to mitigate those risks and capitalize on the opportunities.

A well-developed procurement strategy also helps to improve the transparency and accountability of the procurement process, which can enhance stakeholder trust and confidence. This can be particularly important for businesses that are subject to regulatory oversight, as they must demonstrate that they are following ethical and responsible procurement practices.

In summary, the purpose of a procurement strategy is to ensure that a business can procure the goods and services it needs to operate efficiently and effectively while managing risk, ensuring compliance with regulations, and promoting transparency and accountability in the procurement process.

## Typical Content of a Procurement Strategy

The content of a procurement strategy can vary depending on the size, complexity, and industry of the business. However, most procurement strategies will include the following key elements:

a. Procurement Objectives: The procurement objectives outline the business goals that the procurement strategy aims to achieve. For example, the procurement strategy may aim to reduce costs, improve supplier quality, or increase efficiency in the procurement process.

b. Procurement Methodology: The procurement methodology outlines the approach that the business will take to procure goods and services. This may include the use of competitive bidding, negotiation, or strategic sourcing.

c. Supplier Management: The supplier management section outlines how the business will select and manage suppliers. This may include supplier selection criteria, supplier performance metrics, and procedures for monitoring and evaluating supplier performance.

d. Risk Management: The risk management section outlines how the business will identify, assess, and mitigate procurement risks. This may include risks related to supplier performance, market volatility, or supply chain disruptions.

e. Procurement Policies and Procedures: The procurement policies and procedures section outlines the policies and procedures that govern the procurement process. This may include procurement standards, ethical guidelines, and procurement reporting requirements.

f. Procurement Performance Metrics: The procurement performance metrics section outlines how the business will measure the success of its procurement strategy. This may include metrics such as cost savings, supplier performance, and procurement cycle time.

In summary, a typical procurement strategy will include objectives, methodology, supplier management, risk management, policies and procedures, and performance metrics. These elements provide a roadmap for how the business will procure goods and services, manage suppliers, mitigate risks, and measure procurement performance.

## IMPORTANCE OF A PROCUREMENT STRATEGY FOR BUSINESSES

A procurement strategy is essential for businesses of all sizes and across all industries. The following are some of the key reasons why a procurement strategy is important:

a. Cost Reduction: One of the primary benefits of a procurement strategy is cost reduction. A well-developed procurement strategy can help businesses to identify cost savings opportunities, negotiate better deals with suppliers, and implement cost-effective procurement processes.

b. Improved Supplier Relationships: A procurement strategy can help businesses to build stronger and more effective relationships with their suppliers. By establishing clear supplier selection criteria, performance metrics, and communication channels, businesses can work collaboratively with their suppliers to achieve common goals.

c. Risk Management: Procurement involves many risks, such as supplier non-performance, supply chain disruptions, and compliance issues. A procurement strategy helps businesses to identify and mitigate these risks, reducing the likelihood of negative impacts on operations and reputation.

d. Compliance: A procurement strategy helps businesses to ensure compliance with regulatory requirements and ethical standards. By establishing policies and procedures that govern the procurement process, businesses can ensure that they are following ethical and responsible procurement practices.

e. Enhanced Transparency and Accountability: A procurement strategy can enhance the transparency and accountability of the procurement process, promoting stakeholder trust and confidence. By establishing clear procurement policies, procedures, and performance metrics, businesses can demonstrate that they are committed to responsible procurement practices.

f. Strategic Advantage: Finally, a procurement strategy can provide businesses with a strategic advantage. By aligning procurement goals with overall business objectives, businesses can leverage procurement as a competitive advantage, driving innovation, and growth.

In summary, a well-developed procurement strategy is critical for businesses to achieve cost reduction, improved supplier relationships, risk management, compliance, enhanced transparency and accountability, and strategic advantage.

# 9.2 UNDERSTANDING DIFFERENT METHODS OF SUPPLIER REIMBURSEMENT

In any business, the procurement of goods and services from external sources is a common practice. Suppliers play a critical role in ensuring that businesses have access to the materials and resources they need to function effectively. However, payment is a critical aspect of the supplier relationship, and companies need to choose the appropriate payment method based on the nature of the supplier relationship, the product or service being purchased, and the risk associated with the transaction.

There are several methods of supplier reimbursement, each with its own advantages and disadvantages. The four primary methods of supplier reimbursement include fixed price, cost plus fee, per unit quantity, and target cost. Understanding each of these methods is essential to make informed decisions when selecting a supplier reimbursement method that works best for your business.

## FIXED PRICE REIMBURSEMENT METHOD

The fixed price reimbursement method is perhaps the most common payment method used in supplier relationships. In this method, the supplier and the buyer agree on a fixed price for the product or service being purchased. This price remains unchanged throughout the term of the contract, regardless of any fluctuations in the cost of raw materials, labour, or any other factors that may impact the cost of production.

This method of supplier reimbursement is beneficial in situations where the buyer has a good understanding of the market and can negotiate a fair price with the supplier. It is also useful when the product or service being purchased has a stable cost structure and is not likely to fluctuate significantly over the course of the contract. However, if there are any unforeseen circumstances or changes in the market that impact the supplier's cost structure, the supplier bears the financial risk.

The fixed price reimbursement method is straightforward and easy to administer, which makes it an attractive option for many businesses. However, it may not be the most suitable option for all supplier relationships. For example, in situations where the supplier has limited market knowledge or a lack of bargaining power, a fixed price reimbursement method may result in lower profits and may limit the supplier's ability to invest in future growth.

## COST PLUS FEE REIMBURSEMENT METHOD

In the cost plus fee reimbursement method, the buyer reimburses the supplier for the actual cost of the product or service being provided, as well as an additional fee that covers the supplier's overhead costs and profit margin. The fee may be a fixed percentage of the cost of production or may be negotiated separately between the buyer and the supplier.

This method of supplier reimbursement is beneficial in situations where the buyer has limited knowledge of the market or where the product or service being purchased has a variable cost structure. The supplier bears the financial risk associated with any unforeseen circumstances or changes in the market, but is also compensated for their efforts.

The cost plus fee reimbursement method is also advantageous for long-term supplier relationships, as it allows the supplier to make investments in their business with a degree of financial stability. This method is also transparent, as both parties can easily understand the cost breakdown and the fee structure.

However, the cost plus fee reimbursement method may also be disadvantageous in certain situations. If the supplier overestimates their overhead costs, the buyer may end up paying more than necessary. Additionally, this method may not be suitable for short-term contracts or for suppliers who are unable to accurately forecast their costs.

## PER UNIT QUANTITY REIMBURSEMENT METHOD

The per unit quantity reimbursement method involves the buyer reimbursing the supplier for each unit of product or service delivered, based on a predetermined price per unit. This method is commonly used for products or services that have a fixed or predictable cost structure, such as raw materials or labour costs.

This method of supplier reimbursement is beneficial in situations where the buyer wants to maintain a high level of control over the costs associated with the product or service being purchased. The per unit quantity reimbursement method is also advantageous for short-term contracts, where a fixed price or cost plus fee reimbursement method may not be feasible.

However, the per unit quantity reimbursement method may be disadvantageous for suppliers who have a variable cost structure or for products or services that have a high level of uncertainty associated with them. This method may also incentivize the supplier to prioritize quantity over quality, which can negatively impact the overall value of the product or service being provided.

The per unit quantity reimbursement method is best used in situations where the buyer has a good understanding of the market and can negotiate a fair price per unit with the supplier. This method is also useful for products or services that have a predictable demand or cost structure.

## TARGET COST REIMBURSEMENT METHOD

The target cost reimbursement method is a more complex supplier reimbursement method that involves the buyer and supplier agreeing on a target cost for the product or service being purchased. The target cost includes the supplier's estimated cost of production, as well as their desired profit margin. The buyer then reimburses the supplier for the actual costs of production, up to the agreed-upon target cost. If the actual cost of production exceeds the target cost, the supplier bears the additional cost.

This method of supplier reimbursement is beneficial in situations where the buyer and supplier are in a long-term relationship and have a high level of trust and collaboration. The target cost reimbursement method incentivizes the supplier to work efficiently and to manage their costs effectively, as any cost overruns are borne by the supplier.

However, the target cost reimbursement method may also be disadvantageous in certain situations. If the supplier underestimates their costs, they may not make a profit on the transaction. This method may also be difficult to administer, as it requires close collaboration and communication between the buyer and supplier.

The target cost reimbursement method is best used in situations where the product or service being purchased has a variable cost structure and where the buyer and supplier have a good understanding of the market and the cost drivers associated with the transaction. This method is also useful for long-term supplier relationships, where both parties have a vested interest in the success of the transaction.

## FACTORS TO CONSIDER WHEN CHOOSING A SUPPLIER REIMBURSEMENT METHOD

When choosing a supplier reimbursement method, there are several factors that businesses should consider to ensure that they select the method that best suits their needs. These factors include:

a. Nature of the product or service being purchased: The product or service being purchased may have a stable or variable cost structure, which can impact the choice of reimbursement method.

b. Risk associated with the transaction: Some reimbursement methods place more financial risk on the supplier, while others place more risk on the buyer. Businesses need to assess the level of risk they are willing to accept and choose a reimbursement method that reflects their risk tolerance.

c. Length of the contract: The length of the contract may impact the choice of reimbursement method. Short-term contracts may require a different reimbursement method than long-term contracts.

d. Level of collaboration between buyer and supplier: The level of collaboration between the buyer and supplier can impact the choice of reimbursement method. Some reimbursement methods require a high level of collaboration and communication between the parties.

e. Market knowledge and bargaining power: The buyer's market knowledge and bargaining power can impact the choice of reimbursement method. In situations where the buyer has more bargaining power, a fixed price reimbursement method may be more appropriate.

f. Desired level of control over costs: Some reimbursement methods offer more control over costs than others. Businesses need to consider how much control they want to exert over the costs associated with the transaction.

By considering these factors, businesses can choose a supplier reimbursement method that best suits their needs and the nature of the transaction.

## PROS AND CONS OF EACH REIMBURSEMENT METHOD

Each supplier reimbursement method has its own set of advantages and disadvantages. Here are the pros and cons of each method:

Fixed Price Reimbursement Method: Pros:

- Simple and straightforward

- Offers financial stability to the supplier

- Easy to administer

Cons:

- May not be suitable for products or services with a variable cost structure

- Limits the supplier's ability to invest in future growth

- Supplier bears the financial risk associated with any unforeseen circumstances or changes in the market

Cost Plus Fee Reimbursement Method: Pros:

- Transparent

- Supplier compensated for their efforts

- Suitable for long-term contracts

Cons:

- Supplier may overestimate their overhead costs, leading to higher costs for the buyer

- May not be suitable for short-term contracts or for suppliers who are unable to accurately forecast their costs

Per Unit Quantity Reimbursement Method: Pros:

- Provides control over costs

- Suitable for short-term contracts

- Useful for products or services with a predictable demand or cost structure

Cons:

- May not be suitable for suppliers with a variable cost structure

- Incentivizes the supplier to prioritize quantity over quality

- May not be suitable for products or services with a high level of uncertainty associated with them

Target Cost Reimbursement Method: Pros:

- Incentivizes the supplier to work efficiently and manage costs effectively

- Suitable for long-term relationships

- Offers a high level of collaboration and communication between buyer and supplier

Cons:

- Supplier may underestimate their costs, leading to lower profits

- Difficult to administer

- Requires a high level of collaboration and trust between the parties

By understanding the pros and cons of each reimbursement method, businesses can make informed decisions about which method is most suitable for their needs. It is essential to consider the nature of the product or service being purchased, the level of risk associated with the transaction, the length of the contract, the level of collaboration between the parties, the market knowledge and bargaining power, and the desired level of control over costs.

## CONCLUSION: CHOOSING THE RIGHT SUPPLIER REIMBURSEMENT METHOD FOR YOUR BUSINESS

When choosing a supplier reimbursement method, businesses should carefully consider the nature of the product or service being purchased, the level of risk associated with the transaction, the length of the contract, the level of collaboration between the parties, the market knowledge and bargaining power, and the desired level of control over costs.

Each reimbursement method has its own set of advantages and disadvantages, and businesses should weigh these factors carefully before making a decision. Fixed price reimbursement method is simple and straightforward, but may not be suitable for products or services with a variable cost structure. Cost plus fee reimbursement method is transparent, but may not be suitable for short-term contracts or for suppliers who are unable to accurately forecast their costs. Per unit quantity reimbursement method provides control over costs, but may not be suitable for suppliers with a variable cost structure. Target cost reimbursement method incentivizes the supplier to work efficiently and manage costs effectively, but requires a high level of collaboration and trust between the parties.

Ultimately, the choice of supplier reimbursement method will depend on the unique needs of each business and the specific transaction at hand. By carefully considering the pros and cons of each method and weighing the factors that impact the choice of reimbursement method, businesses can select the reimbursement method that best suits their needs and ensures a successful and profitable supplier relationship.

# 9.3 Understanding Different Contractual Relationships in Project Procurement

Project procurement contracts are legal agreements between a buyer (the entity that needs goods or services) and a seller (the entity that provides goods or services) for the purpose of acquiring goods or services to fulfil the needs of a project. Procurement contracts are an essential component of project management, as they establish the parameters for project delivery and define the obligations and responsibilities of both the buyer and the seller.

In project procurement, it is crucial to understand the different types of contractual relationships that can exist between a buyer and a seller. These relationships determine the degree of risk and control that each party assumes in the project, as well as the payment structure for the work being performed. By understanding the different contractual relationships available, project managers can choose the right contract for their project, negotiate the terms effectively, and manage the project with greater efficiency and success.

## Types of Contractual Relationships in Project Procurement

There are several types of contractual relationships that can exist between a buyer and a seller in project procurement. These relationships are differentiated based on the payment structure, the degree of risk and control assumed by each party, and the performance standards that are expected. The four main types of contractual relationships in project procurement are:

a. Fixed-Price Contracts: In this type of contract, the buyer agrees to pay a fixed price to the seller for the completion of a specific scope of work. This type of contract places most of the risk on the seller, who must deliver the work within the agreed-upon budget. Fixed-price contracts are commonly used when the scope of work is well-defined, and the buyer has a clear idea of what they want.

b. Cost-Reimbursement Contracts: In a cost-reimbursement contract, the buyer reimburses the seller for the actual costs incurred in performing the work, plus a fee or profit margin. This type of contract places most of the risk on the buyer, who assumes the cost overrun risk. Cost-reimbursement contracts are commonly used when the scope of work is uncertain, and the buyer needs flexibility in the project's requirements.

c. Time and Materials Contracts: In this type of contract, the buyer pays the seller for the actual time and materials used in performing the work. This type of contract places most of the risk on the buyer, who assumes the cost overrun risk. Time and materials contracts are commonly used when the scope of work is not well-defined, and the buyer needs flexibility in the project's requirements.

d. Performance-Based Contracts: In a performance-based contract, the buyer pays the seller based on the successful completion of specific project milestones or objectives. This type of contract places most of the risk on the seller, who must meet the performance standards to receive payment. Performance-based contracts are commonly used when the buyer wants to incentivize the seller to achieve specific project goals.

Understanding the different types of contractual relationships in project procurement is essential for project managers to select the right type of contract for their project. By selecting the appropriate type of contract, project managers can ensure that the project is completed within budget, on time, and to the required performance standards.

## FIXED-PRICE CONTRACTS

A fixed-price contract, also known as a lump-sum contract, is a type of contract where the buyer agrees to pay a fixed price to the seller for the completion of a specific scope of work. This price includes all costs associated with the completion of the work, including labour, materials, and overhead costs. Fixed-price contracts are commonly used in project procurement when the scope of work is well-defined, and the buyer has a clear idea of what they want.

One advantage of fixed-price contracts is that they provide a clear budget for the project, which allows for easier financial planning and budgeting. Additionally, because the price is fixed, there is less risk of cost overruns, which can be a significant concern in other types of contracts. Fixed-price contracts can also encourage sellers to work more efficiently, as they are motivated to complete the work within the budget to maximize their profits.

However, fixed-price contracts also place most of the risk on the seller, who must deliver the work within the agreed-upon budget. This can be a significant disadvantage for sellers, as unexpected problems or changes in the project scope can significantly impact their profitability. As a result, sellers may be hesitant to bid on fixed-price contracts or may charge a premium to compensate for the risk.

Overall, fixed-price contracts can be a useful tool in project procurement when the scope of work is well-defined and both the buyer and the seller are willing to accept the associated risks and rewards. Project managers must carefully evaluate the scope of work and project requirements before selecting a fixed-price contract to ensure that it is the best option for their project.

## COST-REIMBURSEMENT CONTRACTS

Cost-reimbursement contracts are a type of contract where the buyer reimburses the seller for the actual costs incurred in performing the work, plus a fee or profit margin. This type of contract is commonly used when the scope of work is uncertain, and the buyer needs flexibility in the project's requirements.

In a cost-reimbursement contract, the buyer assumes most of the cost overrun risk, as the seller is reimbursed for all actual costs incurred in performing the work. This can be a significant advantage for sellers, as they are not responsible for the project's cost overruns. However, the buyer maintains control over the project's scope and can adjust the project's requirements as needed to meet changing needs.

One of the challenges of cost-reimbursement contracts is that they can be challenging to administer. Project managers must carefully monitor costs to ensure that they are reasonable and necessary, as the buyer is responsible for reimbursing all actual costs incurred. Additionally, the fee or profit margin that the seller receives is typically negotiated upfront and may not be adjusted based on the actual costs incurred, which can lead to disputes between the buyer and the seller.

Cost-reimbursement contracts can be useful in project procurement when the scope of work is uncertain, and the buyer needs flexibility in the project's requirements. However, they require careful administration and monitoring to ensure that costs are reasonable and necessary and that the buyer is not overpaying for the work performed. Project managers must carefully evaluate the project's requirements and risks before selecting a cost-reimbursement contract to ensure that it is the best option for their project.

## TIME AND MATERIALS CONTRACTS

A time and materials contract is a type of contract where the buyer pays the seller for the actual time and materials used in performing the work. This type of contract is commonly used when the scope of work is not well-defined, and the buyer needs flexibility in the project's requirements.

In a time and materials contract, the buyer assumes most of the cost overrun risk, as the seller is reimbursed for all actual costs incurred in performing the work. This can be an advantage for sellers, as they are not responsible for the project's cost overruns. However, the buyer maintains control over the project's scope and can adjust the project's requirements as needed to meet changing needs.

One of the challenges of time and materials contracts is that they can be challenging to administer. Project managers must carefully monitor costs to ensure that they are reasonable and necessary, as the buyer is responsible for reimbursing all actual costs incurred. Additionally, because the fee or profit margin that the seller receives is typically negotiated upfront, there may be less incentive for the seller to work efficiently.

Time and materials contracts can be useful in project procurement when the scope of work is not well-defined, and the buyer needs flexibility in the project's requirements. However, they require careful administration and monitoring to ensure that costs are reasonable and necessary and that the buyer is not overpaying for the work performed. Project managers must carefully evaluate the project's requirements and risks before selecting a time and materials contract to ensure that it is the best option for their project.

## PERFORMANCE-BASED CONTRACTS

Performance-based contracts are a type of contract where the buyer pays the seller based on the successful completion of specific project milestones or objectives. This type of contract is commonly used when the buyer wants to incentivize the seller to achieve specific project goals.

In a performance-based contract, the seller assumes most of the risk, as they must meet the performance standards to receive payment. This can be an advantage for the buyer, as it ensures that the project meets specific performance standards. Additionally, because the seller is incentivized to achieve the project goals, they may work more efficiently and effectively.

However, performance-based contracts can be challenging to administer. Project managers must carefully define the project goals and milestones to ensure that they are achievable and measurable. Additionally, because the seller assumes most of the risk, they may be hesitant to bid on performance-based contracts or may charge a premium to compensate for the risk.

Performance-based contracts can be useful in project procurement when the buyer wants to incentivize the seller to achieve specific project goals. However, they require careful administration and monitoring to ensure that the project goals are achievable and measurable and that the seller is not overcompensated for the work performed. Project managers must carefully evaluate the project's requirements and risks before selecting a performance-based contract to ensure that it is the best option for their project.

## CHOOSING THE RIGHT CONTRACTUAL RELATIONSHIP FOR YOUR PROJECT

Choosing the right contractual relationship is a crucial aspect of project procurement. Project managers must consider several factors when selecting the appropriate type of contract for their project, including the project's scope, complexity, and risk profile. Here are some key considerations when choosing the right contractual relationship for your project:

   a. Project Scope: The scope of work is one of the most critical factors to consider when selecting a contractual relationship. If the project scope is well-defined and relatively stable, a fixed-price contract may be the best option. However, if the project scope is uncertain or likely to change, a cost-reimbursement or time and materials contract may be more appropriate.

b. Risk Profile: Different contractual relationships place varying levels of risk on the buyer and the seller. Project managers must evaluate the project's risk profile and determine which contractual relationship is best suited to mitigate those risks. For example, a performance-based contract may be appropriate if the project's success depends on achieving specific project goals.

c. Complexity: The complexity of the project is another critical factor to consider when selecting a contractual relationship. Complex projects may require more flexibility in the project's requirements, which may be better suited to a cost-reimbursement or time and materials contract.

d. Cost: The cost of the project is also a critical factor to consider when selecting a contractual relationship. Fixed-price contracts provide a clear budget for the project, which can be advantageous for managing costs. However, if the project's costs are uncertain or likely to change, a cost-reimbursement or time and materials contract may be more appropriate.

Ultimately, project managers must carefully evaluate their project's requirements and risks before selecting the appropriate type of contract. By selecting the right contractual relationship, project managers can ensure that their project is completed on time, within budget, and to the required performance standards.

## RISKS AND BENEFITS OF DIFFERENT CONTRACTUAL RELATIONSHIPS

Each contractual relationship has its own set of risks and benefits. It's essential for project managers to understand these risks and benefits when choosing the appropriate type of contract for their project. Here are some of the risks and benefits associated with different contractual relationships:

a. Fixed-Price Contracts: Benefits of fixed-price contracts include clear budgeting, reduced risk of cost overruns, and incentivizing sellers to work efficiently. However, the risks associated with fixed-price contracts include the potential for disputes over the scope of work, a lack of flexibility in project requirements, and the potential for sellers to cut corners to maximize their profits.

b. Cost-Reimbursement Contracts: Benefits of cost-reimbursement contracts include greater flexibility in project requirements, reduced risk of incomplete work, and the ability to provide payment to the seller for all actual costs incurred. However, the risks associated with cost-reimbursement contracts include the potential for cost overruns, difficulty in determining actual costs, and disputes over the seller's profit margin.

c. Time and Materials Contracts: Benefits of time and materials contracts include greater flexibility in project requirements, the ability to pay the seller for all actual costs incurred, and incentivizing sellers to work efficiently. However, the risks associated with time and materials contracts include the potential for cost overruns, difficulty in determining actual costs, and disputes over the seller's profit margin.

d. Performance-Based Contracts: Benefits of performance-based contracts include incentivizing sellers to achieve specific project goals, ensuring project success, and encouraging sellers to work efficiently. However, the risks associated with performance-based contracts include the potential for disputes over project goals, difficulty in measuring performance, and the potential for sellers to cut corners to achieve project goals.

Project managers must carefully evaluate the risks and benefits associated with each contractual relationship when choosing the appropriate type of contract for their project. By understanding these risks and benefits, project managers can select the contractual relationship that best suits their project's requirements and risks.

## NEGOTIATING CONTRACTUAL TERMS

Negotiating contractual terms is an essential component of project procurement. Project managers must ensure that the contract reflects the project's requirements and risks while protecting the interests of both the buyer and the seller. Here are some key considerations when negotiating contractual terms:

a. Scope of Work: The scope of work should be clearly defined in the contract to avoid disputes over project requirements and deliverables. Project managers should include a detailed description of the project's objectives, deliverables, and timeline to ensure that both parties understand the project's requirements.

b. Payment Terms: Payment terms should be clearly defined in the contract to avoid disputes over payment. The contract should specify the payment structure, payment schedule, and any incentives or penalties for meeting or failing to meet project milestones.

c. Intellectual Property: Intellectual property ownership and rights should be clearly defined in the contract to avoid disputes over ownership and use of project deliverables. Project managers should include provisions to protect both parties' intellectual property rights, including the use, transfer, and ownership of project deliverables.

d. Risk Allocation: Risk allocation should be clearly defined in the contract to ensure that both parties understand their obligations and responsibilities. Project managers should consider the project's risks and allocate them appropriately between the buyer and the seller.

e. Dispute Resolution: Dispute resolution procedures should be included in the contract to avoid disputes and ensure that they are resolved quickly and fairly. Project managers should consider including provisions for mediation or arbitration to resolve disputes outside of the court system.

Negotiating contractual terms requires careful consideration of the project's requirements and risks. Project managers should work closely with legal and procurement teams to ensure that the contract reflects the project's needs while protecting the interests of both parties.

## CONCLUSION AND RECOMMENDATIONS

In conclusion, choosing the right contractual relationship is a critical aspect of project procurement. Project managers must carefully evaluate their project's requirements and risks to select the appropriate type of contract. Understanding the risks and benefits associated with each contractual relationship can help project managers make informed decisions about which type of contract to use.

Once the appropriate type of contract has been selected, negotiating the contractual terms is essential to ensure that the contract reflects the project's requirements and risks while protecting the interests of both parties. Project managers should work closely with legal and procurement teams to ensure that the contract is fair and equitable for both the buyer and the seller.

Recommendations for project managers include:

a. Evaluate the project's requirements and risks before selecting a contractual relationship.

b. Understand the risks and benefits associated with each contractual relationship.

c. Negotiate the contractual terms to ensure that they reflect the project's requirements and risks while protecting the interests of both parties.

d. Work closely with legal and procurement teams to ensure that the contract is fair and equitable for both the buyer and the seller.

e. Monitor the project's progress and costs to ensure that the project is completed on time, within budget, and to the required performance standards.

By following these recommendations, project managers can successfully navigate the project procurement process, select the appropriate type of contract, and negotiate contractual terms that reflect the project's requirements and risks while protecting the interests of both parties.

# 9.4 NAVIGATING THE SUPPLIER SELECTION PROCESS IN PROJECT PROCUREMENT

Project procurement involves the acquisition of goods, services, or works from external suppliers to support the execution of a project. The supplier selection process is a critical component of project procurement, as it involves the identification, evaluation, and selection of the most suitable supplier(s) to meet the project's requirements. The process of supplier selection should be conducted in a structured and systematic manner to ensure that the project team selects the most appropriate supplier(s) that can deliver the required quality, quantity, cost, and timeliness of goods, services, or works.

In this section, we will explore the importance of the supplier selection process in project procurement and provide an overview of the steps involved in the process. We will also highlight the key considerations that project teams need to make when selecting suppliers and the benefits of conducting an effective supplier selection process.

## IDENTIFYING PROJECT REQUIREMENTS AND SUPPLIER CRITERIA

The first step in the supplier selection process is to identify the project's requirements and the criteria that the supplier(s) must meet. This involves defining the scope of the project, the type of goods, services, or works required, and the quality, quantity, cost, and delivery timeframe of the products or services. It also involves identifying any specific technical or regulatory requirements that the supplier(s) must meet.

Once the project requirements are identified, the project team can begin to develop the criteria that the supplier(s) must meet to be considered for the project. These criteria may include factors such as:

- Experience and expertise in providing the required goods, services, or works

- Financial stability and capacity to deliver

- Quality assurance and control processes

- Compliance with legal and regulatory requirements

- Health, safety, and environmental policies and practices

- Reputation and references

- Price and delivery terms

The criteria should be tailored to the specific needs of the project and should be objective and measurable to facilitate the evaluation of potential suppliers. The project team may also assign weights to each criterion to reflect its relative importance in the supplier selection process.

By clearly defining the project requirements and the supplier criteria, the project team can ensure that the supplier selection process is focused and effective, and that the selected supplier(s) can meet the project's needs.

## CONDUCTING MARKET RESEARCH AND IDENTIFYING POTENTIAL SUPPLIERS

After defining the project requirements and supplier criteria, the project team can begin conducting market research to identify potential suppliers that can meet the project's needs. This involves gathering information about the market for the required goods, services, or works, including:

- The number and types of suppliers in the market

- The supplier's capabilities and capacity

- The supplier's financial stability

- The supplier's reputation and references

- The current market prices for the required goods, services, or works

Market research can be conducted through various channels, such as industry reports, trade associations, online databases, and personal contacts. The project team may also issue a request for information (RFI) to potential suppliers to gather additional information about their capabilities and capacity.

Once potential suppliers have been identified, the project team can evaluate them against the predefined supplier criteria. The evaluation may involve a preliminary screening to eliminate suppliers that do not meet the minimum requirements, followed by a more detailed assessment of the remaining suppliers.

The project team may also consider other factors, such as the supplier's location, cultural fit, and potential for collaboration when evaluating potential suppliers. The goal of this process is to shortlist the most qualified suppliers that can meet the project's needs and move to the next phase of the supplier selection process.

## PRE-QUALIFICATION AND SHORTLISTING OF SUPPLIERS

The next step in the supplier selection process is to pre-qualify potential suppliers and create a shortlist of the most qualified suppliers. Pre-qualification involves verifying that the potential suppliers meet the predefined supplier criteria and can deliver the required goods, services, or works. This may include requesting additional information from the suppliers, such as financial statements, references, and proof of compliance with legal and regulatory requirements.

Once the potential suppliers have been pre-qualified, the project team can create a shortlist of the most qualified suppliers that will be invited to participate in the next phase of the supplier selection process. The shortlisting process may involve assigning weights to each of the supplier criteria and scoring each potential supplier against the criteria. The suppliers with the highest scores may be shortlisted for the next phase of the supplier selection process.

The project team may also conduct a site visit or an interview with the shortlisted suppliers to assess their facilities, processes, and capabilities. This can help the project team gain a better understanding of each supplier's strengths and weaknesses and make a more informed decision about which supplier(s) to select.

The goal of pre-qualification and shortlisting is to identify a pool of qualified suppliers that can deliver the required goods, services, or works and meet the project's needs. By creating a shortlist of the most qualified suppliers, the project team can streamline the supplier selection process and focus their efforts on evaluating the most promising candidates.

## ISSUING REQUESTS FOR PROPOSALS (RFPS) AND EVALUATING SUPPLIER RESPONSES

Once the shortlist of qualified suppliers has been created, the project team can issue a request for proposal (RFP) to each supplier on the list. An RFP is a document that outlines the project requirements and invites the supplier(s) to submit a proposal outlining how they will meet those requirements. The RFP may include information about the project scope, technical specifications, delivery requirements, pricing, and evaluation criteria.

The suppliers are given a deadline to submit their proposals, which are then evaluated by the project team. The evaluation process may involve scoring each proposal against the predefined evaluation criteria and assigning weights to each criterion. The project team may also conduct a detailed review of each proposal to ensure that it meets the project requirements and that all necessary information has been provided.

The project team may also hold a meeting with the shortlisted suppliers to clarify any questions or issues related to the RFP and to gain a better understanding of each supplier's proposal. This can help the project team make a more informed decision about which supplier(s) to select.

After evaluating the supplier proposals, the project team can select the most suitable supplier(s) based on the evaluation criteria and the project requirements. The selection may be based on various factors, such as price, quality, delivery timeframe, and the supplier's ability to meet the project requirements.

The project team may also negotiate with the selected supplier(s) to finalize the contract terms, including the price, delivery terms, payment terms, and any other relevant terms and conditions.

The goal of this phase of the supplier selection process is to select the most suitable supplier(s) that can meet the project's requirements and deliver the required goods, services, or works at a reasonable cost and within the required timeframe.

## NEGOTIATING CONTRACTS AND FINALIZING SUPPLIER SELECTION

Once the most suitable supplier(s) have been selected, the project team can begin negotiating the contract terms with the supplier(s). This phase involves finalizing the price, delivery terms, payment terms, and any other relevant terms and conditions. The goal is to ensure that the contract is fair and balanced and that it meets the project's requirements and objectives.

The contract negotiation process may involve multiple rounds of discussions and negotiations between the project team and the supplier(s). The project team should ensure that the contract terms are clearly defined and that any potential issues or risks are identified and addressed. The project team may also seek legal advice to ensure that the contract is legally binding and enforceable.

After the contract terms have been negotiated and finalized, the project team can issue the contract to the selected supplier(s) and finalize the supplier selection process. The project team should ensure that all parties understand their obligations and responsibilities under the contract and that the supplier(s) can deliver the required goods, services, or works as specified in the contract.

The final step in the supplier selection process is to manage the contract and supplier relationship throughout the project's lifecycle. This may involve monitoring the supplier's performance, resolving any issues or disputes that may arise, and ensuring that the supplier(s) meet the project's requirements and objectives.

The goal of this phase of the supplier selection process is to ensure that the selected supplier(s) can deliver the required goods, services, or works at a reasonable cost and within the required timeframe and that the contract is fair and balanced and meets the project's requirements and objectives. By effectively managing the contract and supplier relationship, the project team can ensure that the project is completed successfully and that the project's objectives are achieved.

## CONTRACT MANAGEMENT AND POST-SELECTION ACTIVITIES

The supplier selection process does not end once the contract has been signed. Effective contract management is essential to ensure that the supplier(s) deliver the required goods, services, or works in accordance with the contract terms and that any issues or disputes are resolved in a timely and efficient manner.

The contract management phase may involve regular monitoring and reporting of the supplier's performance against the contract terms and the project's requirements. This may include conducting site visits, reviewing progress reports, and conducting performance reviews with the supplier(s). The project team should also establish clear communication channels with the supplier(s) to ensure that any issues or concerns are addressed promptly.

In addition to contract management, the project team should also conduct post-selection activities to evaluate the supplier selection process and identify opportunities for improvement. This may involve conducting a post-project evaluation to assess the supplier's performance, the effectiveness of the supplier selection process, and the overall project outcomes. The project team should also document lessons learned and best practices to inform future supplier selection processes.

The goal of this phase of the supplier selection process is to ensure that the project is completed successfully, that the supplier(s) meet the project's requirements and objectives, and that any issues or disputes are resolved in a timely and efficient manner. By effectively managing the contract and supplier relationship and conducting post-selection activities, the project team can improve the effectiveness of the supplier selection process and achieve better project outcomes in the future.

In conclusion, the supplier selection process is a critical component of project procurement. By following a structured and systematic approach, project teams can ensure that the most suitable supplier(s) are selected that can deliver the required goods, services, or works at a reasonable cost and within the required timeframe. Effective contract management and post-selection activities are also essential to ensure that the project is completed successfully and that any issues or disputes are resolved in a timely and efficient manner.

## BEST PRACTICES FOR SUCCESSFUL SUPPLIER SELECTION IN PROJECT PROCUREMENT

To ensure successful supplier selection in project procurement, project teams should follow best practices that help them to make informed decisions and select the most suitable supplier(s) for the project. Some of the best practices include:

1. Define clear project requirements and supplier criteria: To ensure that the supplier selection process is focused and effective, project teams should clearly define the project requirements and the criteria that the supplier(s) must meet. The criteria should be objective and measurable, and the project team should assign weights to each criterion to reflect its relative importance.

2. Conduct thorough market research: Conducting thorough market research helps project teams to identify potential suppliers that can deliver the required goods, services, or works. Market research should be conducted through various channels, such as industry reports, trade associations, online databases, and personal contacts.

3. Pre-qualify potential suppliers: Pre-qualification involves verifying that the potential suppliers meet the predefined supplier criteria and can deliver the required goods, services, or works. This helps project teams to create a shortlist of the most qualified suppliers that can be invited to participate in the next phase of the supplier selection process.

4. Issue clear and concise RFPs: The RFP should clearly outline the project requirements and the evaluation criteria. The RFP should

also include any other relevant information, such as the project timeline, technical specifications, and pricing.

5. Evaluate supplier proposals objectively: The evaluation process should be objective and based on the predefined evaluation criteria. The project team should assign weights to each criterion and score each proposal against the criteria. The project team should also conduct a detailed review of each proposal to ensure that it meets the project requirements and that all necessary information has been provided.

6. Negotiate the contract terms effectively: The contract negotiation process should be conducted in a transparent and collaborative manner. The project team should ensure that the contract terms are clearly defined and that any potential issues or risks are identified and addressed. The project team may also seek legal advice to ensure that the contract is legally binding and enforceable.

7. Manage the contract and supplier relationship effectively: Effective contract management is essential to ensure that the supplier(s) deliver the required goods, services, or works in accordance with the contract terms and that any issues or disputes are resolved in a timely and efficient manner. The project team should establish clear communication channels with the supplier(s) to ensure that any issues or concerns are addressed promptly.

8. Conduct post-project evaluation: Conducting a post-project evaluation helps project teams to assess the supplier's performance, the effectiveness of the supplier selection process, and the overall project outcomes. The project team should document lessons learned and best practices to inform future supplier selection processes.

By following these best practices, project teams can ensure that the supplier selection process is effective and that the most suitable supplier(s) are selected that can deliver the required goods, services, or works at a reasonable cost and within the required timeframe. Effective supplier selection can help project teams to achieve better project outcomes and improve the overall success of the project.

# CHAPTER TEN

## *MANAGING RISKS AND ISSUES IN PROJECT MANAGEMENT*

# 10.1 UNDERSTANDING THE RISK MANAGEMENT PROCESS: FROM IDENTIFICATION TO CLOSURE

Risk management is a process of identifying, assessing, and prioritizing risks that may impact an organization's objectives or projects. It is an essential process that helps organizations understand and manage the potential risks that they face.

The risk management process involves several stages, starting from risk identification and ending with risk closure and evaluation. This process helps organizations to develop effective risk management strategies that can help them minimize the impact of potential risks on their operations and projects.

Effective risk management can help organizations to reduce uncertainty, improve decision-making, and increase their chances of achieving their objectives. It involves a proactive approach to identifying and managing risks, rather than simply reacting to them when they occur.

In the following subheadings, we will explore each stage of the risk management process in detail.

## STAGE 1: RISK IDENTIFICATION

Risk identification is the first stage of the risk management process. In this stage, organizations need to identify potential risks that may affect their projects, operations, or objectives. This stage involves a systematic and comprehensive approach to identify all possible risks that may impact the organization.

Risk identification can be done through various methods, including brainstorming sessions, risk checklists, historical data analysis, and expert opinions. The goal of this stage is to develop a comprehensive list of potential risks that may impact the organization.

It is essential to involve all relevant stakeholders in the risk identification process to ensure that all potential risks are identified. This includes project managers, team members, subject matter experts, and other key stakeholders.

The output of the risk identification stage is a list of identified risks, including their description, likelihood, and potential impact. This information will be used in the next stage of the risk management process, risk analysis.

Effective risk identification helps organizations to develop a better understanding of potential risks and develop risk management strategies to mitigate them.

## STAGE 2: RISK ANALYSIS

Risk analysis is the second stage of the risk management process. In this stage, the identified risks are analysed to determine their likelihood of occurrence, potential impact, and overall risk level. This stage helps organizations to prioritize risks and develop effective risk management strategies.

Risk analysis involves two key elements: risk assessment and risk evaluation. Risk assessment is the process of determining the likelihood and potential impact of identified risks. This is done by analysing historical data, expert opinions, and other relevant information. Risk evaluation is the process of comparing the identified risks against predetermined risk criteria to determine their level of significance and priority.

During the risk analysis stage, organizations need to evaluate the potential impact of identified risks on their operations, projects, or objectives. This includes analysing the financial impact, schedule impact, and any other potential impacts on the organization. The goal is to develop a clear understanding of the risks that require the most attention and resources.

Based on the results of the risk analysis, organizations can develop risk response strategies to manage and mitigate identified risks. This may involve developing risk mitigation plans, transferring risk to a third party, accepting the risk, or avoiding the risk altogether.

The output of the risk analysis stage is a prioritized list of risks, including their likelihood and potential impact, as well as risk response strategies to manage and mitigate identified risks.

Effective risk analysis helps organizations to prioritize risks and develop effective risk management strategies that can help them reduce the impact of potential risks on their operations, projects, or objectives.

## STAGE 3: RISK RESPONSE PLANNING

Risk response planning is the third stage of the risk management process. In this stage, organizations develop risk response strategies to manage and mitigate identified risks. This stage involves developing a proactive approach to address potential risks, rather than simply reacting to them when they occur.

Risk response planning involves four key elements: risk mitigation, risk avoidance, risk transfer, and risk acceptance.

Risk mitigation involves taking actions to reduce the likelihood and/or impact of identified risks. This may include developing contingency plans, improving processes, or implementing additional controls to reduce the likelihood of the risk occurring.

Risk avoidance involves taking actions to eliminate the risk altogether. This may involve changing project plans, processes, or activities to avoid the potential risk altogether.

Risk transfer involves shifting the risk to a third party, such as an insurance company or a subcontractor. This strategy can help organizations to reduce the financial impact of potential risks.

Risk acceptance involves accepting the risk and developing contingency plans to manage the risk if it occurs. This strategy is used when the potential impact of the risk is low or when it is not possible to mitigate or avoid the risk altogether.

The output of the risk response planning stage is a detailed plan that outlines the specific actions that will be taken to manage and mitigate identified risks. The plan should include the risk response strategy, the responsible party, the timeline, and the expected outcomes.

Effective risk response planning can help organizations to proactively address potential risks and reduce their impact on operations, projects, or objectives. It is essential to regularly review and update the risk response plan to ensure that it remains effective and relevant.

## STAGE 4: RISK MONITORING AND CONTROL

Risk monitoring and control is the fourth stage of the risk management process. In this stage, organizations need to monitor identified risks and implement appropriate controls to manage and mitigate them. This stage involves continuous monitoring of potential risks to ensure that they are effectively managed.

Risk monitoring and control involves two key elements: risk control and risk communication. Risk control is the process of implementing appropriate controls to manage identified risks. This may involve developing additional contingency plans, implementing additional controls, or adjusting project plans to address potential risks. Risk communication involves keeping stakeholders informed about the status of identified risks and the actions being taken to manage them.

During the risk monitoring and control stage, organizations need to regularly review and update the risk response plan to ensure that it remains effective and relevant. This involves monitoring the effectiveness of implemented controls, evaluating the status of identified risks, and making necessary adjustments to the risk response plan.

The output of the risk monitoring and control stage is regular status reports that provide stakeholders with up-to-date information about the status of identified risks and the effectiveness of implemented controls. These reports should include information about any changes to the risk response plan and any new risks that have been identified.

Effective risk monitoring and control helps organizations to proactively manage and mitigate potential risks, reducing their impact on operations, projects, or objectives. It is essential to establish a regular review process to ensure that the risk response plan remains effective and relevant.

## STAGE 5: RISK CLOSURE AND EVALUATION

Risk closure and evaluation is the final stage of the risk management process. In this stage, organizations need to evaluate the effectiveness of the risk management process and close out identified risks. This stage involves assessing the success of risk management strategies and identifying areas for improvement.

Risk closure and evaluation involves two key elements: risk closure and lessons learned. Risk closure involves confirming that identified risks have been effectively managed and closed out. This includes verifying that implemented controls have been effective in managing identified risks and that the risk response plan has been successfully executed.

Lessons learned involve assessing the effectiveness of the risk management process and identifying areas for improvement. This includes evaluating the success of risk management strategies, assessing the accuracy of risk assessments, and identifying any gaps in the risk management process.

The output of the risk closure and evaluation stage is a report that outlines the effectiveness of the risk management process and any areas for improvement. This report should include information about the success of implemented controls, any new risks that have been identified, and recommendations for improving the risk management process.

Effective risk closure and evaluation can help organizations to continuously improve their risk management strategies and ensure that they are better equipped to manage potential risks in the future.

In conclusion, the risk management process involves several stages, starting from risk identification and ending with risk closure and evaluation. Effective risk management is essential for organizations to manage potential risks and ensure that they are better equipped to achieve their objectives. By following a systematic and comprehensive approach to risk management, organizations can proactively identify and manage potential risks, reduce the impact of those risks on their operations, projects, or objectives, and continuously improve their risk management strategies.

## IMPORTANCE OF CONTINUOUS RISK MANAGEMENT

Continuous risk management is an essential aspect of the risk management process. It involves regularly monitoring and evaluating potential risks and implementing appropriate controls to manage them. Effective risk management is not a one-time event; it is an ongoing process that requires continuous monitoring and evaluation.

Continuous risk management allows organizations to stay proactive and better equipped to manage potential risks. It helps organizations to identify new risks as they arise, and develop effective risk management strategies to manage them. By continuously monitoring and evaluating risks, organizations can ensure that their risk management strategies remain effective and relevant.

Continuous risk management also helps organizations to better understand the impact of potential risks on their operations, projects, or objectives. This can help organizations to make better-informed decisions and allocate resources more effectively.

It is essential to establish a regular review process to ensure that the risk management process remains effective and relevant. This involves regularly reviewing and updating the risk response plan, assessing the effectiveness of implemented controls, and identifying any new risks that may have arisen.

In today's fast-paced and constantly changing business environment, continuous risk management is more important than ever. By regularly monitoring and evaluating potential risks, organizations can stay proactive and better equipped to manage potential risks, reduce the impact of those risks on their operations, projects, or objectives, and improve their overall risk management strategies.

In conclusion, continuous risk management is a critical component of the risk management process. It enables organizations to proactively identify and manage potential risks, remain agile in a constantly changing business environment, and continuously improve their risk management strategies.

# 10.2 PROACTIVE AND REACTIVE RESPONSES TO RISK: STRATEGIES FOR MANAGING UNCERTAINTY

Risk refers to the potential of an event or circumstance to have an adverse effect on an organization's objectives. These objectives could be related to financial performance, reputation, operations, or legal compliance. In any case, it is essential for organizations to identify, assess, and manage risks to minimize their negative impact.

Effective risk management involves developing a robust understanding of the types of risks an organization faces and the likelihood and potential severity of those risks. This understanding forms the basis for selecting appropriate risk response strategies.

There are two main categories of risk response strategies: proactive and reactive. Proactive strategies aim to prevent or mitigate risks before they occur, while reactive strategies aim to address risks after they have materialized. Both types of strategies have their place in a comprehensive risk management approach, and the choice of strategy will depend on the organization's risk appetite, resources, and objectives.

The following subheadings will explore proactive and reactive risk response strategies in more detail, providing examples of each and outlining the factors to consider when selecting a response strategy.

## PROACTIVE RISK RESPONSE STRATEGIES

Proactive risk response strategies focus on preventing or mitigating risks before they occur. This approach aims to reduce the likelihood and potential impact of adverse events. There are four main types of proactive risk response strategies:

- Avoidance: This strategy involves eliminating or bypassing a risk altogether. For example, an organization might choose to avoid the risk of data breaches by not storing sensitive information in digital form.

- Reduction: This strategy involves taking steps to reduce the likelihood or potential impact of a risk. For example, an organization might implement cybersecurity measures to reduce the risk of a data breach.

- Transfer: This strategy involves transferring the risk to another party, such as an insurance company. For example, an organization might purchase cyber insurance to transfer the financial risk of a data breach to an insurer.

- Acceptance: This strategy involves accepting the risk and its potential consequences. For example, an organization might accept the risk of a certain level of employee turnover if the cost of reducing that risk outweighs the benefits.

When selecting a proactive risk response strategy, organizations must consider various factors, including the cost and feasibility of each strategy, the potential benefits and drawbacks of each strategy, and the organization's risk appetite and objectives.

Proactive risk response strategies can be effective in reducing the likelihood and potential impact of adverse events. However, it is essential to recognize that these strategies cannot eliminate all risks, and organizations must also be prepared to implement reactive strategies to address risks that materialize despite proactive measures.

## REACTIVE RISK RESPONSE STRATEGIES

Reactive risk response strategies focus on addressing risks after they have materialized. These strategies aim to minimize the negative impact of adverse events and ensure that the organization can recover as quickly as possible. There are four main types of reactive risk response strategies:

- Exploitation: This strategy involves taking advantage of a risk to achieve some benefit. For example, a company might exploit a natural disaster in a particular region to gain a competitive advantage over other companies in that region.

- Enhancement: This strategy involves taking steps to improve the organization's ability to respond to a risk. For example, an organization might enhance its cybersecurity protocols after a data breach to reduce the likelihood of future breaches.

- Sharing: This strategy involves sharing the risk with another party, such as a business partner or vendor. For example, an organization might share the risk of supply chain disruptions with its suppliers by requiring them to have contingency plans in place.

- Rejection: This strategy involves refusing to accept the risk and its potential consequences. For example, an organization might reject a proposed business venture if the potential risks outweigh the potential benefits.

When selecting a reactive risk response strategy, organizations must consider various factors, including the severity and impact of the risk, the resources and capabilities needed to implement the strategy, and the organization's risk appetite and objectives.

Reactive risk response strategies can be effective in minimizing the negative impact of adverse events and helping organizations recover as quickly as possible. However, it is essential to recognize that reactive strategies cannot eliminate all risks, and organizations must also implement proactive strategies to prevent or mitigate risks before they occur.

## CHOOSING THE RIGHT RISK RESPONSE STRATEGY

Choosing the right risk response strategy is a critical component of effective risk management. The selection process involves analysing the organization's risks and evaluating the potential benefits and drawbacks of each response strategy. Several factors should be considered when selecting a response strategy:

a. Risk Appetite: The organization's risk appetite will influence the choice of risk response strategy. Some organizations may be willing to accept higher levels of risk to achieve their objectives, while others may be more risk-averse and prioritize risk avoidance.

b. Resources: The resources available to the organization will also influence the choice of response strategy. Some strategies may require significant financial or human resources, while others may be more feasible with fewer resources.

c. Cost and Feasibility: The cost and feasibility of each response strategy must also be considered. Some strategies may be prohibitively expensive or difficult to implement, while others may be more affordable and straightforward.

d. Potential Benefits and Drawbacks: The potential benefits and drawbacks of each strategy must be evaluated. Some strategies may have significant potential benefits but may also come with significant drawbacks or limitations.

e. Timing: The timing of the response strategy must also be considered. Some strategies may be more effective if implemented before a risk materializes, while others may be more effective in the aftermath of an adverse event.

It is also important to recognize that effective risk management requires a balanced approach that includes both proactive and reactive risk response strategies. Organizations should strive to strike a balance between preventing and mitigating risks before they occur while also being prepared to respond quickly and effectively to risks that materialize despite proactive measures.

Ultimately, the choice of risk response strategy will depend on the specific circumstances of each risk and the organization's unique objectives and risk appetite. Organizations should regularly review and update their risk response strategies to ensure they remain effective and aligned with their goals.

## IMPLEMENTING RISK RESPONSE STRATEGIES

Once a risk response strategy has been selected, it must be effectively implemented to ensure that the organization is prepared to manage the risk. The implementation process should be carefully planned and executed to ensure that the response strategy is successful. The following are the key steps involved in implementing a risk response strategy:

1. Planning and Execution: The first step in implementing a risk response strategy is to develop a detailed plan for execution. This plan should outline the resources needed to implement the strategy, the timeline for implementation, and the roles and responsibilities of team members involved in the process. It is crucial to communicate the plan to all stakeholders to ensure that everyone understands their roles and responsibilities.

2. Monitoring and Review: After the response strategy has been implemented, it is essential to monitor its effectiveness and review its impact regularly. This monitoring and review process should be ongoing to ensure that the response strategy is working as intended and to identify any areas for improvement.

3. Continuous Improvement and Adaptation: Effective risk management requires a continuous improvement and adaptation approach. As new risks emerge, or the effectiveness of response strategies changes, organizations must be prepared to adapt their strategies accordingly.

Successful implementation of risk response strategies requires strong leadership, effective communication, and a commitment to ongoing improvement. It is crucial to involve all stakeholders in the process to ensure that everyone is aligned with the organization's risk management goals and strategies.

Organizations should also consider using technology to support the implementation of risk response strategies. For example, risk management software can help automate the process of monitoring risks, implementing response strategies, and reviewing their effectiveness.

In conclusion, implementing risk response strategies requires a comprehensive and well-planned approach. By carefully selecting the right response strategy, planning for execution, monitoring and reviewing effectiveness, and continuously improving and adapting, organizations can effectively manage risks and achieve their objectives.

## CONCLUSION

Effective risk management is critical to the success of any organization. By understanding the types of risks they face, organizations can select appropriate proactive and reactive risk response strategies to minimize their negative impact. Proactive strategies aim to prevent or mitigate risks before they occur, while reactive strategies aim to address risks after they have materialized.

When selecting a risk response strategy, organizations must consider several factors, including their risk appetite, resources, cost and feasibility, potential benefits and drawbacks, and timing. It is also essential to strike a balance between proactive and reactive strategies to ensure comprehensive risk management.

Implementing risk response strategies requires careful planning, execution, monitoring, and review, as well as a commitment to ongoing improvement and adaptation. Strong leadership, effective communication, and the use of technology can all support the implementation process.

Overall, effective risk management is an ongoing process that requires a comprehensive and proactive approach. By developing a robust understanding of their risks and selecting appropriate response strategies, organizations can achieve their objectives and minimize the negative impact of adverse events.

# 10.3 THE IMPORTANCE OF RISK MANAGEMENT IN PROJECT SUCCESS

Risk management is a critical process that is integral to project management. In the context of project management, risk management refers to the identification, assessment, and prioritization of risks and the implementation of strategies to minimize, monitor, and control the impact of these risks on the project's objectives.

Project risk management involves identifying potential risks that could occur during the project, analysing and evaluating those risks to determine their potential impact on the project, and developing plans to mitigate those risks or minimize their impact on the project.

Effective risk management is critical to the success of any project because it helps project teams identify and address potential issues before they become significant problems. By proactively addressing potential risks, project teams can stay on track, reduce costs, and deliver the project on time and within budget.

## BENEFITS OF RISK MANAGEMENT IN PROJECTS

Implementing a robust risk management process provides many benefits to projects, including:

a. Improved Project Planning: Risk management helps identify potential risks that may occur during the project lifecycle. This enables project managers to develop contingency plans and allocate appropriate resources to handle any potential issues. Effective risk management helps project teams to proactively address potential issues and improves their ability to plan and execute the project successfully.

b. Better Decision Making: Risk management helps project managers make better decisions by providing them with a more comprehensive understanding of potential risks and their impact on the project. By identifying potential risks and evaluating their potential impact, project teams can make informed decisions on how to allocate resources and adjust project plans to minimize risks and maximize project success.

c. Increased Project Success: Effective risk management can significantly increase the chances of project success. By identifying potential risks and implementing strategies to mitigate those risks, project teams can reduce the likelihood of cost overruns, schedule delays, and quality issues. As a result, project stakeholders are more likely to be satisfied with the project outcomes, which can improve project success rates.

d. Improved Communication: Risk management involves identifying potential risks and communicating them to project stakeholders. This helps ensure that all project team members are aware of potential risks and their potential impact on the project. Effective communication can help project teams develop a shared understanding of potential risks and their impact, which can improve collaboration and decision-making.

e. Better Resource Allocation: Effective risk management enables project managers to allocate resources more efficiently. By identifying potential risks and developing contingency plans, project teams can allocate resources to address potential issues, reducing the likelihood of over-allocation or under-allocation of resources. As a result, project teams can optimize the use of resources and improve project outcomes.

In summary, effective risk management is essential for project success. It helps project teams identify potential risks, evaluate their impact, and develop strategies to mitigate those risks. This leads to improved project planning, better decision-making, increased project success rates, improved communication, and better resource allocation.

## MITIGATING RISKS AND ENHANCING PROJECT SUCCESS

Effective risk management involves identifying potential risks and implementing strategies to mitigate those risks. Mitigating risks can enhance project success by minimizing the likelihood of cost overruns, schedule delays, and quality issues. Here are some ways that risk management can help mitigate risks and enhance project success:

a. Risk Identification: The first step in effective risk management is identifying potential risks. This involves reviewing the project plan, conducting risk assessments, and engaging stakeholders to identify potential risks. Once identified, risks should be documented and categorized according to their likelihood and potential impact on the project.

b. Risk Analysis: Once risks have been identified, the next step is to analyze them. This involves evaluating the likelihood of the risk occurring and the potential impact on the project if it does occur. By analyzing risks, project teams can prioritize risks and develop appropriate strategies to mitigate them.

c. Risk Mitigation: Once risks have been identified and analyzed, the next step is to develop strategies to mitigate those risks. This may involve developing contingency plans, revising the project plan, or allocating additional resources. Effective risk mitigation strategies should be developed in consultation with project stakeholders and should be reviewed regularly to ensure their effectiveness.

d. Risk Monitoring: Risk monitoring involves tracking the identified risks and assessing their impact on the project. Project teams should regularly review the risk management plan and update it as necessary to reflect any changes in the project environment. This helps ensure that risk mitigation strategies remain effective and that the project remains on track.

e. Risk Communication: Effective risk communication is critical to successful risk management. All project stakeholders should be informed of potential risks and their impact on the project. Communication should be clear and concise, and stakeholders should be encouraged to provide feedback on the risk management plan.

In conclusion, mitigating risks is essential to enhancing project success. Effective risk management involves identifying potential risks, analysing them, developing strategies to mitigate those risks, monitoring risks, and communicating with stakeholders. By implementing effective risk management strategies, project teams can minimize the likelihood of cost overruns, schedule delays, and quality issues, and deliver projects successfully.

## KEY COMPONENTS OF EFFECTIVE RISK MANAGEMENT

Effective risk management requires a structured approach that includes several key components. Here are some of the essential components of effective risk management:

a. Risk Assessment: Risk assessment is the process of identifying and evaluating potential risks. This involves reviewing the project plan, conducting risk assessments, and engaging stakeholders to identify potential risks. Risks should be categorized according to their likelihood and potential impact on the project.

b. Risk Mitigation Plan: Once risks have been identified and analyzed, a risk mitigation plan should be developed. This plan should outline specific strategies for mitigating risks and reducing their impact on the project. It should also include contingency plans for addressing risks that cannot be mitigated.

c. Risk Monitoring: Risk monitoring involves tracking identified risks and assessing their impact on the project. Regular reviews of the risk management plan should be conducted, and updates should be made as necessary to reflect any changes in the project environment.

d. Risk Reporting: Effective risk reporting is essential to successful risk management. All project stakeholders should be informed of potential risks and their impact on the project. Communication should be clear and concise, and stakeholders should be encouraged to provide feedback on the risk management plan.

   e. Risk Management Culture: A risk management culture is critical to effective risk management. This involves promoting a culture of risk awareness and encouraging stakeholders to report potential risks and concerns. All team members should be trained in risk management principles and should be encouraged to participate in risk management activities.

In summary, effective risk management requires a structured approach that includes risk assessment, risk mitigation planning, risk monitoring, risk reporting, and a risk management culture. By implementing these key components of risk management, project teams can minimize the likelihood of cost overruns, schedule delays, and quality issues, and deliver projects successfully.

## IMPLEMENTING RISK MANAGEMENT IN YOUR PROJECT

Implementing effective risk management requires a systematic approach that involves several steps. Here are some steps to consider when implementing risk management in your project:

1. Establish Risk Management Policies and Procedures: The first step in implementing risk management is to establish risk management policies and procedures. This involves defining the roles and responsibilities of the project team, developing guidelines for risk assessment and reporting, and establishing processes for monitoring and managing risks.

2. Identify Risks: Once the risk management policies and procedures are in place, the next step is to identify potential risks. This involves reviewing the project plan, conducting risk assessments, and engaging stakeholders to identify potential risks.

3. Analyze Risks: Once risks have been identified, the next step is to analyze them. This involves evaluating the likelihood of the risk occurring and the potential impact on the project if it does

occur. By analyzing risks, project teams can prioritize risks and develop appropriate strategies to mitigate them.

4. Develop a Risk Mitigation Plan: Once risks have been identified and analyzed, a risk mitigation plan should be developed. This plan should outline specific strategies for mitigating risks and reducing their impact on the project. It should also include contingency plans for addressing risks that cannot be mitigated.

5. Monitor and Review Risks: Once the risk management plan has been implemented, risks should be monitored regularly, and the risk management plan should be reviewed and updated as necessary. Regular reviews of the risk management plan should be conducted, and updates should be made as necessary to reflect any changes in the project environment.

6. Train Project Team Members: All team members should be trained in risk management principles and should be encouraged to participate in risk management activities. This helps ensure that all team members have a shared understanding of potential risks and their impact on the project.

In conclusion, implementing effective risk management requires a systematic approach that includes establishing risk management policies and procedures, identifying risks, analysing risks, developing a risk mitigation plan, monitoring and reviewing risks, and training project team members. By implementing these steps, project teams can minimize the likelihood of cost overruns, schedule delays, and quality issues, and deliver projects successfully.

# 10.4 UNDERSTANDING ISSUE MANAGEMENT: KEY ASPECTS AND BEST PRACTICES

Issue management refers to the process of identifying, prioritizing, and resolving problems or challenges that may arise within an organization or project. These issues can range from minor obstacles to major crises, and can impact various aspects of an organization's operations, such as finances, reputation, customer satisfaction, and productivity.

Effective issue management is essential for ensuring that an organization can operate efficiently and sustainably in the face of adversity. By proactively addressing issues as they arise, organizations can prevent small problems from escalating into larger ones, minimize the impact of crises, and maintain the trust and confidence of stakeholders.

In this section, we will explore the key aspects of issue management, including how to identify and categorize issues, prioritize them based on their urgency and importance, develop an action plan to address them, communicate and collaborate with stakeholders, implement solutions, monitor and evaluate progress, and continuously improve and learn from the process. We will also discuss best practices for effective issue management and provide practical tips and examples.

## IDENTIFYING AND CATEGORIZING ISSUES:

The first step in issue management is to identify and categorize issues. This involves gathering information about problems or challenges that may be affecting the organization or project, and categorizing them based on their nature, severity, and impact.

To identify issues, organizations can use various methods such as surveys, feedback forms, customer complaints, incident reports, and performance metrics. It is important to involve stakeholders in the identification process, including employees, customers, suppliers, and partners, as they can provide valuable insights and perspectives on potential issues.

Once issues have been identified, they should be categorized based on their nature and impact. Common categories include financial issues, operational issues, legal and regulatory issues, reputational issues, and safety and security issues. Categorizing issues allows organizations to prioritize them and allocate resources accordingly.

For example, a financial issue such as cash flow problems may require immediate attention to prevent a crisis, while an operational issue such as a production delay may be less urgent but still require a plan of action to minimize the impact on customers and stakeholders.

By identifying and categorizing issues, organizations can gain a better understanding of the challenges they face and develop a focused approach to issue management.

## PRIORITIZING ISSUES:

Once issues have been identified and categorized, the next step is to prioritize them based on their urgency and importance. Prioritizing issues ensures that resources are allocated to the most critical problems first, reducing the risk of larger problems developing.

To prioritize issues, organizations can use various criteria such as the impact on stakeholders, the likelihood of the issue escalating, the cost of addressing the issue, and the strategic importance of the issue. It is important to involve key stakeholders in the prioritization process to ensure that their perspectives are taken into account.

One common tool for prioritizing issues is a risk matrix, which maps the likelihood and impact of an issue on a scale and categorizes them into high, medium, or low priority. High-priority issues should be addressed first, followed by medium and low-priority issues.

When prioritizing issues, it is important to be realistic about the organization's resources and capabilities. Addressing all issues at once may not be feasible, and some issues may need to be deferred or delegated to others.

For example, if an organization is experiencing a financial crisis, cash flow problems may be prioritized over other operational issues. Similarly, if there is a safety concern, addressing it may take priority over other issues that are less urgent.

By prioritizing issues, organizations can focus their resources and efforts on the most critical problems and minimize the risk of larger issues developing.

## DEVELOPING AN ACTION PLAN:

Once issues have been identified and prioritized, the next step is to develop an action plan to address them. An action plan outlines the steps that will be taken to resolve the issue, including the resources needed, the timeline, and the responsible parties.

When developing an action plan, it is important to involve key stakeholders and ensure that their perspectives are taken into account. This can help to ensure that the plan is realistic, feasible, and has buy-in from those who will be responsible for implementing it.

The action plan should include specific, measurable, achievable, relevant, and time-bound (SMART) goals. Each goal should be broken down into smaller tasks and assigned to specific individuals or teams. The action plan should also include a timeline that specifies when each task should be completed and by whom.

Communication is also important when developing an action plan. All stakeholders should be kept informed of the progress and any changes to the plan. Regular communication can help to ensure that everyone is on the same page and can make any necessary adjustments to their own work.

For example, if an organization has identified a problem with their customer service, an action plan may include steps such as conducting customer surveys to identify specific issues, training staff on customer service best practices, and implementing a system for monitoring customer feedback. Each step would be broken down into specific tasks and assigned to specific individuals or teams.

By developing an action plan, organizations can ensure that they have a clear and focused approach to resolving issues. A well-developed action plan can help to ensure that resources are used efficiently, and that progress can be tracked and measured over time.

## COMMUNICATING AND COLLABORATING:

Effective communication and collaboration are essential for successful issue management. This involves keeping all stakeholders informed of the issue and the steps being taken to address it, and working collaboratively to develop and implement solutions.

Communication should be clear, transparent, and timely. All stakeholders should be kept informed of the status of the issue, any changes to the action plan, and any other relevant information. Communication can be in the form of meetings, emails, progress reports, or other methods, depending on the nature of the issue and the stakeholders involved.

Collaboration involves working together to develop and implement solutions. This can include involving stakeholders in the decision-making process, seeking input and feedback from stakeholders, and working collaboratively to identify and implement solutions.

Effective collaboration requires trust, respect, and open communication. All stakeholders should have a clear understanding of their roles and responsibilities, and be willing to work together to achieve the common goal of resolving the issue.

For example, if an organization is facing a reputational issue due to negative media coverage, collaboration may involve working with PR experts to develop a messaging strategy, involving senior leadership in communicating with stakeholders, and working with legal counsel to address any legal issues that may arise.

By communicating and collaborating effectively, organizations can ensure that all stakeholders are working towards a common goal and that everyone is aware of their roles and responsibilities. This can help to ensure that solutions are developed and implemented efficiently, and that everyone is working towards the same goal.

## IMPLEMENTING SOLUTIONS:

After an action plan has been developed and communication and collaboration have taken place, the next step is to implement the solutions. Implementing solutions involves carrying out the tasks outlined in the action plan, monitoring progress, and making adjustments as needed.

Implementation requires careful planning and coordination. All stakeholders should have a clear understanding of their roles and responsibilities, and the necessary resources should be available to carry out the tasks outlined in the action plan. A timeline should be established, and progress should be regularly monitored and reported on.

During implementation, it is important to be flexible and make adjustments as needed. This may involve re-evaluating priorities, adjusting timelines, or reallocating resources. Open communication is essential during implementation to ensure that everyone is aware of any changes or adjustments.

It is also important to involve stakeholders in the implementation process where appropriate. This can help to ensure that solutions are tailored to the specific needs and concerns of stakeholders, and that they are more likely to be successful.

For example, if an organization is implementing a new system to address a problem with supply chain management, stakeholders such as suppliers and customers may need to be involved in the implementation process to ensure that the new system is effective and meets their needs.

By implementing solutions effectively, organizations can resolve issues and prevent them from becoming more significant problems. Careful planning, coordination, and monitoring can help to ensure that solutions are implemented efficiently and effectively.

## MONITORING AND EVALUATING PROGRESS:

Once solutions have been implemented, the next step is to monitor and evaluate progress. Monitoring and evaluation involves assessing the effectiveness of the solutions, identifying any further issues that may arise, and making any necessary adjustments.

Monitoring and evaluation should be based on the goals and objectives outlined in the action plan. Key performance indicators (KPIs) should be established to measure progress and success. KPIs may include metrics such as customer satisfaction, employee engagement, financial performance, or other relevant measures.

Regular reporting and feedback should be provided to all stakeholders to keep them informed of progress and any further issues that may arise. Feedback from stakeholders can also be used to identify areas for improvement.

If the solutions have not been effective, it may be necessary to re-evaluate the action plan and make adjustments. This may involve revisiting the initial identification and categorization of the issue, re-prioritizing solutions, or involving additional stakeholders.

For example, if an organization has implemented a new system to address supply chain management issues, monitoring and evaluation may involve tracking metrics such as delivery times, product quality, and customer satisfaction. If delivery times have not improved, it may be necessary to re-evaluate the system and identify any further issues that may be impacting delivery times.

By monitoring and evaluating progress, organizations can identify areas for improvement and make adjustments as needed. This can help to ensure that the solutions are effective and sustainable over the long-term.

## CONTINUOUS IMPROVEMENT AND LEARNING:

Continuous improvement and learning are an essential aspect of issue management. It involves using feedback and data to identify areas for improvement, learning from past experiences, and continuously refining and improving processes.

To facilitate continuous improvement, organizations should establish a culture of learning and innovation. This can involve encouraging employees to share ideas and feedback, conducting regular performance evaluations, and investing in training and development opportunities.

Organizations can also use data analytics and other tools to identify trends and patterns that may indicate areas for improvement. For example, if customer complaints have increased over time, it may indicate that there are underlying issues with the organization's products or services that need to be addressed.

Learning from past experiences is also important for continuous improvement. Organizations should conduct post-mortems or after-action reviews to evaluate the effectiveness of their responses to issues. These evaluations can help identify areas where improvements can be made and provide insights for future issue management.

For example, if an organization experienced a crisis related to a product recall, a post-mortem may identify the need for better communication with customers, more robust quality control processes, or improved crisis management plans.

By continuously improving and learning, organizations can become more resilient and better equipped to address future issues. A culture of learning and innovation can also help to attract and retain talented employees, enhance the organization's reputation, and improve overall performance.

## Best Practices in Issue Management:

Effective issue management requires a structured and comprehensive approach that incorporates best practices. Some of the best practices in issue management include:

a. Proactive identification: Issues should be identified proactively rather than reactively. This involves establishing a system for identifying potential issues and risks, and regularly reviewing performance metrics and feedback from stakeholders.

b. Clear communication: Communication is critical during issue management. All stakeholders should be kept informed of the issue, the action plan, and progress made in resolving the issue. Communication should be clear, transparent, and timely.

c. Collaboration: Collaboration is important during issue management. All stakeholders should be involved in the process and work together to develop and implement solutions.

d. SMART goals: Action plans should be developed with specific, measurable, achievable, relevant, and time-bound (SMART) goals. This helps to ensure that the plan is focused and that progress can be tracked and measured.

e. Regular monitoring and evaluation: Progress should be regularly monitored and evaluated using key performance indicators (KPIs). This helps to ensure that the solutions are effective and that any further issues can be identified and addressed.

f. Continuous improvement: Organizations should strive for continuous improvement and learning. This involves using feedback and data to identify areas for improvement, learning from past experiences, and continuously refining and improving processes.

g. Flexibility and adaptability: Issue management requires flexibility and adaptability. Plans should be adjusted as needed based on new information or changing circumstances.

By incorporating these best practices into their approach to issue management, organizations can minimize the impact of issues and crises, maintain stakeholder trust, and achieve better overall performance.

## CONCLUSION:

In conclusion, effective issue management is essential for organizations to operate efficiently and sustainably in the face of adversity. Key aspects of issue management include identifying and categorizing issues, prioritizing them based on urgency and importance, developing an action plan, communicating and collaborating with stakeholders, implementing solutions, monitoring and evaluating progress, and continuously improving and learning from the process.

To ensure effective issue management, organizations should incorporate best practices such as proactive identification, clear communication, collaboration, SMART goals, regular monitoring and evaluation, continuous improvement, and flexibility and adaptability.

By adopting a structured and comprehensive approach to issue management, organizations can minimize the impact of issues and crises, maintain stakeholder trust, and achieve better overall performance.

.

# CHAPTER ELEVEN

## *ACHIEVING EXCELLENCE THROUGH QUALITY MANAGEMENT*

# 11.1 UNDERSTANDING QUALITY PLANNING

Quality planning is the process of determining the quality objectives and requirements for a project or organization, and then developing a plan to meet those objectives and requirements. It involves identifying the quality standards and criteria that need to be met in order to deliver a product, service, or project that meets customer expectations, regulatory requirements, and industry best practices.

Quality planning is a proactive approach to quality management, aimed at preventing defects and errors before they occur, rather than relying solely on inspection and correction after the fact. It is an integral part of the overall quality management system and is typically performed during the project definition phase, before any work begins.

Quality planning includes the development of a quality management plan, which outlines the quality policies, procedures, and standards that will be used to achieve the desired level of quality. This plan also identifies the resources, roles, responsibilities, and timelines required for successful implementation.

In summary, quality planning is the process of defining, documenting, and communicating the quality objectives, criteria, and methods to be used in a project or organization. It is a critical component of effective quality management and is essential for ensuring that the end product or service meets or exceeds customer expectations.

## THE IMPORTANCE OF QUALITY PLANNING

Quality planning is essential for the success of any project or organization. It provides a framework for achieving and maintaining a high level of quality in products, services, and processes. The following are some of the key reasons why quality planning is important:

a. Meeting Customer Expectations: Quality planning helps to ensure that the end product or service meets or exceeds customer expectations. By identifying and documenting customer requirements and quality standards, the organization can ensure that it delivers products and services that meet the needs of its customers.

b. Reducing Costs: Quality planning can help to reduce costs associated with quality defects, rework, and customer complaints. By identifying and addressing quality issues early in the definition phase, the organization can prevent problems from occurring and avoid costly corrective action later on.

c. Enhancing Reputation: Quality planning can enhance the reputation of the organization by demonstrating a commitment to quality and customer satisfaction. A reputation for quality can lead to increased customer loyalty, repeat business, and positive word-of-mouth recommendations.

d. Meeting Regulatory Requirements: Quality planning can help to ensure that the organization meets regulatory requirements and industry standards. This can help to avoid legal and financial penalties, as well as reputational damage.

e. Improving Efficiency: Quality planning can improve efficiency by identifying and eliminating unnecessary or redundant processes. By streamlining processes and focusing on quality, the organization can improve productivity and reduce waste.

In summary, quality planning is important because it helps to ensure that the end product or service meets or exceeds customer expectations, reduces costs, enhances reputation, meets regulatory requirements, and improves efficiency. It is a critical component of effective quality management and is essential for achieving long-term success.

## KEY ELEMENTS OF QUALITY PLANNING

Effective quality planning requires the consideration of several key elements. These elements help to ensure that the organization establishes and achieves its quality objectives. The following are some of the key elements of quality planning:

a. Establishing Quality Objectives: The first step in quality planning is to establish quality objectives that are aligned with the organization's strategic goals. These objectives should be specific, measurable, achievable, relevant, and time bound. Quality objectives can be related to product quality, service quality, process quality, or a combination of these.

b. Identifying Quality Requirements: Quality requirements are the specific characteristics that the end product or service must possess to meet customer expectations and regulatory requirements. Quality requirements can include performance, safety, reliability, durability, usability, and other factors that are important to the customer.

c. Defining Quality Standards: Quality standards are the specific criteria that must be met to ensure that the end product or service meets the quality requirements. Quality standards can be established by the organization or by regulatory bodies. They can include industry standards, customer specifications, and internal quality policies and procedures.

d. Developing a Quality Management Plan: The quality management plan outlines the quality policies, procedures, and standards that will be used to achieve the quality objectives. The plan should also identify the resources, roles, responsibilities, and timelines required for successful implementation.

e. Identifying Risks and Opportunities: Quality planning involves identifying potential risks and opportunities that could impact the quality objectives. Risks can include issues related to product design, manufacturing, distribution, or customer use. Opportunities can include potential improvements to quality, efficiency, or customer satisfaction.

f. Defining Quality Metrics: Quality metrics are the measurements that will be used to evaluate the success of the quality plan. Metrics can include customer satisfaction ratings, defect rates, process cycle times, and other indicators of quality performance.

In summary, effective quality planning requires the consideration of several key elements, including the establishment of quality objectives, the identification of quality requirements and standards, the development of a quality management plan, the identification of risks and opportunities, and the definition of quality metrics. By addressing these elements, the organization can establish a roadmap for achieving its quality objectives and ensuring customer satisfaction.

## THE QUALITY PLANNING PROCESS

The quality planning process involves several steps that are designed to ensure that the organization establishes and achieves its quality objectives. The following are some of the key steps in the quality planning process:

a. Identify Stakeholders: The first step in the quality planning process is to identify the stakeholders who are involved in or impacted by the project or organization. This can include customers, employees, suppliers, regulatory bodies, and other relevant parties.

b. Define Quality Objectives: Once the stakeholders have been identified, the organization must define its quality objectives. These objectives should be specific, measurable, achievable, relevant, and time bound. They should also be aligned with the organization's strategic goals.

c. Determine Quality Requirements: The next step is to determine the quality requirements that must be met to achieve the quality objectives. This involves identifying the specific characteristics that the end product or service must possess to meet customer expectations and regulatory requirements.

d. Establish Quality Standards: Quality standards are the specific criteria that must be met to ensure that the end product or service meets the quality requirements. The organization must establish clear and measurable quality standards that are aligned with its quality objectives.

e. Develop a Quality Management Plan: The quality management plan outlines the policies, procedures, and standards that will be used to achieve the quality objectives. This plan should identify the resources, roles, responsibilities, and timelines required for successful implementation.

f. Identify Risks and Opportunities: The organization must identify potential risks and opportunities that could impact the quality objectives. Risks can include issues related to product design, manufacturing, distribution, or customer use. Opportunities can include potential improvements to quality, efficiency, or customer satisfaction.

g. Define Quality Metrics: Quality metrics are the measurements that will be used to evaluate the success of the quality plan. Metrics can include customer satisfaction ratings, defect rates, process cycle times, and other indicators of quality performance.

h. Implement Quality Plan: Once the quality plan has been developed, the organization must implement it. This involves ensuring that the policies, procedures, and standards are followed, and that the quality objectives are being met.

i. Monitor and Evaluate Quality Plan: Finally, the organization must monitor and evaluate the quality plan to ensure that it is achieving the desired results. This involves collecting and analyzing quality metrics, identifying areas for improvement, and making necessary adjustments to the plan.

In summary, the quality planning process involves several steps, including the identification of stakeholders, the definition of quality objectives, the determination of quality requirements and standards, the development of a quality management plan, the identification of risks and opportunities, the definition of quality metrics, the implementation of the quality plan, and the monitoring and evaluation of its success.

## BENEFITS OF QUALITY PLANNING

Quality planning is an important process that provides several benefits to organizations. The following are some of the key benefits of quality planning:

a. Improved Customer Satisfaction: Quality planning helps to ensure that the end product or service meets or exceeds customer expectations. By identifying and documenting customer requirements and quality standards, the organization can ensure that it delivers products and services that meet the needs of its customers.

b. Reduced Costs: Quality planning can help to reduce costs associated with quality defects, rework, and customer complaints. By identifying and addressing quality issues early in the definition phase, the organization can prevent problems from occurring and avoid costly corrective action later on.

c. Enhanced Reputation: Quality planning can enhance the reputation of the organization by demonstrating a commitment to quality and customer satisfaction. A reputation for quality can lead to increased customer loyalty, repeat business, and positive word-of-mouth recommendations.

d. Improved Efficiency: Quality planning can improve efficiency by identifying and eliminating unnecessary or redundant processes. By streamlining processes and focusing on quality, the organization can improve productivity and reduce waste.

e. Better Risk Management: Quality planning can help to identify potential risks and opportunities that could impact the quality objectives. By identifying risks early in the definition phase, the organization can develop strategies to mitigate those risks and take advantage of opportunities.

f. Compliance with Regulatory Requirements: Quality planning can help to ensure that the organization meets regulatory requirements and industry standards. This can help to avoid legal and financial penalties, as well as reputational damage.

g. Improved Communication: Quality planning involves the documentation and communication of quality objectives, requirements, and standards. This helps to ensure that all stakeholders are on the same page and working towards a common goal.

In summary, quality planning provides several benefits to organizations, including improved customer satisfaction, reduced costs, enhanced reputation, improved efficiency, better risk management, compliance with regulatory requirements, and improved communication. By investing time and resources in quality planning, organizations can establish a roadmap for achieving their quality objectives and ensuring long-term success.

## CHALLENGES OF QUALITY PLANNING

While quality planning provides several benefits to organizations, it also poses several challenges. The following are some of the key challenges of quality planning:

a. Lack of Resources: Quality planning requires the allocation of resources, including time, personnel, and funding. Organizations may struggle to dedicate sufficient resources to quality planning, particularly if they are facing budget constraints or competing priorities.

b. Changing Requirements: Quality planning involves identifying and documenting quality requirements and standards. However, these requirements and standards may change over time, particularly if customer needs or regulatory requirements change. Organizations must be prepared to adapt their quality plans to these changing requirements.

c. Complexity of Products and Services: Some products and services may be complex and difficult to define in terms of quality requirements and standards. This can make it challenging to develop a comprehensive quality plan.

d. Lack of Stakeholder Buy-In: Quality planning involves the identification and engagement of stakeholders. However, stakeholders may not always buy into the quality plan or may have conflicting priorities. Organizations must work to ensure that all stakeholders are aligned and committed to the quality plan.

e. Lack of Quality Expertise: Quality planning requires specialized knowledge and expertise in quality management. Organizations may struggle to find personnel with the necessary skills and experience to develop and implement a quality plan.

f. Resistance to Change: Quality planning may require changes to processes and procedures. However, employees may be resistant to change, particularly if they perceive that the changes may impact their job responsibilities or workload.

In summary, quality planning poses several challenges, including the lack of resources, changing requirements, complexity of products and services, lack of stakeholder buy-in, lack of quality expertise, and resistance to change. Organizations must be aware of these challenges and develop strategies to overcome them in order to effectively implement a quality plan.

## STRATEGIES FOR SUCCESSFUL QUALITY PLANNING

Effective quality planning requires the consideration of several strategies. These strategies help organizations to establish and achieve their quality objectives. The following are some of the key strategies for successful quality planning:

a. Align Quality Objectives with Strategic Goals: Quality objectives should be aligned with the organization's strategic goals. This helps to ensure that quality planning is integrated into the overall business strategy, rather than being seen as a separate activity.

b. Involve Stakeholders: Quality planning involves the identification and engagement of stakeholders. Organizations should involve all relevant stakeholders, including customers, employees, suppliers, and regulatory bodies. This helps to ensure that the quality plan is comprehensive and meets the needs of all stakeholders.

c. Use a Systematic Approach: Quality planning should be approached in a systematic and structured manner. This involves following a defined process, using tools and techniques to identify quality requirements and risks, and documenting all aspects of the quality plan.

d. Continuously Monitor and Evaluate Quality Plan: Organizations should continuously monitor and evaluate the quality plan to ensure that it is achieving the desired results. This involves collecting and analyzing quality metrics, identifying areas for improvement, and making necessary adjustments to the plan.

e. Focus on Continuous Improvement: Quality planning should be viewed as an ongoing process of continuous improvement. Organizations should constantly look for ways to improve quality, reduce costs, and enhance customer satisfaction.

f. Invest in Quality Expertise: Quality planning requires specialized knowledge and expertise in quality management. Organizations should invest in training and development for personnel involved in quality planning to ensure that they have the necessary skills and experience to develop and implement a quality plan.

g. Use Quality Tools and Techniques: Quality planning involves the use of various tools and techniques, such as quality function deployment, failure mode and effects analysis, and statistical process control. These tools and techniques can help organizations to identify quality requirements, risks, and opportunities, and develop effective quality plans.

In summary, successful quality planning requires the consideration of several strategies, including aligning quality objectives with strategic goals, involving stakeholders, using a systematic approach, continuously monitoring and evaluating the quality plan, focusing on continuous improvement, investing in quality expertise, and using quality tools and techniques. By implementing these strategies, organizations can establish a roadmap for achieving their quality objectives and ensuring long-term success.

## EXAMPLES OF QUALITY PLANNING IN ACTION

Quality planning is an essential process for any organization that wants to ensure that its products and services meet or exceed customer expectations. The following are some examples of quality planning in action:

1. Automotive Industry: The automotive industry is an example of an industry that relies heavily on quality planning. Automobile manufacturers use quality planning to ensure that their vehicles meet safety and performance standards, as well as customer expectations. They use tools such as quality function deployment and failure mode and effects analysis to identify quality requirements and risks.

2. Healthcare Industry: The healthcare industry is another example of an industry that relies on quality planning. Hospitals and other healthcare organizations use quality planning to ensure that their services meet patient needs and regulatory requirements. They use tools such as patient satisfaction surveys and quality metrics to monitor and evaluate the success of their quality plans.

3. Construction Industry: The construction industry is an example of an industry that uses quality planning to ensure that buildings and infrastructure meet safety and quality standards. Construction companies use quality planning to identify and address potential risks, such as structural defects or safety hazards.

4. Software Industry: The software industry is an example of an industry that relies heavily on quality planning to ensure that its products meet customer requirements and are free of defects. Software companies use quality planning to identify and document customer requirements, as well as to test and evaluate the quality of their products.

5. Manufacturing Industry: The manufacturing industry is an example of an industry that uses quality planning to ensure that its products are of high quality and meet customer expectations. Manufacturers use quality planning to identify and address potential defects, as well as to ensure that their products are safe and reliable.

In summary, quality planning is used in a wide range of industries and organizations to ensure that products and services meet customer expectations and regulatory requirements. The examples given above demonstrate how quality planning can be applied in different contexts and industries to achieve quality objectives and improve customer satisfaction.

## INTEGRATING QUALITY PLANNING WITH OTHER BUSINESS PROCESSES

Quality planning is an essential component of effective quality management. However, it is important to integrate quality planning with other business processes to ensure that it is fully aligned with the organization's overall strategy and goals. The following are some of the key business processes that should be integrated with quality planning:

a. Strategic Planning: Quality planning should be integrated with the organization's strategic planning process. This involves aligning quality objectives with strategic goals and ensuring that quality planning is integrated into the overall business strategy.

b. Product Development: Quality planning should be integrated with the product development process. This involves identifying quality requirements early in the product development process and ensuring that quality is integrated into the design and development of the product.

c. Supply Chain Management: Quality planning should be integrated with the organization's supply chain management process. This involves ensuring that suppliers meet quality standards and that quality is maintained throughout the supply chain.

d. Human Resources: Quality planning should be integrated with the organization's human resources process. This involves ensuring that personnel are trained in quality management and that they have the necessary skills and experience to implement the quality plan.

e. Customer Relationship Management: Quality planning should be integrated with the organization's customer relationship management process. This involves identifying customer requirements and using quality metrics to monitor and improve customer satisfaction.

f. Continuous Improvement: Quality planning should be integrated with the organization's continuous improvement process. This involves using quality metrics to identify areas for improvement and developing strategies to continuously improve quality.

In summary, integrating quality planning with other business processes is essential for ensuring that quality objectives are fully aligned with the organization's overall strategy and goals. By integrating quality planning with strategic planning, product development, supply chain management, human resources, customer relationship management, and continuous improvement, organizations can establish a comprehensive approach to quality management that is fully integrated into all aspects of the business.

# EXAMPLES OF QUALITY PLANNING TOOLS AND TECHNIQUES

Quality planning involves the use of various tools and techniques to identify quality requirements, risks, and opportunities, and to develop effective quality plans. The following are some examples of quality planning tools and techniques:

a. Quality Function Deployment (QFD): QFD is a tool that helps organizations to translate customer needs and requirements into specific design and production requirements. QFD helps organizations to identify and prioritize customer requirements, and to develop a comprehensive quality plan that meets those requirements.

b. Failure Mode and Effects Analysis (FMEA): FMEA is a technique that helps organizations to identify potential failure modes and their effects on product or service quality. FMEA helps organizations to identify and prioritize potential risks, and to develop strategies to mitigate those risks.

c. Statistical Process Control (SPC): SPC is a technique that helps organizations to monitor and control quality during the production process. SPC involves using statistical methods to analyze production data and identify quality trends, as well as to identify and correct quality defects.

d. Six Sigma: Six Sigma is a methodology that helps organizations to improve quality and reduce defects by identifying and eliminating sources of variation in processes. Six Sigma involves using statistical methods and tools to identify and quantify quality problems, and to develop strategies to reduce or eliminate those problems.

e. Total Quality Management (TQM): TQM is a management philosophy that focuses on continuous improvement and customer satisfaction. TQM involves the use of various quality planning tools and techniques, as well as a focus on employee empowerment, customer focus, and continuous improvement.

f. Lean Manufacturing: Lean manufacturing is a methodology that focuses on reducing waste and improving efficiency in the production process. Lean manufacturing involves the use of various quality planning tools and techniques, such as value stream mapping and continuous flow manufacturing.

In summary, quality planning involves the use of various tools and techniques to identify quality requirements, risks, and opportunities, and to develop effective quality plans. The examples given above demonstrate how these tools and techniques can be applied in different contexts and industries to achieve quality objectives and improve customer satisfaction.

# 11.2 QUALITY CONTROL VS QUALITY ASSURANCE: UNDERSTANDING THE KEY DIFFERENCES

Quality control (QC) refers to the set of activities that are undertaken to ensure that a product or service meets the specified quality standards. The main aim of quality control is to detect and eliminate defects or discrepancies in the final product or service. QC activities may include inspecting, testing, and evaluating products or services to identify any deviations from the quality standards.

On the other hand, quality assurance (QA) is a set of planned and systematic activities that are implemented to ensure that a product or service meets the customer's expectations. QA is focused on preventing defects or deviations from quality standards from occurring in the first place. QA activities may include creating and implementing quality plans, performing audits, and monitoring and analysing data to identify areas for improvement.

While QC and QA are both important components of a quality management system, they differ in their approach and objectives. QC focuses on detecting and correcting problems after they occur, while QA focuses on preventing problems from occurring in the first place.

## OBJECTIVES OF QUALITY CONTROL AND QUALITY ASSURANCE

The primary objective of quality control is to ensure that the final product or service meets the specified quality standards. QC activities aim to detect and eliminate defects, errors, or discrepancies in the final product or service before it is released to the customer. QC is focused on identifying and addressing quality issues to minimize the risk of customer complaints, returns, or product recalls.

The primary objective of quality assurance, on the other hand, is to ensure that the product or service is designed, produced, and delivered according to the customer's requirements and expectations. QA activities aim to prevent defects or deviations from quality standards from occurring in the first place. QA is focused on implementing processes and procedures that can help to improve the quality of the final product or service, reduce waste, and increase efficiency.

Both QC and QA have a common goal of improving the quality of products or services, but they differ in their approach. QC aims to identify and correct problems after they occur, while QA aims to prevent problems from occurring in the first place. Both are essential to achieving high levels of quality in any product or service.

## SCOPE OF QUALITY CONTROL AND QUALITY ASSURANCE

Quality control focuses on the final product or service and is typically performed at the end of the production process. QC activities are aimed at detecting defects, errors, or discrepancies in the final product or service, and correcting them before the product is released to the customer. QC activities may include inspections, testing, and other methods of evaluating the quality of the final product or service.

Quality assurance, on the other hand, has a broader scope that encompasses the entire production process. QA activities are designed to prevent defects or deviations from quality standards from occurring in the first place. QA activities may include developing quality plans, creating quality standards and procedures, conducting audits, and monitoring and analysing data to identify areas for improvement.

The scope of quality control is limited to the final product or service, while the scope of quality assurance is broader, encompassing the entire production process from start to finish. QA activities are designed to ensure that quality is built into the product or service at every stage of production, while QC activities are designed to detect and correct problems in the final product or service.

Both QC and QA are important to achieving high levels of quality in any product or service, but they differ in their scope and focus. QC is focused on the final product or service, while QA is focused on the entire production process.

## PROCESS OF QUALITY CONTROL AND QUALITY ASSURANCE

The process of quality control typically involves the following steps:

1. Planning: This involves defining the quality standards and determining the methods to be used to measure quality.

2. Implementation: This involves carrying out the planned QC activities, which may include inspecting, testing, and evaluating the final product or service.

3. Evaluation: This involves reviewing the results of the QC activities to determine if the final product or service meets the specified quality standards. If there are defects or discrepancies, they are documented and corrective actions are taken to address them.

The process of quality assurance, on the other hand, typically involves the following steps:

1. Planning: This involves defining the quality standards, creating quality plans, and developing procedures for implementing the plans.

2. Implementation: This involves carrying out the planned QA activities, which may include conducting audits, monitoring and analyzing data, and identifying areas for improvement.

3. Evaluation: This involves reviewing the results of the QA activities to determine if the production process is meeting the

specified quality standards. If there are issues or areas for improvement, they are documented and corrective actions are taken to address them.

The processes of QC and QA are similar in that they both involve planning, implementation, and evaluation, but they differ in their focus. QC is focused on the final product or service, while QA is focused on the entire production process. Both processes are important to achieving high levels of quality in any product or service, and they should be implemented in conjunction with each other for the best results.

## TOOLS AND TECHNIQUES USED IN QUALITY CONTROL AND QUALITY ASSURANCE

Quality control and quality assurance both use a variety of tools and techniques to achieve their objectives. Some of the most commonly used tools and techniques are:

Tools and Techniques used in Quality Control:

a. Statistical Process Control (SPC): SPC is a method of measuring and controlling quality by monitoring and analyzing data during the production process.

b. Inspection: Inspection involves examining the final product or service to ensure that it meets the specified quality standards.

c. Testing: Testing involves subjecting the final product or service to various tests to check its quality.

d. Sampling: Sampling involves selecting a representative sample of the final product or service to check its quality.

e. Root Cause Analysis: Root cause analysis is a method of identifying the underlying cause of defects or quality issues in the final product or service.

Tools and Techniques used in Quality Assurance:

a. Quality Planning: Quality planning involves developing quality plans and procedures to ensure that quality is built into the production process.

b. Quality Audits: Quality audits involve evaluating the production process to ensure that it meets the specified quality standards.

c. Process Mapping: Process mapping involves creating a visual representation of the production process to identify areas for improvement.

d. Statistical Process Control (SPC): SPC is used in quality assurance to monitor and analyze data during the production process to identify areas for improvement.

e. Continuous Improvement: Continuous improvement involves continually reviewing and improving the production process to ensure that it meets the specified quality standards.

Both QC and QA use different tools and techniques to achieve their objectives. QC focuses on detecting and correcting defects in the final product or service, while QA focuses on preventing defects from occurring in the first place by implementing quality plans and procedures. Both are essential to achieving high levels of quality in any product or service, and they should be used in conjunction with each other for the best results.

## KEY SIMILARITIES AND DIFFERENCES BETWEEN QUALITY CONTROL AND QUALITY ASSURANCE

While quality control and quality assurance have different objectives and scopes, they also share some similarities. Here are some key similarities and differences between QC and QA:

Similarities:

 a. Both QC and QA are focused on improving the quality of products or services.

 b. Both QC and QA use tools and techniques to achieve their objectives.

 c. Both QC and QA are important components of a quality management system.

Differences:

 a. QC is focused on detecting and correcting defects in the final product or service, while QA is focused on preventing defects from occurring in the first place.

 b. QC activities are performed at the end of the production process, while QA activities are implemented throughout the production process.

 c. QC activities are reactive, while QA activities are proactive.

 d. The scope of QC is limited to the final product or service, while the scope of QA is broader and encompasses the entire production process.

 e. QC activities are designed to ensure that the final product or service meets the specified quality standards, while QA activities are designed to ensure that the production process is meeting the customer's requirements and expectations.

In summary, while QC and QA share some similarities, they have different objectives, scopes, and approaches. Both are essential to achieving high levels of quality in any product or service, and they should be used in conjunction with each other for the best results.

## IMPORTANCE OF QUALITY CONTROL AND QUALITY ASSURANCE IN BUSINESS AND INDUSTRY

Quality control and quality assurance are critical components of any business or industry that produces products or services. Here are some reasons why QC and QA are important:

a. Customer satisfaction: High-quality products and services result in satisfied customers, which can lead to repeat business and positive word-of-mouth referrals.

b. Cost savings: Implementing effective QC and QA measures can help businesses to identify and correct quality issues early, reducing the cost of rework, scrap, and returns.

c. Competitive advantage: Businesses that are known for producing high-quality products or services are more likely to stand out in the market and gain a competitive advantage.

d. Compliance: In some industries, such as healthcare and pharmaceuticals, regulatory bodies require businesses to implement quality control and quality assurance measures to ensure compliance with safety and quality standards.

e. Continuous improvement: Implementing QC and QA measures can help businesses to identify areas for improvement and continuously improve their production processes.

f. Brand reputation: A business's brand reputation is often tied to the quality of its products or services. Implementing effective QC and QA measures can help to protect and enhance a business's brand reputation.

In summary, QC and QA are important for businesses and industries that produce products or services because they can lead to increased customer satisfaction, cost savings, competitive advantage, compliance with safety and quality standards, continuous improvement, and protection of brand reputation.

# IMPLEMENTING EFFECTIVE QUALITY CONTROL AND QUALITY ASSURANCE MEASURES

Implementing effective quality control and quality assurance measures requires a structured approach that involves the following steps:

1. Define quality standards: The first step in implementing effective QC and QA measures is to define the quality standards that products or services must meet. This includes determining the criteria that will be used to measure quality.

2. Develop quality plans and procedures: Quality plans and procedures outline the steps that will be taken to ensure that products or services meet the specified quality standards. This may include specifying inspection and testing procedures, developing process control plans, and establishing quality control checkpoints.

3. Train employees: Effective QC and QA measures rely on the skills and knowledge of employees. Providing training on quality control and quality assurance procedures is essential to ensure that employees understand their roles and responsibilities and can effectively implement QC and QA measures.

4. Monitor and measure quality: Monitoring and measuring the quality of products or services is essential to identifying and addressing quality issues. This may include performing inspections, conducting tests, and collecting data to analyze quality trends.

5. Analyze data and implement corrective actions: Analyzing data on product or service quality can help to identify areas for improvement. If quality issues are identified, corrective actions must be taken to address the root cause of the problem.

6. Continuously improve: Effective QC and QA measures require continuous improvement to ensure that products or services meet or exceed the specified quality standards. This involves

analyzing data, identifying areas for improvement, and implementing changes to improve the production process.

In summary, implementing effective QC and QA measures requires a structured approach that involves defining quality standards, developing quality plans and procedures, training employees, monitoring and measuring quality, analysing data and implementing corrective actions, and continuously improving. By following this approach, businesses and industries can achieve high levels of quality in their products or services and gain a competitive advantage in the market.

Printed in Great Britain
by Amazon

33127301R00331